Middle Powers and the Rise of China

MIDDLE POWERS AND THE RISE OF CHINA

BRUCE GILLEY and ANDREW O'NEIL
Editors

GEORGETOWN UNIVERSITY PRESS
WASHINGTON, DC

© 2014 Georgetown University Press. All rights reserved. No part of this book may be reproduced or utilized in any form or by any means, electronic or mechanical, including photocopying and recording, or by any information storage and retrieval system, without permission in writing from the publisher.

LIBRARY OF CONGRESS CATALOGING-IN-PUBLICATION DATA

Middle powers and the rise of China / Bruce Gilley and Andrew O'Neil, editors.
pages cm
Includes bibliographical references and index.
ISBN 978-1-62616-083-5 (hardcover : alk. paper) — ISBN 978-1-62616-084-2 (pbk. : alk. paper) — ISBN 978-1-62616-085-9 (ebook)
1. China—Foreign relations—Developed countries. 2. Developed countries—Foreign relations—China. 3. Middle powers. 4. China—Foreign relations—21st century. 5. Developed countries—Foreign rrelations—21st century. I. Gilley, Bruce, 1966–, author, editor of compliation. II. O'Neil, Andrew, author, editor of compilation.
DS779.47.M54 2014
327.51—dc23

2013048880

15 14 9 8 7 6 5 4 3 2 First printing

Contents

Illustrations

Tables

Figures

Acknowledgments

THIS BOOK was conceived over a series of conversations about the significance of middle power interactions with China and what these tell us about the nature of China's rise in international relations. This culminated in a two-day workshop in Brisbane in July 2012, funded by Griffith University's Program of Asian Politics, Security and Development. We would like to thank the following people for providing detailed comments on each of the papers presented at the workshop: Baogang He, Alex Bellamy, Nick Bisley, Colin Brown, Michael Heazle, Martin Griffiths, Haig Patapan, Russell Trood, Vlado Vivoda, and Xu Yi-chong. We are grateful to Don Jacobs at Georgetown University Press for his outstanding support and continuing belief in the value of the project as it evolved through various iterations. The quality of the final product was improved considerably by the extensive feedback provided by two anonymous reviewers from Georgetown University Press. Finally, we would like to thank Daniela di Piramo for preparing the index and Andrea Haefner for research assistance.

CHAPTER 1

China's Rise through the Prism of Middle Powers

Bruce Gilley and Andrew O'Neil

Introduction

When Egypt's newly elected president Mohammed Morsi made his first overseas trip outside of the Middle East in 2012, the destination was not Washington but Beijing. "International relations between all states are open and the basis for all relations is balance," he said before leaving. "We are not against anyone but we are for achieving our interests."[1] China's top leader, Hu Jintao, hailed the decision as showing "that your country attaches great importance to the desire to develop relations with China." China's *Global Times* was more blunt, saying that the trip "signifies that there is a major shift in Egypt's foreign policy, which used to be firmly in Washington's camp, and that the nation is reasserting itself as a regional power."[2] Indeed, US officials, noted the *Wall Street Journal*, "are finding themselves in the rare situation of vying with their Chinese counterparts for Cairo's attention."[3]

Morsi's trip was not merely a tributary visit to a great power. While there, he discussed political developments in the Middle East, since China had disagreed with Egypt over the ongoing civil war in Syria. Egypt believed it could reshape China's views on Middle East politics. "The friends of the Syrian people in China and Russia and other states," Morsi said, needed to support "ordinary Syrians" rather than the Bashar al-Assad regime. China seemed more open to the views of the elected Egyptian regime than it had been to its US-backed predecessor. "China supports Egypt to play a bigger role on the international arena," said China's parliamentary chairman.[4]

The rise of China as an increasingly confident and powerful international actor presents a number of challenges for member states of the international system. From a systemic perspective, the ascent of great powers is never easy and has traditionally been characterized by increased potential for interstate conflict as emerging and existing great powers vie for influence. States are generally wary of the "unknown quantity" accompanying the rise of great powers: How will they seek to interact with other states as their power expands? Will they seek to dominate as their new-found status evolves? In the case of China, these questions have sparked an intense and wide-ranging debate. About the only point on which observers agree is that a system where China is a near equal to the United States will be very different from the US-led international order the world experienced for most of the post-1945 period.

Perhaps understandably in view of the central role of larger powers in shaping international relations, the lion's share of research on responses to China's rise has focused on the role of the United States. To the extent that analysis has looked beyond great powers, it has been concerned with China's impact on specific regions in the international system, particularly Asia, but also Africa and Latin America, as well as China's bilateral relationships with individual states.

Absent from these debates has been detailed analysis of the rise of China in relation to the group of states often referred to as "middle powers"—of which Egypt is a prime example. Middle powers are countries with capabilities immediately below those of great powers, but still far above most secondary states in the international system. Middle powers are missing in action in the study of China's rise.

This book seeks to fill that void. It addresses how middle powers are both responding to, and endeavoring to reshape, a rising China. It argues both that the middle power concept is indispensable for understanding the rise of China and that actually existing middle powers are critical players in reshaping the international context that will determine the consequences of China's rise. It finds that middle powers are experiencing similar economic, security, and political challenges as a result of the rise of China that are unique to them as a result of their status in the international system. The responses, far from being mere varieties of realignment, show a distinctive middle power propensity (and capacity) for autonomous and multipronged initiatives that seek, above all, to maintain an orderly international system. Moreover, these responses, while having little direct or measurable impact on China's foreign policy, are shaping the regional contexts in which China's rise is occurring. In short, this book both elucidates the nature of China's rise as seen in its relationships with middle powers and affirms the utility of the middle power prism in understanding systemic transformation in the international system.

In this chapter we have two aims: first, to identify what middle powers are and how the concept generates testable hypotheses for international relations theory (a task elaborated by James Manicom and Jeffrey Reeves in chapter 2); and second, to link that theory to the study of China in the form of four key questions that can be taken up in case studies of China's relations with different middle powers. The purpose of this chapter is to define, hypothesize, and then operationalize the key questions about middle powers and the rise of China.

The middle power concept, which delinks middle power foreign policies from inevitable alignments with great powers, has never been popular with great powers (as David Cooper and Toshi Yoshihara in chapter 4 show is the case in the United States and as Gilley shows in chapter 3 may prove true in China as well). But the questions posed here matter for both China and the United States because middle powers are emerging as a new arena of rivalry for Sino-US relations. China's ability to woo middle powers through deeper relationships, and, in some cases, an effective presentation of an alternative narrative of state-led capitalism, will continue to have an impact for as long as strong economic relations with China remain critical to the national development strategies of middle powers and others. For this reason, Washington needs to understand the contours of relations between middle powers and China in order to formulate a set of appropriate responses and to appreciate the nature of the challenges it faces in responding to China's rise.

This book seeks also to refract China's rise through middle power theory to better understand the nature of China's rise and its future trajectory, as well as the structure of the international system itself. From this perspective, middle powers play a double role in China's rise. As influential agents in international politics, they have the potential to reshape and redirect the way in which China's ascent evolves. In addition, the foreign policy behavior of middle powers provides an important bellwether for charting the rise of China, just as middle powers have often been used as barometers to measure other changes in the international system.[5] More able because of their material power capabilities to take issue with China's preferences, but less able than great powers to balance China's influence unilaterally, middle powers rely on adept diplomatic means, with an emphasis on building coalitions with like-minded powers, to differentiate their policy preferences from great powers. How middle powers use these means is thus a valuable indicator of how they perceive China's rise, and how China is rising.

Seeing China's rise through the prism of middle powers, in other words, provides a novel way to identify important research questions, organize descriptive information, and generate new insights. The utility of this approach goes beyond simply recounting and explaining China's bilateral relationships with middle powers. There are examples in the literature where this has been undertaken, and this book does not purport to contribute to this body of scholarship. Rather, the focus of the chapters here is on understanding the middle power category, China's rise, and the nature of the international system.

Traditional realist approaches to international relations often discount by omission the role of middle powers and instead categorize all nongreat power actors as secondary states. Traditional approaches to area studies, by contrast, focus on national and regional particularities while ignoring the commonalities of similar states. Middle power theory provides a third approach that may explain phenomena that other approaches cannot. In the process we hope to better understand China's power and purpose in the early part of the twenty-first century.

Middle Power Capabilities

Like many important concepts in the social sciences, the idea of middle powers and middle power theory is contested. But its continued use in real-world political debates and diplomacy suggests that it has a relevance and utility grounded in some objective characteristics. The US National Intelligence Council, for instance, predicted in a 2012 report that in the period to 2030, "many of the middle powers [will] . . . rise above the line [of expected diplomatic influence] as both their hard and soft powers increase."[6]

Middle powers have long been identified using one of two approaches: positional (the power they have) and behavioral (the policies they pursue).[7] It is the former that will be taken to define the category here, while the latter will be treated as a set of hypotheses. Positional dimensions refer to the material power capabilities that middle powers possess relative to both great powers and the scores of average, small, and weak states. Positional, or material, capabilities approaches are the natural departure point for defining middle powers because they are the necessary condition for middle powers to be seen as objects of strategic diplomacy by great powers; to have sufficiently broad sets of interests at stake; and for their initiatives to be credible and thus feasible. As Denis Stairs has written: "Having middling capabilities determines not what middle power states *will* do, but what, in principle, they *can* do."[8] What distinguishes middle powers from other secondary states is their greater relative power that gives them a qualitatively greater degree of foreign policy capacity and autonomy.

On the positional approach, middle powers logically include that tier of countries that rank immediately below the eight countries generally acknowledged as established or emerging great powers; namely, the United States and China plus the six other great powers—Britain, France, Germany,

Russia, Japan, and India. Assuming this tier is roughly two to three times as populous as the one above it, middle powers, then, should consist of those states with a ranking roughly in the tenth to thirtieth range across a range of capability indicators. Middle powers, in this view, belong to the set of all "primary states" in the world system when contrasted to the "secondary states" category to which all others belong.

A mean-based cluster analysis that divides the world into four main groups using economic size comes closest to generating what we expect to be a middle powers list, including many of the cases treated in this volume (see figure 1.1). The most contested state is Brazil, which we treat as a middle power here because of its tenth to thirtieth ranking in most material indicators other than economic size.

Several further capabilities-related indicators can be used to identify middle powers. In table 1.1 we can see that the nine countries included in this study generally map with the capabilities typology of middle powers quite well. Across a broad range of indicators, they generally fall into the tenth to thirtieth range out of the world's 190-plus sovereign states.

Since this capabilities-based measure is global, it does not take into account the regional contexts that may magnify or diminish the power of a state at the regional level.[9] Some middle powers are not regional powers

Figure 1.1. The Middle Power Level Using Cluster Analysis

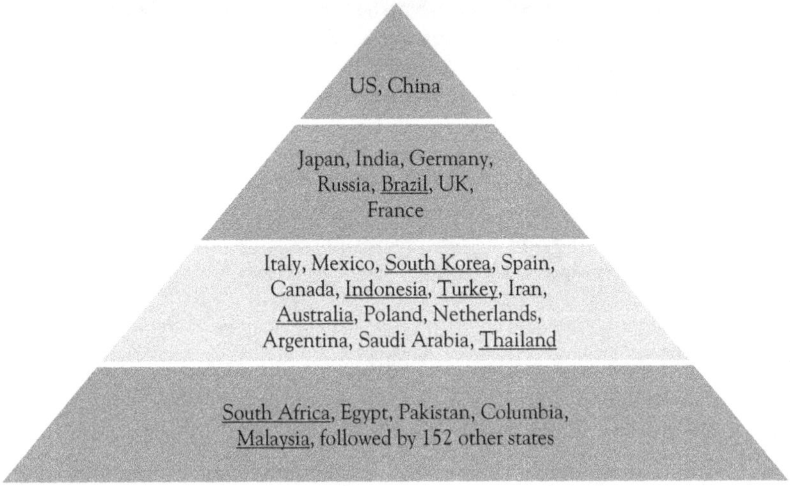

Data Source: IMF World Economic Outlook, April 2012; total GDP (2010, PPP, US$) mean-based partition clustering into four groups. Countries are listed by rank within each cluster. Case studies in this book are underlined.

Table 1.1. Capabilities of Middle Power Cases

(Global Rank)	South Korea	Brazil	Australia	Turkey	Indonesia	Thailand	South Africa	Malaysia
Total GDP	12	7	18	16	15	24	25	29
Defense Spending	12	11	14	15	31	34	35	39
Composite Index of National Material Capabilities	8	6	28	12	14	25	31	41
National Security Index	6	20	12	25	33	38	47	34
Integrated State Power	13	12	10	28	14	36	29	33
AVERAGE SCORE	**10**	**11**	**16**	**19**	**21**	**31**	**33**	**35**
G20 Member	Y	Y	Y	Y	Y	N	Y	N
Number of Times on UNSC since 1989	2	4	1	1	2	0	2	2

Notes:

- GDP: US$ PPP share of world total, IMF World Economic Outlook Database. Figures for 2010.
- Defense Spending: 2010 Defense Spending. Stockholm International Peace Research Institute, *Military Expenditure Database*. Available at www.sipri.org/research/armaments/milex/milex_database.
- Composite Index of National Material Capabilities: Correlates of War National Material Capabilities Index, v3.02. Available at www.correlatesofwar.org/COW2%20Data/Capabilities/nmc3-02.htm.
- National Security Index: India National Security Council. From Karl Hwang, "Measuring Geopolitical Power in India: A Review of the National Security Index (NSI)," *German Institute of Global and Area Studies Working Papers*, no. 136, May 2010.
- Integrated State Power: Karl Hwang, "New Thinking in Measuring National Power," *World International Studies Committee Second Global International Studies Conference*, Ljubljana, Slovenia, July 23–26, 2008, at www.wiscnetwork.org/papers/WISC_2008-137.pdf.

(Poland and Canada, for example) whereas some regional powers are not middle powers (Nigeria and Ethiopia, for example). However, for the most part, middle powers play outsized roles in their regions. In addition, there are several "softer" measures of power that may be particularly pertinent to middle powers. Kim, for instance, has argued that "network power," the strength of the position that a country enjoys within international networks of influence, is particularly important in the ranking of middle powers because of their reliance on coalitions of like-minded states to pursue their foreign policy aims.[10]

While there are many informal groups of middle powers, the closest formal recognition of middle power capabilities in recent international politics has been the formation of the G20, of which six of our eight countries (except Malaysia and Thailand) are members.[11] The emergence of the G20, a Canadian idea from 1999, as the central forum for global economic governance decisions has brought middle powers into what might be called a second golden age, after the first golden age of postwar reconstruction.[12] The players have changed, but the idea—that the unique position of middle powers in the international system gives them an outsized role in global governance—has not. Of the nineteen member states of the G20 (the European Union also sits), eleven are middle powers. Andrew Cooper and Jongryn Mo argue that the range of cross-cutting cleavages within the G20 may "give more opportunity for political entrepreneurship by middle powers," particularly the "Middle 7" of Australia, Canada, South Korea, Indonesia, Argentina, Mexico, and Turkey.[13] Indeed, as Cooper argues elsewhere, the incremental rather than rupture-based creation of the G20 lends itself to the sorts of leadership that middle powers excel at.[14] Early evidence of this can be seen in Middle 7 initiatives within the G20 on financial regulation and global development and in the creation in 2013 of the MIKTA Initiative composed of Mexico, Indonesia, South Korea, Turkey, and Australia to advance their shared agenda on global governance.

Given its relational and material nature, the set of middle powers will fluctuate over time. Indeed, the category itself is no longer defined mainly by the traditional Western middle powers. Some European middle powers have been absorbed into the European Union, although a weakening or disintegration of the EU may lead to a reemergence of traditional European middle powers like Italy or new ones like Poland.[15] Others have simply declined in material power terms and influence, in part because the ranks of non-Western states with significant capabilities have swelled. Switzerland was clearly a middle power in the post–World War II period but is no longer today. India was a solid middle power in the postwar period and its foreign policy continues to be deeply contoured by recognizably middle power behavior, evidenced most recently in the creation of the India-Brazil-South Africa (IBSA) Dialogue Forum in 2003.[16] But it is now generally considered to be an emerging great power and faces concomitant pressures to play the part, evidenced by its quest for a permanent seat on the UN Security Council. Yugoslavia was probably a middle power but none of its successor states are.

Finally, the rise of China is one of the factors that has further churned up the ranks of middle powers—both because Asian middle powers have gained capabilities as a result of economic links to China and because (as Gilley shows in chapter 3) China's own definition of middle powers may become self-fulfilling as its global influence grows. In short, while middle powers can be defined using stable and readily observed criteria, their relative influence depends in part on relational criteria that are much harder to assess.

Middle Power Behavior

If great powers like the United States are "bound to lead," to borrow Nye's optimistic phrase, does this mean that middle powers are "bound to follow" or, as some scholars posit, to choose among a fixed menu of options concerning degrees of alignment with great powers?[17] The core behavioral prediction of middle power theory is that the answer to this question is no. Indeed, the alternative behavioral hypotheses are the reason why the category of middle powers is of interest.

As with all causal claims in the social sciences, hypotheses about middle power behavior can be either deduced from a set of logical propositions and then tested through detailed case studies, or observed from a large set of cases and then investigated for the presence of causal mechanisms. Given the changing international environments in which middle powers have always operated, the latter approach is problematic, both because it assumes an ability to observe and measure all relevant regularities and because as with all such approaches the empirical regularities of today are subject to change tomorrow. Such accounts rapidly become anachronistic. The deductive approach, by contrast, holds more promise because it begins with a theory of what middle power behavior *should* look like across contexts and then opens it to empirical testing. Much of the criticism of middle power theorizing has concerned its failure to begin with empirical regularities. But the deductive or nomological approach does this by design. Cooper and colleagues, for instance, deduced a theory of middle power behavior from first principles rather than attempting to begin with empirical regularities.[18]

As outlined here by Manicom and Reeves (chapter 2), the behavior expected of middle powers in power transitions theory revolves around their role in mediating disputes (typically between great powers) and building bridges (typically between the developed and developing worlds). In other words, power transition theory predicts that all nongreat powers behave in similar ways, the only difference being that middle powers do more. The problem with seeing the world through this prism is that it leaves so much of the world unexplained, in particular why great powers like the United States and China are so often frustrated by middle power foreign policies that do not "get into line" and why new norms, policies, and institutions emerge that are not initiated by great powers. In "seeing beyond hegemony," this book seeks to test an alternative set of hypotheses that do not revolve around great power alignments. Those hypotheses have often gone under the label of "middle power theory."

The interest in middle power theory, to quote Cooper and colleagues, lies in the possibility that middle powers "can be significant in catalyzing the processes of reform and change—especially those requiring considerable cooperation and collaboration—in a variety of issue areas on the international agenda."[19] Robert Keohane, writing in 1969, defined middle (or "system influencing") powers as states that "cannot hope to affect the system acting alone [but] can nevertheless exert significant impact on the system by working through small groups or alliances or through universal or regional international organizations."[20] (He named Canada, Sweden, Pakistan, Brazil, and Argentina.) This system-influencing nature of middle powers is often seen as a result of their status as nongreat powers, which lends them significant persuasive leverage or "soft power."[21]

The specific content of middle power theory has long been deduced from the logic of international trade and traditional security issues. In general, the rise of more actors and more issue-areas in international politics since the end of the Cold War has been a driving force behind new behavioral predictions concerning the rise and uniformity of middle power diplomacy.[22] Bernard Wood included regional leadership, functional leadership, and system stabilization as predicted middle power behaviors.[23] In recent years discussions of the "rise of the South" in the international political economy have been the basis for new theorizing about the role that middle powers are playing in international politics. The rise of China is one of many new developments in world politics that will define what it means to act like a middle power.

Generating hypotheses about the specific content of middle power behavior depends not only on the nature of the international system, but also on the distinctive domestic political, economic, and cultural conditions that are present in the ranks of middle powers. Denis Stairs argued that middle powers would be most likely to engage in middle power behavior if they were free from volatile domestic conflicts, not seen as proxies for great powers, had noncontroversial foreign policy pasts, and thrived within a pluralistic international politics.[24] Cooper and colleagues, meanwhile, argued that middle power behavior depended on whether a state could create policy capacity and civic engagement, and had broad global interests (such as by liberalizing trade).[25] It is also clear that geographical proximity is a key aspect of middle power behavior on any given issue—as the differing Australian and Canadian responses to China show.[26]

In other words, we should expect that the specific behavioral predictions are only probabilistically present in most middle powers and are contingent on international conditions. Many middle powers will not behave according to the predictions of middle power theory but will still be middle powers. By the same token, many smaller and even great powers may engage in middle power–like behavior without being middle powers. That said, there has been a remarkable consistency in the general and unique *expectations* of middle power behavior since World War II, with only some modification of the language used.

The reason for this consistency, as Carsten Holbraad argued in *Middle Powers in International Politics*, is that the combination of sharing with small states a vulnerability to international pressures, but sharing with great powers an ability to influence the system in which they operate, produces probabilistically common patterns of behavior: "Variously threatening their interests and offering possibilities of securing some of their goals, these pressures can sometimes be strong and general enough to produce observable tendencies in the systemic conduct of the middle powers."[27] In other words, the hypothesized behavioral characteristics are inextricably linked to capabilities. The possibility of wielding influence in discrete areas in which they have task-specific capabilities—by acting as either catalyst, facilitator, or manager—generates a proactive diplomacy that has been variously described as "niche diplomacy," or "middle power activism."[28] Former Australian prime minister Gareth Evans described middle power behavior in terms of not just opportunity and imagination (something they might share with small powers) but also capacity and credibility (something more likely to diverge).[29] Robert Cox wrote that middle powers could be influential because they "were not suspected of harboring intentions of domination and . . . had resources sufficient to enable them to be functionally effective."[30]

Beyond the general prediction that middle powers will be overactive in mediation, initiation, and consensus-building, the first specific dimension of predicted middle power behavior is what we will call the *peace initiatives and conflict mediation* role. One of the earliest theorists of middle power behavior, Giovanni Botero (who variously used the Italian terms *mezano* and the less flattering *mediocro*), was a Jesuit-trained Piedmontese teacher of philosophy and rhetoric, who in his 1589 book *The Reason of State* argued that middle powers were peace-promoting because "they are exposed neither to violence by their weakness nor to envy by their greatness, and their wealth and power being moderate, passions are less violent, ambition finds less support and license less provocation than in large states."[31] This notion was subsequently expanded to embrace a more active promotion of peace.

During the Cold War, the middle power peace role was often associated with peacekeeping and peace negotiations. Even today, the incidence of peacekeeping commitments among middle powers is higher than that among either great powers or small powers: in 2012, for instance, eight of the seventeen countries not from sub-Saharan Africa with more than a thousand troops committed to UN peacekeeping operations were middle powers in the definition used here (three were great powers and six small powers).

In the post–Cold War period the peace role increasingly came through leadership in new areas like counterinsurgency and stabilization operations as well as through the promotion of new initiatives such as the Chemical Weapons Convention, Responsibility to Protect (R2P) doctrine, the Ottawa land mines ban, and the Proliferation Security Initiative (PSI).[32] Ban, for instance, argues that South Korea has been active in peacekeeping and counterinsurgency because of its unique middle power status that gives it the legitimacy of a small power and the capabilities of a great power.[33] Behringer argues that the broader "human security" agenda is a middle power creation.[34] Others argue that middle powers will play a key role in forging an international consensus on "climate security."[35]

The second specific hypothesized dimension of middle power behavior is what we will call the *counterhegemonic* or *pro-multipolarity* role. In his consideration of the behavior of middle powers in five distinct global and regional systems in the nineteenth and twentieth centuries, Carsten Holbraad found that middle powers have generally avoided playing balance-of-power games. Sometimes they joined with hegemons, and other times they stood aloof. This idea of middle powers being separate from the predictions of great power balancing or bandwagoning was the beginning of a rethink in which the primary interest of middle powers is to diminish the hegemony of great powers per se, something from which they stand to benefit the most. George Glazebrook, writing in 1947, classified middle powers by "their opposition to undue great power control."[36]

Multipolarity is most obviously in the interests of middle powers since it widens the group of what David Dewitt and John Kirton called "principal powers" in the international system, those that possess the ability to have a decisive influence on specific issues.[37] Middle powers may engage in *simultaneous* initiatives that seek to reshape great powers and their relations among themselves because, unlike smaller powers, middle powers have the capacity to effect such changes. Moreover, multipolarity as an end is consistent with the multilateralism that is the preferred means of middle powers. Not only do middle powers prefer to build a world that looks more like a (multipolar) beehive rather than a (unipolar) spider's web, they also act more effectively under such conditions.

This prediction is especially relevant in the case of China and new middle powers because the previous category-defining middle powers like Canada and Australia may now appear as aberrant because of their close alignment to the United States. Indeed, some analysts in China increasingly leave them out of middle power analysis. In many ways, this brings middle power theory back to the modest tactical hypotheses of some of the earlier writers like Holbraad, who worked from pre-twentieth-century European experiences and assumed nonalignment. The question of whether great power alliances help or hinder middle power diplomacy is one of the most complex, and interesting, of the corollaries of this hypothesis. Can a middle power effectively promote multipolarity while being an ally of a great power?

The pro-multipolarity tendency is also why middle power theory so often receives a cold reception in great power capitals. As both Gilley (chapter 3) and Cooper and Yoshihara (chapter 4) show, neither Beijing nor Washington particularly likes middle power theory because it proposes an ordering mechanism of international relations that does not revolve around the interests and alignments of great powers themselves. Beijing, because it is the weaker of the two, may take the concept more seriously for now, but that may change. Theoretically, this hypothesis lays bare the cleavage in international relations theory between more realist-oriented approaches that stress great power centrality and alternative approaches that stress other factors.

A third, commonly noted feature of middle powers has been their emphasis on diplomatic initiatives that seek to constrain the exercise of power through "rules and institutions." Tow and Rigby describe middle powers as exercising "leadership on key issues relating to international rule-building and rule-adherence."[38] Wanting a more rules-based order is something middle powers share with those below them, but not one that smaller states can generally lead. Moreover, since middle powers tend to have more opportunities for leadership in such institutions than small powers, they arguably benefit more. In particular, such efforts are increasingly manifest at the regional level, where middle powers often take the lead in building regional institutions that have been freed from Cold War–era constraints.

Thus, middle powers are expected to be "status quo" powers when it comes to preserving the rules and institutions of the international system, but "revisionist" powers when it comes to undue great power influence. At times, as we will see, this can lead them in multiple directions, as is the case with Asian middle power efforts to both reinforce the US role in Asian security (reinforcing world order) as well as adjust that system to accommodate China (encouraging multipolarity). This does not mean that middle powers have no preferences among different great power arrangements. They may prefer one to another. But compared to great power condominium, they generally prefer a multipolar world order—a G20 rather than a G2.

These three dimensions—peace and conflict management, multipolarity, and rules-building—were articulated in an earlier form by Cooper, Higgott, and Nossal, who wrote of middle powers' "tendency to pursue multilateral solutions to international problems, their tendency to embrace compromise positions in international disputes, and their tendency to embrace notions of 'good international citizenship' to guide their diplomacy."[39] In sum, middle powers are hypothesized to be both entrepreneurs and defenders of a rules-based international order, and because of their counterhegemonic instincts liable to engage not in reactive responses so much as transformative initiatives designed to reduce the stakes of great power alignments (see figure 1.2). Unlike small and great powers, middle powers are generally not expected to engage in combative diplomacy, preferring instead constructive engagement and consensus-building in pursuit of peace and conflict management, multipolarity, and rules-building.[40]

Of course, middle power behavior is dependent not just on inherent capabilities but also on needs and opportunities for middle power leadership. Without this, as Cooper wrote in 1997, "there remain serious reservations about the ability of these second-tier powers to supply an abundant measure of international leadership."[41] Even with such openings, middle powers require the political will to lead, something that is learned over time. While capabilities may be necessary in a functional sense of giving middle powers the necessary interests to have a motivation to act, it is domestic politics and domestic leadership that are the sufficiency conditions.

Figure 1.2. Three Hypothesized Behavioral Dimensions of Middle Powers

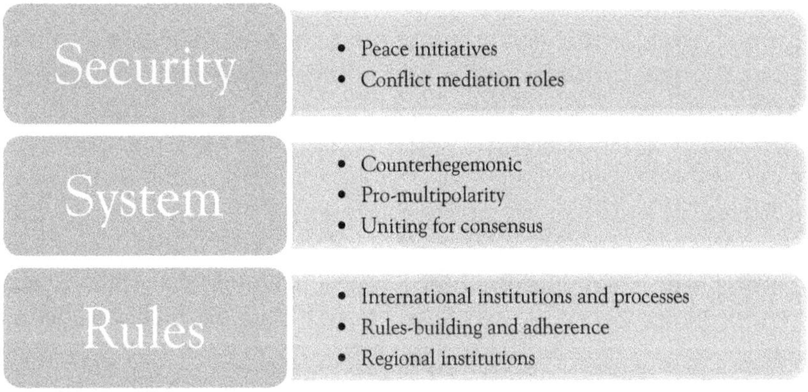

Security
• Peace initiatives
• Conflict mediation roles
System
• Counterhegemonic
• Pro-multipolarity
• Uniting for consensus
Rules
• International institutions and processes
• Rules-building and adherence
• Regional institutions

While the G20 membership list reflects middle power capabilities, two other international groups reflect middle power behavioral theory. One is the Uniting for Consensus (UfC) group that introduced a formal proposal for UN Security Council Reform in 2005.[42] The UfC is led by middle powers such as Argentina, Pakistan, Turkey, Mexico, Egypt, South Korea, and Canada as well as EU middle powers Italy and Spain. Of the countries in this study, only Brazil (which on this issue is swayed by its great power ambitions) stands outside of the UfC group. The UfC aims to widen the membership of the UN Security Council while limiting its role—a furtherance of the existing "middle power principle" of the Security Council that chooses ten non-permanent members primarily on the basis of their "contribution" to international peace and security. Another group of middle powers is the New Agenda Coalition of Brazil, Egypt, Ireland, Mexico, New Zealand, South Africa, and Sweden that works to eliminate nuclear weapons and has been backed by the Middle Powers Initiative coalition of international nongovernmental organizations that have targeted middle powers as the most likely supporters of such a goal.

Several behavioral dimensions of middle power theory are absent here. The most obvious is a promotion of liberal democratic values. This is a conscious removal of a dimension that is self-evidently not present in "new middle powers" in particular.[43] Middle powers today more often reflect skepticism about liberal values, even though they are virtually all democracies. The counterhegemonic instincts of new middle powers are often framed in terms of a *resistance* to values seen as emanating in the West, notably in our cases by Malaysia and South Africa. Liberalism may be more instrumental and contingent in the foreign policies of middle powers, embraced for practical purposes at given times but not as a consistent foreign policy theme. For this reason, liberal great powers often see middle powers as "irresponsible stakeholders" in the international system.[44]

Closely related to this, middle powers today are not likely to be interested in pursuing new "North-South" initiatives of global development, as was the case in the past.[45] In part this is because most come from the South. In part it is because of wide differences within middle power ranks about the appropriate role of aid and trade concessions in global development.[46]

The absence of liberalism and global poverty alleviation as behavioral predictions ties into a larger missing dimension: good international citizenship or the idea of middle powers as "moral actors." The idea that middle power behavior was more ethical than that of great powers was long a staple of middle power theorizing as it related to peace building, human rights, and development. But with the latter two missing, the moral character of middle power behavior becomes less obvious. We are left then with only a positivist prediction of the promotion of peace-building initiatives, multipolarity, and institutions that *may* lead to better outcomes for global citizens, but may not. In other words, the middle power behavioral hypothesis does not imply "good" outcomes, much less "good" intentions. There is no reason to suppose that middle powers are more ethical than great powers.

Another item—not behavioral but related to behavior—missing here is a self-identity among a country's intellectual or foreign policy elites as a middle power. The term elicits storms of protest in Brasilia but is warmly embraced in Seoul. Scholars in Western middle power countries more schooled in traditional realism are skeptical of the concept, while those in non-Western middle powers have found it useful and relevant to their diplomatic status and aims. Pakistan embraces this description of itself, but only with the politically loaded caveat that the same description applies to India.

In short, being a middle power does not depend on the subjective acceptance or proper use of the concept in the country concerned, whether by politicians or analysts. It is the position of middle powers in the international system, not their "national role conception," that should shape their behavior.[47] Brazil is the best test of this because it so strenuously rejects the middle power label. Iran too, despite its clear middle power capabilities, has long cherished a Persian great power dream, which makes it a test case in Middle East politics of middle power behavioral predictions. Japan and India, by contrast, strain to conceive of themselves as middle powers despite being great powers, thus providing further hard test cases for middle power theory.

Nonetheless, as Manicom and Reeves point out, the fully formed ideal-type middle power would not only possess the necessary positional capabilities and act in the hypothesized ways, but also would be analytically and strategically astute enough to recognize itself as a middle power and embed this in its national role conception in a way that becomes self-reinforcing. In the present context, Australia and South Korea may come closest to meeting this fully formed ideal.

Eight Middle Power Cases

Having deduced a theory of middle power behavior, the confirmation of whether the theory holds any value depends on detailed comparative case studies. Is "middle power behavior" typical of middle powers? There has never been agreement on this, but as Stairs noted, "the impression that there really are powers of secondary rank with similar capabilities and similar minds, and with a similar approach to the maintenance of the international system seems somehow to survive exposure to the 'real world' observation that things are in fact a jumble."[48] Neak found statistical evidence in support for middle power behavior in studies of 1992 and 1993.[49] At a time of systemic transformation with the rise of China and of a shifting membership of middle power ranks, it is time to revisit this testing.

Of necessity, this study could not include all middle powers. Our case selection, however, was not without justification. The intention was to sample a geographical cross section of middle powers. They have been arranged here from those closest to China to those farthest away.

South Korea (chapter 5) is the middle power of perhaps preeminent interest in this book. Not only does it have classical middle power capabilities and an emerging identity as such, but it sits on China's doorstep while being allied to the United States. Alongside it is Indonesia (chapter 7), regional heavyweight of Southeast Asia, whose other two middle powers, Thailand and Malaysia (chapter 6), face similar challenges from the rise of China. While Thailand and Malaysia might normally be thought of as marginal cases, their location in Asia, near China, and their role in the "middle power regionalism" of the Association of Southeast Asian Nations (ASEAN) make them particularly important to consider.[50] Moreover, Thailand and Malaysia are important because they have recently entered the middle power ranks, having been far out of the tenth to thirtieth rank on most measures as recently as 1980. Within the Asian region, Australia (chapter 8) is another key case, combining as it does both a robust middle power status and an intentional middle power policy.

The cases of South Africa (chapter 9) and Turkey (chapter 10) deserve careful scrutiny because they are both excellent examples of "new middle powers" that nonetheless are not geographically close to China. By filtering out regional proximity, they provide a window on the importance of middle power status alone.

Finally, Brazil (chapter 11) serves as a useful test case for middle power behavior. Brazil, as mentioned, is a top-tier middle power that seeks to be a great power (just as Japan is a lower-tier great power that seeks to be a middle power).[51] Brazil's inclusion allows a way to test the strength of the link between capabilities and behavior (just as South Africa may play that same role at the lower end of capabilities).

In addition to the middle power members of the European Union—specifically, Italy, Spain, the Netherlands, and Poland—excluded because of the foreign policy coordination within the EU, other important cases omitted for reasons of space include Iran, Pakistan, and Mexico.

Therefore, the first question we have posed to our contributors is: How would you characterize the capabilities and behavior of their selected countries when compared to the ideal type of the middle power as outlined in this chapter and in the chapter by Manicom and Reeves? This is an important starting point to grasp the nature of the new membership of middle powers, which may differ fundamentally from the traditional Western middle powers.

Responses to China

The descriptive part of middle power theory sees them as particularly sensitive to changes in great power relations and the broader international system. In general, the China challenge for middle powers has involved common threads. These include the economic challenge of trade imbalances and industrial hollowing out; the security challenges of managing other security commitments while building closer diplomatic ties with Beijing; and the political challenges of protecting domestic liberal values and regional leadership. Middle powers may benefit from China's rise and its blandishments, strengthening their capabilities especially vis-à-vis regional neighbors. Yet, this in turn thrusts them into roles of responsibility in managing the rise of China and may raise new tensions in their regional relations if they are seen as Beijing's proconsuls for the region. Middle powers face the dilemma of needing to tread carefully in their ties with China so as not to upset their regional neighbors and, in several cases, their alliance partner.

The second question we pose for our contributors to address is: How has the rise of China affected their middle power's domestic, regional, and global environment? Answering this question requires careful attention to the principles of good causal analysis so that the discrete "China effect" is properly measured. In some cases, as with trade and economic impacts, these are more easily measured. In more complex situations, such as the country's regional leadership, teasing out the China factor involves consideration of several interacting variables.

Quite apart from its impact on their relations with China is the more general impact on the foreign relations of middle powers. How will the rise of China affect the role of middle powers in international affairs? How does it affect each of their relations with the United States? What are the impacts on the foreign policy initiatives and global governance networks of middle powers? The ultimate purpose is to elicit from the chapters an on-the-ground sense of the nature of China's rise as seen through the experiences of middle powers. By virtue of their being moderately vulnerable, the middle power experience may give us the greatest clues about whether China's rise will promote illiberalism, revisionism, and security threats, as opposed to cooperation, rule-abidance, sovereignty, and harmony.

As Manicom and Reeves argue, middle power theory generates a set of testable hypotheses, most of them indicated in the behavioral predictions above. *The third question, then, is: How have middle powers responded to the rise of China?* In particular, how does this response differ from that of smaller powers? The counterhegemonic hypothesis noted above, for instance, runs in direct contrast to the typical hypothesis of power transition theory that middle powers will seek to balance the rising power. From this perspective, it makes sense for middle powers to simultaneously bandwagon and balance because their interest is not balancing per se but countering great power hegemony. By pursuing diplomatic initiatives with the rising power (China), they aim to socialize it into norms of cooperation. By simultaneously maintaining, and in some instances strengthening, ties to the existing power (the United States), middle powers seek to offset the rising influence of the new great power. Middle power responses in a power transition may tell us about whether a power transition is in fact taking place since they are the most free-floating actors in the international system.[52] Moreover, all countries carefully scrutinize middle power responses as bellwethers for constructive approaches to foreign policy. The more that middle powers are responding to China, the more we have reasons to believe that China is rising.

Here, we have asked our contributors to focus on the essential point of agency, leadership, and choice that in many ways is the central feature that distinguishes middle power theory from more structurally determinative theories of great powers and secondary states. Is there evidence of middle power "niche diplomacy" or diplomatic entrepreneurship in relation to China that is qualitatively different from great or smaller powers? Moreover, while each of our middle powers (with perhaps the exceptions of Malaysia and Thailand) is a democracy, the role of civil society in contesting and shaping responses to China varies. How does civil society activism shape middle power responses to China?

In his remarks to the Shangri-La Security Dialogue in 2012, quoted in Ann Marie Murphy's chapter, Indonesian president Susilo Bambang Yudhoyono said that "the relations of major powers are not entirely up to them." He pointed to the role of Indonesia and other powers in pushing the great powers to take measures that enhance trust and cooperation among them. *The fourth question, then, is: Does evidence exist of a "middle power effect" in China's rise?* How has enmeshment, socialization, or constraint by middle powers operated on China? If China's rise is in part a social construction—people believe it will rise and thus begin to behave accordingly, which in turn makes it more likely—how have its purposes as well as its reception been changed by interactions with middle powers?[53] If middle powers laid claim to more than their fair share of UN Security Council nonpermanent seats based on their "contributions" to international peace and security, then what are those contributions with respect to the rise of China?

Again, the principles of good causal analysis apply here, and we expect that this effect will be modest at best when properly measured. Middle powers may be pursuing many initiatives with respect to China—itself notable in terms of power transitions theory—but the question of their effects is separate. We expect that any middle power effect on China's rise will be of modest magnitude, difficult to observe, and mostly indirect. The nature of middle power behavior is that it is limited in capabilities, works through coalitions, and is mainly directed at reshaping great powers by reshaping the international system.

This book, then, is both an exploration of China's rise through the middle power prism (using theory to interpret reality) as well as an exploration of middle power behavior in a variety of different cases (revising theory in light of reality). To put it plainly, in order to be useful, the middle power prism should have something novel and important to contribute. Our intention is both to contribute to international relations theorizing and to address the practical challenges of the world in responding to the rise of China.

Notes

1. Samia Nakhoul and Edmund Blair, "Morsi Pursues 'Balanced Foreign Policy,'" *Reuters News Agency*, August 28, 2012.

2. Yang Jingjie, "Morsi Kicks Off Visit to China," *Global Times*, August 28, 2012.

3. Brian Spegele, "Egypt's Morsi Firms Up Ties to China," *Wall Street Journal*, August 29, 2012.

4. "China Supports Egypt's Choice of Political System: Legislator," *People's Daily Online*, August 30, 2012, http://english.peopledaily.com.cn/90883/7929316.html.

5. Y. St. Pierre, "Caught in the Storm: Middle-Powers as Barometers for the West's Changing Attitudes towards Security and Human Rights after 9/11," in *Human Rights in the 21st Century: Continuity and Change since 9/11*, eds. Michael E. Goodhart and Anja Mihr (New York: Palgrave Macmillan, 2012).

6. National Intelligence Council, *Global Trends 2030: Alternative Worlds* (Washington, DC: National Intelligence Council, 2012), 19.

7. Adam Chapnick, "The Middle Power," *Canadian Foreign Policy* 7, no. 2 (1999): 73–82.

8. Denis Stairs, "Of Medium Powers and Middling Roles," in *Statecraft and Security: The Cold War and Beyond*, 270–86, 275, ed. Ken Booth (New York: Cambridge University Press, 1998).

9. David Cooper, "Somewhere between Great and Small: Disentangling the Conceptual Jumble of Middle, Regional, and 'Niche' Powers," *Journal of Diplomacy and International Relations* 14, no. 2 (2013): 32–58.

10. Sang-bae Kim, "Middle Powers from a Network Perspective," Paper presented at the conference The Role of Middle Powers in 21st Century International Relations (Seoul, April 19–20, 2013).

11. An example is the Constructive Powers Initiative that includes Australia, New Zealand, Brazil, Canada, Japan, Indonesia, South Korea, Mexico, Norway, South Africa, Switzerland, and Turkey.

12. John Ibbitson and Tara Perkins, "How Canada Made the G20 Happen," *Globe and Mail*, June 18, 2010.

13. Andrew Cooper and Jongryn Mo, "The Middle Seven Initiative," in *Middle Powers and G20 Governance*, 105–21, 109, ed. Jongryn Mo (Seoul: Asian Institute for Policy Studies, 2012).

14. Andrew Cooper, "Squeezed or Revitalised? Middle Powers, the G20 and the Evolution of Global Governance," *Third World Quarterly* 34, no. 6 (2013): 963–84.

15. Giampiero Giacomello and Bertjan Verbeek, *Italy's Foreign Policy in the Twenty-First Century: The New Assertiveness of an Aspiring Middle Power* (Lanham, MD: Lexington Books, 2010); Marcin Zaborowski and David H. Dunn, *Poland: A New Power in Transatlantic Security* (London; Portland, OR: Frank Cass, 2003).

16. Charalampos Efstathopoulos, "Reinterpreting India's Rise through the Middle Power Prism," *Asian Journal of Political Science* 19, no. 1 (2011): 74–95.

17. Joseph S. Nye, *Bound to Lead: The Changing Nature of American Power* (New York: Basic Books, 1990); Kristen P. Williams, Steven E. Lobell, and Neal G. Jesse, *Beyond Great Powers and Hegemons: Why Secondary States Support, Follow or Challenge* (Stanford, CA: Stanford University Press).

18. Andrew Fenton Cooper, ed. *Niche Diplomacy: Middle Powers after the Cold War, Studies in Diplomacy* (New York: St. Martin's Press, 1997).

19. Andrew Fenton Cooper, Richard A. Higgott, and Kim Richard Nossal, *Relocating Middle Powers: Australia and Canada in a Changing World Order*, Canada and International Relations (Vancouver: UBC Press, 1993), 13.

20. Robert Keohane, "Lilliputians' Dilemmas: Small States in International Politics," *International Organization* 23, no. 2 (1969): 291–310, 295.

21. Joseph S. Nye, *Soft Power: The Means to Success in World Politics*, 1st ed. (New York: Public Affairs, 2004).

22. Cooper, Higgott, and Nossal, *Relocating Middle Powers*, 14, 21.

23. Bernard Wood, *The Middle Powers and the General Interest* (Ottawa: North-South Institute, 1988).

24. Stairs, "Of Medium Powers and Middling Roles," 279–80.

25. Cooper, Higgott, and Nossal, *Relocating Middle Powers*, chap. 2.

26. James Manicom and Andrew O'Neil, "China's Rise and Middle Power Democracies: Canada and Australia Compared," *International Relations of the Asia-Pacific* 12, no. 2 (2012): 199–228.

27. Carsten Holbraad, *Middle Powers in International Politics* (New York: St. Martin's Press, 1984); Andrew Fenton Cooper and Timothy M. Shaw, *The Diplomacies of Small States: Between Vulnerability and Resilience* (New York: Palgrave Macmillan, 2009); Holbraad, *Middle Powers in International Politics*, 5.

28. Cooper, Higgott, and Nossal, *Relocating Middle Powers*, 24–25; Andrew Fenton Cooper, *Niche Diplomacy: Middle Powers after the Cold War* (New York: St. Martin's Press, 1997); John Ravenhill, "Cycles of Middle Power Activism: Constraint and Choice in Australian and Canadian Foreign Policies," *Australian Journal of International Affairs* 52, no. 3 (1998): 309–28; Dilek Barlas, "Turkish Diplomacy in the Balkans and the Mediterranean. Opportunities and Limits for Middle-Power Activism in the 1930s," *Journal of Contemporary History* 40, no. 3 (2005): 441–64.

29. Gareth Evans, "Middle Power Diplomacy," *Inaugural Edgardo Boeninger Memorial Lecture*, Chile Pacific Foundation, Santiago, July 5 (2011).

30. Robert W. Cox, "Middlepowermanship, Japan, and Future World Order," *International Journal* 44, no. 4 (1989): 823–62.

31. Giovanni Botero, *The Reason of State*, Rare Masterpieces of Philosophy and Science (New Haven, CT: Yale University Press, 1589 (1956)), 8.

32. David Cooper, "Challenging Contemporary Notions of Middle Power Influence: Implications of the Proliferation Security Initiative for 'Middle Power Theory,'" *Foreign Policy Analysis*, no. 7 (2011): 317–36; Ronald Behringer, "Middle Power Leadership on the Human Security Agenda," *Cooperation and Conflict* 40, no. 3 (2005): 305–42.

33. Kil-Joo Ban, "The ROK as a Middle Power: Its Role in Counterinsurgency," *Asian Politics & Policy* 3, no. 2 (2011): 225–47.

34. Ronald M. Behringer, *The Human Security Agenda: How Middle Power Leadership Defied US Hegemony* (New York: Continuum, 2012).

35. Elizabeth Chalecki and Lisa Ferrari, "More Maple Leaf, Less CO^2: Canada and a Global Geo-Engineering Regime," *Canadian Foreign Policy* 18, no. 1 (2012): 120–32.

36. G. det. Glazebrook, "The Middle Powers in the United Nations System," *International Organization* 1, no. 2 (1947): 307–15, 308.

37. David B. Dewitt and John J. Kirton, *Canada as a Principal Power: A Study in Foreign Policy and International Relations* (Toronto; New York: Wiley, 1983).

38. William Tow and Richard Rigby, "China's Pragmatic Security Policy: The Middle Power Factor," *China Journal* 65, no. 1 (2011): 157–78.

39. Cooper, Higgott, and Nossal, *Relocating Middle Powers*, 19.

40. Charalampos Efstathopoulos, "Middle Powers and Combative Diplomacy: South Africa in the 2003 Cancun Ministerial Conference of the World Trade Organisation," *Diplomacy & Statecraft* 23, no. 1 (2012): 140–61.

41. Andrew Fenton Cooper, "Niche Diplomacy: A Conceptual Overview," in *Niche Diplomacy: Middle Powers after the Cold War*, 1–24, 3, ed. Andrew Fenton Cooper (New York: St. Martin's Press, 1997).

42. United Nations General Assembly, "'Uniting for Consensus' Group of States Introduces Text on Security Council Reform to General Assembly," www.un.org/News/Press/docs/2005/ga10371.doc.htm.

43. Eduard Jordaan, "The Concept of a Middle Power in International Relations: Distinguishing between Emerging and Traditional Middle Powers," *Politikon: South African Journal of Political Studies* 30, no. 2 (2003): 165–81.

44. Stewart Patrick, "Irresponsible Stakeholders?," *Foreign Affairs* 89, no. 6 (2010): 44–53.

45. Cranford Pratt, *Middle Power Internationalism: The North-South Dimension* (Kingston; Buffalo: McGill-Queen's University Press, 1990).

46. Janis van der Westhuizen, "Class Compromise as Middle Power Activism? Comparing Brazil and South Africa," *Government and Opposition* 48, no. 1 (2013): 80–100.

47. K. J. Holsti, "National Role Conceptions in the Study of Foreign Policy," *International Studies Quarterly* 14, no. 3 (1970): 233–309.

48. Stairs, "Of Medium Powers and Middling Roles," 282.

49. Laura Neak, "Empirical Observations on 'Middle State' Behavior at the Start of a New International System," *Pacific Focus* 7, no. 1 (1992): 5–21; "Delineating State Groups through Cluster Analysis," *Social Science Journal* 30, no. 3 (1993): 347–71.

50. Evelyn Goh, "Institutions and the Great Power Bargain in East Asia: ASEAN's Limited 'Brokerage' Role," *International Relations of the Asia-Pacific* 11, no. 3 (2011): 373–401, 380.

51. Yoshihide Soeya, *Nippon No "Midorupawā" Gaikō—Sengo Nippon No Sentaku to Kōsō (Japan's "Middle Power" Diplomacy: Idea Selection and Postwar Japan)* (Tokyo: Chikuma Shobo, 2005).

52. Enrico Fels, "Middle Power Allegiance and the Power Shift in Asia-Pacific—The Case of Australia," *International Studies Association Annual Conference* (2011).

53. Jeffrey Legro, "Purpose Transitions: China's Rise and the American Response," in *China's Ascent: Power, Security, and the Future of International Politics*, 163–90, eds. Robert S. Ross and Feng Zhu (Ithaca: Cornell University Press, 2008).

CHAPTER 2

Locating Middle Powers in International Relations Theory and Power Transitions

James Manicom and Jeffrey Reeves

Introduction

MUCH OF THE LITERATURE on China's rise has centred on the response of great powers to the emergence of a rising power. An alternative body of work has explored how smaller powers neighboring China have responded to a nascent competition between a hegemonic United States and a rising China for primacy in Asia. Conventional international relations theory sees small and middle powers as "policy*takers*" rather than "policy*makers*." Consequently, their direct agency to respond to power transitions is limited; a secondary state's policy options are limited to varieties of bandwagoning with or balancing against the rising power. This misconception is at odds with the literature on middle power foreign policy, which views middle powers as capable actors that contribute to international relations in the spaces overlooked by great powers. In time of great power competition, they can serve as "honest brokers" and are thus integral to the building of confidence that can mitigate great power or "hegemonic" war. Furthermore, acting with like-minded states, these middle-ranking states can constrain the excesses of great and hegemonic powers by enmeshing them in norms and institutions. However, this research paradigm has struggled to maintain relevance due to its enduring definitional and methodological shortcomings and the preoccupation of the international relations discipline with great powers.

This chapter addresses some of these concerns by stripping middle power theory down to its core and proposing a way to use the theory to compare and assess the behavior of a certain category of secondary states under the conditions of a power transition. It begins with an outline of the expectations of power transition theory as it pertains to rising powers, and notes that middle powers are overlooked in this research program. The second section surveys the middle power research program and addresses its definitional and conceptual weaknesses. The final section sets out why this theoretical approach is nonetheless an appropriate lens through which to examine China's rise and advances a threefold middle power typology that guides the comparative approach of the remainder of the volume.

Power Transition Theory: Rising Powers and Secondary States

International relations theory has long divided the world into great powers and the rest, which has meant that the exponentially greater capabilities of middle powers are equated with those of small powers. Rarely afforded agency, middle powers are frequently presented as either pawns on the geostrategic chessboard or actors with extremely limited policy options. At best, middle powers in international relations theory are states that can influence the global order through alliances, security communities, or international organizations. At worst, middle powers are presented as having little choice outside bandwagoning or balancing.

Within international relations theory as a whole, realism offers the bleakest view of middle power's capacities. In his seminal realist work, *Politics among Nations*, Morgenthau specifically relegates middle powers, which he calls "traditional nation states," to a role of reaction rather than action.[1] Within Morgenthau's realist principles, states without the material power to advance their own interests occupy dependent positions incapable of driving change. Drawing on Morgenthau's realist tradition, Stephen Walt notes that secondary states must either bandwagon or balance, with weaker states opting to bandwagon with the stronger power because they can "do little to affect the outcome."[2] Conversely, Kenneth Waltz notes that secondary states, "if they are free to choose, flock to the weaker side," because their support is more greatly appreciated and their potential rewards larger.[3] While these two distinguished realist representations of middle power behavior suggest a divergence in perceptions over what motivates middle powers, their treatment of middle powers' foreign policy options points to a theoretical concurrence that such options are extremely limited.

Within realism, power transition theory also suggests that middle powers lack agency and are beholden to great powers for their strategic maneuver. A. F. K. Organski and Jacek Kugler argue that middle powers are incapable of affecting change in the international system because they lack sufficient material capacity.[4] Even if fully economically and politically developed, Organski and Kugler argued, middle powers cannot influence development at the strategic level in ways that even a great power as limited as India can. Power transition theory removes any scope for maneuver for middle powers to emerge as independent actors as it presents the international system as hierarchical, not anarchic.[5] Given power transition theory's dyadic focus on competition between the system's dominant state and rising powers as the driver for change within the international system, the theory's dismissal of middle powers' agency is not surprising.

While Douglas Lemke's multiple hierarchical model approach to power transition theory is often lauded as a successful attempt to incorporate middle powers into the theory, it does not develop a framework for thinking about middle powers' behavior outside the power transition framework.[6] For Lemke, "the difference between major—and minor—power war is one of degree, not of kind."[7] Lemke's addition to the literature on middle powers is, therefore, minimal.

Neither does Robert Gilpin's writing on power transition assign middle powers any agency. Instead, hegemons and their challengers use middle powers as a means to strengthen their relative positions vis-à-vis one another. Great powers accomplish this through "the use of threats and coercion, the formation of alliances, or the creation of exclusive spheres of influence."[8] At best, middle powers within Gilpin's approach are conscious actors forced to choose between two competing great powers. At worst, they are formless instruments in a great power's arsenal. This dearth of treatment of middle powers is not just confined to theories about power transition. Since Thucydides, writings on international relations have focused on great powers as the forces for change in the international system. Particularly within realism, secondary states were presented as passive actors that could move only in accordance with pervasive power trends within the contemporary international system.[9]

Realism's conceptualization of middle powers is limited, as it defines them in comparison to great powers and by their role in international politics. This view of middle powers does not allow for consideration of middle power influence at a regional level, where middle powers are most active. While middle powers may lack the material power to affect change among great powers at an international level, this limitation is not always present in regions. Subsequent empirical work has revealed that middle powers will often resist efforts by hegemons to consolidate their regional status.[10]

Like realism, liberalism fails to treat middle powers as independent actors in the international system. One notable exception to this oversight is the treatment by complex interdependence theorists of middle power foreign policy. Robert Keohane and Joseph Nye define complex interdependence as occurring when two states have extensive linkages across multiple channels, when cooperation is not confined to military concerns, and when the threat of military conflict between the two states is diminished.[11] Middle powers can engage in linkage strategies with larger states to decrease their vulnerability at relatively low cost and with relatively high return.[12] Yet at its core, complex interdependence is similar to bandwagoning, suggesting the best a middle power can do in the international system is to cast its lot with a greater power in the hope of carving out a security niche. Furthermore, the paradigm's focus on a more diverse array of actors, such as international nongovernmental organizations, multinational corporations, and international institutions, further marginalizes the potential influence of middle powers.

Of the three major approaches, constructivism addresses middle power behavior most directly, but also offers the most muddled account of middle power behavior. One strand of constructivism sees the concept of middle powers as a means used by diplomats in secondary states to raise their countries' status. By arguing that secondary states possess agency to affect change at the international and regional levels, middle power actors have created a middle power identity that serves as the basis for explaining middle power behavior.[13] Likewise, Japanese scholars have used the middle power concept to reduce Japan's status in an effort to project a more benign image and a concomitantly more activist foreign policy role. Aside from this constructed narrative, there is little commonality between middle powers that would suggest they occupy a distinct position in international society.

Conversely, some scholars employ constructivism to explain middle powers' influence as "norm-makers" and the building blocks of security communities.[14] Middle powers operate with a normative-focused foreign policy, which makes them more responsible actors, on this view. Middle powers act as both followers and leaders in the construction of thick multilateralism.[15] Within this strand of constructivism, middle powers are the building blocks of global and regional security, not mere imagined entities. While often consistent with middle power theory, this approach has the weakness of assuming that middle power behavior is normatively attractive, a facet that Gilley and O'Neil reject in chapter 1.

The homogenization of all secondary state foreign policy behavior by international relations theory is in many ways mirrored in contemporary writings on rising China and leads to dangerous oversights. Many accounts of China's rise and power transitions in Asia focus on relations between great powers when conceptualizing the drivers behind the region's strategic architecture. Scholars point to the underlying tensions that result from Sino-US, Sino-Japanese, or Sino-Indian relations, frequently citing theories of power transitions or realism to explain regional security dynamics. John Mearsheimer's famous prediction of conflict between the United States and China in *The Tragedy of Great Power Politics* is a good example.[16] Henry Kissinger's warning of the inevitable conflict that will occur between the United States and China if the two states cannot develop strategic trust is another.[17] Both overlook the importance of the Association of Southeast Asian Nations (ASEAN) to Chinese foreign policy and of the North Atlantic Treaty Organization (NATO) to US foreign policy. Neither analysis can explain China's decade-long "smile offensive" toward its neighbors.[18] The theoretical predisposition toward great powers causes some scholars to miss a key part of the picture.

When addressed, scholars often portray Asian middle powers as practicing traditional middle power strategies aimed at dealing with China's rise. Aaron Friedberg's "Ripe for Rivalry" prediction presented middle power actors as engaged in either bandwagoning or external balancing aimed at China.[19] Indeed, Friedberg's thesis rested on middle powers following this foreign policy path as he predicted such behavior would result in regional conflict. Even writing on middle powers from a distinctly Asian perspective limits their foreign policy options to those presented in classic and neorealist approaches. David Kang, for example, does not provide a detailed treatment of middle powers' foreign policy in Asia despite his insistence that any framework for viewing interstate relations in Asia must be viewed through a lens of Asian norms and history. For Kang, while Asian middle powers' motivations may be distinct, they still engage in foreign policy behavior explicitly outlined in classic realism.[20] These assumptions stand in stark contrast to research on middle power foreign policy.

Middle Power Project: Position, Behavior, and Identity

At its core the middle power research program is an attempt to theorize about the role of a certain category of secondary state in international politics. The program starts with the assumption that nongreat powers are in fact agents in the making of their own foreign policy. Middle powers are states with tangible influence at the international (as distinct from regional) level that possess relative global material power capabilities behind the great powers but still in the top tier of all states (ahead of the vast number of small states). Definitional problems have plagued the middle power research program since its inception.[21] Self-identified middle powers emerged after World War II when Australia and Canada lobbied for a greater role in the postwar international security apparatus as a function of their commitment to the Allied war effort.[22] During the Cold War period, middle powers were described as mediators of disputes and builders of bridges.[23] As détente emerged in the 1970s and early 1980s, middle power behavior took on a normative aspect as these states reached out to develop links with the Non-Aligned Movement or tried to improve relations between Asia and the West. Finally, as the Cold War wound down and the international system became unipolar, middle power behavior was characterized by coalition building within multilateral institutions, by a strong belief in the principles of liberal internationalism, and the pursuit of "niche diplomacy" in areas such as trade and commerce, rule and norm creation, and regime and institution building.[24]

Middle power foreign policy behavior, traditionally defined, includes a tendency toward multipolar preferences, the embrace of mediation or peacebuilding activities, and a predisposition toward good international citizenship often reflected in building and following rules, all guided by a healthy dose of self-interest.[25] Problematically, there is no clear causal link between the root of this behavior and the size of a particular state or its position in the international hierarchy. Whether or not they *believe* in liberal internationalism, middle powers act collaboratively and multilaterally because they have to.[26] Indeed, multilateralism is not a uniquely middle power value; the United States is one of the most multilaterally inclined states in the system. As Kim Nossal has argued, "middlepowermanship is how one defines middle powers, and those who engage in middlepowermanship are middle powers—a classic tautology."[27] As noted below, this book seeks to amend this state of affairs.

Furthermore, the definition reveals a lack of consensus on what material attributes, such as geography, population, military spending, or diplomatic capacity, yield to a middle power.[28] Can a middle power be labeled as such if it is not simultaneously a regional power? Why are materially weaker powers, such as Norway, perpetually linked with the term by virtue of their behavior? Why is Japan even a part of the conversation, despite having the world's third-largest economy?[29] The answer, of course, is that there are those in Japan, as in Australia and Canada, who frame the country's foreign policy as having the characteristics of a middle power. This book seeks to salvage the middle power paradigm as an analytical lens by making no a priori assumptions about the nature of middle power behavior. Rather, we develop hypotheses about how states of considerable capacity might behave under the conditions of a power transition, thus avoiding Nossal's tautology noted above. This section explores the multiple conceptions of the term "middle" and identifies three different types of middle powers that portray related but distinct traits: positional, behavioral, and ideational middle powers.

The definition contains an inherent positional criterion: a basic level of material power is the core-defining feature to wear the label of middle power. Further, the literature on middle powers reveals a hypothesized behavioral aspect—that middle powers behave in particular ways under particular circumstances—and finally an ideational aspect—some states cultivate a middle power foreign policy identity.[30] Although the first criterion is a necessary condition, the existence and impact of the latter two on a given middle power's response to the rise of China is hypothetical—as stated in chapter 1, behavioral traits are not defining of the category, rather they are hypothesized predictions of the category. After exploring these three criteria, the chapter explores the salience of the international system in the development of expectations about the direction of middle power behavior. One of the reasons middle power behavior has been so varied is that the concept has sought to explain the behavior of middle powers under four distinct conditions: the post–World War II world, the Cold War world, the post–Cold War world, and the current state of systemic uncertainty. This approach forms the basis of a comparative methodology that allows authors to locate their subject state within the middle power paradigm and ask what the middle power concept reveals about a given state's relationship with a rising China.

There is an underlying logic to the positional definition of the term middle power. It seems plausible to expect countries in the middle of the international hierarchy to have a greater capacity for autonomy than the smallest states in the system. States with capacity are thus more likely to engage in foreign policy activism than those with less capacity. They are more likely to exercise more agency than weaker states in their alignment strategy toward hegemonic and rising powers. By contrast, weak states are more likely to be concerned with responding to internal and external threats as a source of their alignment strategy.[31] Recent research suggests that a sense of vulnerability primarily motivates small state behavior.[32] Furthermore, middle powers, unlike small states, are less likely to develop a dependent relationship with great powers.[33] It thus remains a pertinent entry point for an attempt to theorize the behavior of such secondary states toward a systemic shift—the rise of a potential challenger to the hegemon.

From a positional standpoint middle powers have certain capabilities that sit below the great powers but above the small powers.[34] The positional criterion is necessary for a given state to adopt the behavioral or ideational components of a middle power; without a basic level of capability, a middle power could not act like one, nor plausibly identify as one. Although there is no causal link between size and foreign policy behavior, there is a logical one.

Middle powers are not powerful enough to act alone, yet not small enough to render the pursuit of their national interests futile. Although both may be less clear than ideal, it is easy to identify what is *not* a twenty-first-century middle power. It is not Somalia; it is not America; it is not China, or Trinidad. Indeed, since they have turned their foreign policymaking over to a supranational government in Brussels, it is not Denmark or the Netherlands.

As one moves down from obvious great powers and up from obvious small powers, one enters the gray area of countries like Brazil (from the top) and Malaysia (from the bottom), both of which are included here. But, as the saying goes, twilight is not proof that night and day do not exist. States that lie roughly within the tenth to thirtieth range of various power capabilities can thus be characterized as "positional middle powers."[35] The behavioral and ideational criteria help clarify which among these are expected to display more traditional aspects of middle power behavior. Some positional middle powers have not or will not adopt the necessarily activist foreign policy role, such as Colombia, Iran, and Saudi Arabia, to be described as a traditional behavioral middle power. Other secondary states, formerly having identified as middle powers, fall outside the necessary capabilities range, including New Zealand, Belgium, Austria, and Norway. For the purposes of this book we identify eight states that are among those that meet the positional criteria: Australia, Brazil, Indonesia, Malaysia, South Africa, South Korea, Thailand, and Turkey. These secondary states have also at times displayed the kind of foreign policy activism that is the hallmark of middle powers: multipolar, mediation oriented, seeking modest reforms and strengthening of the rules-based international system.

This positional criterion is the basis of the remaining aspects of middle powers; it is necessary for a certain type of foreign policy behavior, one that is more activist than those states that lack the necessary capabilities. It does not determine this role, but it is necessary as not all states have the military, diplomatic, and technical expertise required to exercise influence on the world's stage. Whether a state chooses to do so is a function of the latter two criteria. In the absence of the positional criterion, a state does not have the option to act as a middle power. The origin of the behavioral quality of middle powers lies in the first generation of middle power scholarship, which rested on two assumptions.

The first assumption is that middle powers are inherently status quo oriented. This emerged out of their role following World War II as the "first followers" of *Pax Americana*. The United States constructed a system that aimed to prevent the outbreak of another world war while ensuring that communism could be contained. Indeed, middle powers were instrumental in keeping America engaged after the end of World War II, and were particularly active in the creation of the UN.[36] The middle powers were active supporters of this effort and in the process contributed to international order, not least their efforts to enmesh the superpowers into international institutions aimed to curb their excesses.[37] Indeed, this behavioral typology persists to this day. Gilbert Rozman has argued that South Korea's middle power assets allow it to "maneuver among great powers to help them realize elusive goals," thereby allowing it to thrive in Northeast Asia.[38]

The shifting international structure of the post–Cold War period marked the beginning of a second phase of middle power scholarship. As a function of unipolarity, the traditional middle power role became obsolete. Nevertheless, as new economic and security challenges emerged, middle powers embarked on "niche diplomacy."[39] Also called mission-oriented diplomacy, niche diplomacy refers to efforts by entrepreneurial states able to draw on functional expertise in their bureaucracies to act as a catalyst or leader on a given international issue. In the absence of great power competition, middle powers were able to use their residual capacity to pursue their interests while responding to emerging international problems. Middle powers were able to build coalitions that included not only like-minded states, but also nongovernmental organizations and social movements and, in the economic realm, corporations.

In many cases such efforts also included issue linkages across previously unknown relationships, such as gender and development, intellectual property and agriculture, and between trade and the environment.[40] The international effort to ban cluster munitions is one example of mission-oriented diplomacy; NGOs can provide technical expertise and generate momentum behind an initiative while middle powers are well placed to add the issue to the international agenda.[41] In Canada, this agenda was dominated by the "human security" paradigm; in Australia, it was characterized by efforts to drive regionalism in East Asia and cultivate a role as a regional power, while also driving the global arms control agenda.[42]

However, this work exposed a tension in the middle power research agenda: the behavioral criterion became too flexible to be analytically useful. Middle power activism during the Cold War was not driven by altruism but by the calculation that great power war was something to be avoided and that an opportunity existed for middle powers to contribute to international peace and stability while pursuing their interests. Some aspects of post–Cold War middlepowermanship, such as Australia's role in developing the agricultural Cairns Group, are consistent with this behavioral model: a positional middle power state aligning with others to pursue its interests in a multilateral context.[43] However, other aspects of the post–Cold War middle power agenda defied this logic. What national interest is served, for instance, by Canada's support for the international effort to ban landmines, which led to the Ottawa Treaty, which was not signed by its chief ally the United States? Rather, this international activism had a domestic agenda.[44]

This exposes a tension at the heart of the behavioral criterion: there is no underlying logic as to why a middle power engages in "middle-powermanship."[45] Why should analysts expect the middle range of countries, roughly with power capability ranking in the range ten to thirty for the purposes of this book, to behave similarly? How does one explain the apparent altruism behind some elements of classically defined middle power foreign policy? Why did Canada pursue a ban on landmines so strongly? What did Australia gain by being so active in the Cambodian peace process? Why was South Africa so intent on the creation of the new African Union and related regional instruments? These deviations from the more instrumental aspects of middle power behavior that defined its early Cold War permutations can be explained by the conceptualization of an "ideational" middle power.

Centered on the idea of national role conception, states may behave in such ways because they identify as a middle power and have constructed this term to mean certain things relating to the conduct of foreign affairs in an activist, perhaps even altruistic, fashion.[46] Characterizing a state as a middle power may be a useful way for activist diplomats to sell certain foreign policies to the electorate.[47] By the late 1990s, some argued that middle powers were driving a "human security agenda" based on emerging norms of state intervention, the Ottawa process to ban landmines, the International Criminal Court, and attempts to ban small arms.[48] In the Canadian case, for instance, successive governments under Prime Ministers Brian Mulroney and Jean Chrétien constructed a role for Canada as a unique foreign policy actor, based on its noncolonial past, its investment in multilateralism, and its role as a mediator. This role found expression in Canada's belief in peacekeeping, a national belief that far outlasted Canada's actual commitment to UN peacekeeping missions.[49] There is clearly an ideational component to middle powers. Countries like Australia have classically identified themselves as such and have adopted foreign policy roles that reflect this ideational belief.[50] Others use the ideational concept instrumentally. In Japan, those who seek a more internationalist military role for Japan—one that is currently out of reach due to constitutional constraints—have tried to frame Japan as a middle power in an effort to build support for the adoption of such an agenda.[51]

Analytical recognition of this ideational dimension helps clarify some of the definitional issues that have plagued the concept. Those that identify as middle powers may in fact emphasize select behavioral aspects not explicitly linked to the academic concept itself. Thus, Carl Ungerer's formulation of Australia's middle power diplomacy as centering on the twin themes of "a broad commitment to liberal internationalism and a belief in the leadership role that small and middle powers could play in international relations" is in fact a statement of how successive Australian leaders conceived of Australia's middle power role, not an objective assessment of the direction of Australian foreign policy.[52] Indeed, as John Ravenhill has illustrated, even if middle power behavior can be identified, such behavior does not reflect a state's behavior all of the time.[53] Archetypical middle power behavior remains subject to broader considerations and is often opportunistic.

The archetypical middle power thus possesses three characteristics: the material capability, the behavioral element, and the ideational component. For the range of cases in this book, the first is a necessary condition as the latter two are dependent on it, but may not obtain for all states that meet the positional criterion. Although status does not determine behavior, it may provide a window into state interests under certain conditions. As illustrated by Robert Cox, middlepowermanship is a reflection of middle power status.[54] Classically defined middle powers have a more status quo orientation than other secondary states by virtue of their status. In the latter part of the Cold War, and in the post–Cold War period, the opportunity arose for middle powers to play a more active role, hence the behavioral typology noted above. In order to pursue activism in multilateral forums, such forums need to exist and a given middle power needs to have the institutional literacy to pursue their objectives. In the current global order these forums are an extension of American hegemony. Although much of their activism is related to reformist activity, this is reform that follows an international consensus among those states active in the system that change needs to occur.

Middle power modifications to international order are not necessarily identical to the hypothesized revisionist ambitions of rising powers. Indeed, it is when this system is threatened by reformist activity that deviates too far from the status quo that middle powers act to rein in the excesses of great powers. In other cases they can drive systemic reform themselves. Middle powers have a stake in the international system; it has made them wealthy, it has kept them relatively secure, and they thus have a vested interest in maintaining its stability. If change is afoot, they have an interest in managing that change so that the system that emerges on the other side is one in which they can thrive.[55] This is what underwrites their proclivity for multilateralism, their drive for consensus, and their support of the international system. Thus, although a middle power's status may not determine its behavior, it may offer clues about its interests toward the challenge posed by the emergence of a rival to the hegemon.

Whether twenty-first-century middle powers share this status quo orientation remains to be seen. Not all states that qualify as positional middle powers may in fact share this foreign policy predisposition. Indeed many may seek, when confronted with a rising hegemon, to bandwagon with its efforts to remake international order. Second-generation middle powers may be less predisposed to the broadly liberal foreign policy role of their first-generation counterparts.[56] It was previously possible to identify subtle differences in style between the broadly liberal coalition of first-generation middle powers. States such as Australia, Norway, Sweden, and Canada applied their activism in different forms across specific or a broad range of issue areas.[57]

As a product of the diffusion of economic power to the developing world, the same international process that underwrites the rise of China, formerly developing states are becoming positional middle powers. Many of these powers are concomitantly more activist than previously, but may not perceive system reform in the same way as first-generation middle powers.[58] If first-generation middle powers were archetypical "liberal internationalist" states, second-generation middle powers may be better described as simply "internationalist" states. Whether these second-generation middle powers will behave in ways similar to their first-generation counterparts can be evaluated when weighed against a common phenomenon—the rise of China.

This book is thus an attempt to move the middle power paradigm beyond the "first-generation" middle powers in the Western European and Anglophone tradition to "second-generation" middle powers, to include Brazil, Malaysia, Indonesia, South Africa, Thailand, and Turkey.[59] The question of what, if anything, is distinctive about middle power behavior is asked with respect to new middle powers and a new issue in international relations—the rise of China. Since the states and the phenomenon here are both so central to the categories of middle powers and international order, respectively, the results can lay claim to defining what middle power theory means today. Although middle powers have acted together to reform the international system in a broadly liberal fashion, via the ban on landmines or the creation of the International Criminal Court, no such assumption is made with regard to the second-generation middle powers that are characterized by varied domestic political orientations. The list of "second-generation" middle powers contains both US allies and states that pride themselves on independent foreign policy traditions.

This book also jettisons the geographic criterion of a middle power physically located between great powers, and the normative criterion, the assumption that middle powers somehow have a more virtuous foreign policy definition than other states in the system.[60] Indeed, unlike their first-generation predecessors, the second-generation middle powers are far more powerful relative to their regional neighbors than the first-generation middle powers.[61] Nevertheless, these states seem to be engaged in activist foreign policies that at times mirror the middle power style of old.[62] Some have argued that the India-Brazil-South Africa Dialogue Forum is illustrative of an effort by these states to drive the global agenda against agricultural subsidies, but which came to represent a broader set of reforms to international order that were rooted in the developing world experience.[63]

The rise of China presents a common empirical phenomenon against which these states' behaviors can be evaluated. The rise of China presents a number of challenges across numerous issue areas, including economic, political, and strategic.[64] Within the middle power typology, different states may have more or less concern about different aspects of China's rise. Western middle powers have struggled to balance the economic and political dimensions of China's rise due to sensitivities about human rights.[65] Does this hold for second-generation middle powers? What is the relationship between a state's middle power qualities and its reaction to efforts by China to alter the international system? Does China's recognition of the importance of middle powers, in contrast to America's ambivalence, say anything about the future of multilateral attempts to solve world problems?

Why Now? Middle Powers and Power Transitions

Power transitions are important because the rising power will seek to modify the international system as it emerges. Rising powers affect international order in a number of ways. By definition, rising powers affect the strategic calculations of all other states in the system by virtue of their increased military expenditure and expanded foreign policy agenda. Rising powers can also present compelling economic challenges. If the rising state has revisionist aspirations, it can advance opposing models of economic order to that of the hegemonic state as the Soviet Union did during the Cold War period. Alternatively, if the rising power is an active participant in the dominant economic order, its economic growth will almost certainly present opportunities and challenges to other trading states. For example, according to one scholar, China is advancing an economic order in the energy sector that suboptimizes the American system.[66] This alternative economic order is rooted in a set of political preferences that privilege the state over the market and collective good over individual liberty.[67] Thus, despite the staying power of the current liberal democratic order, because a rising power finds within the system the tools required to fulfill its objectives and by extension does not develop revisionist aspirations, it may seek to form new coalitions to modify select aspects of international order.[68] Given the absence of a coherent research program on secondary states during power transitions, and the assumption that middle powers possess agency, the latter is a natural fit to address the former. In this context there are two compelling reasons to study middle powers and the rise of China.

First, the structural changes under way in international relations mean that the capacity of middle powers to affect a rising great power—given the diffusion of power to a multitude of state and nonstate actors, institutions, and norms—may be unprecedented in world history.[69] As Joseph Nye cogently illustrates, the international system is defined by an increasingly diverse set of actors in different issue areas. Although the global strategic order will remain unipolar, there is ample evidence that the economic order is becoming more diffuse and multipolar; global civil society is becoming increasingly turbulent as actors proliferate.[70] Furthermore, the salience of multilateral institutions is on the decline as regional institutions increasingly become the legitimizers of behavior.[71] As noted by Holbraad, middle powers are most prominent under the conditions of restrained rivalry, a condition that undoubtedly exists between the United States and China. Many middle powers owe their status to the international system that has been backed by the United States. That some second-generation middle powers have reformist ambitions toward this order makes them potential allies of a rising China. It is thus unsurprising that, as Bruce Gilley notes in chapter 3, a number of Chinese scholars take the middle power concept seriously. Middle powers may thus emerge as key players if, as some expect, China seeks to delegitimize American hegemony.[72]

Regardless of reformist ambitions, no rising power has ever been as conscious of promoting a benign appearance of its rise as China. Middle powers, as norm-makers and enforcers, are the targets of China's strategy to ensure a peaceful external environment to focus on domestic development. Middle powers are the audience that China seeks not to alarm by its rise.[73] This was true for Southeast Asian states for much of the late 1990s and the first decade of the twenty-first century. As David Lampton has observed, China's relations with its neighbors are the "canary in the coal mine" for the rest of the world.[74] Sino-ASEAN interactions led to shared experiences between the two and eventually enmeshed China into normative frameworks not of its own making.[75] This assessment seems to support some of the more optimistic assessments of the middle power foreign policy agenda outlined above, which indicates that middle powers, acting collectively rather than alone, can transform the international system in subtle ways. Middle powers are thus potential partners and potential rivals regarding China's efforts to reform the international system.

Second, these new international conditions have arguably given rise to a new kind of middle power. The second wave of middle power scholarship—which looked for a role for middle powers in the post–Cold War era—was centered on the assumption that power in the international system was becoming more diffuse and that in such a climate, secondary states had more latitude to pursue their foreign policy interests, while making slight modifications to international order. Similarly, this book is written at a time of uncertainty and arguably greater diffusion of power through the international system. However, unlike the early 1990s when middle powers acted independently of the hegemon in new "low-politic" issue areas, middle powers are now confronted with a dramatically different set of international circumstances. Although the system is confronted with greater uncertainty, the emergence of multiple poles of power, centered in particular in Asia, presents new unfamiliar challenges.

Likewise, the domestic capacity of many traditional middle powers is itself threatened by their exposure to the global financial crisis.[76] Middle powers are thus as active as ever in international institutions, but the diffusion of power has created unfamiliar coalitions based on national interests. It seems there is little appetite in the current international system for the kind of internationalist behavior witnessed in the 1990s. As a consequence, we may be at the cusp of a third wave of middle power scholarship that explores second-generation positional middle powers engaged in a new kind of middle power behavior. There is no better case against which to explore this issue than middle power reactions to the rise of China, a country that has a decidedly mixed interaction with international order.[77]

The prospects for the socialization of China are a vital part of this story. China has sought to soften concern about its rise by settling border disputes, emphasizing its domestic challenges, and broadly adhering to international norms.[78] For much of the 1990s, China embarked on a "charm offensive" designed to improve relations with its neighbors.[79] Although many believed that this enmeshment of China would constrain its behavior in the South China Sea, subsequent events raised new uncertainties. However, it could be argued that China has been affected by middle power diplomacy at the systemic level. This is best illustrated by its posture toward the Responsibility to Protect (R2P), which originated as a middle power normative project. China has long been a staunch defender of the traditional, Westphalian norms of noninterference and nonintervention in the domestic affairs of other states. This dictum was evident in its five principles of peaceful coexistence and arguably underwrites the "ASEAN way." Nevertheless, as international attitudes shifted, so did China's. Although China has not wholly endorsed intervention on humanitarian grounds, Rosemary Foot and

Andrew Walter argue that China can be seen as the more conservative end of the R2P spectrum.[80] Importantly, it has not sought to block or delegitimize the norm, but rather has emphasized the high standard for intervention and the preventative aspects of capacity building within problematic state. Second-generation middle powers are also active in modifying this norm and may be partners or adversaries for Chinese efforts, illustrated by Brazil's notion of "responsibility while protecting."[81]

The threefold typology of middle powers developed above yields the following hypothesized behavior toward a rising China. First, positional middle powers are expected to be able to exercise influence by virtue of their disproportionate size and contribute to the building of international order in a way that reflects their interests. Second, behavioral middle powers are expected to do the above plus build coalitions with like-minded states, look for niche areas in which to exercise disproportionate influence, and act as bridge builders between great powers. Third, ideational middle powers are expected to do the above plus claim a degree of moralism in their foreign policy (the claim of good international citizenship), adhere to liberal internationalist values, and frame themselves as leaders on a given issue.

These three ideal types allow the authors of the case study chapters to classify their secondary state and analyze its response to the rise of China through the middle power prism. This should shed insight on the suitability of the middle power paradigm for the analysis of secondary-state interactions with a rising power. Specifically, is there variation between first- and second-generation middle powers with reference to the rise of China? Has the rise of China given middle powers disproportionate influence that they might otherwise not have? Is this influence directed at China or at the hegemonic United States?

Conclusion

The time is right to dust off the middle power concept and assess its ability to explain the response of powerful secondary states to the rise of China. The international system is in a state of flux and the relationship between a rising China and the hegemonic United States is characterized by a restrained rivalry. Under these conditions, middle power theory should be able to inform students of international politics about the impact of these secondary states on great power behavior. The exercise has added salience because the past two decades have witnessed the emergence of secondary states that meet the positional benchmark of a middle power, yet lack the historical origins of the first-generation middle powers, and by extension may not share the traditional behavioral or ideational traits.

If a coherent research program on secondary states is to emerge, middle power theory seems to be a rich testing ground. How will these second-generation middle powers behave under these international conditions? Will these states adopt middle power identities in an effort to carve out niches in a more fluid international context? If not, what explains the appeal of middle power diplomacy to some secondary states and not others? Finally, in the litmus test for any theory of secondary state behavior, have these powers affected a rising China and if they have, what does this tell us about middle power theory? Rather than simply applying extant middle power theory, with all its definitional problems and conceptual murkiness, this chapter has instead developed a threefold typology of middle powers with the aim of assessing the value of conceptualizing the role of secondary powers under the conditions of power transition.

Middle powers matter because they are the constituent parts of an international system in flux. Small powers lack the capacity to influence the system; great powers have the capacity to shape the system unilaterally. There is little doubt of the ability of rising powers to modify the system as they rise. These modifications may be embraced, resisted, or amended by middle powers. Some may seek to work with China to manage normative change so that the system reflects Chinese interests. This is already occurring as Brazil sides with China in its quest for more democratic International Monetary Fund representation; Malaysia has worked with China to perpetuate the norm of noninterference. Thailand's recent ratification of the UN Convention on the Law of the Sea was received in Washington as evidence that China's limited interpretation of navigational freedoms in coastal waters is gaining support in East Asia to the detriment of American security interests.[82]

In this context the role of middle powers as supporters of emerging norms becomes more important. The study of the relationship between China and middle powers can shed light on the relationship between a class of state and a rising power. By comparing reactions to the rise of China across the positional, behavioral, and ideational criteria of middle powers, it may also be possible to assess what, if anything, the middle power paradigm has to say about the role of secondary states in power transitions. The remaining chapters in this book explore both sides of this equation.

Notes

1. A distinction is drawn between this, "ministates," and the two superpowers. See Hans Morgenthau and Kenneth W. Thompson, *Politics among Nations: The Struggle for Power and Peace*, 6th ed. (New York McGraw Hill, 1985), 8.

2. Stephen Walt, *Origin of Alliances* (Ithaca, NY: Cornell University Press, 1987), 29.

3. Kenneth Waltz, *Theory of International Politics* (Long Grove, IL: Waveland Press, 2010), 127.

4. A. F. K. Organski and Jacek Kugler, *The War Ledger* (Chicago: University of Chicago Press, 1980), 21.

5. Richard Ned Lebow and Benjamin Valentino, "Lost in Transition: A Critical Analysis of Power Transition Theory," *International Relations* 23, no. 3 (2009): 389–410.

6. Colin Elman, *Progress in International Relations Theory: Appraising the Field* (Cambridge, MA: MIT Press, 2003), 133.

7. Douglas Lemke, "Small States and War: An Expansion of Power Transition Theory," in *Parity and War: Evaluations and Extensions of the War Ledger*, 77, eds. Jacek Kugler and Douglas Lemke (Ann Arbor: University of Michigan, 1996).

8. Robert Gilpin, *War and Change in World Politics* (Cambridge: Cambridge University Press, 1983), 24.

9. Kristen Williams, Steven Lobell, and Neal Jesse, *Beyond Great Powers and Hegemons: Why Secondary States Support, Follow, or Challenge* (Stanford: Stanford University Press, 2012), 1.

10. David R. Mares, "Middle Powers under Regional Hegemony: To Challenge or Acquiesce in Hegemonic Enforcement," *International Studies Quarterly* 32, no. 4 (1988): 453–71.

11. Robert O. Keohane and Joseph S. Nye, *Power and Interdependence* (London: Longman, 2011) 24.

12. Ibid., 26.

13. Laura Neack, *The New Foreign Policy: U.S. and Comparative Foreign Policy in the 21st Century* (Lanham, MD: Rowman & Littlefield, 2003), 170.

14. Emanuel Adler and Michael Barnett, *Security Communities* (Cambridge: Cambridge University Press, 1998), 280.

15. John Gerard Ruggie, "Multilateralism: The Anatomy of an Institution," *International Organization* 46, no. 3 (1992): 561–98.

16. John Mearsheimer, *The Tragedy of Great Power Politics* (New York: W. W. Norton & Co., 2003), 375–77.

17. Henry Kissinger, *On China* (Toronto: Penguin, 2011), 517.

18. See David Shambaugh, "China Engages Asia: Reshaping the Regional Order," *International Security* 29, no. 3 (2004–5): 64–99; Evelyn Goh, "Great Powers and Hierarchical Order in Southeast Asia," *International Security* 32, no. 3 (2007/8): 113–57.

19. Aaron L. Friedberg, "Ripe for Rivalry: Prospects for Peace in a Multipolar Asia," *International Security* 18, no. 3 (1993): 5–33.

20. David C. Kang, "Between Balancing and Bandwagoning: South Korea's Response to China," *Journal of East Asian Studies* 9, no.1 (2009): 1–28.

21. Nikola Hynek, "Humanitarian Arms Control, Symbiotic Functionalism, and the Concept of Middlepowerhood," *Central European Journal of International and Security Studies* 1, no. 2 (2007): 132–55.

22. Adam Chapnick, *The Middle Power Project: Canada and the Founding of the United Nations* (Vancouver: UBC Press, 2005); G. Det Glazebrook, "The Middle Powers in the United Nations System," *International Organization* 1, no. 2 (1947): 307–15.

23. Carsten Holbraad, *Middle Powers in International Politics* (London: Macmillan, 1984); Jennifer Welsh, *At Home in the World: Canada's Global Vision for the 21st Century* (Toronto: HarperCollins Publishers, 2004).

24. Carl Ungerer, "The 'Middle Power' Concept in Australian Foreign Policy," *Australian Journal of Politics and History* 53, no. 4 (2007): 538–51; Andrew F. Cooper, "Niche Diplomacy: A Conceptual Overview," in *Niche Diplomacy: Middle Powers after the Cold War*, 9–13, ed. Andrew F. Cooper (Houndmills, UK: Macmillan Press, 1997).

25. Andrew F. Cooper, Richard A. Higgott, and Kim Richard Nossal, *Relocating Middle Powers: Australia and Canada in a Changing World Order* (Vancouver: UBC Press, 1993), 20–25.

26. Robert O. Keohane, "Lilliputians' Dilemmas: Small States in International Politics," *International Organization* 23, no. 2 (1969): 291–310, 296.

27. See Kim Richard Nossal, "'Middlepowerhood' and 'Middlepowermanship' in Canadian Foreign Policy," in *Canada's Foreign and Security Policy: Soft and Hard Strategies of a Middle Power*, 20–34, eds. Nikola Hynek and David Bosold (Toronto: Oxford University Press, 2010).

28. David A. Cooper, "Challenging Contemporary Notions of Middle Power Influence: Implications of the Proliferation Security Initiative for 'Middle Power Theory,'" *Foreign Policy Analysis* 7, no. 3 (2011): 317–36, 319.

29. Soeya Yoshihide, "Diplomacy for Japan as a Middle Power," *Japan Echo*, 35, no. 2 (2008).

30. In this way it adds a further dimension to Kim Nossal's distinction between "middlepowerhood" (positional) and "middlepowermanship" (behavioral). See Nossal, "'Middlepowerhood' and 'Middlepowermanship' in Canadian Foreign Policy," 20–34.

31. Steven R. David, "Explaining Third World Alignment," *World Politics* 43, no. 2 (1991): 233–56.

32. Andrew Fenton Cooper and Timothy M. Shaw, *The Diplomacies of Small States: Between Vulnerability and Resilience* (New York: Palgrave Macmillan, 2009).

33. Bruce E. Moon, "The Foreign Policy of the Dependent State," *International Studies Quarterly* 27, no. 3 (1983): 315–40.

34. Chapnick, *The Middle Power Project*, 76–79.

35. For alternative sets of measures see Bernard Wood, "Middle Powers in the International System: A Preliminary Assessment of Potential," *Wider Working Paper*, no. 11 (1987); Jonathan H. Ping, *Middle Power Statecraft: Indonesia, Malaysia and the Asia-Pacific* (Aldershot, UK: Ashgate, 2005).

36. Chapnick, *The Middle Power Project*.

37. John W. Holmes, *The Shaping of Peace: Canada and the Search for World Order*, vol. 1 (Toronto: University of Toronto Press, 1979).

38. Gilbert Rozman, "South Korea and Sino-Japanese Rivalry: A Middle Power's Options within the East Asian Core Triangle," *Pacific Review* 20, no. 2 (2007): 197–220, 216.

39. Cooper, ed. *Niche Diplomacy*.

40. Richard Higgott, "Issues, Institutions and Middle Power Diplomacy: Action and Agendas in the Post-Cold War Era," in *Niche Diplomacy*, ed. Andrew F. Cooper.

41. Matthew Bolton and Thomas Nash, "The Role of Middle Power-NGO Coalitions in Global Policy: The Case of the Cluster Munitions Ban," *Global Policy*, 1, no. 2 (2010): 172–87.

42. Ronald M. Behringer, "Middle Power Leadership on the Human Security Agenda," *Cooperation and Conflict*, 40, no. 3 (2005): 305–42; Allan Gyngell and Michael Wesley, *Making Australian Foreign Policy*, 2nd ed. (Cambridge: Cambridge University Press 2007), 214–17.

43. Richard A. Higgott and Andrew Fenton Cooper, "Middle Power Leadership and Coalition Building: Australia, the Cairns Group and the Uruguay Round of Trade Negotiations," *International Organization* 44, no. 4 (1990): 589–632.

44. Lloyd Axworthy, "Canada and Human Security: The Need for Leadership," *International Journal* 52, no. 2 (1997): 183–96; Fen Osler Hampson and Dean F. Oliver, "Pulpit Diplomacy: A Critical Assessment of the Axworthy Doctrine," *International Journal* 53, no. 3 (1998): 379–406.

45. David R. Black and Heather Smith, "Notable Exceptions? New and Arrested Directions in Canadian Foreign Policy Literature," *Canadian Journal of Political Science* 26, no. 4 (1993): 745–74, 760. John Wendell Holmes is credited with the first articulation of the term. Early articulations date to J. King Gordon, ed., *Canada's Role as a Middle Power* (Toronto: Canadian Institute of International Affairs, 1966).

46. K. J. Holsti, "National Role Conceptions and the Study of Foreign Policy," *International Studies Quarterly* 14, no. 3 (1970): 233–309; Ronald L. Jepperson, Alexander Wendt, and Peter J. Katzenstein, "Norms, Identity, and Culture in National Security," in *The Culture of National Security: Norms and Identity in World Politics*, 33–75, ed. Peter J. Katzenstein (New York: Columbia University Press, 1996).

47. Mark Neufeld, "Hegemony and Foreign Policy Analysis: The Case of Canada as a Middle Power," *Studies in Political Economy* 48 (1995): 7–29.

48. Behringer, "Middle Power Leadership on the Human Security Agenda"; Edward Newman, "Human Security and Constructivism," *International Studies Perspectives*, 2 (2001): 239–51.

49. See, for instance, Adam Chapnick, "The Canadian Middle Power Myth," *International Journal* 55, no. 2 (2000): 188–206.

50. Ungerer, "The 'Middle Power' Concept in Australian Foreign Policy," 538–51.

51. See Richard Samuels, "Securing Japan: The Current Discourse," *Journal of Japanese Studies*, 33, no. 1 (2007): 125–52. The classic statement is Yoshihide Soeya, *Nihon-no Middle Power Gaiko (Japan's Middle Power Diplomacy)* (Chikuma-shobo, 2005).

52. Ungerer, "The 'Middle Power' Concept," 519.

53. John Ravenhill, "Cycles of Middle Power Activism: Constraint and Choice in Australian and Canadian Foreign Policy," *Australian Journal of International Affairs* 52, no. 3 (1998): 309–27.

54. Robert T. Cox, "Middlepowermanship, Japan and the Future of World Order," *International Journal* 44, no. 4 (1999): 823–62, 827.

55. Cox, "Middlepowermanship," 825. For an outline of this system, see G. John Ikenberry, *After Victory: Institutions, Strategic Restraint and the Rebuilding of Order after Major Wars* (Princeton: Princeton Universisty Press, 2001); Ian Clark, *The Post-Cold War Order: The Spoils of Peace* (Oxford: Oxford University Press, 2001); G. John Ikenberry, "Power and Liberal Order: America's Postwar World Order in Transition," *International Relations of the Asia-Pacific* 5, no. 2 (2005): 133–52.

56. Eduard Jordaan, "The Concept of a Middle Power in International Relations: Distinguishing between Emerging and Traditional Middle Powers," *Politikon: South African Journal of Political Studies* 30, no. 2 (2003): 165–81.

57. Cooper, "Niche Diplomacy," 9–13.

58. Tom Keating and Edward Akuffo, "Revisioning International Order: The Role of (Re)emerging Powers and Regional Institutions." Paper presented at the Annual Conference of the International Studies Association, San Diego, April 2012.

59. See Cooper, "Niche Diplomacy," 13–20; Ryerson Christie and David Dewitt, "Middle Powers and Regional Security," paper presented at Conference IBSA, Argentina and Regional Security, Buenos Aires, Argentina, May 2006; Ping, *Middle Power Statecraft*; Kim Richard Nossal and Richard Stubbs, "Mahathir's Malaysia: An Emerging Middle Power?," in *Niche Diplomacy*, ed. Andrew F. Cooper.

60. See David Capie and Paul Evans, *The Asia-Pacific Security Lexicon*, 2nd ed. (Singapore: ISEAS Publishing 2007): 155–58; Carsten Holbraad, "The Role of Middle Powers," *Cooperation and Conflict* 6, no. 1 (1971): 77–90; Gareth Evans and Bruce Grant, *Australia's Foreign Relations in the World of the 1990s* (Carlton, Australia: Melbourne University Press, 1991).

61. Christie and Dewitt, "Middle Powers and Regional Security," 27.

62. See, for instance, Janis Van Der Westhuizen, "South Africa's Emergence as a Middle Power," *Third World Quarterly* 19, no. 2 (1998): 435–55.

63. Daniel Flemes, "Emerging Middle Powers' Soft Balancing Strategy: State and Perspectives of the IBSA Dialogue Forum," *GIGA Working Papers* no. 57 (2007).

64. Robert S. Ross, "Balance of Power Politics and the Rise of China: Accommodation and Balancing in East Asia," *Security Studies* 15, no. 3 (2006): 355–95.

65. James Manicom and Andrew O'Neil, "China's Rise and Middle Power Democracies: Canada and Australia Compared," *International Relations of the Asia-Pacific* 12, no. 2 (2012): 199–228.

66. Vlado Vivoda, "China Challenges Global Capitalism," *Australian Journal of International Affairs* 63, no. 1 (2009): 22–40.

67. See Martin Jacques, *When China Rules the World: The End of the Western World and the Birth of a New Global Order* (New York: Penguin, 2009); Stephen Halper, *The Beijing Consensus: How China's Authoritarian Model Will Dominate the*

Twenty-First Century (New York: Basic Books, 2010); Ian Bremmer, *The End of the Free Market: Who Wins the War between States and Corporations?* (London: Portfolio, 2010).

68. Fareed Zakaria, "The Future of American Power: How America Can Survive the Rise of the Rest," *Foreign Affairs* 87, no. 3 (2008): 18–43; G. John Ikenberry, "The Rise of China and Future of the West," *Foreign Affairs* 87, no. 1 (2008): 23–37.

69. Richard N. Hass, "The Age of Nonpolarity: What Will Follow US Dominance," *Foreign Affairs* 87, no. 3 (2008): 44–56.

70. Joseph Nye, *The Future of Power* (New York: Public Affairs, 2011).

71. Ian Bremmer, *Every Nation for Itself: Winners and Losers in a G-Zero World* (New York: Portfolio, 2011).

72. Randall Schweller and Xiaoyu Pu, "After Unipolarity: China's Visions of International Order in an Era of US Decline," *International Security* 36, no. 1 (2011): 41–72.

73. See, for instance, William Tow and Richard Rigby, "China's Pragmatic Security Policy: The Middle Power Factor," *The China Journal* 65, no. 1 (2011): 157–78.

74. David M. Lampton, *The Three Faces of Chinese Power: Might, Money and Minds* (Berkeley: University of California Press, 2008), 166.

75. Sarah Eaton and Richard Stubbs, "Is ASEAN Powerful? Neo-realist Versus Constructivist Approaches to Power in Southeast Asia," *Pacific Review* 19, no. 2 (2006): 135–55.

76. Indeed, some note that niche diplomacy is appealing in times of fiscal austerity. See Evan H. Potter, "Niche Diplomacy and Canadian Foreign Policy," *International Journal* 52, no.1 (1996–97): 25–38.

77. Rosemary Foot and Andrew Walter, *China, the United States, and Global Order* (Cambridge: Cambridge University Press, 2011); Ann Kent, *Beyond Compliance: China, International Organizations and Global Security* (Stanford: Stanford University Press, 2007); Alastair Iain Johnston, *Social States: China in International Institutions, 1980–2000* (Princeton: Princeton University Press, 2007).

78. Foot and Walter, *China, the United States, and Global Order*, 58.

79. Shambaugh, "China Engages Asia," 64–99.

80. Foot and Walter, *China, the United States, and Global Order*, 60.

81. Ambassador Maria Luiza Ribeiro Viotti, "Letter from the Permanent Representative of Brazil to the United Nations Addressed to the Secretary General," November 9, 2011.

82. Peter Dutton, "Cracks in the Global Foundation: International Law and Instability in the South China Sea," in *Cooperation from Strength: The United States, China and the South China Sea*, 67–82, 74, ed. Patrick Cronin (Washington, DC: Center for a New American Security, 2012).

CHAPTER 3

China's Discovery of Middle Powers

Bruce Gilley

Introduction

SINCE THE EARLY 2000s, Chinese analysts have been engaged in a low-profile discussion about ties to pivotal middle powers through which Beijing might manage and enhance its global role. This discovery of middle powers among international relations scholars in China is in part motivated by a recognition that middle powers may bandwagon with different great powers on different issues or areas, thus creating scope for expanding or reshaping alignments. As time passes, a new theoretical discussion has arisen in China that positions middle powers in a strategically complex view of China's grand strategy. In particular, this new discussion emphasizes middle powers as key determinants of international order and institutions. It also identifies middle power relations as a key litmus test of China's "peaceful rise."

This chapter describes the main lines of debate on middle powers in China. While it is too early to tell if Beijing will incorporate an explicit middle power approach into its foreign policy, there is clearly more interest in the concept among leading international relations scholars in China than in the United States. As such, it suggests that middle power approaches may find a more hospitable environment in the international system as a result of China's rise. Nonetheless, as a rising great power with a historical identity as a hegemon, China will find it difficult to fully embrace the middle power agenda. The chapter concludes with implications for middle powers themselves.

Middle Power Writings

China began what became known as a "charm offensive" (or "smile diplomacy") in Asia in the 1990s as a result of a realization that its aggressive policies on everything from trade negotiations to Taiwan were causing concern among neighbors and reducing its global influence.[1] A multipronged diplomacy begun in the later years of Jiang Zemin (party general secretary from 1989 to 2002) and then accelerated under his successor Hu Jintao (2002 to 2012) was an attempt to decenter its foreign policy from excessive dependence on ties to the United States and to build up trust with non-Western states. Among the targets were great powers like India and Russia. Beyond them, leading middle powers became a new focus of diplomatic outreach.

From a strategic standpoint, the logic was simple: Beijing risked creating a global coalition against it and needed to tread more carefully. The coalition that China has sought to build might best be described as a coalition of "principal non-Western powers," for which it has used the term "principal newly emerging market economy countries" (*zhuyao xinxing shichang jingji guojia*). This term includes great or major powers like China, Russia, and India, but also middle powers like Brazil, South Africa, Mexico, Turkey, and Indonesia. Yabin Liang of the International Institute for Strategic Studies at the Central Party School, for instance, argues that these "newly rising countries" (using the shortened form *xinxing guojia* or *xinxing jueqi guojia*) are the key to whether US hegemony can be maintained in the future because of their pivotal role in upholding US financial and military power globally.[2]

In the course of working out how to deploy its diplomatic resources for this multiregional charm offensive, Chinese strategic thinkers discovered the concept of middle powers. Since about 2009, there has been a cottage industry of "middle power studies," emerging primarily from international relations scholars. This debate taps into a deeper question about whether, as a rising great power, China's foreign relations should replicate the hegemonic assumptions of US foreign policy or accept the counterhegemonic aims of middle powers. Scholars in senior institutions like the Central Party School and the People's Liberation Army are studying middle powers for insights into strategic choices for China.[3] China can never be a middle power, but like Japan and India, it may choose to mimic or slipstream with middle powers on certain issues. The framing and terms of the debate provide useful insights into how China sees its future role in international society. Middle powers as seen from Beijing are both a potential target as well as a possible determinant of China's future foreign relations. They are strategically and normatively attractive as partners of China's "peaceful rise" and yet a threat to the hierarchical preeminence that China seeks in the new international order.

The term "middle power" is a relatively new one in China's foreign policy lexicon. Indeed, it is fair to say that with rare exceptions, China has never had an explicit view about middle powers *as* middle powers. The Chinese term for middle power is *zhongdeng qiangguo*, which literally translated means "middle-level powerful state."[4] This is a more accurate description of middle powers than the English term because it makes clear that these countries rank among the cohort of all "powerful states" and are "middle" only within this upper echelon. On this conception, middle powers occupy a special position between superpowers (*chaoji daguo*) and great powers (*daguo*) on one side and the large number of normal (*putongguo*), small (*xiaoguo*), and weak (*ruoguo*) states on the other. From this terminological perspective, middle powers are an important piece of the global power pie because they *are* powers.

Given that Thomas Christensen has described China as the "high church of realpolitik," it is no surprise that the definition of middle powers by analysts in China centers on their power capabilities (which provides added reasons beyond the theoretical ones for adopting that same approach in this volume).[5] Zhongbo Zhu, of Peking University's School of International Studies, and Yunheng Zhou, of Fudan University's School of International Relations and Public Affairs, identify middle powers primarily in terms of their positional capabilities (land, resources, economy, military, population, etc.).[6] Zhou sees Canada, for instance, as a middle power not because of its behavioral or normative commitments, most often cited by others outside of China, but because of its capabilities.

By far the most influential thinker on middle powers is Ding Gong, a researcher at the Central Party School whose writings on middle powers have been "sent to senior leaders" (*shangbao*).[7] Ding argues that middle powers have power capabilities that put them in the "upper middle class" (*zhongjian pianshang jieceng*) of all states.[8] This means that middle powers are uniquely positioned to influence international affairs because they have sufficient independence and capabilities as well as national interests to expend diplomatic resources, usually in concert with other like-minded middle powers. Ding lists the following as middle powers: Turkey, Saudi Arabia, Pakistan, South Korea, Egypt, Iran, South Africa, Nigeria, Mexico, Argentina, Indonesia, and Australia. India and Brazil, he believes, are borderline cases because they have sought to throw off their post–World War II middle power identity to pursue great power status. Canada and the European middle powers, meanwhile, are too closely integrated into the maintenance of the Western-dominated order to qualify as independent, in his view.

All three authors make clear that the predicted behavior of middle powers is what makes them of interest, in particular the predictions of an independent foreign policy and a proactive diplomacy. Ding argues that middle powers have an abiding interest in maintaining the status and effectiveness of international institutions.[9] This is usually evidenced through regional leadership, which in his view is the single most important indicator that a middle power has taken on a "middle power identity."[10] Gang Tang of Shanghai International Studies University sees counterhegemony, multilateralism, and regional leadership as key behavioral attributes of middle powers, noting how this behavioral approach is a departure for China, which is used to seeing the world in terms of capabilities alone.[11] Likewise, Changsen Yu, a professor of Asian studies at Zhongshan University, notes that China-Australia relations are driven on the Australian side by the "middle power need to maintain the status quo" of international institutions through which China's rise can be managed in typical middle power fashion.[12] Although an affinity for a rules-based international order is in the interests of middle powers, they gain a soft power advantage as a result because such an order is also favored by small powers and weak powers. As a result, middle powers often serve as "rule-makers" in the international system, he writes.

One result, noted by Hao Qian, a professor of international relations and diplomacy at Shanghai Foreign Languages University, is that middle powers are distinguished by their ability to constrain great power unilateralism and aggression through both soft power as well as their use of international and regional institutions.[13] "Middle powers can use their soft power advantages to exert soft balancing in areas where the hard power of hegemonic powers is useless or degraded. At the same time, middle powers can make use of various kinds of multilateral frameworks to constrain or block the unilateralism of hegemons," he writes.

This also means that middle powers have a tendency toward nonalignment. At the regional level, middle powers are usually powerful enough to stand as equals with great powers while at the global level they maximize their influence by promoting an institutionalized, rules-based, multilateral international order rather than alliances with great powers. Middle powers are seen as promiscuous free agents, shifting their allegiances issue by issue in order to maximize their influence.

In this sense, Chinese observers see Canada and Australia not as archetypal middle powers (as mentioned, Ding does not consider Canada a middle power at all) but as aberrant middle powers by virtue of their close alliances with the United States. Xiaosong Tang and Ke Bin, professors of international relations at Guangdong Foreign Languages and Trade University, ascribe the failure of Australian prime minister Kevin Rudd's "middle power diplomacy" in Asia to his country's dependence on the US alliance, which made other countries suspicious of Australian motives. "Without the explicit or tacit approval of the US, no matter how much it is claimed to be 'independent,' the Australian policy will face all sorts of challenges."[14] However, Australia attracts far more attention than Canada from middle power scholars in China because of a view that it is more likely to escape from this "traditional middle power" alignment and emerge, along with countries like South Korea and Turkey, as a "new middle power." This, however, makes Australia a more complicated topic for Chinese strategists. Xiaohui Yang of Shanghai University of Political Science and Law, for instance, argues that Australia's muscular middle power diplomacy complicates its relations with China compared to a policy of strict US alignment.[15]

In a dynamic sense, several Chinese scholars argue that middle powers are a "rising force" in international politics in both number and influence because of the end of the Cold War and the rise of new regional and international institutions where middle power activism is most effective. Ding cites South Africa, South Korea, and Turkey as emblematic of "new middle powers." They had "transformed from peripheral or semi-peripheral aspirants to critical rule-makers" of the international system.[16] In particular as global order was increasingly devolved to regional orders, global power politics was becoming less important than regional power politics where middle powers often played a critical role. The unstated assumption is that since China has no intention of asserting global leadership, more responsibility will fall to middle powers if the US role declines.

Using an operatic metaphor, Ding argues that increasingly "regional organizations erect the stage and great powers direct the action, but middle powers sing the opera." In support of Ding's view, one might note that while it was China and the United States that reached the key agreement at the Copenhagen climate change summit in 2009, it was only acceptable to the conference as a whole, and thus enacted, because India, South Africa, and Brazil signed on to make it look like a consensus accord. From a policy sciences perspective, this could imply a greater de facto role for middle powers than for great powers since it is often the agents rather than the architects who determine a policy's success.

In a similar vein, Shenggang Bao, a former Huadong Teacher's University international relations professor, argues that the world is entering "the era of middle powers" because of the shift away from a "strategic world" dominated by power and security concerns to a world dominated by legitimacy and equality concerns.[17] Middle powers have the advantage of public opinion and legitimacy in the world system. Moreover, the ranks of middle powers are swelling as a result of the benefits of globalization. From being "followers, opponents, or revolutionaries" of the world system, these new middle powers have become "participants, revisionists, and determinants" of it. Parallel to the emergence of a middle class in domestic politics, the emergence of middle powers causes a "change in the political structure" of world politics, he argues.

The view of middle powers among this group of international relations scholars in China, then, tends to focus on their role in constraining great powers and setting and implementing new international agendas. Canada and Australia, with their liberal commitments and US ties, are an anachronism amidst the rising number of unaligned new middle powers. Chen Zhao of the Chinese Academy of Social Sciences, for instance, argues that Canada's liberal political culture and its "complicated dependence" on the United States causes it to pursue global governance initiatives in areas like human rights and nongovernmental organization participation that other middle powers do not.[18] From this perspective, the "typical" middle power today is something more like South Africa, Indonesia, or Turkey. Chinese president Xi Jinping's description of Turkey in 2012, cited by Yitzhak Shichor in this volume, reflects this view: "safeguarding regional stability and promoting common development," helping to resolve "international and regional hot issues," engaging in a "proactive, flexible, and all-dimensional foreign policy," and having "a more and more important role in international and regional affairs."

It is notable that this view of middle powers is almost entirely political in nature. While Beijing is certainly interested in closer relations with mineral-rich middle powers such as Australia, Canada, Brazil, and South Africa, this is not mentioned in its theorizing of middle powers because mineral-rich nongreat powers where China can invest without great power security complications is a category that also covers many smaller powers. In this sense, China's middle power theorists reflect a classical diplomatic thinking that harkens back to the origins of the concept.

Integrating Middle Powers into China's Foreign Policy

China's foreign policy has focused on several groups of states—bordering states, which deliver territorial security; great powers, which deliver strategic stability; and developing countries, which provide natural resources and UN votes. The result of this is that middle powers per se do not have a special place in China's foreign policy even if some, like South Korea, are bordering states while others, like South Africa and Egypt, are leaders of the developing world. No official foreign policy document refers to "middle powers" and the foreign ministry website deems the term "illegal" when used in a search.

Both Ding and Shanrong Jin, a professor of international relations at People's University of China, worry that Beijing has a blind spot for middle powers.[19] "We cannot find the place of middle powers" in China's foreign policy, notes Ding. This means, he continues, that China's foreign policy does not focus on the most important characteristic of these powers, namely their role in setting rules and in carrying out regional mandates.

For example, several Chinese authors note that as Association of Southeast Asian Nations (ASEAN) chair in 2011, Indonesia resisted a Philippines push at the annual summit for a "zone of peace, freedom, friendship and cooperation" in the South China Sea that would delineate disputed areas of the sea for joint development. Jakarta also ensured that the final communiqué acknowledged Beijing's preference for bilateral talks, not the multilateral ones sought by the Philippines and Vietnam.[20] In this case, middle power activism defused what could have been a sharper military conflict between China and the Philippines. Ding notes that the "more cautious attitude" by Indonesia ensured that ASEAN had maintained a "balanced attitude so that the issue has not become a common cause among ASEAN." This proved to be crucial to the 2012 Sino-Philippines dispute over Scarborough Shoal, when ASEAN, especially through the ASEAN Plus Three Defense Ministers forum, played a neutral, mediatory role, despite pleas from Manila for the body to "issue a statement" saying China was in violation of ASEAN-China agreements on the South China Sea.[21] "By seeing Indonesia as just a bordering state [bordering on China's claims in the South China Sea] or a developing nation," writes Ding, China's foreign policy "will lead to inadequate attention to Indonesia's positive role in regional affairs and hinder the effective enhancement of China's diplomacy with neighboring countries as a whole." While outside analysts, including Ann Marie Murphy (in this volume), do not see any evidence that China has moderated its behavior in response to Indonesian diplomatic initiatives, the view of analysts in China is that it has. For instance, in 2013, China abandoned its long-stated view that it would deal with the issue on bilateral terms by agreeing to joint talks with ASEAN as a whole convened by Thailand and Indonesia on a legally binding code of conduct to replace the nonbinding code signed in 2002.

Likewise in its relations with Europe, according to Ding, China is too focused on major powers like Germany, France, and the United Kingdom, ignoring the role of middle powers like Spain and Italy that are often its staunchest allies. Ding notes that Spain initiated an attempt to lift the post-Tiananmen European Union arms embargo on China when it assumed the EU presidency in early 2010, which was rejected by Germany and the United Kingdom.[22] He also notes that Spain has been a key advocate within the European Union to have China accepted as a full-market economy. (China agreed to adopt nonmarket status for fifteen years when joining the World Trade Organization in 2001.) In 2005, the Spanish president of the European Commission, Jose Manuel Barroso, said he was "hopeful that we can find a pragmatic way to grant market economy status to China."[23] In 2011, Premier Wen Jiabao said that in return for buying Spanish and other European bonds, the European Union "should recognize China's full market economy status. . . . To show one's sincerity on this issue . . . is the way a friend treats another friend."[24]

Jin too argues that middle powers (he cites South Korea, Canada, and Turkey) should be given "sufficient attention" in China's foreign policy. In particular South Korea, by being slotted into the "bordering" countries category, is misperceived by Beijing's georealist viewpoint, because its significance to China's rise goes far beyond its immediate geography given that it is a major economic and even political power in Asia. Jin reflects a rising awareness among Chinese analysts about this diplomatic dynamo emerging on China's doorstep, which under President Lee Myung-bak launched a "global Korea" foreign policy and which is sensitive to being perceived by China as a tributary state. As Jin puts it bluntly: "Laos may be happy to be put into the category of a bordering state in China's foreign relations, but South Korea is not."[25]

Ding and Zhang, a Hong Kong political analyst and board member of the pro-Beijing Hong Kong Development Forum, argue that by focusing on "bordering states" as its regional security strategy for Asia, Beijing has put geographic determinism ahead of political realities. Ding notes that it is far more important to focus on the three middle powers that surround China—South Korea, Indonesia, and Pakistan—than the array of middle, great, and small powers because it is these middle powers that the United States is building ties with to "contain" China's rise. Countering this by strengthening its own ties to these middle powers would therefore exert a "radiation effect" on China's regional security. "The absence of the 'middle power' concept represents a hole in China's regional security strategy," writes Zhang.[26]

Ding highlights the case of Turkey as particularly "embarrassing" for China's conventional foreign policy worldview because of its pivotal role as a regional powerbroker and as a bridge between several competing world blocs. "The scope of China's cooperation with Turkey is very limited and the degree very low."[27] This highlights the central problem:

> China's current diplomatic framework ignores the whole set of middle powers and its foreign policy decisions are lagging behind changes in the world situation, especially after the global financial crisis. This negatively impacts the

> optimal allocation of China's diplomatic resources, undermining the ability of China to convert its rising comprehensive national strength into sustainably developing international influence.[28]

By not conceptualizing middle powers as pivotal players in China's rise, he argues, Beijing has allowed petty disputes (he cites trade dumping disputes with Mexico and human rights differences with Turkey) to weaken its relations with countries since "other large countries" use such disputes to "signal the need to contain a rising China." While not as important as relations with the United States, Russia, Japan, Europe, and India, he argues, middle power relations "nonetheless have an effect that cannot be underestimated."[29]

More generally, Ding argues that by targeting middle powers throughout the developing world, Beijing could avoid the "distractions" of trying to curry favor with the scores of small and weak states. He notes that South Africa and Egypt have both played leading roles as "representatives" of their developing regions. By advancing a focused diplomacy with these powers, Beijing could simplify its developing country diplomacy.

Middle Power Bandwagoning and Its Risks

The role of middle powers in constraining hegemons (*baquan guo*), as emphasized by Qian and others, obviously refers to the United States. But China too aspires to being a great power with hegemonic potential, especially in Asia. This points up the fundamental challenge for China to pursue a middle power–like diplomacy: as a historical great power and a contemporary rising one, it is just as likely as the United States to scorn the concept. Moreover, unlike rising India, which has been able to retain its middle power identity and middle power–style "niche diplomacy" of multipolarity and peace building despite its positional rise because of domestically determined cosmopolitanism and emphasis on compromise, China has neither of these attributes.[30] Its self-identity is built upon an exclusive form of nationalism and its domestic politics are characterized by finality and coercion. While the United States shares with China a self-identity built on unique national characteristics, the pursuit of those aims by Washington is significantly constrained by its democratic character.

China looked something like an aligned middle power (like today's Canada or Australia) from 1949 until it began to detach itself from the Soviet Union with the first Khrushchev-Mao meeting in Beijing in 1958. This was followed by a period from 1958 until 1972, when China played a role in world politics that, but for its size, has been described as akin to that of a middle power.[31] For instance, its high profile at the Afro-Asian Conference begun at Bandung in 1955 signified its commitment to multilateralism, sovereign equality, and nonalignment. China's return to great power status with the Sino-US reconciliation meant that it lost its leadership role within the nonaligned movement. But in a sense, China has never stopped *thinking* of itself as a counterhegemonic great power with middle power sensibilities.

From 1997 to 2001, China promoted a "new security concept" in Asia. The soft edge of this was a reiteration of "the ASEAN Way" of consensus, mutual respect, Westphalian noninterference, and multilateralism. But the hard edge was the attempt to dismantle the United States–centered hub-and-spoke alliances of the San Francisco System as the region's security architecture.[32] China subsequently dropped this hard edge, having been told by ASEAN states about the indispensability of the American presence.[33] Middle and small powers in Asia seek a continued US presence not just to hedge against a rising China, but also to avoid Japanese rearmament and to manage nongreat power rivalries within the region—between Malaysia and Indonesia, for instance, or Cambodia and Thailand.[34]

Jakarta's notion of a "dynamic equilibrium" in Asian politics is one that gradually accommodates China's great power role but only alongside a continued American one.[35] The more closely US-aligned South Korea, meanwhile, signed military cooperation agreements with Indonesia in 2008 and with Australia in 2011. In the latter case, the defense ministers said in a joint statement that the two countries are "like-minded middle powers" and "natural security partners."[36] Yet neither country has been willing to pursue the maintenance of the US-centric regional security architecture that Washington desires. This is consistent with middle power nonalignment.

China's intention continues to be a widening of its acknowledged sphere of influence and "core interests" in Asia at the expense of the United States. This is where middle powers come in, Ding believes. By bandwagoning with middle powers, China would gain "global strategic space." Specifically, cooperation with middle powers on "secondary" issues like the environment, human rights, development, and foreign aid, Beijing could "weaken some of the pressures that great powers use to squeeze China."

Beyond Asia, Ding argues, the middle power desire for a more equitable UN system also plays to China's advantage. As the weakest permanent member of the UN Security Council, China is hostage to Western dominance and agenda-setting. Adding countries like India, Brazil, Japan, and Germany as permanent members would make matters worse for China. The Uniting for Consensus (UfC) group on UN reforms, led by prominent middle powers like Indonesia, Canada, Pakistan, Egypt, Turkey, and South Korea, which wants only nonpermanent Security Council members increased and the body's powers reduced, is thus consistent with China's interests in a multipolar world in which it could exercise its rising power more effectively. China's long-standing appeals for the "democratization of international relations" are intended to expand its great power ambitions. This has created a "Baptists and bootleggers" coalition—a coalition sharing the same aims but for different reasons—of China and the UfC group on this issue. Since 2011, China has been participating in the UfC meetings. Beijing has publicly supported the aims of the UfC group as taking UN reform in a "very important and right direction."[37] Says Ding: "Since the UfC encompasses almost all middle powers, by initiating a middle power diplomacy, China could strengthen its communication and coordination with the UfC, increasing its ability to push forward UN reform and to give it more leeway to oppose hasty changes to the UN system." Jiantao He of Fujian Normal University argues that China should work assiduously to resurrect the role of middle powers in UN peacekeeping operations because doing so would prevent those operations from becoming dominated by NATO, which undermines China's aspirations to global leadership.[38]

The G20, meanwhile, provides the ideal forum in which a China allied with key middle powers would provide a formidable force to manage global affairs. During the global financial crisis of 2008 to 2009, Beijing put out many signals that it considered the G20 as the preeminent forum for discussing global economic issues.[39] As Ding puts it: "With the sudden emergence of the G20 as the primary forum for the management of global economic cooperation, China can use this forum to move from the periphery to the center of global governance. China should draw closer to the middle powers of the G20 in order to influence the operations of this forum from the inside, strengthening China's ability to set the agenda which will further and safeguard China's interests in all aspects of policy formulation and implementation."

There is other evidence of this middle power bandwagoning in China's foreign policy in Beijing's policies toward South Korea and Australia. For Tow and Rigby, China's policies toward South Korea and Australia reflect the "middle power factor" in China's foreign policy—meaning the extent to which China has rejected great power rulemaking attempts in favor of rule and norm-abiding diplomacy. In its hosting the Six-Party Talks on North Korea and its collaboration on countering terrorism, piracy, and other non-traditional security threats, they write, "Chinese policymakers have clearly developed entrepreneurial postures increasingly compatible with middle-power viewpoints."[40] In the realm of peacekeeping, China's behavior has been described as "consistent with that of a middle power in its policy development, which has been defined as professing a multilateral approach to building peace, a willingness to compromise, an understanding of middle-power limitations, and a tendency to take a targeted approach to international problems through what has been called 'niche diplomacy.'"[41]

The strategic rationale for China to bandwagon with middle powers is that it could strengthen the perception of Beijing's benign intentions and thus achieve China's broader strategic goals. To borrow Ding's metaphor, if Beijing's ultimate aim is to promote Peking Opera, then it should begin by establishing its credibility with the singers by directing performances of Puccini. Segal famously dismissed China as "at best a second rank middle power that has mastered the art of diplomatic theatre."[42] That was intended as an insult. From another perspective, being thought of as a benign middle power might be exactly what China wants. Beijing should canonize Segal for his attempts to downplay China's hegemonic potential.

Challenges and Risks

The attempt to integrate middle power agendas into its foreign policy will bring several difficulties to Beijing. "Middle powers represent an opportunity as well as a challenge for China," notes Ding.[43] One obvious risk is that Beijing would be wasting its time. Guangqi Wei of the School of International Studies at Nanjing University is one of the few writers openly skeptical of the benefits of middle power diplomacy by China. He argues that the significance of middle powers (he identifies Canada, Brazil, Australia, South Africa, and Mexico as examples) is overblown because at a time of shifting great power relations, rising nonstate actors, and growing issue complexity, the attempts at "niche diplomacy" that depend on a relatively stable world order will more often fail than succeed. "As a result of these external pressures, middle powers may well lose their autonomy or even become marginalized."[44] This is a reminder that to some extent, middle powers will matter depending on whether Beijing chooses to make them matter.

The opposite danger is paying too little attention to middle powers. Jin and Ma describe the "mass rise of middle powers" (*zhongdeng qiangguo quntixing jueqi*) as one of six key trends in world affairs in the decade from 2012.[45] Pointedly excluding Western middle powers in their list (they identify India, Brazil, South Africa, Mexico, Turkey, Vietnam, Indonesia, Nigeria, Saudi Arabia, Argentina, and Egypt), they argue that this sudden eruption into world affairs will make managing global order more difficult since they would become the object of courtship by great powers: "Whoever obtains the support of middle powers will gain the upper hand in the great power game."

Arguably, and discussed by David Cooper and Toshi Yoshihara in chapter 4, the United States has been just as active in courting traditional middle powers like Indonesia and Australia as well as emerging middle powers like Vietnam. There is even evidence of a realignment between Canada and the United States in response to the rise of China.[46] One further example of Washington's agility is that it was quick to sign up with the Climate and Clean Air Coalition on so-called "short-lived climate forcers" (black carbon, methane, hydrofluorocarbons) led by Canada, Mexico, Bangladesh, Sweden, and Ghana in 2012, agreeing to pay $12 million of the $15 million project cost. China, by contrast, was unwilling to join because it was suspicious that the initiative would produce recommendations that would unduly burden China.[47] The European Union is also alert to the potential of middle powers to leverage its own great power status: one unofficial strategy document identifies South Africa, Turkey, and the three ASEAN middle powers of Indonesia, Thailand, and Malaysia as objects of outreach.[48] The EU's trump card with middle powers is that it includes several middle powers itself and has been a vehicle for their internal modernization and nonhegemonic external influence, neither of which China can promise.

Coopting middle power agendas to advance geostrategic positioning thus requires not just diplomatic agility but also policy prescience from China. China has interests in maintaining the preeminence of great powers in the international system. It is torn between its hierarchical great power identity and its egalitarian middle power costume. Ding notes that "within certain limits and over a certain time, the expansion and extension of China's national power will be at odds with the interests of some middle powers."[49] Jin worries that with the expansion in the number of middle powers, there is a danger of weak leadership in international politics because international power would go beyond multipolar to being "nonpolar."[50] China cannot encourage multipolarity (*shijie duojihua*) without undermining its great power ambitions.

On many of the issues that China may wish to engage middle powers, it has shown a willingness to be socialized into cooperative norms. These include the use of multilateral (rather than bilateral) approaches to resolve territorial claims; the acceptance of limited doctrines of humanitarian intervention and human rights promotion; the rejection of state subsidies in international trade; and the indispensable leadership role of the United States in global security. In all of these cases, middle power agendas mesh with US interests. But in other cases, middle power agendas may worsen Beijing's relations with Washington. When Brazil and Turkey, as rotating nonpermanent members of the UN Security Council, struck a deal in 2010 to temporarily resolve the crisis over Iran's nuclear program, for instance, China rebuffed the effort by siding with a US proposal for a new round of sanctions. In retrospect, the brusk US dismissal of the proposal, whatever its shortcomings, was probably a mistake given that it offered a means to build trust and deescalate the conflict. China's opportunity to stand tall by backing the peacemakers was lost. By siding with great power bargains, Beijing demonstrated the difficulties it will face in reaching out to middle powers.

In addition, Beijing will need to recognize that the more it bandwagons with illiberal middle powers, the more it risks alienating the liberal ones. Beijing, for instance, is working closely on economic and development policy positions with the essentially anti-Western BRICS group (Brazil, Russia, India, China, and South Africa). The more it does so, the more it will find cooperation with liberal middle powers like Indonesia and South Korea, not to mention Australia, Canada, and the would-be middle powers of the European Union, becomes difficult.

Finally, Beijing must tread carefully in the complex politics of middle power–small power relationships. For most small powers the "hegemon" they worry about is a middle power with regional influence—South Africa in southern Africa, Brazil in Latin America, and Iran in the Middle East. In East Asia alone, there are six small or weak states (North Korea, Myanmar, Cambodia, Laos, East Timor, and Brunei) in addition to four small powers (Singapore, Philippines, Taiwan, and Vietnam) dealing with the regional hegemony of four middle powers (South Korea, Indonesia, Thailand, and Malaysia) and four great powers (China, Japan, Russia, and the United States). One Singaporean analyst worries about plans by China "to create a hierarchical structure or a concert of the major and middle powers which would presumably 'rule' over the less powerful states of the region."[51] Beijing may indeed want to avoid the "distractions" of dealing with small and weak states to focus on middle powers. But doing so requires an acute sensitivity to the subregional relationships that this diplomacy may upset.

Policy Options for Middle Powers

China, then, remains more intrigued by the middle power concept than the United States, and there is some evidence of a middle power shift in its foreign policy. There is a growing cottage industry in middle power theorizing that recognizes the strategic value of foreign policy planning from a middle power perspective.

One risk of the "middle power factor" in China's foreign policy is that it may discredit middle powers themselves. As Hirono and Lanteigne put it, if China uses middle power offices and middle power behavior to enlarge its own great power status, then "the area of overlap between the two power perspectives will gradually minimize, and the middle-power status will become meaningless."[52] However, just as middle power engagement poses risks and rewards for China, so too engagement with China poses risks and rewards for middle powers. The ability to socialize and constrain China is a significant potential payoff. So too is the multiplier effect on the middle power agenda. The understanding of China's views suggests two different options for middle powers that seek a "dynamic equilibrium" between great powers.

One would be to recognize China's need for middle power alliances and collaboration and to work assiduously with Beijing on many fronts. This would be to put aside the problem of China's great power ambitions and hope that through a process of socialization and institutionalization, any revisionist impulses can be tamed. The other option would be to draw a clearer line between middle power values and interests so that collaboration with China is "firewalled" against great power taint. This will be more the case the more liberal is the middle power itself, or the more that it sees itself as committed to the liberal international order.

These two options can be optimally combined so that middle powers selectively engage with China on issues where the risk/reward calculus makes it worthwhile. Within the G20, for instance, Australia and Turkey cochair the International Financial Architecture Working Group that has the potential to shape China's stances in international financial institutions and policies. Bringing it closely into those discussions may be well worth the risks. China is grappling with middle powers because they reflect deeply on its own emergence and grand strategy. How middle powers respond will shape China's rise.

Notes

1. Jing Sun, *Japan and China as Charm Rivals: Soft Power in Regional Diplomacy* (Ann Arbor: University of Michigan Press, 2012); Yunling Zhang, *Making New Partnership: A Rising China and Its Neighbors* (Beijing: Social Sciences Academic Press, 2008).

2. Yabin Liang, "Xinxing Guojia Jueqi Yu Meiguo Baquande Tuichi" [The rise of new powers and the maintenance of US hegemony], *Xin Yuanjian* [*New Long-term Thinking*], no. 3 (2012): 23–31.

3. See the articles by Ding Gong cited here. Erjie Hu, "Zhongdeng Guojiade Gonggong Waijiao: Dui Jianada, Helan, Yu Nanfei San Guode Anli Yanjiu" [The public diplomacy of middle powers: case studies of Canada, the Netherlands, and South Africa], in *People's Liberation Army College of International Relations* (Beijing, 2011).

4. Sometimes *zhongdeng guojia* or "middle country" is used; however, for the most part in Chinese this term refers to middle-income countries and is used in discussions of economic development.

5. Thomas J. Christensen, "Chinese Realpolitik," *Foreign Affairs* 75, no. 5 (1996): 37–52.

6. Zhongbo Zhu and Yunheng Zhou, "Jianada Zhongdeng Guojia Shenfen Kaoxi" [An analysis of Canada's middle power identity), *Shangrao Shifan Xueyuan Xuebao* [*Journal of Shangrao Normal University*] 30, no. 1 (2010): 29–34.

7. Interview with Professor He Baogang, Brisbane, July 24, 2012.

8. Gong Ding, "Tuerqi Zhongdeng Qiangguo Waijiaode Xianshixing He Kenengxing" (The possibility and reality of Turkey's middle power diplomacy], *Heping yu Fazhan* [*Peace and Development*] 127, no. 3 (2012): 63–68, 63.

9. "Zhongdeng Qiangguo Jueqi Ji Qi Dui Zhongguo Waijiao Bujude Yingxiang" [The rise of middle powers and its effect on China's foreign policy framework], *Xiandai guoji guanxi* [*Contemporary International Relations*], no. 10 (2011): 47–53.

10. "Zhongdeng Qiangguode Jueqi Yu Zhongguo Waijiao Bujude Tiaozheng" [The rise of middle powers and the adjustment of China's foreign policy], *Guoji Guanxi Xueyuan Xuebao* [*Journal of the College of International Relations*], no. 5 (2011): 66–71.

11. Gang Tang, "Quanqiu Zhili Beijingxiade Qiangguo Jinian Zaidingyi" [Redefining middle powers in global governance], *Bijie Daxue Xuebao* [*Journal of Bijie University*] 14, no. 6 (2013): 32–38.

12. Changsen Yu, "Aodaliya Dui Zhongguo Jueqide Renzhi Yu Fanying" [Australian views and reactions to the rise of China], *Dangdai Yatai* [*Journal of Contemporary Asia Pacific*], no. 4 (2010): 129–42.

13. Hao Qian, "Zhongdeng Qiangguo Canyu Yu Guoji Shiwude Lujing Yanjiu" [Middle power approaches to international affairs], *Shijie jingji yu zhengzhi* [*World Economics and Politics*] 6 (2007): 47–54.

14. Xiaosong Tang and Ke Bin, "Lukewen Zhongdeng Qiangguo Waijiao Pingxi" [An evaluation of Rudd's middle power diplomacy], *Xiandai guoji guanxi* [*Contemporary International Relations*] 10 (2008): 14–19, 18.

15. Xiaohui Yang, "'Zhongdeng Qiangguo' Audaliyade Haijun Zhengce Yu Shili Jiqi Dui Zhongguode Yingxiang" ['Middle power' Australia's naval policy and strength and its effects on China], *Shanghai Jiaotong Daxue Xuebao (Zhexue Shehui Kexue Ban)* [*Journal of Shanghai Jiaotong University*, Philosophy and Social Sciences edition] 12, no. 4 (2013): 65–70.

16. Gong Ding, "Zhongdeng Qiangguo Jueqi Ji Qi Dui Zhongguo Waijiao Bujude Yingxiang" [The rise of middle powers and its effect on China's foreign policy framework], *Xiandai guoji guanxi* [*Contemporary International Relations*] 10 (2011): 47–53.

17. Shenggang Bao, "Shijie Zoujin Zhongdeng Qiangguo Shidai" [The world is entering the era of middle powers], *Quanqiu Shibao* [*Global Times*], January 25, 2008.

18. Chen Zhao, "Guonei Zhengzhi Wenhua Yu Zhongdeng Qiangguode Quanqiu Zhili: Jiyu Jianadade Kaocha" [Domestic political culture and middle power

global governance: The case of Canada], *Shijie jingji yu zhengzhi* [*World Economics and Politics*] 10, no. 158 (2012): 80–94.

19. Ding, "Zhongdeng Qiangguo Jueqi Ji Qi Dui Zhongguo Waijiao Bujude Yingxiang" [The rise of middle powers and its effect on China's foreign policy framework]; Shanrong Jin, "Zhongguo Waijiao Xu Geiyu Zhongdeng Qiangguo Qiadang Dingwei" [China's diplomacy should afford middle powers an appropriate status], *Guoji zhanxue* [*International Strategy*], no. 5 (2010): 20–21.

20. Peter Alford, "ASEAN Bid to Calm Waters on Sea Claims," *Australian*, November 18, 2011.

21. Thai News Service, "Philippines: Gazmin, Chinese Counterpart Vow to Keep Communication Lines Open," May 31, 2012; "Ph Exhorts Asean: Step into Dispute," *Manila Standard Today*, April 27, 2012.

22. Carlos Cue, "US Pressed European Union to Keep Chinese Arms Ban Intact," *El País—English Edition*, December 16, 2010.

23. Dennis Eng, "EU Leader Seeks More Progress," *South China Morning Post*, July 19, 2005.

24. Ambrose Evans-Pritchard, "China States Price for Italian Rescue," *Daily Telegraph*, September 15, 2011.

25. Shanrong Jin, "Tuchu Zhongdeng Qiangguo: Wo Guo Waijiao Ying Caiqude Xin Celue" [Emphasizing middle powers: A new strategy that should be adopted in China's foreign policy], *Zhongguo yu Shijie Jingji Yanjiu Zhongxin* [*Journal of the Center for China in the World Economy*] 9, no. 9 (2009).

26. Zhigang Zhang, "Hua Xu Yingdui Zhongdeng Qiangguo Jueqi" [China needs to recognize the rise of middle powers], *Taiyang bao* [*Hong Kong Sun*], November 8, 2011.

27. Ding, "Zhongdeng Qiangguode Jueqi Yu Zhongguo Waijiao Bujude Tiaozheng" [The rise of middle powers and the adjustment of China's foreign policy)," 70.

28. Ibid.

29. Ibid.

30. Charalampos Efstathopoulos, "Reinterpreting India's Rise through the Middle Power Prism," *Asian Journal of Political Science* 19, no. 1 (2011): 74–95.

31. Carsten Holbraad, *Middle Powers in International Politics* (New York: St. Martin's Press, 1984), 71.

32. Michael Yahuda, "Chinese Dilemmas in Thinking about Regional Security Architecture," *Pacific Review* 16, no. 2 (2003): 189–208.

33. David L. Shambaugh, "China Engages Asia: Reshaping the Regional Order," *International Security* 29, no. 3 (2004): 64–99.

34. Renato Cruz De Castro, "Managing 'Strategic Unipolarity': The Asean States' Responses to the Post-Cold War Regional Environment," in *Southeast Asian Perspectives on Security*, ed. Derek da Cunha (Singapore: Institute of Southeast Asian Studies, 2000).

35. BBC Monitoring Service, "Indonesian Paper Backs Jakarta's Vision of 'Dynamic Equilibrium' in Asia," June 7, 2011.

36. Rod McGuirk, "South Korean and Australian Defence Ministers Agree to More Exercises and Deeper Cooperation," *Associated Press*, December 14, 2011.

37. Permanent Mission of the People's Republic of China to the UN, "Remarks by Ambassador Wang Guangya at Meeting on 'Uniting for Consensus,'" April 11, 2005.

38. Jiantao He, "Zhongdeng Qiangguo Zai Lianheguo Weihe Xingdongzhong Diwei Bianluhuade Genyuan: Yi Jianada Weilie" [The marginalization of middle powers in UN peacekeeping operations: The case of Canada], *Waijiao pinglun* [*Foreign Affairs Review*] 23, no. 4 (2013): 18–32.

39. Maoqing Zhou, "From G8 to G20," *Beijing Review* 53, no. 27 (2010): 12–13.

40. William Tow and Richard Rigby, "China's Pragmatic Security Policy: The Middle Power Factor," *China Journal* 65, no. 1 (2011): 157–78, 159.

41. Miwa Hirono and Marc Lanteigne, "China and UN Peacekeeping," *International Peacekeeping* 18, no. 3 (2011): 243–56, 249.

42. Gerald Segal, "Does China Matter?," *Foreign Affairs* 78, no. 5 (1999): 24–36, 24.

43. Ding, "Zhongdeng Qiangguode Jueqi Yu Zhongguo Waijiao Bujude Tiaozheng" [The rise of middle powers and the adjustment of China's foreign policy], 70.

44. Guangqi Wei, "Zhongdeng Guojia Yu Quanqiu Duobian Zhili" [Middle powers and multilateral global governance], *Taipingyang Xuebao* [*Pacific Journal*] 18, no. 12 (2010): 36–44, 44.

45. Shanrong Jin and Xin Ma, "Weilai Shinian Shijie Liu Da Yousi" [Six big concerns for world affairs in the next decade], *Guoji Guanxi Xueyuan Xuebao* [*Journal of the College of International Relations*], no. 1 (2012): 1–5, 3.

46. Bruce Gilley, "Middle Powers during Great Power Transitions: The Rise of China and Canada-US Relations," *International Journal* 66, no. 2 (2011): 245–64.

47. David G. Victor, Charles F. Kennel, and Veerabhadran Ramanathan, "The Climate Threat We Can Beat," *Foreign Affairs* 91, no. 3 (2012): 112–21.

48. Adam Balcer, "Golden Age of Middle Powers?," *Centre for European Strategy Papers*, no. February (2012): 1–16.

49. Ding, "Zhongdeng Qiangguode Jueqi Yu Zhongguo Waijiao Bujude Tiaozheng" (The rise of middle powers and the adjustment of China's foreign policy), 71.

50. China Business News, "Shanghai Jiaotong University: Prof. Jin Canrong Talks about International Situation at Sjtu," *China Business News*, February 18, 2012.

51. Tommy Koh, "Building Fraternity among East Asians," *Straits Times*, April 7, 2010.

52. Hirono and Lanteigne, "China and UN Peacekeeping," 251.

CHAPTER 4

US Responses to Middle Powers and China

David A. Cooper and Toshi Yoshihara

Introduction

IN THE PRECEDING chapter Bruce Gilley notes that Chinese strategic thinkers have recently discovered the "middle power" concept, thus suggesting that China may increasingly use this conceptual lens to inform its engagement with such actors as part of a broader strategic vision. By contrast, in this chapter we argue that for the United States the middle power concept generally lacks salience.[1] The current chapter therefore offers a somewhat contrarian perspective to the book as a whole by sounding a cautionary note about applying insights derived from middle power theory for purposes of shaping, informing, or explaining the American understanding of, or behavior toward, this category of international actor. To be clear, we are not suggesting that the various countries examined in the chapters that follow are seen as unimportant by the United States; to the contrary, most have one or more important relationships with Washington—for example, as major trading partners, allies or coalition partners, influential regional players, or host nations for basing or supporting US military forces. From a US perspective, however, the foundations of these relationships are not necessarily (or even mostly) grounded in these states' hierarchical standing as global middle powers. Consequently, we contend that using the conceptual lens of their "middlepowerness" is more likely to obscure than to illuminate US responses to these actors. We posit that this is especially true in the *meta*geostrategic context of a protracted transition in global and regional polarity implied by the ongoing rise of China.

The chapter begins by conceptualizing the perspectives of US scholars and policy elites on middle powers generally, with particular emphasis on American perceptions of their roles during the widely surmised global power transition that is being brought about by the recent or incipient graduation of several middle powers to the great power ranks in parallel to the prospective emergence of China as a regional hegemon and global superpower. It then offers an overview of US strategic responses to a rising China, with illustrative examples of how different strata of Asia-Pacific powers (great, middle, and otherwise) fit into this picture.

Why the "Middle Power" Concept Does Not Resonate in Washington

It has been said that international relations is an American social science, and as James Manicom and Jeffery Reeves explore at length in chapter 2, the major contemporary schools of international relations evince little interest in middle powers, either as a concept or as a category.[2] In the following discussion we posit that this general lack of resonance is especially acute within the mainstream of American international relations scholarship per se, and even more so in terms of how this manifests in the perspectives of US policy elites.

Various strands of international relations realism and liberalism differ in their interpretation of the role and implications of various types of "power" in international relations, but they all share basic structural assumptions about world order that lend themselves to seeing middle powers (in this book defined by their position within a global hierarchy) as largely ineffectual actors on the world stage, lacking the wherewithal to exercise significant independent agency at the level of the international system to warrant much attention. The simple truth is that, from any structural international relations perspective, middling powers are of middling interest compared to more significant global players. Such disinterest is especially pronounced within the most unabashedly structural school of international relations theory, neorealism, which we would argue remains the dominant international relations paradigm in the United States.

Although the mainstreaming of social constructivism in the 1990s promised to expand American scholarly interest in middle powers in light of its deemphasis of structural explanations of international relations, this manifestly has not been the case. In fact, as Manicom and Reeves observe, constructivism "offers the most muddled account of middle power behavior" and many constructivist scholars implicitly refute the validity of the middle power concept.[3] Far from being a cruel twist of fate, this constructivist ambivalence is an entirely logical reflection of the structural underpinnings of the middle power concept going back to its modern international relations origins in A. F. K. Organski's power transition theory (which conceives of a hierarchical global power continuum in which middle powers are called out as a distinct category). Although Organski sees beyond the purely military power confines of structural realism by factoring economic and political sources of power, he nonetheless cleaves to the inherently structural notion that relative international power is derived from tangible national attributes. This leads him to focus on the rise or realignment of great powers as challenges to the dominance of what we would now term global superpowers, with scant attention for the middle or lower echelons.[4] In other words, the structural assumptions embedded within the very concept of middle-powerness relegate it by definition to peripheral importance to structural understandings of international relations, while rendering it conceptually incompatible with nonstructural approaches like constructivism.

In the final analysis, the only major branch of international relations theory that is conceptually compatible with the concept of middle powers, while at the same time offering a basis for caring much about their systemic role, is the English School. The latter reframes classical realist assumptions about anarchy and power in part through conceiving of world politics in sociological terms, as a complex web of interactions among states comprising an international society, wherein the raw use of power in pursuit of naked national interests is tempered by societal norms arising from primary international institutions such as diplomacy, international law, and alliances. In this "society of states," while middle powers may not belong to high society, nevertheless, like so many Jane Austen heroines, they are still respectable enough to move in the right social circles and thereby, through combinations of charm, cleverness, talent, virtue, and verve—using "soft power" to exasperate and beguile the high and mighty—can contrive to make a mark above their station. Thus it should not be surprising that, in exploring the relationships among the Southeast Asian states, China, and the United States (in a sense a microcosm of this book), Goh soundly rejects both neorealist and neoliberal explanations. Instead, he points to the seminal English School theorizing of the Australian scholar Hedley Bull as the only suitable theoretical lens for this type of asymmetric comparative analysis.[5] The rub here of course is that the English School has been largely marginalized within the US sphere of the international relations discipline since being on the losing methodological side of the Second Great Debate of the 1960s between traditionalists and behavioralists. To be sure, English School theorizing retains a loyal American cult following, but it lacks any broad influence within contemporary US international relations scholarship.

This marginalization of the English School is symptomatic of the comparatively narrow structural and positivist boundaries of American international relations theorizing. The "inter-paradigm debate" of the 1970s and 1980s had by the mid-1990s been resolved in what Wæver terms a "neo-neo synthesis" (between neorealism and neoliberalism) as a broad mainstream consensus.[6] Others might argue that neorealism won outright. In a survey of international relations scholarship near the end of the first post–Cold War decade, British scholar Steve Smith judges the American incarnation of the discipline to be markedly more restrictive than in Britain and elsewhere. "The so-called cutting edge of international theory has little impact on what happens in the 2000 or so institutions that teach IR in the US," he observes, characterizing American international relations as "far more unquestioning of the dominance of realism and positivism."[7] As for the postpositivist debate that has frothed up in the intervening years with the likes of postmodernist, feminist, and environmentalist international relations theorizing, this trend has certainly spurred sundry critiques of the rigid "neorealist orthodoxy" in American international relations. As Hamati-Ataya observes, however, the fact that neorealism remains the most widely criticized approach merely serves to confirm its enduring dominance.[8] Even within this general challenge to neorealist orthodoxy, there are unmistakable signs of a (neo)structural backlash against postpositivism, for example, the renewed interest in power transition theory, structural security complexes at the regional level, or the emergence of neoclassical realism as a more nuanced variation of metastructuralism. Moreover, a growing number of scholars suggest that the prospect of a looming transition to global multipolarity—especially in the context of an unusually large number of emerging or resurging great powers by historical standards, and combined with post–Iraq/Afghanistan intervention fatigue and the concurrent constraints of long-term fiscal austerity—is if anything likely to further revitalize structural realist proclivities in US international relations thinking with particular emphasis on balancing with great powers.[9] In other words, the dominance of structural realism in one form or another may be on the upswing, which would not bode well for increasing scholarly interest in middling powers.

Of course our interest in American international relations scholarship for purposes of this book includes the influence that it exerts on the worldview of official Washington. Walt makes a compelling case that, while policymakers do not always realize it, the underlying assumptions of international relations theory can exert significant influence on them.[10] In this regard neorealist, or at the least neo-neo dominance, is more pronounced. Rather than theory-heavy PhD programs, the US foreign and national security policy elites hail disproportionately from terminal master degree programs at a small cluster of top public policy schools with concentrations in international affairs. These applied professional programs focus on interdisciplinary areas such as security studies or international political economy where, as with strategic studies master degree programs in the professional military education system (America's war and staff colleges), the esoterica of avant-garde international relations theory attracts little interest.[11] Finally, as one prominent Canadian scholar-practitioner observes, America's political elites of all stripes are edging away even from neoliberalism. He laments, "A dwindling band of liberal internationalists still keep the faith, but an unlikely convergence of left and right has emerged to leave them isolated. . . . This alliance of opposites leaves the American constituency who still believes in international institutions weak and exposed."[12] In sum, even more so than in international relations scholarship, neorealist assumptions increasingly dominate American strategic and foreign policy thinking, albeit tempered by residual strands of neoliberalism.

So where does all of this leave US policy elites in thinking about middle powers and the rise of China? In a nutshell they are alarmed by the dire realist implications of inevitable confrontation as epitomized by the stark predictions of structural realist John Mearsheimer, tempered somewhat by the revivification of interest in power transition theory and its promise of a successful countervailing coalition between the United States and the emerging constellation of like-minded (read: democratic) great powers and others.[13] All the while, they cling to fading neoliberal hopes for peaceful enmeshment through deepening economic and cultural globalization and political institutionalism. Perhaps nothing captures this American zeitgeist better than the popularity and influence of geostrategic bestsellers such as Robert Kagan's *The World America Made*, Robert Kaplan's *The Revenge of Geography*, and Zbignew Brzezinski's *Strategic Vision*, which generated keen interest within US strategic circles.[14] Kaplan, for example, urges a return to classical geopolitical thinking in American grand strategy, such as Nicholas Spykman's rimland theory (discussed below), the intellectual foundation for the US Cold War containment strategy. Kaplan characterizes China as an "über-realist power" that is inexorably destined to be "propelled abroad" by its core economic and security interests unless it is checked by the combined naval power of the United States, India, Japan, and other democracies.[15]

This surge of renewed US interest in geostrategic thought does not prominently feature global middle powers. Instead, American strategic thinking is increasingly focusing on the very actors that Bruce Gilley and Andrew O'Neil in chapter 1 classify as great powers. Only two of their putative middle powers, Brazil and Iran, can be said to command significant American interest at the international system level. But these are really the exceptions that prove the rule. In the first place, as Gilley and O'Neil readily acknowledge, many now see Brazil as an emerging great power that is transcending the middle power category, and significantly this is precisely Washington's view.[16] Even so, its claim to US attention probably derives as much from its status as the dominant power of a contiguous region, just as interest in Iran is primarily driven by its efforts to challenge US dominance in the geostrategically vital Middle East region. Consider that while Canada and Mexico are both global middle powers, this is far less relevant for Washington than their overland commerce and "homeland security" importance as immediate neighbors. Put simply, we would assert that, to the extent that hierarchical global middle powers matter to the United States, it is mostly in cognate guises. This observation has significant conceptual implications for US perceptions of, and responses to, middle powers in relation to China.

Why Middle Powers (May) Matter to Washington . . . But Not *as* "Middle Powers"

We argue that, rather than viewing middle powers through the conceptually unifying lens of their hierarchical global middlepowerness, the United States sees these actors mostly through a refracting prism of diverse cognate guises, for instance, multilateral activist, regional power, ally or coalition partner, or perhaps merely as a strategically important geographic location.[17] Pronounced diversity in the combinations and levels of such cognate guises across middle powers implies correspondingly diverse US responses to these actors. It necessarily follows that it is their cognate guises that must be taken heavily into account when explicating US responses to any particular middle power in relation to China.

Of the myriad cognate guises in which Washington sees middle powers, the role of multilateral activist is most closely aligned with the long-standing tenets of classical middle power theory. A few recent studies suggest that the importance of this role might be on the rise in that middle powers may prove to be especially adept at working in the expanding milieu of informal "network" multilateralism, as embodied by the nascent Group of Twenty (G20) summit process, which many observers speculate could evolve into a sort of de facto steering committee for global governance with most top-tier middle powers in the mix.[18] Consistent with the idea of an enduring neoliberal influence in American thinking (Wæver's neo-neo synthesis), many observers suggest that multilateralism generally, and norm-building in particular, is already part and parcel of an evolving US neorealist balancing strategy against China. This suggests a potential area of synergy between US interests and a surmised middle power tendency. For example, Manicom and Reeves (chapter 2) suggest that, because the current international system reflects the dominant American status quo, any norm-building efforts by middle powers within this system inherently tend to support long-term US interests. In principle this can even be true when their efforts are at odds with immediate US policy goals, for instance, the International Criminal Court or the Ottawa Convention against landmines. While this benign view of middle power meddling is unlikely to be appreciated by US policymakers when it manifests at cross purposes with their goals, Washington certainly welcomes normative activism that complements its priorities, for example, in areas like counterproliferation or humanitarian intervention.

Normative confluence between specific US interests vis-à-vis China and general middle power inclinations could resonate powerfully with the residual neoliberal strands of US strategic thinking. For instance, in a classic articulation of neo-neo synthesis, Miller argues that, even as the United States focuses on balancing other great powers, it is pursuing a concurrent agenda to promote democratization and liberal norms as a means to assess which great powers it deems threatening such that they require balancing.[19] Along the same lines, Kreps shows that multilateralism has become an ingrained normative element to US power balancing irrespective of its necessity in strictly neorealist terms.[20] A small number of explicitly neoliberal analysts take this thinking to its logical extreme, arguing that American dominance can only be extended in a global power transition by normatively enmeshing China and other potential status quo challengers, but that this will require Washington to move adroitly to strengthen, rely upon, and submit to the web of global institutions that underpin the American liberal world order.[21] Particularly if China is becoming more assertive multilaterally as some observers suggest, and given the demonstrated effectiveness of the "traditional" middle powers at harnessing global civil society in international norm-building causes (e.g., Responsibility to Protect, conflict diamonds, child soldiers), it is plausible that the United States will increasingly look to some middle powers as key norm-building partners.[22] Given the underdeveloped nature of Asia-Pacific multilateral architecture, this dynamic could be especially important regarding China and the further incremental development of regional multilateralism, which President Obama's former deputy secretary of state, James Steinberg, identifies as one pillar of the emerging US security strategy in Asia.[23]

At the same time, a cautionary note is in order about the pertinence of middlepowerness in any apparent normative confluence. Whereas middle power theory is on solid ground in predicting multilateral activism as a common tactic of middle power statecraft, numerous scholars decisively refute any claim that middle powers tend to share inherent underlying normative or political interests.[24] Thus the multilateral activism that middle powers may bring to bear could just as easily be employed against US interests to challenge the status quo, including worrisomely from a US viewpoint as part of a deliberate bandwagoning strategy with an ascendant China. Indeed, there are several emerging informal multilateral groupings of middle and great powers that exclude the United States and include China, for instance, the new BRICS grouping (Brazil, Russia, India, China, South Africa) summit process, or the recently elevated Indian Ocean Rim Association for Regional Cooperation (where China is an observer), that could veer in just such a troubling direction.

From the dominant realist perspective of US strategic thinking, by far a more important cognate role of (some) middle powers is that of regional power, wherein a global middle power may possess vastly greater proportional "hard" power attributes relative to the smaller structural dynamics of a regional security order.[25] (This logic also applies from a neoliberal perspective in terms of the proportionately greater political influence that regional powers can exert through regional multilateralism.) The significance of regional power hierarchies is especially relevant for the United States in the context of China. While US perspectives vary about whether China is poised to emerge as a truly global peer, there is widespread consensus that Beijing, having already surpassed Washington's regional economic clout, could soon be in a position to challenge American strategic and political supremacy in the Asia-Pacific region or parts thereof. From a structural perspective, the issue boils down to whether a rising regional hegemon can peacefully coexist with a global hegemon within the same geographic space. Holslag, for one, predicts that structurally the Asia-Pacific security dynamic will "become increasingly bipolar, but there will be a multipolar sub-structure in which other powers will make their independent choices about whether to balance, hedge, or jump on the bandwagon."[26] On the other hand, Huntington's diagnosis of a protracted uni-multipolar stalemate—during which the United States fails to achieve global hegemony while rising powers fail to become its global peers—could prove more enduring than even he imagined.[27] Whatever the answer, the realist logic of US thinking suggests that the most plausible path for China to challenge American global dominance is by first challenging its regional influence.[28] In other words, as embodied by the US "pivot to Asia" strategy, any power transition involving China—irrespective of whether it comes about antagonistically, competitively, or cooperatively, or how it eventually plays out globally—for the foreseeable future will from Washington's perspective be perceived *primarily as a regional dynamic*.

This regional focus in US responses to China collides headlong with one of the more glaring weaknesses in extant middle power theory, namely, the failure to grapple with confluences and distinctions between the concept of a global middle power and a regional power. Too frequently these categories are used interchangeably, but because the latter is based on idiosyncratic regional norms, roles, reputations, and power hierarchies, the categories can manifest differently and must therefore be distinguished accordingly.[29] For example, Australia is at one and the same time a quintessential middle power globally, a secondary peripheral regional power within the greater Asia-Pacific, and a hegemonic subregional power in the South Pacific; Canada, by contrast, is also a quintessential global middle power without being any kind of regional power; whereas Nigeria can barely be considered a global middle power and Ethiopia is certainly not one, but both are nonetheless major regional and dominant subregional powers. The implication being that the United States, seeing the rise of China as a largely regional dynamic, is more apt to focus its attention on proximate lesser regional powers like the Philippines or Vietnam, even though they are not global middle powers, than on distant global middle powers such as Argentina or South Africa that exercise less regional sway in Asia.

Some regional players may have important roles for US responses to China that have little or nothing to do with traditional power hierarchies, regional or otherwise. Australia, Japan, the Philippines, South Korea, and Thailand run the hierarchical gamut from global great power to minor power (or at best marginal middle power), but all are formal allies in the hub-and-spoke US system of bilateral Asian alliances. Other smaller powers like Singapore and Vietnam are moving rapidly to cement alliance-like relationships with the United States, including basing or supporting US military forces. A fundamental aspect of the long-term US strategy in Asia is to reenergize its long-standing bilateral alliances while actively seeking new bilateral arrangements.[30] Washington is also working deliberately to trilateralize key bilateral alliances, most notably with Japan/Australia and Japan/South Korea, and may be in the fledgling stages of multilateralizing its expanding Asian alliance network.[31] Finally and notwithstanding US denials that it is pursuing a Chinese containment strategy, simple geography may also matter far more than relative global or regional power attributes when it comes to strategically positioned states, as demonstrated not only by the likes of Singapore and Vietnam, but also the recent attention that Washington has lavished on its rapprochement with Myanmar.

Three important themes emerge from the preceding analysis. First, geostrategic thought and the attendant focus on great power politics are enjoying a kind of renaissance in the US policymaking community. Second, the United States conceives of China's rise largely in the regional context. Or, to put it another way, Washington feels Beijing's rise most acutely in Asia. Third, because China must rise in Asia before it can truly rise globally, the United States attaches high value to local Asian powers that can exert direct influence in the region and on China. In this context middle powers resonate with the United States only to the extent that they can produce strategic effects—be they diplomatic, economic, or military—in China's neighborhood. Geography, as it turns out, matters a great deal. The geospatial dimension of strategy is thus essential to understanding Washington's strategic response to China's rise and its alignment with regional powers in Asia.

Spykman's Rimland Theory and US Security Partners in Asia

As noted above, geopolitics has made a comeback in US policy debates. Its resurgence should not be surprising given that geostrategy enjoys deep roots in the American foreign policy tradition. So ingrained is the practice of geopolitics in US statecraft that the assumptions underlying such a seemingly old-fashioned discipline are rarely explicated. The ubiquity of geopolitics in the policy community makes it easy to take the concept for granted. Nevertheless, the geostrategic framework not only informs American policymakers' worldview and how they evaluate power, but it directly influences how Washington engages third parties—middle powers and otherwise—in managing China's rise.

A long-standing geopolitical consensus running through the American academic and policy discourse is that Western Europe and East Asia are the arenas where the struggle for mastery would unfold. Geopolitical logic foretells that a great power's hostile seizure of one of these two regions—the epicenters of military competition and economic wealth in the international system—would equip it with the resources to upend the global order. As such, the primary US aim has been to prevent the rise of a hegemon on the eastern and western fringes of the Eurasian landmass. This basic objective, which verges on a prime directive in America's regional strategies, traces its origins to the emergence of the United States as a global power.

Writing during World War II, Yale University professor Nicholas Spykman offered a prescient geostrategic analysis that would see its key tenets reflected in US strategy throughout the Cold War and even beyond. He built a convincing case for US balancing in the "rimlands," or coastal regions, of Europe and East Asia.[32] America could project military power across the Atlantic or Pacific to prevent aspiring hegemons from wresting away control of the Eurasian landmass. As he looked to the postwar era, Spykman insisted that the United States must mount a standing, forward defense to avert such an outcome. For him the alternative, hemispheric defense was "no defense at all" because it would deprive America of beachheads on the Eurasian landmass.[33]

Spykman believed a hegemon could marshal sufficient maritime resources to reach out across the Atlantic or Pacific, menacing the Western Hemisphere that was geographically surrounded by the larger, more populous, more resource-rich Eurasian landmass.[34] The global war that engulfed the United States as he penned his classic treatise, *The Geography of the Peace*, was the clearest proof of this danger. To Spykman, Washington's neglect of the rimlands during the interwar period when isolationism gripped the nation permitted Nazi Germany and Imperial Japan to seize the most productive seaboards of Eurasia that turned "the geographic embrace of the Western Hemisphere by the Old World into political strangulation."[35]

To preclude "such an encirclement in the future," counseled Spykman, "our constant concern in peace-time must be to see that no nation or alliance of nations is allowed to emerge as a dominating power in either of the two regions of the Old World from which our security could be threatened."[36] He urged the United States to acknowledge that "the power constellation in Europe and Asia is of everlasting concern to her, both in time of war and in time of peace."[37] US statesmen ought to stand ready lest the regional balance tilt dangerously toward hegemony. Spykman, then, premised his strategy on managing events in the western and eastern extremis of the Eurasian rimlands. The Cold War containment strategy, centered on defending Europe and Asia from Soviet dominion, largely validated his vision.

Spykman's assessment with its emphasis on key regional centers of global power has remained a bedrock assumption among many policymakers and academics in the years following the Soviet Union's collapse. To be sure, the rimland strategy and the raw geopolitical calculus that underwrites it do not define entirely nor dominate US security strategy. American foreign policy is certainly far more complex and nuanced than an all-consuming fear of a rival peer competitor. But policymakers look to geopolitical considerations as an important compass to guide the general direction of US regional strategy.

The rimland theory not only illustrates the magnitude of the hegemonic threat, but it also prescribes a certain set of broad policies designed to preclude or to frustrate the rise of a dominant power in Eurasia. Indeed, the theory furnishes Washington with a strategic script that it has followed with fidelity. An important component of the antihegemonic agenda is a formula for choosing the right partners to secure the rimland from an overbearing power.

As an offshore island-continent with the Atlantic and Pacific Oceans separating it from the eastern and western rimlands of Eurasia, the United States must rely on proxy powers residing in those rimlands to counterbalance an aspiring hegemon. Several criteria define the suitability of these proxies. First, they must be physically in or near the region to influence events there. Second, the partners should boast sufficient strategic heft to share the burden of balancing. Third, their location—that affords maritime access in particular—and their willingness to host US military forces must enable Washington to radiate strategic power along the seaboards of Eurasia. Fourth, their ability to interoperate with US forces through shared equipment, doctrine, and training should maximize military effectiveness. Finally, they should ideally (but certainly not necessarily) be like-minded states that share a stake in defending the US-led global order.

Only a few powers meet all criteria, and they are the ones that attract the most policy attention in Washington. But even those that possess one or two of these attributes may be sufficiently important for the purposes of counterbalancing a prospective hegemon. Some middle powers may meet one or more of these benchmarks, thus meriting a place in US strategy and plans. Some may not at all. The bottom line is that middlepowerness by itself is rarely the basis by which Washington chooses its partners when the geopolitical stakes are high as they are with a Eurasian hegemonic threat. Recent US policy toward key partners in Asia shows how such geostrategic calculations inform Washington's thinking about its regional strategy and its response to China's rise. For illustrative purposes, the following examines Japan (a global great power), Australia (a global middle power), and Singapore (a lesser regional power) to understand US regional perspectives along the power hierarchy presented in this book.

Japan, Australia, and Singapore

A key policy consensus arising from the rimland theory is the imperative to keep Japan in America's orbit. Indeed, Japan's strategic importance to the United States is hard to overstate and will remain so for the foreseeable future, despite two decades of Japanese stagnation and relative decline. Various analysts and officials have unstintingly praised Japan as "the indispensable linchpin of our forward military and diplomatic presence in Asia and the foundation of a stable strategic equilibrium in the region," "the cornerstone of peace and stability in the region," and "a platform for US military readiness in Asia."[38] These evocative depictions bespeak Tokyo's centrality to America's strategic posture in the region. According to a study by the prominent Center for a New American Security,

> In Asia, the [US-Japanese] alliance constitutes an unrivaled platform for maintaining the United States as a "resident power." Because Japan hosts American bases, Washington can quickly deploy military assets throughout the region, as epitomized by the dispatch of US ships to Indonesia following the 2004

> tsunami. Moreover, bases in Japan enhance America's capacity to respond to sudden change on the Korean Peninsula and any contingency in the Taiwan Strait.[39]

Japan's proximity to potential flashpoints in Asia, including those involving China, enhances allied deterrence while maximizing early warning, rapid crisis response, and wartime mobilization should deterrence fail. Without Japan the United States would lose a critical, irreplaceable foothold from which to project combat power along the eastern Eurasian seaboard. At the same time allied interoperability benefits enormously from regular interactions, training, and exercises that a substantial US military presence affords. In the eyes of some American strategists, potential adversaries—such as China—must take into account the emergence of a "joint command relationship" that increasingly characterizes the maturing US-Japan alliance, dissuading adventurism and aggression. To them, "This deterrent effect would not be possible without forward deployed US forces in Japan."[40] Japan's strategic location thus underwrites a great deal of its value to US regional strategy.

The influential Armitage-Nye reports—a series issued by bipartisan study groups over the past decade—have pinned high hopes on Japan's continuing leading role in Asia. In 2000, the architects of the report called on the US-Japan alliance to emulate the special relationship between the United States and the United Kingdom.[41] To them Tokyo empowers Washington in the Asian rimland just as London has played a critical role in Europe as an offshore balancer and as an intermediary between Washington and continental European affairs. Six years later, the authors described the alliance as "the keystone of the United States' position in Asia" that could best foster "a balance of power that favors freedom." They warned that neglect of the alliance could lead Japan to "become comfortable as a 'middle power' at best."[42] Despite Japan's inability to reverse its fortunes and the March 2011 triple disaster, Armitage and Nye continued to express hope that Japan would remain a "tier-one nation" defined as a power boasting "significant economic weight, capable military forces, global vision, and demonstrated leadership on international concerns."[43] It is striking that Armitage and Nye equate the concept of middle power—at least as it relates to Japan—to strategic retreat. The US insistence on Japan's centrality to its regional strategy reveals that great power balancing remains the coin of the realm.

If Japan is a standard bearer for US strategy in Asia and for managing China's rise, then Australia could be undergoing a strategic makeover that will make it an important anchor in the region. Canberra is a major component of the ongoing realignment of the US forward presence that will shift a basing infrastructure centered overwhelmingly on Northeast Asia to the southern rimland of Eurasia. Washington appears to be pursuing an ambitious reorientation of its regional strategy that increasingly frames Asia-Pacific affairs in "Indo-Pacific" terms. The Obama administration's southward push has already yielded important initiatives with Australia, including the rotational presence of US Marines and aircraft as well as the advance placement of military assets and supplies. Recent US proposals have included forward-deploying a carrier strike group at the southwestern naval base in Perth.[44] This renewed focus on Australia can be understood only in terms of geostrategy and China's re-rise. The growing military reach of local powers—aided by the proliferation of long-range precision-strike systems—has radically altered the region's strategic geography, exposing large swathes of maritime Asia that were once considered sanctuaries. The shrinkage of Asia has, in turn, brought Australia, traditionally a peripheral regional power, into sharper focus.

Simply put, Australia is a superb location for US naval basing in the Indian Ocean basin as China's military reach and concomitant maritime ambitions extend beyond the "near seas." The island-continent lies at the seam between the Pacific and Indian Ocean theaters, allowing for ready strategic maneuver between the two oceans while circumventing maritime bottlenecks such as the Malacca Strait. It is remote from potential threats like the Chinese conventional ballistic-missile force and other striking arms of the People's Liberation Army. It boasts the resources of a continent-spanning state and a range of critical maintenance and training facilities for naval forces. Perhaps, most importantly, US relations with the host nation are excellent at the political, strategic, and operational levels. How far Australia is prepared to go is unclear, given the concerns of certain domestic constituencies. But Washington is clearly determined to maximize the island-continent's location as it rebalances its focus toward Asia in general and China in particular.

Finally, Singapore, a tiny, nonaligned city-state, is another case of how geography and power elevate a local player's salience to Washington. Located at the narrowest point of the Malacca Strait, the small island-nation sits at the nexus between the Indian Ocean and the western Pacific theaters. From the US perspective, a friendly power there is essential to help keep open a critical chokepoint through which massive volumes of seaborne trade passes. Singapore also punches well above its weight. It boasts a world-class air force and a small but balanced navy capable of exercising limited sea control in and around the Straits of Malacca and Singapore. Bilateral military agreements permit US forces to rotate ships and aircraft through Singapore. Notably, the United States enjoys naval access to the city-state's Changi naval base, the only facility in Southeast Asia capable of docking aircraft carriers. As noted above, Singapore recently agreed to host the rotational presence of four littoral combat ships, furnishing Washington the capacity to maintain good order at sea, engage in naval diplomacy, and, most importantly, keep an eye on China.

Again, geostrategic calculations premised in part on the rimland theory inform US relations and, specifically, basing arrangements with Singapore. Compared to the concentration of American military power in Northeast Asia, the US forward presence in the South China Sea theater has been relatively sparse owing to a decades-long contraction of American power there. After its defeat in the Vietnam War, the United States lost a major foothold on continental Southeast Asia, including the highly prized deep-water port in Cam Ranh Bay. In the early 1990s, Washington pulled out its naval and air forces from Subic Bay and Clark airbase, respectively, in the Philippines after Manila withdrew its consent to host the US military. Since then, it has tightened strategic relations with Singapore to compensate for this loss of access. As China's maritime activism increases along with its ascent, Washington will expand ties with Singapore, to the extent that the city-state is able and willing.

Regional Trilateralism

For over a decade, the United States has sought to link its bilateral security arrangements in Asia by encouraging closer coordination between US security partners that have traditionally looked exclusively to Washington. In theory, regular interactions among American treaty allies and friends would increase mutual trust and foster habits of cooperation. Over time, such a socialization process could eventually help develop more effective regional security institutions. Washington's preferred approach is to expand existing bilateral relationships that possess the capacity—developed over decades with US forces—to leverage commonalities as well as exploit comparative advantages in doctrine, procedures, force structure, and so on.

In the late 1990s, Washington, Tokyo, and Seoul formed the Trilateral Coordination and Oversight Group (TCOG) to jointly manage North Korea's nuclear weapons development. Until then, Japanese and South Korean defense-related contacts had been sporadic due to historical and territorial disputes, even though both maintained close military ties with the United States. Policymakers on all sides welcomed TCOG as a hopeful sign that trilateralism would provide the foundations for more ambitious institution-building in Northeast Asia. Trilateral consultations continued in response to Pyongyang's various provocations over the past decade. In June 2012, Tokyo and Seoul came close to concluding a military pact that would have enhanced intelligence sharing and logistical cooperation. But domestic backlash in South Korea dashed the plans for setting up what would have been routine interactions between two advanced militaries. There is no doubt that Washington would welcome such an accord in the future. Closer defense cooperation between Tokyo and Seoul would clearly advance the larger US aims of building on the hub-and-spoke security architecture.

Other trilateral security arrangements have been forged since, including the US-Japan-Australia (2006) and the US-Japan-India (2011) strategic dialogues. These developments have paralleled enhanced bilateral security accords between US allies and friends featuring joint declarations by Australia-Japan in 2007, Japan-India in 2008, Australia-India in 2009, and Australia-South Korea in 2010. Many of these partnerships involve closer consultations and coordination, basic defense collaboration, and nontraditional security cooperation, including humanitarian assistance, disaster relief, and other lesser-included military operations. All have assiduously avoided steps that would feed perceptions that these agreements were designed to contain China. In theory, a web of overlapping and interlocking ties could deepen political, military, and economic relations across the region while prodding these countries to develop a durable security architecture.

It is worth noting again the geopolitical patterns that emerge from these efforts to link the various "spokes" of the American-led security order. Thus far, the great powers have played the most prominent roles in the trilateral pacts. From the US perspective, Japan has been the preferred strategic conduit through which ties can be extended to great powers like India and to middle powers like Australia and South Korea. It is particularly noteworthy that efforts to push forward a US-India-Australia pact have foundered due in part to New Delhi's reticence to confer the kind of strategic equality to Canberra that such a trilateral framework would imply. Here, too, it is clear great power politics remain the coin of the realm. The most successful and mature non-US bilateral defense relationship is between Japan and Australia. They constitute the northern and southern anchors of the US forward strategy and boast world-class air and naval power that have operated alongside American forces for decades. Geography and power are integral to these developments. But for the unfortunate overhang from the ugly past, Japan and South Korea are natural allies in geographical and strategic terms. In Washington eyes, they would make for a formidable pairing should they ever transcend history.

Conclusion

The central premise of this volume as a whole is that hierarchical global middle powers as a category—in other words, *because* they are hierarchical global middle powers—may play a unique and important systemic role in reshaping the rise of China and the emergent world order that this power transition portends. Our intention in this chapter has not been necessarily to challenge this insight, although its validity certainly remains to be seen. Instead our thrust has been to sound a cautionary note that the United States is unlikely to understand, or respond to, China and middle powers in these terms. Of course, US thinking could evolve if the middle power premise is borne out, and indeed this book may offer the conceptual foundation for just such a shift in Washington's understanding of the role of middle powers in the international relations of the coming decades–or possibly not. The point is that for now, at least, the United States mostly does not think in terms of middle powers as such, even as it keenly perceives the importance of multilateralism (including at the regional level), alliances, regional security dynamics, and strategic geography.

Notes

1. The opinions expressed in this chapter are solely those of the authors and do not reflect official positions of the US Naval War College, US Defense Department, or any government agency.

2. Stanley Hoffman, "An American Social Science: International Relations," *Daedalus* 106, no. 3 (1977): 41–60.

3. David A. Cooper, "Challenging Contemporary Notions of Middle Power Influence: Implications of the Proliferation Security Initiative for 'Middle Power Theory,'" *Foreign Policy Analysis* 7, no. 3 (2011): 317–36.

4. A. F. K. Organski, *World Politics* (New York: Alfred A. Knopf, 1958).

5. Eveyn Goh, "Great Powers and Hierarchical Order in Southeast Asia," *International Security* 32, no. 3 (2007): 113–57.

6. Ole Wæver, "The Rise and Fall of the Inter-paradigm Debate," in *International Theory: Positivism and Beyond*, 149–85, eds. Steve Smith, Ken Booth, and Marysia Zalewski (Cambridge: Cambridge University Press, 1996).

7. Steve Smith, "The Discipline of International Relations: Still an American Social Science?," *British Journal of Politics and International Relations* 2, no. 3 (2000): 374–402, 379.

8. Inanna Hamati-Ataya, "Neorealism Reconsidered: Human Nature or State Behavior?," *International Studies Review* 14, no. 2 (2012): 303–7.

9. See, for example, Dana H. Allin and Erik Jones, *Weary Policeman: American Power in an Age of Austerity* (New York: Routledge, 2012); David Lai, *The United*

States and China in Power Transition (Carlisle, PA: Strategic Studies Institute, 2011); Sebastian Rosato and John Schuessler, "A Realist Foreign Policy for the United States," *Perspectives on Politics* 9, no. 4 (2011): 803–19.

10. Stephen Walt, "The Relationship between Theory and Policy in International Relations," *Annual Review of Political Science* 8 (2005): 23–48.

11. In a scathing rebuke to the wider international relations discipline, the former dean of one of the leading international relations professional schools lambastes recent trends in international relations scholarship as increasingly irrelevant to the needs of policymakers. See Robert L. Gallucci, "How Scholars Can Improve International Relations," *Chronicle of Higher Education*, November 26, 2012.

12. Michael Ignatieff, "The One and the Many" (review of Mark Mazower's *Governing the World: The History of an Idea*), *New Republic* (December 20, 2012), 40.

13. John J. Mearsheimer, *The Tragedy of Great Power Politics* (New York: W. W. Norton, 2001).

14. Robert Kagan, *The World America Made* (New York: Knopf, 2012); Robert D. Kaplan, *The Revenge of Geography: What the Map Tells Us about Coming Conflicts and the Battle against Fate* (New York: Random House, 2012); Zbigniew Brzezinski, *Strategic Vision: America and the Crisis of Power* (New York, Basic Books, 2012). For instance, Joint Chiefs Chair General Martin Dempsey has been referring in speeches to Kaplan's latest opus, Brzezinski and his book have become veritable fixtures on the MSNBC network's influential *Morning Joe* program, and numerous news reports indicate that President Obama has been influenced by Kagan's anti-America-in-decline geohistoric reasoning. These are only a few of the most recent and prominent examples of a wave of geostrategic offerings.

15. Kaplan, *The Revenge of Geography*, 102, 199, 227.

16. See, for example, Peter Dauvergne and Déborah B. L. Farias, "The Rise of Brazil as a Global Development Power," *Third World Quarterly* 33, no. 5 (2012): 903–17; Juliá E. Sweig and Daid Herrero, "Brazil as an Emerging Global Power: Implications for US-Brazil Relations" (Washington, DC: Aspen Institute, 2011), www.aspeninstitute.org/sites/default/files/content/docs/congressional/Sweig%20Essay_0.pdf; Shannon O'Neil, "Brazil as an Emerging Power: The View from the United States," *SAIIA Policy Briefing* 16 (February 2010); Elton Reis, "Competing Regional Integration Alternatives and Power Projection: Brazilian Foreign Policy Strategy Facing FTAA and ALBA," conference paper, www.allacademic.com/meta/p381044_indext.html.

17. This list is intended to be illustrative rather than inclusive. For example, "NAFTA trading partner" or "border security partner" may be the most relevant Mexican roles; just as "rogue state" or "nuclear proliferator" might be the most apropos Iranian guises from a US perspective.

18. For discussion of the adeptness of middle powers in informal multilateralism, see, for example, Katharina Grath and Claudia Schmucker, "The Role of the Emerging Countries in the G20: Agenda-setter, Veto Player or Spectator?," *Bruges Regional Integration and Global Governance Papers* (February 2011); David A. Cooper, "Challenging Contemporary Notions of Middle Power Influence" (2011); Wongi Choe,

"The Role of Korea in the G20 Process and the Seoul Summit," conference paper for G20 Seoul Summit: From Crisis to Cooperation, Seoul, May 2010. For discussion of the potential emergence of the G20 as a leading instrument for global governance involving middle powers, see, for example, Leonardo Martinez-Diaz and Ngasse Woods, "The G20—The Perils and Opportunities of Network Governance for Developing Countries," Global Economic Governance Programme Briefing Paper (Oxford: Department of Politics and International Relations, Oxford University, November 2009); Alan S. Alexandroff, "Stuck in Transition: Conflicting Ambitions for the G20's Future," *Global Asia* 5, no. 3 (September 2010): 42–46; Paul Heinbecker, "The Future of the G20 and Its Place in Global Governance," *CIGI G20 Papers*, no. 5 (April 2011); International Institute for Strategic Studies, "Crisis Over, G20 Struggles to Prove Its Utility," *Strategic Comments* (November 2012); Robert A. Manning, *Envisioning 2030: US Strategy for a Post-Western World* (Washington, DC: Atlantic Council, 2012); Fen Osler Hampson and Paul Heinbecker, "Leadership in a Turbulent Age," *CIGI Papers*, no. 11 (January 2013).

19. Paul D. Miller, "Five Pillars of American Grand Strategy," *Survival* 54, no. 5 (2012): 7–44.

20. Sarah E. Kreps, *Coalitions of Convenience: United States Military Interventions after the Cold War* (Oxford: Oxford University Press, 2011).

21. See, for example, Cesare Merlini, "The Lonely Architect" (review of Robert Kagan's *The World America Made*), *Survival* 54, no. 5 (2012): 143–60; G. John Ikenberry, *Liberal Leviathan: The Origins, Crisis, and Transformation of the American World Order* (Princeton: Princeton University Press, 2011); G. John Ikenberry, "Power and Liberal Order: America's Post War World Order in Transition," *International Relations of the Asia-Pacific* 5, no. 2 (2005): 133–52.

22. Joel Wuthnow, Xin Li, and Lingling Qi, "Diverse Multilateral Diplomacy," *Journal of Chinese Political Science* 17, no. 3 (2012): 269–90; Matthew Bolton and Thomas Nash, "The Role of Middle Power–NGO Coalitions in Global Policy: The Case of the Cluster Munitions Ban," *Global Policy* 1, no. 2 (2010): 172–84.

23. James B. Steinberg, "2012—A Watershed Year for East Asia?," *Asia Policy* 14, no. 2 (2012): 22–25.

24. See, for example, David A. Cooper, "Challenging Contemporary Notions of Middle Power Influence" (2011); Paul Cecelovsky, "Constructing a Middle Power: Ideas and Canadian Foreign Policy," *Canadian Foreign Policy* 15, no. 1 (2009): 77–96; Carl Ungerer, "The 'Middle Power' Concept in Australian Foreign Policy," *Australian Journal of Politics and History* 53, no. 4 (2007): 538–51; Jennifer M. Welsh, "Canada in the 21st Century: Beyond Dominion and Middle Power," *Behind the Headlines* 61, no. 4 (2004): 1–15; David A. Cooper, *Competing Western Strategies against Weapons of Mass Destruction: Comparing the United States to a Close Ally* (Westport, CT: Praeger Publishers, 2002); Adam Chapnick, "The Canadian Middle Power Myth," *International Journal* 55, no. 2 (2000): 188–206; Denis Stairs, "Of Medium Powers and Middling Roles," in *Statecraft and Security: The Cold War and Beyond*, 270–86, ed. Ken Booth (New York: Cambridge University Press, 1998); John Ravenhill,

"Cycles of Middle Power Activism: Constraint and Choice in Australian and Canadian Foreign Policies," *Australian Journal of International Affairs* 52, no. 3 (1998): 309–27.

25. Derek Frazier and Robert Stewart-Ingersoll, "Regional Powers and Security: A Framework for Understanding Order within Regional Security Complexes," *European Journal of International Relations* 16, no. 4 (2010): 731–53.

26. Jonathan Holslag, *Trapped Giant: China's Military Rise* (London: IISS/Routledge, 2010).

27. Samuel P. Huntington, "The Lonely Superpower," *Foreign Affairs* 78, no. 3 (1999): 35–49.

28. John J. Mearsheimer, *The Tragedy of Great Power Politics* (New York: Norton, 2001); William C. Wohlforth, "The Stability of a Unipolar World," *International Security* 24, no. 1 (1999): 5–41.

29. Detlef Nolte, "How to Compare Regional Powers: Analytic Concepts and Research Topics," *Review of International Studies* 36, no. 3 (2010): 881–901; David Shim, "A Shrimp amongst Whales? Assessing South Korea's Regional-power Status," GIGA *Working Papers* 107 (August 2009); Øyvind Østerud, "Regional Great Powers," in *Regional Great Powers in International Politics*, 1–15, ed. Iver B. Neumann (New York: St. Martin's Press, 1992).

30. Steinberg, "2020—A Watershed Year for East Asia?"

31. Nick Bisley, *Building Asia's Security* (London: IISS/Routledge, 2009); Lai, *The United States and China in Power Transition.*

32. Nicholas John Spykman, *The Geography of the Peace*, ed. Helen R. Nicholl, intro. Frederick Sherwood Dunn (New York: Harcourt, Brace, 1944); *America's Strategy in World Politics: The United States and the Balance of Power* (New York: Harcourt, Brace, 1942).

33. Spykman, *America's Strategy in World Politics*, 457.

34. Spykman, *Geography of the Peace*, 19, 22, 33, 60.

35. Spykman, *America's Strategy in World Politics*, 194–95.

36. Spykman, *Geography of the Peace*, 34.

37. Ibid., 19, 22, 33, 60.

38. "Indispensable linchpin": Michael J. Green, Japan Chair of the Center for Strategic and International Studies, *Prepared Statement for Hearing on the Future of Japan*, Foreign Affairs Committee, Subcommittee on Asia and the Pacific, House of Representatives, 11th Cong., 1st sess., May 24, 2011, 2; "Cornerstone": Hillary Clinton, "America's Pacific Century," *Foreign Policy Magazine*, November, 2011: 58–60; "Platform": Emma Chanlett-Avery, *The US-Japan Alliance*, Report to Congress RL33740 (Washington, DC: Congressional Research Service, January 18, 2011).

39. Patrick M. Cronin, Daniel M. Kilman, and Abraham M. Denmark, *Renewal: Revitalizing the US-Japan Alliance* (Washington, DC: Center for a New American Security, October 2010), 9.

40. David J. Berteau and Michael J. Green, *US Force Posture Strategy in the Asia Pacific Region: An Independent Assessment* (Washington, DC: Center for Strategic and International Studies, August 2012), 26.

41. Richard Armitage et al., *The United States and Japan: Advancing toward a Mature Relationship* (Washington, DC: Institute for National Strategic Studies Special Report, National Defense University, October 11, 2000), 3–4.

42. Richard Armitage and Joseph Nye, *The US-Japan Alliance: Getting Asia Right through 2020* (Washington, DC: Center for Strategic and International Studies, February 2007), 15.

43. Richard Armitage and Joseph Nye, *The US-Japan Alliance: Anchoring Stability in Asia* (Washington, DC: Center for Strategic and International Studies, August 2012), 1.

44. Berteau and Green, *US Force Posture Strategy in the Asia Pacific Region: An Independent Assessment*, 74.

CHAPTER 5

South Korea's Middle Power Response to the Rise of China

TongFi Kim

Introduction

SOUTH KOREA is the natural starting point for new middle power theorizing based on responses to the rise of China. Not only have its capabilities expanded rapidly along with its diplomatic ambitions, but it also sits on the doorstep of the rising China while being a formal ally of the United States. Moreover, the country's foreign policy elites increasingly identify their nation as a middle power. At a time when global governance has become more dispersed and more competitive, South Korea provides an excellent case for middle power behavioral predictions.

This chapter discusses the constraints and possibilities for South Korea's foreign policy toward China. South Korea's response to the rise of China shares certain common elements with other middle powers, but this chapter also analyzes unique factors in the bilateral relationship. Like other middle powers, South Korea cannot independently affect systemic changes, and China's rise will affect South Korean policy more than vice versa. However, the stakes of the bilateral relationship are high for both China and South Korea.

South Korea has had a long, close, and complicated history with China. Geography always has made China an important factor in South Korea's foreign policy, but Seoul has felt the presence of its giant neighbor even more strongly in recent years. China is a key player in dealing with North Korea, and it is the largest trading partner for both South and North Korea. Meanwhile, South Korea hosts American troops, and the US military bases in South Korea are the closest ones to Beijing. The rise of China affects every state in the international system, but the stakes in choosing the right strategy are particularly high for Seoul because of this interplay of geography, economic interdependence, the North Korean challenge, and the US alliance.

Chinese influence is stronger in Northeast Asia than elsewhere, and many in the region speculate on the possibility of power transition from the United States to China. Some, therefore, see South Korea's response to the rise of China as a survival strategy in the possible power transition.[1] As a Chinese diplomat pointed out to an American ambassador to Seoul, Korea's Joseon dynasty clung to the Ming dynasty well after the Qing dynasty had replaced it as the ruler of China.[2] Whether and how South Korea keeps its military alliance with the United States is an important question for China.

South Korea's foreign policy has adapted not only to specific international events but also to its own rising capability. As Cooper, Higgott, and Nossal point out, there are several major strands of research that define middle powers, for example, by position (relative capabilities), geography (located between major powers), normative viewpoint, and behavioral patterns.[3] Except for its geographic location, South Korea was not a middle power for a long time, but the country has acquired the capabilities of a middle power in recent decades. As the capabilities of China have rapidly increased, South Korea has also transformed its foreign policy from that of a minor power to one closer to the ideal type of middle power diplomacy.

To some observers the "patterns of South Korean middle power behavior took hold prior to the end of the Cold War" and can be seen as early as the so-called *Nordpolitik* in the 1980s.[4] In 1991, Gareth Evans, the Australian foreign minister, and Bruce Grant wrote that "there are good reasons for including" South Korea in the middle power category. The same year, South Korean president Roh Tae-woo, in a speech to the Hoover Institution, declared that South Korea in the 1990s would "seek new roles as a middle power—between the advanced and developing countries."[5] In 2013, the vice foreign minister Kim Kyou-hyun promised that "middle power diplomacy will be the diplomatic endeavour that will be unleashed at the regional and global level."[6] In this sense, South Korea's response to the rise of China may be as much about the rise of South Korea as about the rise of China.

The paths of South Korea's foreign policy in recent decades might shed new light on the way we define middle powers. Both capability-based and behavior-based definitions of middle powers are popular in the international relations literature, but this chapter emphasizes the importance of capabilities, consistent with this volume's overarching approach.[7] South Korea first became a middle power as its capabilities increased, and the country began to behave according to the patterns associated with "traditional middle powers" as defined by Jordaan.[8] Robertson argues that South Korea during the Kim Dae-jung administration (1998–2003) evolved from a capabilities-based middle power to a behavioral middle power.[9] As Robertson acknowledges, however, South Korea had been actively engaged in multilateral institutions earlier; it was a founding member of the Asia-Pacific Economic Cooperation (APEC) forum in 1989 and G20 in 1999, and Seoul also joined the Organization for Economic Cooperation and Development (OECD) in 1996.[10] Since 1997, South Korea has been part of the Association of Southeast Asian Nations (ASEAN) Plus Three cooperation endeavor along with its larger neighbors, China and Japan.

Middle powers should have certain commonalities in terms of their response to the rise of China. On one hand, they are not powerful enough to balance the rise of China independently, and their China policy significantly depends on US policy toward China. Middle powers' policies, to a large extent, will be reactive to both what China does and what the United States does. On the other hand, middle powers are not so powerless that they become bystanders in the making of a new international order. As nontrivial powers, middle powers collectively have substantial influence over the behavior of China and the United States. South Korean foreign policy experts are wary of being forced to choose between the United States and China, and many seem to prefer mediating the Sino-American relationship as a member of a middle power coalition rather than on its own.[11] South Korean diplomats are wary of being crushed in a great power conflict and thus seek to create room on both sides.

South Korea's middle power diplomacy has contributed to the engagement of China on various issues. South Korea, along with ASEAN and Japan, has established institutional mechanisms for regional cooperation. South Korea, as one of China's major trade partners (third largest, only after the United States and Japan, in 2011), has helped to integrate the Chinese economy into the liberal international economic order. North Korea is the issue on which South Korea's "middle power effect" on China is most obvious. Seoul's active diplomacy played a major role in drawing China away from its traditional alliance with North Korea to the multilateral approach taken by the international society.

The following passages explain various issues in the Sino-South Korean relationship in both historical and contemporary contexts. Aside from the Korean War, the most important political change in the bilateral relationship took place at the end of the Cold War, which led to the two countries' establishment of formal diplomatic ties in 1992. It should be noted, however, that South Korea's foreign policy had started to change before the structural change in the international system. For instance, reflecting its rising economic power, South Korea in the 1980s developed *Nordpolitik* (northern policy, *Bukbang jeongchaek*, named after West Germany's *Ostpolitik* toward East

Germany) and improved its relationships with the Soviet Union and China through economic engagement. South Korea, along with North Korea, joined the UN in 1991, and South Korea has steadily increased its commitments to multilateral international cooperation as its capabilities have increased.

This chapter divides the discussion of Sino-South Korean relations into two periods: the period before and the period after the normalization of their diplomatic relations in 1992. Although the two countries ceased to be hostile to one another and developed economic ties well before the end of the Cold War, the normalization marked a defining moment and set the tone of the current bilateral relationship. After explaining the historical and recent trends in South Korean foreign policy toward China, this chapter concludes with a brief discussion of the importance of South Korea to China and why middle power diplomacy serves South Korea's national interest.

Prologue to Normalization

Due to their geographical contiguity, the historical ties between China and Korea are old and deep. States on the Korean peninsula have suffered numerous invasions by dynasties based in China.[12] On other occasions, for example during the two Japanese invasions of Korea around the end of the sixteenth century (1592–98), China acted as the protector of Korea. By the time of the Three Kingdoms of Korea (first through seventh centuries), the Korean peninsula was, at least informally, part of the China-centered tributary system, and it remained under the system until after the defeat of China in the Sino-Japanese War (1894–95).[13]

Because of the division of the Korean peninsula into two states after the Second World War, South Korea does not share a land border with China, but the role of China is no less significant in South Korea's modern history. Communist China's entry into the Korean War in 1950 made it possible for the North Korean government to survive the counteroffensives of the international coalition led by the United States. China and the Soviet Union were the patron states of the North Korean regime from its earliest days, and they both signed a formal bilateral defense pact with Pyongyang in 1961. Notwithstanding occasional disputes within the socialist bloc and political turmoil within China, Sino-North Korean relations were generally good during the Cold War, and this imposed a limit on political relations between China and South Korea.

The Sino-US rapprochement in the early 1970s was a shock to the South Korean government, and Seoul began to seek ways to improve its relationship with Beijing. Park Chung-hee had already been concerned about the declining US military commitment in Asia since US president Richard Nixon announced his Guam Doctrine in July 1969. The United States seemed to be disengaging from South Vietnam, and in early 1971, twenty thousand of the sixty-two thousand American troops stationed in South Korea were withdrawn. Park reportedly called these US policies "a message to the Korean people that we won't rescue you if North Korea invades again."[14] Consequently, Park initiated policies to improve Seoul's relationships with socialist states. In 1972, for example, the South Korean government legalized trade with communist states, except for North Korea and Cuba. In his special speech on foreign policy on June 23, 1973, Park declared that South Korea would open its door to all states regardless of their ideologies.

China and South Korea began indirect trade in the late 1970s, and the informal economic cooperation between them steadily expanded as both countries' economies rapidly grew. The 1988 Olympic Games in Seoul further facilitated the expansion of contacts and exchanges between them. Through the Olympics, Seoul projected a positive image of South Korea as a successful, growing economy, and Sino-South Korean bilateral relations improved significantly.[15] The South Korean economy had been rapidly developing for an extended period, and its real average annual growth rate peaked at nearly 12 percent between 1986 and 1988.[16] This economic growth made possible the rise of South Korea to middle power status.

Beijing was sensitive to Pyongyang's concerns, but it eventually established diplomatic relations with Seoul in August 1992. As Chinese officials confided to a Japanese diplomat, China used "flattering and saving face" to obtain North Korea's acceptance of the change.[17] With its growing economic power, China continues to support North Korea economically, and North Korea's increased dependence on China has made Beijing more important in South Korea's foreign policy.

Economic Relationships

Economic interdependence between China and South Korea further deepened as a result of the diplomatic normalization. As Samuel Kim points out, South Korea's dependence on trade is much higher than that of larger states such as the United States and Japan, and this "trade or perish" situation magnifies the importance of China as an export market for South Korea.[18] In 2012, China's share in South Korea's total export was 24.5 percent, significantly higher than 10.7 percent for the second-largest export market, the United States.[19] Moreover, South Korea's balance of trade with China has been consistently positive since 1993. As South Korea's economic growth heavily relies on exports, any government in Seoul has a stake in a sound relationship with Beijing.

There is, of course, no guarantee that South Korea's trade with China will continue to positively affect political relationships between the two nations. As Chinese industries acquire more sophisticated technologies, South Korea's trade surplus vis-à-vis China and other states can significantly decrease. The competitive side of the economic relationships can have negative implications for their political relations in the future. Moreover, even the continuation of the present trade surplus for Seoul does not necessarily mean a rosy picture for the export-dependent state. South Korea's asymmetric dependence on the Chinese market creates a bargaining leverage for China. For instance, when South Korea restricted the importation of garlic from China in 2000 at the request of the agriculture lobby, China aggressively retaliated by restricting the importation of mobile phones and polyethylene from South Korea. South Korea was quickly forced to surrender, and the trade dispute soured the bilateral relations.[20] South Korea's trade dependence on China is considered a serious risk that needs to be managed by the South Korean government.[21]

South Korea's investment in China has steadily grown in the last two decades, though with some setbacks after the 1997–98 Asian financial crisis. Seoul and Beijing signed a bilateral investment treaty in May 1992, and the diplomatic normalization in August 1992 further strengthened the confidence of South Korean investors. China became South Korea's top investment destination in 1995, and South Korea became the third-largest investor in China in 2003.[22] China's investment in South Korea is relatively small, but it is growing.[23] These investments increase the mutual dependence of the two states, although technology transfers from South Korea to China could result in more competition in the long run.

Middle power theory might provide a useful context for understanding the increasingly important bilateral economic relations between China and South Korea. South Korea's economic relations with China are defined not only by the rise of China but also by the status of South Korea as a globally engaged economic power, which can be reasonably called a middle power in terms of its capability. In the garlic dispute of 2000, which occurred before China joined the World Trade Organization, South Korea could not bilaterally restrain China with its economic statecraft. South Korea, therefore, has a strong interest in using its middle power capabilities to promote multilateral or institutional economic cooperation.[24]

Seoul's active engagement with regional and global economic cooperation initiatives seems to be a rational response of a middle power to the rising economic influence of China. In addition to engagement with regional multilateral initiatives such as the APEC, ASEAN Plus Three, and East Asia Summit, South Korea has been actively forming free trade agreements (FTAs) across the globe.[25] Seoul already has eight FTAs in effect with entities such as ASEAN, India, European Union, and the United States and has sixteen FTAs under negotiation or consideration.[26] Meredith Woo argues that the Korea-US FTA was an attempt by South Korea to balance against the rise of China, but it should also be noted that South Korea is pursuing institutionalization of economic cooperation with various states.[27]

Seoul's economic foreign policy seems consistent with the predictions of middle power theory, and the development of a liberal economic order, regionally and globally, should help South Korea accommodate the economic rise of China in an institutional framework. The middle power effect of South Korean economic foreign policy may be enhanced by power politics in East Asia as well. For instance, China is eager to pursue a China-Japan-South Korea trilateral FTA because it views the US-led Trans-Pacific Partnership (TPP) to be excluding China.[28] The value of middle powers like South Korea to China will increase as China's relationships with other major powers—in particular, the United States and Japan—become more problematic.

North Korea

The role of China as North Korea's patron has changed in a few important ways since the early 1990s, and China is now an important partner for South Korea in many issues regarding North Korea. South Korea's threat perception of North Korea has changed significantly as North Korea's relative capability declined in the 1990s and as the cost of unification loomed large. Most importantly, neither South Korea nor China wants a destabilized North Korea as its neighbor. South Korea and China also share interests in the denuclearization of North Korea, although nonproliferation is not as important to them as it is to the United States.

As a result of the collapse of the Soviet Union, China became the sole protector of North Korea, and this shift—as well as the end of the Cold War—transformed the alliance between Beijing and Pyongyang.[29] China's 1961 defense pact with North Korea is supposed to involve Beijing automatically when North Korea is attacked. In reality, however, Beijing is increasingly ambivalent about its defense obligation.[30] Chinese public opinion is increasingly critical of North Korea, and the Chinese government has been allowing state-run media and policy experts to criticize North Korea.[31]

Pyongyang's dependence on Beijing for political and military support is still great, but the bilateral relationships between the two neighbors are weaker and more contentious than during the Cold War. Although the Chinese political system is still distant from democracy, North Korea's dynastic political system and isolationist economic policy are alien to the current Chinese leadership. The ideological and strategic forces of the Cold War are long gone and so are the personal ties between the older generations who fought together against the Japanese empire or the United States. Geography still makes North Korea an important strategic partner for China, but the partner is anything but easy to deal with. Given the economic troubles and provocative behavior of Pyongyang, North Korea is more a source of trouble than an asset for China.[32]

China in the early 1990s was somewhat detached from international efforts to denuclearize North Korea, but it has been playing an increasingly important role as North Korea's nuclear development has advanced. In the first North Korean nuclear crisis of 1993–94. China was probably the largest obstacle to sanctions against Pyongyang, although Japan and South Korea were also sensitive to the risk of escalation.[33] China joined the two Koreas and the United States in the four-party talks on peace on the Korean peninsula in 1997. As tensions between the Bush administration and North Korea escalated, China hosted three-party talks with the United States and North Korea in 2003, which were later expanded to the six-party talks including South Korea, Japan, and Russia. China has become more critical toward North Korean nuclear development and has actively engaged in the efforts to denuclearize North Korea.[34]

As mentioned, North Korea is the issue on which South Korea's "middle power effect" on China is most obvious. Seoul proved instrumental in ushering in the six-party talks and in prying China away from North Korea. As a result, China and North Korea no longer have the close relationships that were likened to "lips and teeth," but China is still considered to wield strong leverage over Pyongyang as its military ally and largest trading partner. China needs to avoid the destabilization of North Korea, but it could pressure Pyongyang by simply stopping some of the support it provides. For instance, in 2003, China cut off oil supply to North Korea for three days.[35] China's role in dealing with North Korean nuclear development "enhanced overall positive development in China's relations with" South Korea and the United States, "while managing tensions over the North Korean program in ways that avoided conflict or instability on the peninsula."[36]

It is natural for South Korea and other actors to expect Beijing to have significant influence over Pyongyang when North Korea relies on China for more than 70 percent of its trade, 80 percent of its foreign capital, and much of its oil imports.[37] North Korea's economic dependence on China has increased dramatically since the early 1990s. The share of China in North Korea's total trade increased particularly fast in the 2000s. Whereas North Korea's trade dependence on the Soviet Union was 56 percent in 1990, North Korea's trade dependence on China reached 83 percent in 2010.[38] China's economic support helps reduce the risk of destabilization in North Korea, but it also reduces the effectiveness of the economic pressure that the international society can impose on Pyongyang.

The North Korea factor is unique to the environment South Korea lives in, but the issue is also related to South Korea's middle power status and its response to the rise of China. The rise of South Korea as a middle power has made it possible for Seoul to take active diplomatic initiatives to engage Pyongyang. During the Cold War, as a minor power, South Korea single-mindedly relied on the United States for its foreign policy, and Seoul was not enthusiastic about engaging Pyongyang. If South Korea was a great power, it could pursue a more unilateral policy toward North Korea, but its limited capability requires Seoul to coordinate its policy with other relevant actors.[39] Problems related to North Korea increase the importance of China in South Korean foreign policy. So far, the rise of China seems to have had generally positive effects for Seoul's policy toward Pyongyang, because Beijing and Seoul agree that the destabilization of North Korea would be detrimental to the interests of its neighbors. Once the concerns for the sudden collapse of North Korea decline, however, the rising influence of China over North Korea may become more problematic to South Korea.

US Alliance

A common question asked in Seoul, and by middle powers in general, is whether ties to the United States constrain or strengthen middle power diplomacy. The answer is probably that it depends on the issue. Seoul's improved relationships with Beijing generally serve South Korea's national interest, but they complicate and are complicated by the military alliance with the United States. The United States and South Korea fought China in the Korean War, and they perceived China as an enemy in the early Cold War era. After the Sino-American rapprochement in the early 1970s, China was no longer a serious enemy to the alliance. China even considered the alliance to be a useful check against Japan's remilitarization.[40] With the end of the Cold War, however, China emerged as a rival of the United States and it has become more critical of the alliance. While Seoul has worked hard to strengthen the alliance, it has also cultivated cooperation with

Beijing.[41] China and South Korea have been holding high-level defense exchanges in the "strategic cooperative partnership" since 2008, and the first strategic defense dialogue between the two countries' defense ministers took place in 2011.[42] In 2012, Seoul proposed to Beijing an agreement regarding military supplies for emergency recovery operations.[43]

China has reasons to be concerned about the US-South Korea alliance. In the post–Cold War era, Washington has encouraged its traditional allies to expand the scope of decades-old alliances, such as the North Atlantic Treaty Organization (NATO) and the US-Japan alliance. The alliance with South Korea has not been an exception. The main focus of the alliance continues to be the deterrence of North Korea, but the alliance is "going global" and "meeting new security challenges" in diverse fields.[44] For instance, South Korea sent about thirty-six hundred troops to Iraq in 2004, making it the third-largest military contingent in theater after the United States and United Kingdom. More significantly for China, South Korea agreed to the so-called strategic flexibility of United States Forces Korea (USFK) in 2006, which refocuses the role of the USFK from deterrence and defense against North Korea to a more global one.[45]

The apparent discord between South Korea and the United States during the Roh Moo-hyun (2003–8) administration led some Chinese to predict the weakening of the alliance, but they were then surprised by the reinforcement of the alliance under President Lee Myung-bak (2008–13).[46] In particular, Beijing was worried about the increased military cooperation after the sinking of South Korean navy ship *Cheonan* in 2010 and North Korea's shelling of South Korea's Yeonpyeong Island later the same year. The Chinese Foreign Ministry issued a statement in opposition to US-South Korea naval exercises in the Yellow Sea, which "undermine China's security interests."[47]

China is not alone, however, in worrying that the alliance might entangle South Korea in a conflict between the United States and China.[48] Although the US government announced that it will respect Seoul's "position that it shall not be involved in a regional conflict in Northeast Asia against the will of the Korean people," the presence of US forces in the South Korean territory increases the risk of military entanglement.[49] American military bases in South Korea are the closest ones to Beijing, and this magnifies South Koreans' fear of entanglement. The construction of a naval base on Jeju Island that began in 2011 faced strong domestic protests because it is seen as "serving U.S. regional defense interests against China rather than [South Korean] security needs against North Korea."[50] While the security benefits of the alliance with the United States are more important to Seoul, South Koreans are concerned that the alliance might entangle them in a conflict between China and the United States over North Korea, Taiwan, and other issues. In addition to the risk of military entanglement, the alliance also limits the policy options for Seoul and imposes a cost of political and economic entanglement.[51]

It is difficult but imperative for South Korea to maintain good relationships with both the United States and China. On the one hand, the United States has a democratic political system, the world's top military and economic capabilities, and no territorial ambitions in East Asia in the traditional sense. Maintaining the military alliance with the United States is important to counter the pressure of the rise of China. On the other hand, China's geographic proximity and its rising economic power make a hostile relationship with China costly. Whereas the United States might abandon South Korea in the future, China will always be next to the Korean peninsula.[52] The North Korea factor discussed earlier also looms large in South Korea's strategic calculations. As one Korean scholar points out, "some Koreans are viewing closer relations with China as providing an attractive counterweight to possible U.S. unilateralism on the Korean peninsula."[53] South Korea seeks to balance the risk of abandonment by the United States and the risk of entanglement in a conflict with China not only in military affairs but also in political and economic fields.

Public opinion polls suggest that the South Korean people are torn between the United States and China. Overall, younger generations are more critical toward the United States and more friendly toward China, while policy elites are more concerned about China than the mass public is. There are large fluctuations in public opinion toward China and the United States, and neither country is locked in as the most important country for South Korea's future. Compared with the period between 1997 and 2004, the South Korean public was more critical toward China in the period between 2004 and 2010.[54]

The concept of a middle power might be useful for explaining South Korea's management of the relations with the United States and China since they defy traditional categories of balancing and bandwagoning.[55] Although it is theoretically conceivable that South Korea could benefit from a Sino-American competition for South Korea's loyalty, Sino-American frictions are more likely to cause problems for Seoul. South Korea as a nongreat power will not change the overall balance of power between China and the United States, and South Korea will be the passive actor in the trilateral relationships. On the other hand, South Korea as a middle power has a diplomatic capacity to initiate a multilateral cooperation that could mediate the frictions between China and the United States. Given that siding unequivocally with either of the giants is detrimental to South Korea's national interests,

South Korea's best way out of the dilemmas discussed above may lie in so-called middle power diplomacy, which pursues "multilateral solutions to international problems" and embraces "compromise positions in international disputes."[56] Managing the power transition in Northeast Asia through middle power diplomacy is not just normatively attractive to South Korea but strategically critical.

Like Indonesia, Seoul seeks to build a "dynamic equilibrium" in the region between the superpowers (see chapter 7). President Park Geun-hye in 2013 proposed the initiation of a "Seoul Process" to build confidence in security issues in the region, a not-too-subtle reference to the Helsinki Process that aimed to temper the rivalry between the United States and the Soviet Union during the Cold War. In this and many other ways, including its role in the ASEAN Regional Forum and in the New Asia Initiative of President Lee Myung-bak announced in Jakarta in 2009 to ensure that Seoul coordinated its regional policy more closely with the middle power activism of ASEAN, South Korea avoids the choice between balancing and bandwagoning with respect to the rise of China. Instead, making use of its middle power capabilities and ambition, Seoul has sought to redefine the security situation in Asia in ways that build peace and enmesh great powers in overlapping cooperative arrangements.

Global Governance

South Korea's middle power effects on China's rise are most likely to be observed not in South Korea's direct bilateral relations with Beijing but in its broader diplomatic stance and initiatives relating to regional and global governance. In addition to its role in promoting regionalism in Asia, Seoul has taken prominent "middle power" positions in world affairs that shape the global context in which China's rise is taking place. Having outgrown the Northeast Asian subregion in which its ties to the United States loom largest, Seoul's "Global Korea" brand provides it with opportunities for autonomous foreign policy initiatives that are not derivative of US policy. Seoul's initiation of a "green growth" approach to environmental sustainability, its promotion of a new development assistance model, and its efforts to enhance global cybersecurity provide evidence of middle power activism in three key areas where concerns about the rise of China have been high.

The Global Green Growth Institute began as a South Korean nonprofit foundation in 2010 and turned in 2012 into an international treaty organization backed by the UN with headquarters in Seoul. The initiative bridged

China's (and India's) insistence on continued growth with demands for sustainability by introducing the notion of bottom-up, country-by-country solutions to pressing issues like climate change. In a sense, the South Korean model of growth with sustainability challenges China to live up to its own commitments to reduce greenhouse gas emissions as part of a progrowth strategy.

In the field of aid, the South Korean convening of the Fourth High Level Forum on Aid Effectiveness in 2011 bridged the differences between traditional aid givers (represented by the OECD's Development Assistance Committee, which South Korea joined in 2010) and emerging donors such as China and India.[57] Since then, South Korea has led efforts to pioneer a new "Asian approach" to development aid that grows out of its own experience and has made a point of mainstreaming China within those discussions.[58] Again, while not directed at China, the Seoul model of development assistance may provide the developing world with an attractive non-Western alternative to a "Beijing Consensus" approach to development that is heavy on planning and infrastructure and light on democracy and civil society.

Seoul has also made new international cooperation on cybersecurity (or cyberterrorism) a top diplomatic priority. It took the lead in forming the ASEAN Regional Forum Seminar (ARF) on Cyber Terrorism, which held its first meeting in South Korea in 2004, and hosted the ARF Seminar on Confidence-Building Measures in Cyberspace in 2012. Again, while not directly related to its China relationship, this middle power activism in creating new global governance norms will have a deep impact on China, a main site of both global cybersecurity threats as well as vulnerabilities.

At the 2010 G20 Seoul Summit, South Korea's vice minister of foreign affairs and trade, Kim Sung-han, was explicit in linking these initiatives to a middle power identity: "Solving today's complex challenges will require 'middle powers' to play a greater, more active role. . . . Through various initiatives, such as its programs in green growth and development cooperation, South Korea has demonstrated the influence middle powers may have on global governance . . . and middle powers such as South Korea may be best suited to facilitate consensus building and revitalize momentum for cooperation."[59] While Kim had no intention of linking this middle power activism to the rise of China, in both its conception and its consequences, Seoul's diplomatic dynamism cannot be separated from the global context as seen from South Korea of which the rise of China is the most prominent part.

Outstanding Disputes

The geographic proximity of China and South Korea creates various frictions between them. For example, the two countries' exclusive economic zones (EEZs) overlap in the ocean between them, and they have not been able to agree on how to draw the line of jurisdiction. The two countries have criticized each other's behavior over what South Korea calls the Ieodo Reef and China calls the Suyan Reef.[60] Illegal fishing by Chinese ships in the South Korean EEZ has been a regular problem, and the South Korean public was outraged when Chinese fishermen killed South Korean coast guards in 2008 and 2011.[61] South Korea has been severely affected by environmental pollution from China as well. The yellow dust from China flies over to South Korea every year, and it has caused serious health and economic problems in South Korea. The yellow dust is blamed for increases in respiratory disease and higher rates of defections in the precision manufacturing industry in South Korea.[62]

As a government of a divided nation, South Korea is sensitive to certain issues even when they do not directly involve South Korean territories or citizens. For example, the South Korean public has been critical toward China's handling of North Korean refugees. China considers North Korean refugees as China illegal migrants, and the Chinese police arrest and repatriate them to North Korea, where these refugees face severe punishments as "traitors."[63] China and South Korea share a critical stance toward Japan on the latter's wartime atrocity, but they have disputes over their own history as well.[64] In 2004, South Korean public opinion shifted dramatically against China because of a dispute over the history of the Goguryeo Kingdom (37 BCE to 668 CE), which ruled the northeastern region of China as well as the northern part of the Korean peninsula. The Chinese government had launched the Northeast Borderland History and the Chain of Events Research Project in 2002, and some Chinese scholars began arguing that Goguryeo was a regional government of China. In 2004, the Chinese Ministry of Foreign Affairs eliminated website references to Korean history before the establishment of the South Korean government in 1948 in order to defuse tensions over the interpretation of the Goguryeo history. Ironically this move sparked angry responses from the South Korean public.[65]

While these disputes are important themselves, how China and South Korea handle them will be affected by the two countries' economic interdependence, the necessity for cooperation over North Korea, and the triangular relationships with the United States. In particular, South Korea as a middle power cannot match China's bargaining power in bilateral negotiations, and Seoul will benefit from creating a multilateral framework to dissolve the disputes with its giant neighbor.

Conclusion

In response to the four key questions posed by this book, this chapter concludes that (1) South Korea is a complete middle power by virtue of its robust capabilities, behavior, and self-identity as a middle power; (2) China's rise has profoundly affected South Korea in economic, security, and diplomatic terms by virtue of three key factors—its geographic proximity to China and its traditional close alliance with the United States; (3) South Korea's response to China's rise fits the predictions of middle power theory well (and defies the predictions of power transitions theory) because of its emphasis on multilateralism and changing the terms of the debate; and (4) although South Korea's effect on China's foreign policy has so far been limited to the North Korea issue, its global governance initiatives in areas like cybersecurity, aid, and climate change will be important in indirectly shaping the context in which China's foreign policy operates.

South Korea's evolution as a middle power has influenced how the country responds to the rise of China. South Korea's engagement of China was largely unsuccessful during the Cold War for a variety of reasons. There was a sharp division between two blocs, although the socialist bloc was far from monolithic. Even after Chinese foreign policy became more pragmatic in the late 1970s, Beijing still had to be sensitive to the concerns of Pyongyang. South Korea on its part lacked diplomatic leverage, as it was a minor state heavily dependent on the United States. Fortunately for South Korea, Seoul's *Nordpolitik* began to bear fruit in the late 1980s, and the end of the East-West confrontation, the Sino-Soviet rapprochement, and the subsequent collapse of the Soviet Union all made it easier for Beijing to adopt a friendly policy toward Seoul at the expense of the Sino-North Korean alliance. Whereas South Korea's failed attempt to engage socialist states in the 1970s was in reaction to international events and defensive in nature, *Nordpolitik* in the 1980s reflected South Korea's growing confidence and capability. South Korea's China policy after the normalization in 1992 is consistent with the behavior often attributed to middle powers, whose capabilities are limited but not negligible.

Like all middle powers, South Korea's relationship to the rise of China has certain national particularities. Most notably, the factors that make China important to South Korea also give Seoul a more significant influence over China than any other middle power, an impact disproportionate to South Korea's size. Beijing and Seoul share many concerns over the future of North Korea, and they are sound partners in their endeavor to avoid regional chaos arising from a sudden collapse of the North Korean regime. There is no guarantee that the shared interests will continue to exist, but South Korea's strategic importance to China will not decline even if China establishes a control over North Korea or South Korea reunifies the Korean peninsula. South Korea is a close military ally of the United States and provides China's primary competitor with military bases close to Beijing. Having a good relationship with Seoul is important to Beijing also because China's relations with Japan are likely to remain difficult for historical and power-political reasons.

South Korea's national interest lies in middle power diplomacy and creating a multilateral and institutional framework to accommodate the rise of China. Surrounded by major states, Koreans have traditionally perceived themselves to be a shrimp among whales. The shrimp, however, is not as powerless as it used to be, and it can contribute to the development of a stable regional order. Because conflicts between China and the United States will be costly to South Korea, Seoul's middle power diplomacy in East Asia will be vital to the future of the country.

Notes

1. On power transition theory and South Korea as a middle power, see Woosang Kim, "Korea as a Middle Power in the Northeast Asian Security Environment," in *The United States and Northeast Asia: Debates, Issues, and New Order*, 123–42, eds. G. John Ikenberry and Chung-In Moon (Lanham, MD: Rowman & Littlefield, 2007).

2. The Chinese diplomat was commenting on North Korea's reluctance to reform, but it is interesting to see that a Chinese diplomat thinks of Korea's tradition as the following: "the Korean response when confronted with a rapidly changing environment was to hunker down out of fear that it would cease to exist if it succumbed to change." See "Chinese Envoy in Seoul Slammed N. Korea's Botched Currency Reform," *Chosun Ilbo English*, January 5, 2011, http://english.chosun.com/site/data/html_dir/2011/01/05/2011010 501028.html.

3. Andrew Cooper, Richard Higgott, and Kim Nossal, *Relocating Middle Powers: Australia and Canada in a Changing World Order* (UBC Press, 1993), 16–19. Cooper, Higgott, and Nossal emphasize the importance of behavioral patterns, the tendency of middle powers to "pursue multilateral solutions to international problems, their tendency to embrace compromise positions in international disputes, and their tendency to embrace notions of 'good international citizenship' to guide their diplomacy" (1993, 19). Jordaan identifies an even larger number of criteria in the literature: "considerations of state capacity, position in the world order, the normative composition of the middle power state–societal complex, domestic class interests, and the role and influence of foreign policy-makers." See Eduard Jordaan, "The Concept of a Middle Power in International Relations: Distinguishing between Emerging and Traditional Middle Powers," *Politikon: South African Journal of Political Studies* 30, no. 2 (2003), 165–81, 166.

4. William Tow and Richard Rigby, "China's Pragmatic Security Policy: The Middle Power Factor," *China Journal* 65, no. 1 (2011), 157–78, 173. *Nordpolitik* (northern policy), in which South Korea approached North Korea's socialist allies for normalization, was named after West Germany's *Ostpolitik*.

5. Gareth Evans and Bruce Grant, *Australia's Foreign Relations: In the World of the 1990s*, 2nd edition (Melbourne: Melbourne University Press, 1995), 397.

6. Kim Kyou-hyun, "Keynote speech," conference on The Role of Middle Powers in 21st Century International Relations, Seoul, April 2013.

7. Jeffrey Robertson "South Korea as a Middle Power: Capacity, Behavior, and Now Opportunity," *International Journal of Korean Unification Studies* 16, no. 1 (2007): 151–74.

8. Jordaan, "The Concept of a Middle Power."

9. Robertson, "South Korea as a Middle Power," 158.

10. Ibid., 156.

11. This author's interviews in Seoul in November 2012. To a certain extent, South Korean progressives are more likely to be pro-China and anti-American than conservatives, but both the left and right agree that South Korea should avoid the choice between the United States and China.

12. As Jae-ho Chung notes, the South Korean public sees China in a more favorable light than it sees Japan; many of more than nine hundred foreign invasions Korea suffered came from China or dynasties established by tribes in its northern region. Jae Ho Chung, *Joongkuk Ui Busang Gwa Han Bando Ui Mirae* [The rise of China and the future of the Korean Peninsula] (Seoul: Seoul National University Press, 2011), 17.

13. On the premodern history of Korea, see, for example, Keith Pratt, Richard Rutt, and James Hoare, *Korea: A Historical and Cultural Dictionary* (London: Curzon Press, 1999); Michael Seth, *A History of Korea: From Antiquity to the Present* (Lanham, MD: Rowman & Littlefield, 2010).

14. Don Oberdorfer, *The Two Koreas: A Contemporary History*, revised and updated edition (New York: Basic Books, 2001), 13.

15. Jae Ho Chung, *Between Ally and Partner: Korea-China Relations and the United States* (New York: Columbia University Press, 2007), 43–45.

16. Young-lob Chung, *South Korea in the Fast Lane: Economic Development and Capital Formation* (New York: Oxford University Press, 2007), 15.

17. Oberdorfer, *The Two Koreas*, 247.

18. Samuel Kim, "Globalization Helps Korea Create New Identity," *Korea Herald*, July 17, 2007.

19. South Korea's export dependency on China was 24.1 percent in 2011 and 25.1 percent in 2010. Korea Customs Service, www.customs.go.kr/kcshome/.

20. Scott Snyder, "The Insatiable Sino-Korean Economic Relationship: Too Much for Seoul to Swallow?" *Comparative Connections* 2, no. 3 (2000): 79–84; Si-joong Kim, "Economic and Trade Relations as an Arena of Korea-China Contention," *Asian Perspective* 36, no.2 (2012): 237–62.

21. Byung Il Choi, "Muyok Jungguk Euijon Gukga Risk Ro Gwanli Haeya" [Trade dependence on China needs to be managed as a state risk], *Chosun Ilbo*, January 1, 2011.

22. Chung, *Joongkuk Ui Busang*, 237–38.

23. Qingfen Ding, "China Eyes Bigger Investment in South Korea," *China Daily*, April 14, 2012.

24. Si-joong Kim, "Economic and Trade Relations," 258.

25. "South Korea is now linked to free trade networks that account for 61 percent of the world's GDP. Only Chile and Mexico have concluded more FTAs with other countries. These trade networks can be useful resources for South Korea to play a bridging or mediating middle power role, at least on trade issues." Sook-Jong Lee, "South Korea as New Middle Power Seeking Complex Diplomacy," East Asia Institute, Asia Security Initiative Working Paper (September 2012), 17.

26. South Korea is also considering FTAs with China and Japan. "FTA Status of ROK," Ministry of Foreign Affairs and Trade, Republic of Korea, www.mofat.go.kr/ENG/policy/fta/status/overview/index.jsp?menu=m_20_80_10&tabmenu=t_1.

27. Meredith Jung-En Woo, "East Asia after the Financial Crisis," in *Insight into Korea: Understanding Challenges of the 21st Century*, 126–27, ed. Korea Herald (Seoul: Herald Media, 2007).

28. "Hopeful China Wants Japan, S. Korea in Own Trade Pact," *Asahi Shimbun*, March 18, 2013, http://ajw.asahi.com/article/behind_news/politics/AJ201303180007. South Korea has been invited but has not joined the negotiations for the TPP.

29. Cuba has a defense pact with North Korea, but the alliance is likely to be ineffective. See the Alliance Treaty Obligations and Provision dataset, http://atop.rice.edu.

30. Michael R. Chambers, "Dealing with a Truculent Ally: A Comparative Perspective on China's Handling of North Korea," *Journal of East Asian Studies* 5, no. 1 (2005): 35–75.

31. "More within China Criticizing Support of North Korea," *Hankyoreh*, March 1, 2013, http://english.hani.co.kr/arti/english_edition/e_northkorea/5 76150.html.

32. Deng Yuwen, a deputy editor of *Study Times*, the journal of the Central Party School of the Communist Party of China, wrote an article titled "China Should Abandon North Korea" in the *Financial Times*, February 27, 2013.

33. Joel Wit, Daniel Poneman, and Robert Gallucci, *Going Critical: The First North Korean Nuclear Crisis* (Washington, DC: Brookings Institution, 2004), 194.

34. Hui Zhang, "Ending North Korea's Nuclear Ambitions: The Need for Stronger Chinese Action," *Arms Control Today*, July/August 2009, www.armscontrol.org/act/2009_07-08/zhang.

35. Jonathan Watts, "China Cuts Oil Supply to North Korea," *Guardian*, April 1, 2003.

36. Robert Sutter, *China's Rise in Asia: Promises and Perils* (Lanham, MD: Rowman & Littlefield, 2005), 156.

37. Chung, *Joongkuk Ui Busang*, 334.

38. Bomi Lim, "North Korean Dependence on China Trade Rises as Sanctions Worsen Isolation," *Bloomberg News*, May 27, 2011.

39. Even a great power such as the United States has difficulty in its dealing with North Korea and needs multilateral cooperation to pressure Pyongyang. It is, however, generally more difficult for weaker states to engage in unilateral foreign policy.

40. Sung-joo Han, "The State of the US-ROK Alliance: Current Issues in US-ROK Relations," (2011), www.cfr.org/south-korea/state-us-rok-alliance/p26204.

41. The US-ROK alliance has experienced minor crises, most recently during Roh Moo-hyun's presidency, but it has been overall fairly stable. Despite the widely shared perception that he was anti-American, Roh actually accommodated many American requests, including the dispatch of South Korean troops to Iraq.

42. In May 2011, China and South Korea began a diplomatic exchange program between junior foreign ministry officials, making South Korea the third country to have such a program with China, only after North Korea and Mongolia. See Scott Snyder and See-won Byun, "A Fragile China-ROK Strategic Partnership," *Comparative Connections* 13, no. 2 (2011): 101–10.

43. He-suk Choi, "Seoul Seeks to Boost Military Ties with China," *Korea Herald*, May 21, 2012.

44. See Kurt Campbell et al., "Going Global: The Future of the US-South Korea Alliance" (Center for a New American Security, 2009) and Scott Snyder, ed. *The US-South Korea Alliance: Meeting New Security Challenges* (Boulder, CO: Lynne Rienner Publishers, 2012).

45. The threat of North Korea makes it difficult for South Korea to refuse US requests, despite Seoul's reluctance to alienate China. See Hyon-joo Yoo, "The Korea-US Alliance as a Source of Creeping Tension: A Korean Perspective," *Asian Perspective* 36, no. 2 (2012): 331–51.

46. See Jae Ho Chung, "Korean Views of Korea-China Relations: Evolving Perceptions and Upcoming Challenges," *Asian Perspective* 36, no. 2 (2012): 219–36, 230; Keyu Gong, "The Korea-US Alliance from a Chinese Perspective," *Asian Perspective* 36, no. 2 (2012): 309–30.

47. Foreign Ministry Spokesperson Qin Gang's Regular Press Conference, July 8, 2010, www.fmprc.gov.cn/eng/xwfw/s2510/t715219.htm.

48. In the US-ROK alliance, South Korea was traditionally concerned about being abandoned by the United States, but since the 1990s it has been increasingly fearful of being entrapped into a conflict with North Korea over US interests in nuclear nonproliferation.

49. Joint United States-Republic of Korea statement on the launch of the Strategic Consultation for Allied Partnership, January 19, 2006, http://2001-2009.state.gov/r/pa/prs/ps/2006/59447.htm.

50. Snyder and Byun, "A Fragile China-ROK Strategic Partnership."

51. Entanglement is defined here as the process whereby a state is compelled to aid an ally in a costly and unprofitable enterprise because of the alliance. TongFi

Kim, "Why Alliances Entangle but Seldom Entrap States," *Security Studies* 20, no. 3 (2011): 350–77. For discussions of nonmilitary entrapment (entanglement), see Glenn Snyder, *Alliance Politics* (Ithaca, NY: Cornell University Press, 1997), 357; Galia Press-Barnathan, "Managing the Hegemon: NATO under Unipolarity," *Security Studies* 15, no. 2 (2006): 271–309, 280–81.

52. For the effects of geography on strategic relationships in East Asia, see Robert S. Ross, "The Geography of the Peace: East Asia in the Twenty-First Century," *International Security* 23, no. 4 (1999): 81–118.

53. Geun Lee, "The Rise of China and Korea's China Policy," in *The Rise of China and a Changing East Asian Order*, 198, eds. Ryosei Kokubun and Jisi Wang (Tokyo: Japan Center for International Exchange, 2004).

54. Chung, *Joongkuk Ui Busang*, 355–61.

55. Acharya argues that ASEAN states are trying "to enmesh both China and the United States in regional interdependence and institutions" in order to avoid choosing between the two giants. What he calls "double-binding" and "institutional-binding" are crucial to South Korea as well. Amitav Acharya, "Will Asia's Past Be Its Future?," *International Security* 28, no. 3 (2003):149–64, 153.

56. Cooper, Higgott, and Nossal, *Relocating Middle Powers*, 19.

57. Mark Tran, "China and India to Join Aid Partnership on New Terms," *Guardian*, December 1, 2011.

58. See, for instance, *Pro-Poor Growth and Development Cooperation: Experience and Lessons from Asia*, report from the Asian Approaches to Development Cooperation Dialogue, June 27–29, 2012, Beijing, http://asiafoundation.org/resources/pdfs/ProPoorGrowthandDevelopm entCooperatio n.pdf.

59. "Global Governance and Middle Powers: South Korea's Role in the G20," Council on Foreign Relations, New York, www.cfr.org/south-korea/global-governance-middle-powers-south-koreas-role-g20/p30062.

60. Jeremy Page, "China, South Korea in Row over Submerged Rock," *Wall Street Journal Asia*, March 14, 2012; Scott W. Harold, "Ieodo as Metaphor? The Growing Importance of Sovereignty Disputes in South Korea—China Relations and the Role of the United States," *Asian Perspective* 36, no. 2 (2012): 287–307.

61. BBC News Asia, "Chinese Fisherman Jailed for South Korea Stabbing," April 19, 2012, www.bbc.co.uk/news/world-asia-17766167.

62. Scott Snyder, "A Dark Turn in Political Relations," *Comparative Connections* 9, no. 1 (2007): 111–12.

63. Sang-hun Choe, "China Should Not Repatriate North Korean Refugees, Seoul Says," *New York Times*, February 22, 2012.

64. On Chinese writings on South Korea and its history, see Gilbert Rozman, "History as an Arena of Sino-Korean Conflict and the Role of the United States," *Asian Perspective* 36, no. 2 (2012): 263–85.

65. See Scott Snyder, "A Turning Point for China-Korea Relations?" *Comparative Connections* 6, no. 3 (2004): 109–16; Chung, *Joongkuk Ui Busang*, 302–12. China has its own concerns about South Korea's nationalism in relation to ethnic Koreans in China. See Zhimin Chen, "Embracing the Complexities in China-ROK Relations: A View from China," *Asian Perspective* 36, no. 2 (2012): 195–218, 197.

CHAPTER 6

Malaysia, Thailand, and the ASEAN Middle Power Way

Amy L. Freedman

Introduction

OVER THE LAST twenty years there has been an explosion in the amount of literature published on the rise of Chinese power and what this will mean for international relations. China's meteoric rise from being a poor, agrarian economy enmeshed in ideological warfare against itself, to being the world's second-largest economy, has produced both admiration and consternation. There are scholars and policymakers who see the growth of Chinese power as a threat to regional and possibly global stability.[1] And there are those who see China's resurgence as an opportunity for new relationships, new configurations of power, and new ways of thinking about balance of power.

What we may be seeing in Asia is neither the balancing that realists expect, nor clear cases of bandwagoning. Instead, countries in Asia are behaving in a variety of ways in reaction to the growth of Chinese power. For the countries of Southeast Asia in particular, the question of how to react to China is especially interesting as many of these states fall into the "middle power" category. This chapter looks at the role of two such middle powers, Malaysia and Thailand, in order to understand the changing dynamics in the region and how middle powers can impact regional relations.

Not surprisingly, much of the early literature on middle powers examined the role of Canada, Australia, and Scandinavian countries and their role in international relations. Part of the source of influence and credibility of these traditional middle powers came from their high level of economic development and wealth, their political and social stability, and their social democratic norms and practices.[2] There is a newer body of literature on emerging middle powers that moves the focus away from Europe and North America to look at late developers, including Malaysia, Saudi Arabia, South Korea, Chile, Mexico, Indonesia, and Thailand. Emerging middle powers may be more peripheral than traditional middle powers, they may be "materially inegalitarian" and only partly democratic, but they have increasing regional influence, particularly in regional organizations.

Malaysia and Thailand are two examples.[3] As Bruce Gilley and Andrew O'Neil mention in chapter 1, these two countries have moved only recently into the ranks of middle powers as measured by total gross domestic product.[4] While these rankings might make Malaysia and Thailand seem less important, their position in Asia and their activity in the regional Association of Southeast Asian Nations (ASEAN) makes them important in relation to China's rise.

Malaysia's position regarding China might be best described as neutral, pushing for greater economic links with China, while maintaining greater independence in foreign and defense policy. Thailand has fostered strong economic ties to China, and has opted for greater military cooperation as well. What Malaysia and Thailand share is a common desire to benefit economically from China's rising financial position, and both countries want to include China in, and anchor it to, regional organizations like ASEAN and others.

The capabilities and behavior of Malaysia and Thailand differ from other middle powers. As noted, their economic power is near the bottom of the middle power cohort, and neither country commands significant soft power resources such as being a source of prestige, norms, or influence. However, both Malaysia and Thailand's behavior within ASEAN and within other regional forums is critically important. Both countries demonstrate elements of what Gilley and O'Neil discuss in chapter 1 as counterhegemonic behavior. Ping describes this dynamic in terms of behavior that is "antihegemonic" and it includes actions that demonstrate bad international citizenship (among other behaviors).[5] Spanakos and Marques in chapter 11 note similar behavior from Brazil. A good example of this behavior can be seen when Malaysia and Thailand signaled continuing support for China even in the wake of the massacres at Tiananmen Square in 1989. This did not mean that Malaysia and Thailand were bandwagoning with China or reneging on their relationship with the United States, but rather it showed a refusal to conform to Western pressure.

This chapter looks at the rise of China, followed by an examination of Malaysia and Thailand's evolving relationships with it, including their efforts to include China in regional organizations. The chapter finds that Malaysia and Thailand are exerting influence on China by imposing norms of regional cooperation on Beijing's foreign policy in Asia.

Rise of China

Literature on the growth of Chinese power has become an industry in and of itself. At the outset of China's economic reforms in 1978, it accounted for less than 1 percent of the world's economy, and its total foreign trade was worth $20.6 billon. By 2012, China's total foreign trade was worth $308.6 billon and its economy is the second largest in the world.[6] Despite these changes, China remains (in Susan Shirk's words) a fragile superpower.[7] While there is no doubt that China has been playing a more significant role in global affairs, China's main preoccupation is in maintaining order and stability at home. The Chinese Communist Party (CCP) maintains a monopoly on power and it remains highly vigilant about social problems within the vast country. There is no doubt that China has significant domestic problems: rural-urban inequality, labor issues, pollution, lack of a culture and system of rule of law, corruption, and center-periphery power struggles, just to name a few. But being able to manage these problems, Shirk argues, is what the Chinese government is largely concerned with. So, while there is a great deal of speculation (particularly in the United States) about what China's strategic intentions are, for the most part Chinese leaders are motivated by wanting to stay in power and being able to keep a lid on social discontent.

Chinese leaders are quick to point out that they have only peaceful intentions and that the growth of Chinese power has been beneficial for all of Asia. There are, however, a few reasons for concern among China's neighbors. First, and most simply, China's economy is so large that almost all aspects of its economy have effects outside China's borders—from the value of the renminbi, the wages earned by laborers, the need for natural resources (oil, natural gas, minerals, food, etc.). Second, as communism has lost legitimacy as a motivating ideology in China, it has been replaced by resurgent nationalism. Nationalism has served the CCP well as the party has created a discourse based on the following narrative: after overcoming a hundred years of victimization at the hands of foreigners, China has finally stood up. Through the wise leadership of the CCP, China has overcome its previously weak position and is now reclaiming its position as a leader in Asia and the rest of the world. This casting and recasting of modern history has served the CCP's purpose of retaining power and creating a large reservoir of support at home for their policies. However, nationalism can be hard to control. Over the last ten years, public demonstrations and activism have illustrated that nationalist sentiment in China is easy to inflame and the targets of public anger can be China's neighbors. This may then intensify the regime's territorial claims and make it harder to envision China compromising on potential solutions.

Additionally, as China's economy has grown, so have its military spending and efforts to modernize military capabilities. There may be little fear of China invading any of its neighbors, but there are a number of long-standing territorial disputes throughout Asia, and countries do not want to see China bully its way militarily into an armed conflict over these territories. Singaporean prime minister Goh Chok Tong has been quoted as saying that "in Asia, China's rising power and arms build-up has stirred anxiety. . . . It is important to bring into the open this underlying sense of discomfort, even insecurity, about the political and military ambitions of China."[8] Foremost among the disputes are the conflicts over territorial and sovereignty claims between Japan and China over the Diaoyu/Senkaku Islands, and conflicts between China and Vietnam; China and the Philippines; China and Malaysia; and China and Brunei over outcroppings in the South China Sea known as the Spratly and Paracel Islands. More will be discussed later on this dispute, but the overarching point is that China's neighbors have good reasons to feel trepidation at the growth of Chinese power (and Chinese nationalism) and what this will mean for their own interests. Perhaps even more significantly, there is variation among China's neighbors as to how each views the growth of Chinese power. All countries want to benefit from China's booming economy, and to a significant extent Southeast Asia has been buffered by China's continued economic growth in the face of a wider global economic slowdown since 2008. But there are different levels of concern when it comes to how China is perceived and exactly how cozy one should be with this looming giant.

China has long borders with Burma and Vietnam and a shorter one with Laos. Southeast Asian states have troubled histories with China stemming from internal discomfort with large overseas Chinese populations, and from internal struggles with communist movements. From 1949 to 1990, the ideological and strategic rivalries among great powers played out in the region, forcing countries to choose sides. China was not always on the sidelines of this "great game." With the Cold War over, and with Vietnam's agreement to withdraw from Cambodia in 1989, the threat of communist interference has all but disappeared in the region. Now there is a common perception that, regardless of how countries feel about Chinese power and influence, all nations would like to see China involved in international institutions. All countries hope that China's involvement will anchor China to both a way of thinking and a way of behaving, and that international institutions will serve as a constructive way to settle disputes and potentially constrain aggressive Chinese behavior. Ultimately, the hope is that they will serve to socialize China to Southeast Asian norms of behavior.

Malaysia and China

Malaysia's history and approach to China are somewhat typical for Southeast Asia. After Mao Zedong's successful revolution in 1949, Malaysia feared (legitimately so) Chinese intervention in Malaysia's own internal struggle against a communist insurgency. Malaysia was the first member of ASEAN to normalize relations with China, in 1974. Malaysia's motivation for this rapprochement was the hope that improved relations with China would lead to Beijing terminating its support for the Communist Party of Malaysia (CPM). This did not happen and relations between the two countries could be best characterized from 1974 to 1985 as one of détente and political acclamation.[9] Relations did not improve until the 1980s under the leadership of Prime Minister Mahathir. In 1984, Prime Minister Mahathir commissioned a major reassessment of relations between Malaysia and China that resulted in a report titled "Managing a Controlled Relationship with the PRC." The report recommended strengthening economic ties while remaining vigilant of China's support for communist movements and their claims in the South China Sea.[10] In 1985, Mahathir endorsed the report and it ushered in a new era of pragmatic thinking about China. Mahathir sought to cooperate economically with China, but ambivalence remained. By 1989, the CPM had dissolved and the fear of communism in the region had declined. Mahathir downplayed the possibility of China being a threat in the region and he hoped to enmesh China in regional security and economic institutions.

From 1985 to 1989, levels of trade between the two countries doubled to $1 billion. Mahathir's "Vision 2020" aimed for Malaysia to become a developed country by that year. Economic cooperation with China would become the focal point of the two countries' relations. Despite the atrocities committed by the Chinese regime in the wake of the Tiananmen Square demonstrations in the spring of 1989, Malaysia lifted travel bans with China in 1990, and in 1993, Malaysia lifted the ban on Malaysian investment in China. More important perhaps was the rhetoric and symbolism of these gestures. Mahathir warmed up to China just as the West was criticizing the Chinese for human rights atrocities. Mahathir saw this as an opportunity to promote "Asian values" of working for the good of the group and having deference and respect for authority (as distinct from Western values, which aim to protect rights of the individual over the state).[11] Mahathir further appreciated Chinese support in the wake of the 1997 Asian financial crisis, as China refrained from devaluing its currency, and spoke harshly against Western actors (whom Mahathir had been lambasting for the crisis).

In 1999, on the twenty-fifth anniversary of normalization of relations, Malaysia and China reaffirmed their bilateral cooperation. Over the last twelve years, there have been numerous high-level meetings and visits between heads of state from both nations. Economic relations have continued to deepen and expand. The implementation of the China-ASEAN Free

Trade Agreement on January 1, 2010, increased these links. Malaysia became China's biggest trading partner in ASEAN.[12]

It is clear that Malaysia, first under Mahathir and then continuing under Abdullah Badawi and now Najib Razak, wants to reap as much economic benefit from China's economic power as possible. Areas of cooperation between the two countries include trade in machinery, the energy sector, fisheries, and forestry.[13] There is also cooperation between the two countries on antiterrorism, marine enforcement, and law enforcement in drug interdiction. In April 2012, China and Malaysia launched their first joint industrial park, Qinzhou Industrial Park in Guangxi Zhuang autonomous region. The industrial park aims at coordinating manufacturing, information technology, and service of a multitude of projects.[14]

Closer relations between China and Malaysia coincide with a preference (particularly under Mahathir) for "looking East" for ideas about modernization and development, rather than looking at the West for models to emulate. Current Malaysian foreign policy may reflect what Yitzhak Shichor (chapter 10) describes in the case of Turkey as being both Western and Eastern in orientation. In Malaysia this may also be the case, although any "Western" orientation tends to be downplayed by most political leaders for fear of seeming too close to the United States. There are of course pitfalls to "looking East" as well.

Despite all the smiling diplomatic photos of Malaysian and Chinese leaders, Malaysia is not close to bandwagoning with China. Malaysia may be vigorously pursuing better economic ties with China, but they are also updating and modernizing their military and forging stronger relations with the United States.[15] Malaysian forces regularly conduct joint training with US counterparts, and the United States enjoys access to Malaysian airfields and ports. Between 2010 and 2012, relations between the United States and Malaysia became warmer, with Secretary of State Hillary Clinton going out of her way to praise Malaysian leaders for their cooperation in Afghanistan (there was a small medical team serving there), and for their leadership in Southeast Asia.[16] What is most important about Malaysia's relationship with China is the desire from Kuala Lumpur's perspective to see China cement their institutional ties to the larger Southeast Asian region.

Kim Nossal and Richard Stubbs see Malaysia's foreign policy as demonstrating middle power traits. Mahathir's forceful voice in the 1980s and 1990s as a leader in the Non-aligned Movement (NAM) and expanding Malaysian ties to the Middle East and Africa, demonstrated the country's ability to assert power and influence internationally. Malaysia's middle power diplomacy has had a more "acerbic" side, as it has often taken anti-Western positions.[17] This, however, plays directly into Malaysia's ability to forge better ties with China. Its ability to strike an independent foreign policy path also enhances its leadership and position within ASEAN and its leadership toward developing countries globally, traits that characterize middle power behavior.

Thailand and China

Thailand is known in Asia for having a flexible foreign policy.[18] Avoiding outright colonization and occupation by Japan, Thailand has demonstrated an ability to accommodate great powers while still holding on to some measure of sovereignty. Like other countries in Southeast Asia, from the 1930s to the 1970s Thailand had a resentful, suspicious, and hostile relationship with its ethnic Chinese population. Likewise, anticommunist fears kept Thailand from recognizing the Central Communist Party in China. Thailand forged close relations with the United States, going so far as sending Thai troops to the US-led efforts in Korea in 1950. Thailand was later a key player in the creation of (the now-defunct) Southeast Asian Treaty Organization (SEATO), and was a key ally and staging ground for the US war effort in Vietnam. Mao and Chinese military leaders vehemently denounced US-Thai links.

By the 1970s, Thailand's concerns about rising Vietnamese power in Southeast Asia prompted Bangkok to rethink its relationship with China. US president Nixon's decision to disengage from Vietnam (the Nixon Doctrine), coupled with improved Sino-US relations, were cause for alarm in Bangkok. Conversations began between Thailand and China in 1971, which led to restoration of trade between the two countries and later to other travel and cultural links. The fall of Saigon in 1975 seemed to signal to Thai officials that the United States was unable and unwilling to defend regional allies, and perhaps more importantly, the reunification of Vietnam seemed to be a more significant threat than Chinese power. Thus Thailand decided to formally recognize the Peoples Republic of China. As Ian Storey notes, "by the second half of the 1970s, Thai and Chinese threat perceptions had begun to converge."[19]

This became even clearer in the late 1970s with Vietnam's invasion of Cambodia. China became Thailand's most important security partner; Thailand worked with China to deliver weapons and supplies to the Khmer Rouge in resisting Vietnamese-backed forces in Cambodia, which lasted until the 1991 Paris Peace Accords that ended the horrific conflict in Cambodia. The Thai-China alignment lost its common focus and instead of sharing military/strategic goals, the two countries shifted their focus to economic concerns.

Between 1990 and 1999, trade between Thailand and China tripled and there was a tremendous amount of Thai investment in China.[20] With security concerns largely out of the picture, the two countries developed close economic ties. Thailand has even gone several steps further in fostering strong relations with China, loudly supporting China's position on the "One China" issue vis-à-vis Taiwan, and echoing China's condemnation of the Dalai Lama and groups like the Falun Gong. Like Malaysia, Thailand strongly appreciated China's gestures of support during the 1997 financial crisis (not devaluing the renminbi, and contributing $1 billion to the International Monetary Fund's rescue package).[21]

Throughout the chaotic postfinancial crisis years, Thailand continued to strengthen its ties to China. In 1999, China and Thailand signed a Joint Communiqué on a Plan of Cooperation for the 21st Century. This was a diplomatic statement from the two countries' foreign ministries pledging military cooperation, further economic ties, and disaster assistance. The relationship between China and Thailand deepened. This was particularly true under Thailand's controversial prime minister Thaksin Shinawatra. Business tycoon–turned–politician Thaksin and his family hailed from southern China and he viewed it as the best country to tap for help in achieving rapid economic growth for Thailand. Contravening previous custom, Thaksin visited China twice before making it to Washington, DC, for an official visit. The terrorist attacks on September 11, 2001, forced a review of Thailand's foreign relations. After initially declaring Thailand "neutral" in President Bush's "war on terror," Thailand later offered the United States full support for its antiterrorist efforts, allowing it rights to fly over Thai territory and providing access to Thai military bases; and Thailand even deployed two contingents of army medical and engineering units to assist with reconstruction efforts in Iraq.[22] The United States then granted Thailand Major Non-NATO Ally (MNNA) status in October 2003.

The United States and Thailand have conducted yearly joint military exercises called "Cobra Gold" since 1981. These training exercises have been expanded and now include many states in the region, including Indonesia, Malaysia, Singapore, Japan, and South Korea.[23] Since 2003, China has sent a small number of observers to Cobra Gold while Thailand has sent observers to China's military exercises in Inner Mongolia since 2003.[24] This military cooperation deepened in 2005, when the two countries held joint military exercises, a joint naval search-and-rescue drill conducted in the Gulf of Thailand; and in July 2007, the two countries conducted "Strike 2007," a two-week drill in southern China that involved special forces from both countries.[25] China has responded to closer US-Thai relations with a charm offensive of its own. The ousting of Prime Minster Thaksin resulted in Thai foreign policy taking a back seat to internal political instability. China's response to the 2006 military coup was (predictably) to announce that the coup was an internal affair and that China would respect Thai sovereignty and maintain a policy of noninterference. Since Thaksin had been such a good friend to China, one might have expected some distress from Beijing at the loss of their ally. However, Sino-Thai relations continued on a relatively even (if not improved) footing from 2006 to 2010. Over the last ten years the two countries have refrained from criticizing each other's internal problems,[26] which the Thais appreciate after listening to criticism from the United States on their subversion of democracy, weaknesses in dealing with human trafficking, and intellectual property rights violations.

When Thaksin's sister, Yingluck Shinawatra, and the Pheu Thai Party won the 2011 election, China refocused on its relationship with Thailand and has come through with a significant show of support for the Yingluck government. There have been high-level visits between Thai and Chinese leaders over the last year, and there seems to be a renewed sense of closeness between the two countries. During the 2011 floods in Thailand, China responded quickly and provided the largest assistance to Thailand, ahead of Japan and US efforts. In December, Thailand and China signed a 325 billion baht swap deal allowing import-export settlements in Chinese renminbi. The two countries have started joint military exercises and training, especially with Thai special forces. With Laos and Burma, both countries also coordinated joint patrols along the Mekong River (following the attack and murder of thirteen Chinese sailors). Beginning in 2012, Thailand took over as the country coordinator for ASEAN-China relations.[27] This is a significant role as tensions have heated up over conflicts in the South China Sea, and clearly China hopes that Thailand will promote an accommodationist policy rather than a confrontational one.

ASEAN: Malaysia and Thailand Attempt to Anchor China

Ann Marie Murphy has written (in chapter 7) on Thailand's response to China's rise and she has clearly laid out a framework for understanding Thailand's position. Murphy finds that Thailand is neither balancing nor bandwagoning in the (realist) conventional uses of those terms—while Thailand wants positive and close relations with China for both economic gains and politically motivated reasons. Murphy argues that Thailand views China's rise as an opportunity. While Thailand does not view China as a threat, nor are the Thais willing to let China have its way on all issues.[28] Murphy asks an important question: Is Thailand simultaneously balancing and bandwagoning? Thailand has not been forced to choose an alliance with the United States or China, instead it has been able to pursue both. Murphy argues against using the term "hedging" to describe Thai policies toward China, though there are additional reasons her critique is correct. Murphy argues that hedging (which is used by Medeiros and Goh[29] to mean a mixed strategy of both balancing and bandwagoning) is not the right lens through which to view Thai relations with China since there is no clear evidence that Thailand is in fact balancing against China.

If "hedging" is balancing *and* bandwagoning, one would expect to see behaviors consistent with each strategy, but both of these terms require knowing the actor's motivations behind the behavior. In the case of Thailand's (and Malaysia's) behavior, there could be multiple explanations. For example, increased military spending in Thailand and Malaysia could be interpreted as an effort to balance against China; but it could also reflect strong economic growth in the region and regimes that want the symbolic boost that comes from enhanced military upgrades. As both countries have sought to improve their military posture by buying new equipment and increasing the number of routine patrols by air force aircraft and navy vessels, this could be due to efforts to improve interoperability with the United States, it could also be to improve reaction time in South China Sea contingencies, and it could also be that these upgrades are symbolic of state power and so serve a domestic political purpose as much as an international one.[30]

A better analytical tool to understand Thai and Malaysian relations with China is to move away from the polarizing terms of balancing and bandwagoning and instead think in terms of the concept of "bonding." Thailand, and to a lesser extent Malaysia, has fostered closer ties to China seeking economic gains and friendly security relations, but better relations does not mean any inclination to compromise sovereignty and it does not imply or result in weaker relations with the United States. Neither Thailand nor Malaysia sees relations with China and the United States as a zero-sum game where closeness to one would preclude closeness to the other.[31] And part of this strategy of bonding involves linking China to regional organizations such as ASEAN.

The idea of bonding is consistent with behavior of middle powers in seeking to assert influence and protect interests in the larger international arena. In this spirit middle powers are not hedging so much as they are countering hegemony using a variety of resources both domestically and regionally. In order to take advantage of the peaceful rise of China, Thailand and Malaysia have pursued policies of engagement. The aim of engagement is to draw China closer to both countries and to bring them into the institutional fold of ASEAN to integrate China into the regional community at the political, economic, and security levels (classic middle power behavior), thereby sensitizing and socializing the Chinese government into accepting regional norms. The most important regional norms include respecting national sovereignty and territorial integrity, the nonuse of force, and the peaceful settlement of conflict through negotiation.[32]

ASEAN was originally formed in 1967 by Malaysia, Thailand, the Philippines, Indonesia, and Singapore as an anticommunist club. By the 1990s ASEAN was largely viewed as a "talk shop," long on rhetoric and diplomatic niceties, but short on tangible achievements. That has fundamentally changed. The shift in ASEAN's importance has come about for several reasons. First was the 1991 withdrawal of Vietnamese forces from Cambodia. This signaled an end to the Cold War in Southeast Asia and with it the end to the polarization, conflict, and divisiveness of great-power rivalries and ideological battles. The year 1991 saw China's foreign minister first attend ASEAN meetings as a consultative partner, which was part of larger efforts by China to reengage with the world after being shunned for the Tiananmen Square crackdown in 1989. In 1993–94, ASEAN proposed establishing joint committees with China to promote functional cooperation in economics, trade, science, and technology and in 1996, China was promoted from a consultative partner to a dialogue partner (along with India and Russia).[33] These events coincided with the significant expansion of ASEAN membership and the proliferation of off-shoot organizations. The ASEAN Regional Forum (ARF) was created in 1994 to promote a security dialogue between ASEAN and other Asian neighbors (including the United States, Russia, China, Japan, and India). It was created partly out of the angst and uncertainty of the end of the Cold War, but also because of the new reality of a growing China and a refocusing of US priorities so that the US commitment to Asia was unclear. The ARF's creation marked a turning point for ASEAN in acknowledging that security matters now fell within its purview and it was an attempt to socialize the new participant (China) to the ASEAN norms and for setting new norms to bring China into the conversation.[34] Thailand and Malaysia were both supportive of these efforts to include China. As Storey relates:

> At the ARF's inaugural meeting in 1994, participating states adopted the "ASEAN Way" of decision making by consultation and consensus, and the norms of behavior outlined in the TAC (Treaty of Amity and Cooperation). Although unstated, the primary objective of the ARF was to promote regional stability by keeping the United States engaged in the security affairs of Asia, and to encourage China's participation as part of the socialization process. As Foreign Minister Abdullah noted at the first ARF meeting: "As a potential

> economic and political superpower, [China] has to be reckoned with. It would be in the interests of the Asia Pacific countries to ensure that China becomes constructively engaged in regional affairs."[35]

By the end of 1999, Brunei, Vietnam, Laos, Cambodia, and Myanmar had become ASEAN members, thus making ASEAN truly a regional organization. In 1997, ASEAN Plus Three (APT)—the three being China, Japan, and Korea—was initiated. China had initially seemed like a wary participant in regional organizations and meetings, but through the end of the 1990s China had become used to the organization's way of operating. This does give support for the effectiveness of middle powers approaching and dealing with great powers through the prism of international institutions. Where China initially viewed ASEAN, the ARF, and APT with some hesitation, it is clear that the APT has become one of China's favorite institutions. This is largely the case because the United States is not a part of APT and China has found it a welcoming forum for them to promote their vision of a stable Asia that is economically prosperous and open to Chinese influence.[36]

China proposed the China-ASEAN Free Trade Agreement (CAFTA) in 2000. The goal was to promote cooperation and economic partnership among Southeast Asian countries and China. China realized that countries in Southeast Asia felt threatened by China's growing economic clout and competitiveness. CAFTA was an attempt to reassure Asian countries that China was committed to economic growth across the region. CAFTA was accepted by ASEAN in late 2001 and came into force on January 1, 2010. Singapore, Malaysia, and Thailand (in that order) have the highest levels of trade with China, but as in the rest of the region, China sells more to each of these countries than vice versa.

China wants to see greater economic integration in Asia and wants to lead that effort. Working mostly through APT China is promoting Chinese standards and harmonization objectives. It provides technical training to better promote Chinese interpretations of trading structures such as competition laws, indigenous innovation, and other regulatory rules.[37]

Other institutions in the region are also incorporating China into their frameworks: The ASEAN Defense Ministers' Meeting-Plus (ADMM-Plus) and the East Asia Summit (EAS) aim to continue dialogs on a range of issues. The ADMM-Plus is designed to discuss regional security architecture and to develop confidence-building measures to help solve potential disputes. The EAS aims to meet yearly after ASEAN meetings and it incorporates APT countries, plus the United States, Russia, India, Australia, and New Zealand. Topics include a wide range of issues from economic cooperation, to environmental issues, energy, and climate problems.[38] There have been contentious questions raised in both ADMM-Plus and EAS about which nations should be included and which excluded. China ultimately acquiesced to expanding participation, but again China prefers the smaller grouping of APT that does not include the United States, India, or Russia.

From 2000 to 2010, China was attuned to the "ASEAN way" and had settled into the regional institution and its norms. In 2003, China became the first great power to accede to the Treaty of Amity and Cooperation, and hopes were high in the region that China would continue to be a good neighbor.[39] By 2010, optimistic views were being tempered. China's economic clout was increasingly difficult to compete against, the growth and modernization of the People's Liberation Army were impressive and even intimidating to some in Southeast Asia, and increasingly countries were coming to realize that there was a gap between Chinese rhetoric and reality. For example, CAFTA had initially seemed like a way to improve the trading field between China and Southeast Asia, yet the agreement has been causing domestic difficulties in a number of Southeast Asian countries. For example, Thailand found that Thai farmers were hurt by cheap Chinese imports of things like garlic and other produce, and due to nontariff barriers and other mechanisms, China was not buying as much agricultural output from Thailand as had been hoped. Although there has clearly been domestic political activism in Thailand from disappointed farmers, the reactions have not been as strong in Thailand as in Indonesia, as Murphy describes in her chapter on Indonesia. Likewise, China is moving up the technological ladder faster than was perhaps anticipated, causing concern in Malaysia about increased competition in that sector.

Even more serious than economic concerns is the ongoing dispute in the South China Sea. In the waters south of China, near Vietnam, parts of Malaysia, the Philippines, Brunei, and Taiwan, are various chains of islands and outcroppings. The Spratly and Paracel Islands are the site of overlapping territorial claims among these six countries. The disputes involve sovereignty claims, the potential profit from oil and natural gas deposits (some experts believe that there could be as much as 130 billion barrels of oil and 900 trillion cubic feet of gas under this area), and control over shipping lanes between East/Northeast Asia and the Middle East.[40] The most contentious claims are those between China and Vietnam and between China and the Philippines. China and Vietnam have had sporadic naval clashes going back to the 1970s, and as recently as last year Chinese boats twice sabotaged oil exploration efforts by cutting ship cables in Vietnam's waters.[41] Malaysia too has concerns over China's claims to the Spratlys. In the 1980s, Malaysia occupied Swallow Reef, Mariveles Bank, as well as Ardasier Reef, in a direct challenge to China's claims.[42]

China and the Philippines have repeatedly come close to clashing in areas known as Mischief Reef and the Scarborough Shoal. The most recent dispute occurred in spring 2012 when half a dozen Chinese fishing boats, two Chinese law enforcement vessels, and a (dated) Philippine naval ship confronted each other and almost exchanged fire. While the conflict was nominally about rare corals, clams, and poached sharks, the underlying problem is that both countries claim this area to be part of their territory.[43] A Philippines energy company, Philex Petroleum Corporation, announced in 2012 that they had discovered larger-than-expected natural gas resources during exploration near the disputed waters.[44] In the past, China has expressed some willingness to jointly explore for oil and natural gas and to share the profits from these resources.

The flare-up of territorial disputes is a key test for the middle power diplomacy exhibited by Malaysia and Thailand—whether the strategy of "bonding" China to regional norms can achieve peaceful and satisfactory outcomes better than a more traditional strategy of balancing against it. Countries in Southeast Asia would like to see the conflicts in the South China Sea settled through peaceful and multilateral means. The United States has conducted joint military exercises with the Philippines, and in 2011 announced plans to station a small number of troops in Darwin, Australia. China views both of these actions as directly related to their claims in the South China Sea and Beijing has repeatedly said that it is not an issue with which the United States should be concerned. While China would prefer to deal with the problem bilaterally, Southeast Asian countries would like to see it settled through the legal mechanism of the UN Convention on the Law of the Sea (UNCLOS), of which China and the countries of the region are members. Yet China has been unwilling to address the dispute in a multilateral forum. This is one reason that it is significant that Thailand has taken over this year as the liaison between ASEAN and China. Since Thailand does not have a claim in the South China Sea dispute, the hope is that it can serve as a neutral arbiter. Thailand's neighbors hope that allegiance to ASEAN will prompt the Thais to channel the dispute through international legal mechanisms. So far, Thailand has not acted forcefully either as a neutral actor, or as a proponent of the more favored position within ASEAN of trying to get China to agree to a multilateral code of conduct. There has been some grumbling that Thailand has in fact moved closer to China, and that it is failing to help put pressure on China on behalf of fellow ASEAN members.[45]

The renewed conflict over islands in the South China Sea has demonstrated the divisions within ASEAN. While ASEAN, the ARF, and other institutions have become more important and effective in the last twenty years, they do not represent a security community in the sense that Karl

Deutsch explains it. Deutsch and others list three main characteristics of a community as including: shared identities, values, and meanings; many-sided and direct relations among the groups; and diffuse reciprocity. A community of states is a pluralistic security community when there are reliable expectations of peaceful exchange, when states do not expect and prepare to use violence as a means to solve disputes.[46] Organizations in Southeast Asia are not embedded security communities, as described by Deutsch and others. While that does not mean that a large war could break out in the region, there are still quite significant points of contention in the region that divide countries and can and do trigger the use of violence. The fear is that alignment with China and the disputes in the South China Sea could become such a flash point.

Commonalities and Difference

Malaysia and Thailand have different histories and attitudes toward China. While both viewed China warily after 1949 and Malaysia moved to normalize relations relatively early with China in the 1970s, it was Thailand's decisive action to join with China in balancing Vietnamese power in the region that is the most remarkable difference between Malaysia and Thailand's relations with China until the post-Cold War period. Thailand's military cooperation with China is significantly warmer than anything seen between China and Malaysia. While both Malaysia and Thailand welcome China's oft-stated policy of refraining from others' internal affairs, both countries also have some hesitation in moving more completely into China's orbit. China's reassertion of claims in the South China Sea, and the fact that economic relations with China still appear to benefit China the most, has caused many countries in the region (Burma in particular) to rethink their closeness with the rising giant. Thailand has not yet signaled any increasing reservations about their closeness with China.

Despite few overt diplomatic changes in relations between China and Malaysia and Thailand, we do see actions worth noting: There has been increased government spending throughout the region on military equipment. Malaysia and Thailand have increased their military budgets over the last ten years. In part this reflects changing military requirements, particularly the need to secure sea lanes of communication (SLOCs), shifts in the United States' military posture and attention, and the growing Chinese military presence in the region (particularly the South China Sea). Since economies in the region have continued to grow successfully, there is also more money on the supply side with which to upgrade capabilities. And military spending has an element of status to it for regional leaders.

Malaysia has acquired at least eighteen *Sukhoi* SU-30MKM fighter planes; Thailand has purchased twelve *Gripen* fighter jets. Both have also bolstered their naval hardware: Malaysia bought two British frigates and two *Scorpene* SSKs (submarines), and has plans to build (locally) up to twenty-seven offshore patrol vessels (MEKO 100). Thailand acquired an aircraft carrier (HTMS *Chakri Naruebet*) and submarines. Both countries have also spent money on building up their land power, buying battle tanks, artillery systems, and attack helicopters.[47] While the increased military spending should be watched carefully, it may not reflect balancing behavior or adversarial relations.[48] As Bitzinger points out, these acquisitions do not necessarily reflect a deliberate structuring of armed forces based on an adversary's behavior (or the adversary's military modernizations). However, this military modernization may have two important effects: First, it may increase regional security dilemmas; second, these efforts may improve the ability of Southeast Asian countries to contribute and cooperate with US efforts in the region because these upgrades improve interoperative capabilities for countries to be able to work more seamlessly with US counterparts.[49]

To be clear: It is possible that increased military spending reflects a concern over China's growing military power, but this is not the most compelling explanation. China's military is so much larger and growing so rapidly, it seems that military spending among its neighbors is not really about being able to match or balance these efforts, but instead indicates a level of nuance in regard to how Malaysia and Thailand view their big neighbor. Clearly, the first choice of both these middle powers is to tie China to regional institutions, norms, and frameworks. However, even a country as close to China as Thailand wants to maintain a high degree of autonomy, thus Thailand and Malaysia's increased military spending and continued links to the United States are efforts to do just that. In other words, even middle power behavior has its limits and is itself "hedged" with the possibility of a reversion to more classic balancing. For now, however, these capabilities play into the middle power strategy by offering credibility for initiatives to secure peace.

Conclusions

In response to the four key questions posed by this book, this chapter concludes that (1) Malaysia and Thailand are incomplete middle powers by virtue of their modest capabilities and reluctance to self-identify as middle powers, even though their international behavior often conforms to middle power expectations; (2) China's rise has led to a deep integration with ASEAN economies like Malaysia and Thailand, while reviving the importance of the organization in regional security questions; (3) the response of Malaysia and Thailand, reflecting a general ASEAN response, has been to seek to "bond" or "enmesh" China into multilateral regionalism that seeks to socialize it toward cooperative norms in order to protect national interests and prevent a great power conflict in the region; and (4) Malaysia and Thailand's effect on China's foreign policy through both bilateral and multilateral initiatives has been partially successful in moderating Beijing's great power ambitions for preeminence in Asia and in nudging it toward multilateral solutions that include the United States.

To elaborate, this examination of Malaysia and Thailand's relations with China highlights the importance of understanding the role of middle powers in addressing China's rise. The first question to be addressed in these chapters was an assessment of the capabilities and behaviors of the middle powers as they relate to ideal middle powers. Malaysia and Thailand, although possessing less economic clout than other middle powers, are behaving in noteworthy ways by anchoring China to regional organizations as a way out of more conventional international relations choices of balancing against a rising power, or bandwagoning with it. While neither country conforms to the initial typology of an "ideal" middle power, and while both have demonstrated antihegemonic behavior from time to time, both Malaysia and Thailand *are* demonstrating the capabilities to influence regional and global actors and they are choosing to do so in ways very much in keeping with middle power behavior, through international organizations. Questions two and three ask us to consider how China's rise has impacted the domestic, regional, and global environment of Malaysia and Thailand, and how they are reacting to China. This chapter has demonstrated that both Thailand and Malaysia are doing more to accommodate China's rise than they are to counter it; however, they are choosing to do so in ways not really predicted by realist theory, therefore the middle power approach can help us understand their behavior. Both countries are engaging China economically, but are also fostering close relations with the United States, including greater military cooperation and coordination. Most importantly, Malaysia and Thailand are turning to regional organizations like ASEAN, APT, CAFTA, and others to shape and constrain Chinese behavior.

In answering the question about middle powers' ability to have an impact on China and to affect China's rise, what Malaysian and Thai foreign policy shows is that middle power diplomacy is a way of imposing policy preferences on more powerful actors, which fits more with antihegemonic behavior of some newer middle powers (Brazil and Turkey, among others). The way that this is being done in Southeast Asia is through organizations such as ASEAN, APT, and ARF. At least at a rhetorical level, China does seem to care what her neighbors in Southeast Asia think and how China is perceived there. So, we can find some impact of middle power behavior on China's foreign policy. One of the most often-cited examples of this can be seen in China's shift from its "peaceful rise" policy in 2003 to a renamed slogan that replaced the "peaceful rise" with the "harmonious world view." The term "rise" implied the growth of relative power in relation to its neighbors. Former president Hu Jintao first used the phrase "harmonious world view" internationally in Jakarta at an Asia-Africa summit in 2005; analysts believe this reflected Chinese attention to concerns of Southeast Asian neighbors. Similarly, China's increasing participation and activism within regional organizations and actively promoting security dialog in the Asia Pacific region demonstrate that China is paying attention to the norms and preferences of Southeast Asian nations.[50] This should not lead one to believe that China is fully onboard with institutional norms and cooperative behavior. Clearly, there are wide differences in Chinese behavior on issues they perceive as integral to their sense of nationalism and territorial integrity—such as the South China Sea claims, and issues like economic integration where they may be more willing to operate by institutional norms and constraints.

Malaysia and Thailand may be on their way to being in a position to be effective as middle powers, but they are not all the way there yet. Credibility in the case of Malaysia and Thailand may rest with both countries being able to address domestic political tensions. One of the reasons that ASEAN has enjoyed a rebirth of sorts over the last few years is that Indonesia has reestablished its leadership and credibility within Southeast Asia, allowing it to speak more forcefully within ASEAN about the value of democracy, democratic norms and values, and the importance of settling disputes through legal, rational means. Thailand and Malaysia are not yet in positions where the regimes have the internal or international credibility to do likewise.

Malaysia and Thailand are bolstering their military capabilities in order to improve their own security, coordinate more effectively with the United States, and better assist in peacekeeping operations around the world. With growing economies they are better able to spend money on solving regional problems as well; these developments will allow these middle powers to be more active in promoting their foreign policy interests. Malaysia and Thailand's reactions to the growth of Chinese power contribute to the literature on middle powers by showing the choices and variation in how emerging middle powers confront a change in the regional and global distribution of power. Malaysia and Thailand would like to use the collective power of regional organizations to help them best benefit from China's growth, while mitigating the potential dangers of too close a relationship. It is too soon to know how successful this strategy will be.

Notes

1. For a survey of these arguments see Denny Roy, "The China Threat Issue: Major Arguments," *Asian Survey* 36, no. 8 (1996): 758–71.

2. Eduard Jordaan, "The Concept of a Middle Power in International Relations: Distinguishing between Emerging and Traditional Middle Powers," *Politikon: South African Journal of Political Studies* 30, no. 2 (2003): 165–81.

3. Jordaan, "The Concept of a Middle Power."

4. GDP: US$ purchasing power parity (PPP) share of world total, IMF World Economic Outlook database for 2010, www.imf.org/external/pubs/ft/weo/2010/02/weodata/index.aspx.

5. Jonathan H. Ping, *Middle Power Statecraft: Indonesia, Malaysia, and the Asia Pacific* (Burlington, VT: Ashgate, 2005), 191.

6. Bijian Zheng, "China's 'Peaceful Rise' to Great Power Status," *Foreign Affairs* 84, no. 5 (2005): 18–24; Xinhua, "Foreign Trade Growth Slows, Surplus Widens, *English.news.con*, May 10, 2012.

7. Susan L. Shirk, *China: Fragile Superpower* (New York: Oxford University Press, 2007).

8. Quote taken from Ian Storey, *Southeast Asia and the Rise of China: The Search for Security* (London: Routledge, 2011), 42.

9. Editors, "Global Insider: China-Malaysia Relations," *World Politics Review*, June 1, 2011, www.worldpoliticsreview.com/articles/print/9025; see also Lim Tin Seng, "Renewing 35 Years of Malaysia-China Relations: Najib's Visit to China," *EAI Background Brief* (National University of Singapore), no. 460, June 23, 2009.

10. Storey, *Southeast Asia and the Rise of China*, 212.

11. Ibid., 218.

12. "China-Malaysia Relations Eye Brighter Future," Xinhua News Agency, May 22, 2011.

13. For articles on current economic relations between China and Malaysia, see *New Straits Times*, "China Is a Reliable Friend of Malaysia," *New Straits Times*, June 2, 2012; "Malaysia, China Sign Pacts to Boost Investment," April 28, 2011, Abcnews.go.com; "Malaysia Seeks China JVs," *Live Trading News*, April 23, 2012, www.livetradingnews.com/malaysia-seeks-china-jvs; "China, Malaysia Pledge to Seek Stronger Economic Cooperation," Xinhua News Agency, April 19, 2011.

14. There are various sources of articles on the joint industrial park, including *China Daily*, *Sin Chew*, *Sun Daily*, *Asiaone.com*.

15. In the 1980s, Mahathir signed the Bilateral Training and Consultation (BITAC) agreement with the United States. This agreement provided a framework for working with the US military for training and joint exercises. The initial premise

for the agreement was clearly suspicion of China and lingering Cold War tensions in the region. However, the relationship between Malaysia and the United States for military cooperation has continued. In 1994, defense ties between the two countries were strengthened with an additional agreement that allowed US naval ships and aircraft to transit through Malaysia for resupply and maintenance. The United States has utilized this agreement and fifteen to twenty US naval ships visit Malaysian ports every year. The two militaries also conduct join training exercises and US Special Forces conduct training at Malaysia's jungle warfare facility in Johor. This relationship with the United States signals Malaysia's acknowledgment and interest in having the United States play a stabilizing role in the region and it illustrates Malaysia's continued sense of caution in developing overwhelming close ties to China. See Storey, *Southeast Asia and the Rise of China*, 223.

16. For information on the US-Malaysia relationship see John Roberts, "US Praises Malaysia's Autocratic Government," *World Socialist Web Site*, November 29, 2010, www.wsws.org/articles; speech given by Prime Minister Najib Razak when he was defense minister on the occasion of a visit to the United States reprinted in "Malaysia-US Defence Cooperation: A 'Well Kept Secret,'" *Harakah Daily*, http://en.harakahdaily.net/index.php/berita-utama; Daniel Ten Kate, "US Boosts Asian Defense Ties amid Growing Challenge from China Military," *Bloomberg*, July 22, 2010.

17. Kim Richard Nossal and Richard Stubbs, "Mahathir's Malaysia: An Emerging Middle Power," in *Niche Diplomacy: Middle Powers after the Cold War*, 147–63, ed. Andrew F. Cooper (London: MacMillan, 1997).

18. While other countries have "flexible" foreign policy, Thailand has been more successful at it than most other nations. They were able to accommodate the Japanese in World War II, but not be treated as an enemy by the United States in the postwar order. Likewise, they were able to maintain good relations with the United States during the Cold War while simultaneously pivoting toward China when needed.

19. Storey, *Southeast Asia and the Rise of China*, 129; Michael R. Chambers, "The Evolving Relationship between China and Southeast Asia," in *The Legacy of Engagement in Southeast Asia*, 281–310, eds. Ann Marie Murphy and Bridget Welsh (Singapore: ISEAS, 2008); and Michael R. Chambers, "'The Chinese and the Thai Are Brothers': The Evolution of the Sino-Thai Friendship," *Journal of Contemporary China* 14, no. 45 (2005): 599–629.

20. *Direction of Trade Statistics Yearbook* (Washington, DC: International Monetary Fund, multiple issues 1991–2001).

21. Storey, *Southeast Asia and the Rise of China*, 133. It should also be noted here that China's contribution was actually quite small in comparison to Japan's, the United States', and others. But it was significant as marking China's growing clout in the region and in regional cooperative efforts to address the crisis.

22. Storey, *Southeast Asia and the Rise of China*, 134–35.

23. Lance Cpl. Kasey Peacock, III, Marine Expeditionary Force, "Cobra Gold Begins in Thailand," February 8, 2012, www.army.mil/article/73324/.

24. Chulacheeb Chinwanno, "Rising China and Thailand's Policy of Strategic Engagement," in *The Rise of China: Responses from Southeast Asia and Japan*, 81–110, ed. Jun Tsunekawa (Tokyo: National Institute for Defense Studies, 2004).

25. Ann Marie Murphy, "Thailand's Response to China's Rise," *Asian Security* 6, no. 1 (2010): 1–27, 15.

26. Kavi Chongkittavorn, "Thai-China Relations: A Friendship Now Not So Special," *Nation*, June 28, 2010.

27. Kavi Chongkittavorn, "Thailand Is Courting China," *Mizzima*, April 17, 2012, http://mizzimaenglish.blogspot.com/2012/04/thailand-is-courting-china.html; also see "Thailand-China Relationship Has Undergone Continuous Dynamics," *Diplonews*, April 18, 2012.

28. Murphy shows that Thailand has been vocally opposed to China's dam building on the upper Mekong River, and that Thailand has sought Chinese support for their interests vis-à-vis drug interdiction, and issues relating to Thaksin's exile. Murphy, "Thailand's Response to China's Rise," 16–17.

29. Evan S. Medeiros, "Strategic Hedging and the Future of Asia-Pacific Stability," *Washington Quarterly* 29, no. 1 (2005–6): 145–67, 146; Evelyn Goh, "Great Powers and Hierachical Order in Southeast Asia: Analyzing Regional Security Strategies," *International Security* 32, no. 3 (2007/8): 113–57, 131.

30. Renato Cruz De Castro, "Managing 'Strategic Unipolarity': The ASEAN States' Responses to the Post-Cold War Regional Environment," in *Southeast Asian Perspectives on Security*, ed. Derek da Cunha, 60–80 (Singapore: Institute of Southeast Asian Studies, 2000).

31. Neal Jesse, Steven Lobell, Galia Press-Barnathan, and Kristen Williams, "The Leader Can't Lead When the Followers Won't Follow: The Limitations of Hegemony," in *Beyond Great Powers and Hegemons: Why Secondary States Support, Follow, or Challenge*, 1–30, 14, eds. Neal Jesse, Steven Lobell, and Kristen Williams (Stanford, CA: Stanford Security Studies, 2012).

32. Chinwanno, "Rising China and Thailand's Policy of Strategic Engagement."

33. Storey, *Southeast Asia and the Rise of China*, 49.

34. Chinwanno, "Rising China and Thailand's Policy of Strategic Engagement," 97.

35. Storey, *Southeast Asia and the Rise of China*, 49.

36. Ibid., 80–84; Carlyle A. Thayer, "The Rise of China and India: Challenging or Reinforcing Southeast Asia's Autonomy?," in *Strategic Asia 2011–12, Asia Responds to Its Rising Powers China and India*, 313–49, 314, eds. Ashley J. Tellis, Travis Tanner, and Jessica Keough (Seattle, WA: National Bureau of Asian Research).

37. Ernest Bower, "The US-ASEAN Relationship in 2030," in *CSIS Newsletter*, May 10, 2012 (Washington, DC: Center for Strategic and International Studies Southeast Asia Program).

38. Thayer, "The Rise of China and India," 314.

39. TAC is a peace treaty dating back to 1976. "The purpose of the treaty is to promote perpetual peace, everlasting amity, and cooperation among the people of Southeast Asia, which would contribute to their strength, solidarity, and closer relationship. In their relations with one another, the High Contracting Parties shall be

guided by the following fundamental principles: (a) mutual respect for the independence, sovereignty, equality, territorial integrity and national identity of all nations, (b) the right of every State to lead its national existence free from external interference, subversion, or coercion, (c) noninterference in the internal affairs of one another, (d) settlement of differences or disputes by peaceful means, (e) renunciation of the threat or use of force, and (f) effective cooperation among themselves." TAC Treaty, 1976.

40. Jane Perlez, "Beijing Exhibiting New Assertiveness in South China Sea," *New York Times*, May 31, 2012.

41. Ibid.

42. Storey, *Southeast Asia and the Rise of China*, 217.

43. Perlez, "Beijing Exhibiting New Assertiveness in South China Sea"; "State Media Fuel Nationalism in China-Philippines Standoff," *Freedom House Weekly Updates of Press Freedom and Censorship in China*, no. 58, May 17, 2012.

44. CSIS Weekly Newsletter, "South China Sea," May 10, 2012.

45. Joshua Kurlantzick, "South China Sea: From Bad to Worse?," Council on Foreign Relations, July 24, 2012, www.cfr.org/china/south-china-sea-bad-worse-p28739.

46. Karl Deutsch et al., *Political Community and the North Atlantic Area: International Organization in the Light of Historical Experience* (Princeton, NJ: Princeton University Press, 1957); Michael Haas, "Comparing Regional Cooperation in Asia and the Pacific," in *Toward a World of Peace*, 149–68, eds. Jeannette P. Mass and Robert A. C. Stewart (Fiji: University of South Pacific Press, 1986); Sonia Lucarelli, "Peace and Democracy: The Rediscovered Link The EU, NATO and the European System of Liberal-Democratic Security Communities," Report for Forum on the Problems of Peace and War, 2000–2002.

47. Richard A. Bitzinger, *Southeast Asian Military Modernization: A New Arms Race* (Singapore: Rajaratnam School of International Studies, 2011).

48. In fact, Yu Wang finds that increased military spending in Southeast Asia reflects economic, sociopolitical, and strategic motives. Yu Wang, "Determinants of Southeast Asian Military Spending in the Post-Cold War Era: A Dynamic Panel Analysis," *Defence and Peace Economics* 24, no. 1 (2013): 73–87.

49. Bitzinger, "Southeast Asian Military Modernization."

50. Tsai Tung-Chieh, Hung Ming-Te, and Tony Tai-Ting Liu, "China's Foreign Policy in Southeast Asia: Harmonious Worldview and Its impact on Good Neighbor Diplomacy," *Journal of Contemporary Eastern Asia* 10, no. 1 (2011): 25–42.

CHAPTER 7

Indonesia Responds to China's Rise

Ann Marie Murphy

"We have to get something from the rise of China, especially in economic terms."

President Susilo Bambang Yudhoyono

"China respects strength. If they see you as being weak, they will eat you alive."

Dewi Fortuna Anwar, foreign policy adviser to former President Habibie

Introduction

CHINA'S RISE has provided opportunities and challenges to Indonesia as officials in Jakarta seek to elevate Indonesia's international stature. Globally, China's rise is consistent with a long-standing Indonesian desire for multipolarity and greater influence for developing countries in global governance. In Asia, China's rise has been a double-edged sword for Indonesia. As Southeast Asia's largest state and the de facto leader of the Association of Southeast Asian Nations (ASEAN), Indonesia has long served as a linchpin of regional order. As concern over China has led countries such as the United States, South Korea, and Australia to strengthen ties with Indonesia and the regional architecture based on ASEAN, Jakarta's status has risen. At the same time, China's attempts to stake its own claims to regional leadership pose a significant challenge to Indonesia. China's development of a blue-water navy and its claims to virtually the entire South China Sea directly threaten Indonesian interests. As conflicts over competing claims to the South China Sea escalate, it is becoming increasingly difficult for Indonesia to play its traditional middle power role of mediator.

Indonesia ranks as the world's fourth-largest state by population, placing it above the middle power category. Economically, Indonesia ranks as the world's sixteenth-largest state, placing it squarely in the middle power category. The economy has been expanding rapidly, and the World Bank forecasts that it will grow 6.1 percent in 2012.[1] McKinsey Global Institute recently argued that the country's productivity growth and favorable demographics could make Indonesia the world's seventh-largest economy by 2030, placing it ahead of Germany and Great Britain, two countries long considered great powers.[2]

On a series of other dimensions, Indonesia ranks at the top of the international hierarchy. It is the world's third-largest democracy, and with over 88 percent of its people professing the Muslim faith, Islam has more adherents in Indonesia than all of the Middle East. Indonesia's status as the only Muslim majority country that has instituted a successful counterterrorism policy while making a transition to democracy gives it special status in a post-9/11 world.[3] Indonesia is the world's third-largest emitter of greenhouse gases and has more confirmed deaths from avian influenza than any other country, making it a pivotal player in global efforts to respond to climate change and pandemics.

Indonesia, however, has limited military capacity. Despite the prominent role the Indonesian armed forces, *Tentara Nasional Indonesia* (TNI), traditionally played in Indonesian politics, it has always been a small force: its 413,729 military personnel account for less than 1/20 of 1 percent of the country's 240 million people.[4] Military spending was slashed during the 1998 financial crisis, and although it rose from 23 trillion rupiah in 2005 to 40.6 trillion rupiah (US$4.18 billion) in 2010, it accounted for a paltry 0.78 percent of gross national product.[5] The decrease in military spending combined with suspension of military sales by the United States severely degraded Indonesian military capacity. According to one estimate, only half of the military's aircraft are operational at any one time.[6] Indonesia increased the 2012 defense budget by 35 percent and has embarked on a military modernization plan.[7] Indonesia's increased defense spending is driven in part by regional uncertainty but it should not be viewed simply as a response to China. It is also a function of increased budget capacity and the need to enhance Indonesia's military capacity after a long period of decline.

Indonesia's weight in international affairs is enhanced by factors not captured in traditional middle power rankings. Its geographic position sitting astride some of the world's vital sea lanes linking the Pacific and Indian Oceans raises its strategic importance beyond the level to which its weak military might otherwise consign it. If middle powers are countries that rank near but not at the top of the global hierarchy, then Indonesia's size gives it the potential to become something more than a middle power. For now, Indonesian diplomats at least seem to accept the middle power designation: Jakarta joined the Mexico-Indonesia-South Korea-Turkey-Australia (MIKTA) Initiative of like-minded states, formed in 2013, which explicitly recognized the countries as middle powers.

This chapter examines the impact of China's rise on Indonesia, analyzes Jakarta's response to China, and assesses the extent to which these responses can be said to have had a middle power effect on China. First, the chapter briefly reviews the history of Indonesia's relations with China within the broader context of Indonesian foreign policy. Second, the chapter analyzes Indonesia's capabilities and foreign policy behavior. It argues that although Indonesia has the potential to rank among the world's great powers on several dimensions, its foreign policy behavior hews closely to the middle power ideal type outlined in this book. Third, the chapter analyzes the impact of China's rise on Indonesia at the global, regional, and domestic levels. The chapter concludes that China's assertiveness in the South China Sea combined with its negative economic impact have raised Indonesian perceptions of a China threat. There are at least two ways that Indonesia has exerted a "middle power effect" on China—encouraging China's post-1997 "charm offensive" in Southeast Asia, and preventing China from usurping the role of ASEAN's leadership role in East Asian affairs.

Indonesia and China to 1997

Indonesian foreign policy has undergone dramatic swings. During the Sukarno era (1945–65), it was marked by a strident nationalism, calls for third world solidarity, and ultimately for the revolutionary overthrow of the international order. Under Suharto (1965–98), Indonesia took the lead in creating ASEAN to promote regional stability and aligned closely with the West.[8] Since Indonesia's consolidation of democracy under Susilo Bambang Yudhoyono (2004–present), Indonesia is increasingly emphasizing its status as the world's fourth-most-populous country, third-largest democracy, and home to the world's largest Muslim population.

Despite these shifts, the country's key national interests and foreign policy doctrine have exhibited strong continuity.[9] A nation of seventeen thousand islands stretching over three thousand miles, Indonesia's key national interests have always been maintaining the territorial integrity and sovereignty of its far-flung archipelago and promoting the social cohesion of its extremely diverse population. Indonesia's constitution calls for the government to "join in establishing a world order based on freedom, everlasting peace, and social justice."[10] Indonesia's *bebas dan aktif* or free and active foreign policy doctrine was promulgated in 1948. The free component holds that Indonesia should refrain from alliances and chart its own course in international affairs. The active component holds that Indonesia should seek to influence the international system, not simply accept its rules. Key aspects of Indonesia's middle power behavior—a desire to work for justice and peace combined with a conviction that developing states should play an active role in international politics—can be traced to these beliefs.

Indonesia gained sovereignty from the Dutch in 1949 and established diplomatic relations with China in July 1950. Having devoted scarce resources to suppress a communist rebellion in 1948, Indonesia's government was suspicious of communist countries but recognized China in order to give substance to its "independent" foreign policy plank.[11] Despite tensions over Beijing's relationship with Indonesia's ethnic Chinese population, a shared belief that newly independent countries should play a larger role in international politics provided a basis for cooperation. Indonesia's role in creating the Non-Aligned Movement (NAM) and its hosting of the 1955 Bandung Conference of Asian-African countries marked the country's first major step onto the international stage. Chinese Premier Zhou Enlai used the Bandung Conference as an opportunity to promulgate the Five Principles of Peaceful Coexistence as a basis for China's relations with developing countries.

In 1959, President Sukarno imposed an authoritarian political system of "Guided Democracy" and from that time until the end of his rule, he maintained his political authority by balancing the TNI against the Indonesian Communist Party, *Partai Komunis Indonesia* (PKI).[12] Sukarno proclaimed "an anti-imperial axis" among Jakarta-Beijing-Phnom Penh, Hanoi, and Pyongyang in 1965. Sukarno's policies transformed Indonesia into a revisionist state.

In October 1965, an abortive coup and countercoup triggered a series of events that ultimately resulted in the downfall of Sukarno and the rise of the anticommunist General Suharto, who named his regime the "New Order." The TNI took harsh measures against what it perceived as the "triple threat" of the PKI, the ethnic Chinese, and the People's Republic of China.[13] At least five hundred thousand Indonesians suspected of being PKI members were killed and the PKI was made illegal. Suharto banned the use of the Chinese language, closed Chinese schools, and made the importation of Chinese language materials illegal. Chinese were urged to adopt Indonesian names to show their loyalty to Indonesia, and many did so for protection.

Convinced of Chinese complicity in the coup, Indonesia "froze" relations with China in 1967. Throughout the Suharto era, China was perceived as Indonesia's key strategic threat and Suharto rejected proposals to reestablish relations, even after other ASEAN countries and the United States did so in the 1970s.[14] Since Suharto's military-backed regime justified its rule on the basis of having saved the country from communism, recognition of China would have to await new sources of regime legitimacy.

Suharto focused on promoting economic development, which he viewed as an antidote to communism.[15] Over the next three decades, Suharto opened Indonesia to foreign investment, and the economy grew at an average of 7 percent a year, placing it among the ranks of Asia's economic success stories.[16] The United States became the patron of the TNI, providing military aid, equipment, and training to generations of officers, including President Yudhoyono.

To promote the regional stability necessary for development, Suharto took the lead in creating ASEAN in 1967, which joined Indonesia with the anticommunist states of Thailand, Malaysia, Singapore, and the Philippines. ASEAN was a vehicle for Indonesian leadership and a mechanism through which Suharto reassured Indonesia's smaller neighbors of its peaceful intentions after the aggressive policies of the Sukarno era. ASEAN was perceived as a bulwark against China's attempts to export revolution. Over the following decades, Indonesia helped mediate numerous regional disputes.

In 1990, Suharto reestablished diplomatic ties with China. This was based on a number of pragmatic factors, not a significant change in threat perception. First, with strong economic progress legitimizing his rule, Suharto no longer needed to play up the communist threat. Second, China's economic development created opportunities for Indonesia, which had begun direct trade with China in 1985. Finally, by 1990, Suharto was sufficiently confident of Indonesia's domestic achievements and Southeast Asia's regional stability that he sought to elevate Indonesia's international standing and sought the chairmanship of the NAM. China's influence in the NAM is significant, and Indonesia's decision to recognize China was taken in part to remove an obstacle to its bid for the NAM chairmanship, which Indonesia won in 1992.

Despite recognition, Indonesia remained suspicious of China and sensitive to its links with the local Chinese community. In April 1994, when labor unrest in Sumatra led to anti-Chinese riots, China issued a statement of "concern" and called upon Jakarta to defuse the situation. Indonesia responded angrily, warning China that it had "better mind its own internal affairs" and some officials even threatened to freeze bilateral ties again.[17]

Indonesia also remained suspicious of China's irredentist aims, particularly in the South China Sea. Indonesia was a strong advocate in the UN Convention on the Law of the Sea negotiations (UNCLOS) for the adoption of the "archipelagic principle" that would grant island states sovereignty over their internal waterways. Indonesia gained sovereignty over its waterways when UNCLOS came into force in 1994.

At this time China's occupation of Mischief Reef claimed by the Philippines and military clashes with Vietnam led many ASEAN leaders to view China as a revisionist actor. Viewing China's actions as a test for the organization, ASEAN responded collectively by telling China directly at a 1994 meeting in Hangzhou that ASEAN would not tolerate the use of force to resolve regional disputes.[18] As a nonclaimant, Indonesia believed that it had the independence to serve as mediator, and in 1994 began a series of meetings between the disputants to build confidence and set parameters to avoid clashes at sea. Indonesia complemented its diplomatic response with a show of force, holding what was at that time the country's largest military exercise, involving over nineteen thousand soldiers, fifty warships, and forty aircraft in September 1996 around Natuna.[19] Juwono Sudarsono, a respected academic who would later become defense minister, opined that "barring the possibility that China can gain access to resources other than the South China Sea area, then ASEAN countries will have to face the possibility of an imminent military confrontation with China."[20]

By the mid-1990s, Chinese leaders began to realize that its assertive policies were raising concerns in ASEAN. Furthermore, the strong US response during the Taiwan Strait crisis of 1995–96 demonstrated the US resolve to balance against China.[21] Chinese leaders feared that ASEAN states might join a balancing coalition against China, leading to its "encirclement." To forestall such an eventuality, China adopted a "win-win" strategy to convince its Southeast Asian neighbors that it was a benign great power.[22] China's adoption of its "peaceful rise" strategy is variously ascribed to the US "hard power" response on Taiwan and to the "middle power effect" of Indonesia's and ASEAN's strong stance of multilateral resolution through peaceful means.

China's Post-1997 Charm Offensive

The Asian financial crisis hit Indonesia hard. The economy contracted 13.8 percent in 1998, triggering social and political protests that led to Suharto's overthrow in May of that year. The collapse of the Suharto regime was preceded by intense rioting during which the ethnic Chinese became the targets of brutal attacks. China stated that it "attached great importance" to the attacks and the Chinese media responded angrily to President Habibie's statement that the attacks were driven by economic disparity rather than ethnicity.[23] Indonesia responded calmly to China's concerns. In the view of prominent analyst Rizal Sukma, the riots were a test of the newfound maturity of the relationship that both sides passed as they worked to prevent the issue from negatively impacting the broader relationship.[24]

In the early years of Indonesia's democratic era, the country suffered a series of major crises that triggered strong Western pressure. The International Monetary Fund (IMF) provided Indonesia with an economic bailout but imposed strict structural adjustment conditions that Indonesia resented. China contributed $500 million to the IMF's $43 billion bailout, provided $500 million in export credit, $3 million in grant aid to purchase medicine, and agreed not to devalue the yuan, which would have hurt Indonesian exports.[25]

Following East Timor's August 1999 vote for independence, pro-Indonesia militias and their TNI allies forced more than two hundred thousand East Timorese across the border, attacked UN personnel, and destroyed 70 percent of the territory's physical infrastructure. The United States, Australia, and the United Kingdom placed sanctions on the sale of military equipment and demanded Indonesia allow an international force to restore peace. Habibie's acquiescence to international pressure to permit foreign troops into what many Indonesians viewed as their sovereign territory was viewed as a national humiliation and helped lead to his downfall.

In Indonesia's newly free political environment, secessionist, religious, and terrorist challenges erupted, challenging Indonesia's social stability and territorial integrity. Indonesia cracked down militarily, triggering strong Western criticism. A series of terrorist attacks, notably the 2002 Bali bombings perpetrated by *Jemaah Islamiyah*, a Southeast Asian terrorist group with links to al-Qaeda, triggered international demands that Indonesia crack down on terrorists.

To Indonesian officials, the contrast between the unwelcome Western pressure and China's quiet response was stark. As Sukma has argued, China pursued "charming diplomacy."[26] Since it came at a time when Indonesia felt betrayed by its traditional Western supporters, it welcomed China's support. When the devastating tsunami struck in 2004, Prime Minister Wen Jiabao attended the special ASEAN meeting of tsunami pledge donors and pledged $60 million of "unselfish" long-term reconstruction aid with "no added conditions."[27] Indonesia's foreign ministry spokesman stated that China's actions were an example of "a friend in need is a friend indeed."[28]

An integral part of Indonesia's transition to democracy was the expansion of civil and political rights to minority groups, including the ethnic Chinese. Habibie's successor, Abdurrahman Wahid, lifted the restrictions on Chinese language and declared *Imlek*, the Chinese New Year, a national holiday. Restrictions on travel to China were lifted, as were immigration restrictions on Chinese officials, thereby facilitating travel between the two countries. Today, Chinese is taught at Indonesia's major universities and over a hundred language centers including China-funded Confucius Institutes. Close to eleven thousand Indonesians are studying in China.[29] The granting of full civil and political rights to Indonesia's ethnic Chinese community marked a significant break with the past and removed an important barrier to better Sino-Indonesian relations.[30]

The inauguration of Susilo Bambang Yudhoyono as Indonesia's first directly elected president in 2004 ushered in a new era of Indonesian foreign policy. By then the economy had stabilized, social stability had improved, and Indonesia had begun implementing what would become one of the world's most successful counterterrorism policies. With its domestic house in order, the Yudhoyono administration embarked on a concerted effort to repair Indonesia's international reputation. Given the strong influence that domestic politics has traditionally had on its foreign policy, Yudhoyono has emphasized the country's domestic transformation as he has sought to raise Indonesia's international profile, stating:

> We are a proud nation who cherish our independence and national unity. We are the fourth most populous nation in the world. We are home to the world's largest Muslim population. We are the world's third largest democracy. We are also a country where democracy, Islam and modernity go hand-in-hand. We will stay our course with ASEAN as the cornerstone of our foreign policy. And our heart is always with the developing world, to which we belong. These are the things that define who we are and what we do in the community of nations.[31]

As Yudhoyono's comment illustrates, Indonesian officials have drawn on a mix of traditional power indicators, structural characteristics, domestic achievements, and its position in important global issue areas in their efforts to promote Indonesia's rise. In its quest for global influence, the Yudhoyono administration has sought to position Indonesia as a mediator and bridge-builder, classic middle power behavior.[32] It won election to the UN Security Council (UNSC) and Human Rights Council, secured membership in the G20, and is playing a more prominent role in the Organization of the Islamic Conference (OIC). Elevating Indonesia's international status requires enhancing its relations with major powers. After a decade of frayed relations, Indonesia and the United States signed a Comprehensive Partnership in 2010.[33] Indonesia has also sought to enhance its ties with India as well as with other rising powers such as Brazil and South Korea.

The 2005 Sino-Indonesian Strategic Partnership Agreement serves as a framework to expand bilateral political, military, economic, and social relations. Indonesia's entry into the 2005 partnership was motivated by a desire for "balance" in its relations with great powers and to signal to the United States that Indonesia had alternative sources of military equipment.[34] Since then, the leaders of the two countries have made many reciprocal visits, most recently Yudhoyono's March 2012 trip to Beijing, and signed numerous agreements to institutionalize the partnership. A memorandum of understanding (MOU) between the two foreign ministries calls for a range of activities including training of diplomats, policy planning, and the establishment of hotlines. [35] In 2010, the two sides ratified a five-year "plan of action" committing to a bilateral dialogue on technical cooperation and funding arrangements, among other issues. In 2012, the two sides signed six MOUs covering fields as diverse as maritime cooperation, counternarcotics, science and technology, food security, and statistical data exchanges.[36] Both sides have framed their cooperation as an integral part of the historic rise of two of Asia's giant powers. As Premier Wen Jiabao told his Jakarta audience in April 2011, the twenty-first century is "the Asian century," which is driven by a "great rejuvenation of the Oriental Civilization."[37]

Given Indonesia's long-standing perception of China as its key external threat, the development of Sino-Indonesian security relations has made significant progress. Since 2005, agreements have been reached on defense technology cooperation, defense consultation, and joint military training exercises. Indonesia has purchased Chinese antiship missiles, has discussed procuring C-907 missiles to arm its *Sukoi* jet fighters, and the Indonesian navy recently unveiled a locally produced guided-missile boat equipped with Chinese C-705 missiles.[38] In June 2011, the two sides held their first special forces joint exercise, "Sharp Knife," in Indonesia.[39]

Despite this progress, the relationship has not been trouble-free and there are reasons to question whether recent agreements will be fulfilled. In one of its first purchases of Chinese guns, shipments arrived with old, rusty rifles packed beneath the modern arms ordered, leading Indonesian officials to conclude China viewed Indonesia as a dumping ground.[40] Indonesia has not taken China up on its repeated offer of JF-17 jet fighters jointly produced with Pakistan. Indonesia is in the midst of a major military modernization but China ranks low on Indonesia's list of preferred arms suppliers. Furthermore, China's recent assertiveness in the South China Sea has raised perceptions of a Chinese threat, creating an obstacle to further strengthening of security ties.

Impact of China's Rise on Indonesia

Globally, China's rise has helped create a more multipolar system, a longstanding Indonesian aim. China shares many Indonesian goals such as a reduction of Western voting power in the IMF and World Bank, an aversion to sanctions, and a disinclination to vote for the use of military force to resolve domestic conflicts in the UN. Its strong commitment to the principle of sovereignty means that Indonesia will often call for a ceasefire but oppose proposals for military action such as the UN intervention in Libya, even as it offers to participate in UN Peacekeeping Operations (UNPKOs) once a ceasefire is reached.[41]

China's rise is unlikely to have an effect on Indonesia's participation in UNPKOs, which bolsters Indonesia's claim to be a constructive member of the international community as it seeks to elevate its global status. Indonesian peacekeepers have earned a reputation for professionalism and are particularly sought for deployments in Muslim countries. Today, Indonesians rank as the world's seventeenth-largest contributor to UNPKOs and Foreign Minister Marty Natalegawa has stated that Indonesia aims to become one of the top ten contributors to UNPKOs.[42] At the global level, a broad congruence between Sino-Indonesian interests combined with the presence of other powerful actors to dilute Chinese influences when interests do diverge means that China's rise has had a broadly positive effect on Indonesia.

The domestic impact of China's rise on Indonesia has been largely economic. China's demand for raw materials has created significant opportunities for Indonesia to export natural resources. In the wake of the 2010 implementation of the ASEAN-China Free Trade Area (ACFTA), a flood of low-cost Chinese consumer goods has led to the hollowing out of some domestic industries. The resulting pattern of trade in which Indonesia exports primary products and imports manufacturing goods has come under strong criticism as a "neocolonial" one, created perceptions of China as an exploitative economic actor, and led to the adoption of defensive measures.

As two large, export-oriented producers of low-tech manufactures, particularly shoes, textiles, and garments, China and Indonesia compete for foreign direct investment and foreign markets. In the aftermath of the 1997–98 economic crises, Indonesia experienced a displacement of foreign direct investment and exports to OECD countries in those sectors to China. Blame for Indonesia's slow recovery—it did not reach 1997 per capita income until 2004—was placed not on China but on political instability, terrorism, and an uncertain investment environment.[43] The Indonesian economy posted strong economic growth after 2006, and between then and 2011, total trade between Indonesia and China doubled, hitting $49.2 billion in 2011 when China become Indonesia's second-largest trading partner.[44] During the same period, however, Indonesia went from having a trade surplus of $1.1 billion to a deficit of $3.2 billion.[45] Five raw materials—coal, palm oil, gas, crude petroleum, and rubber—composed approximately 60 percent of Indonesian exports to China in 2011.[46] This "neocolonial" pattern has stoked Indonesian economic nationalism and created perceptions of China as an exploitative economic power. The influence of Indonesian civil society on policy toward China is strongest in foreign economic policy.

Indonesians place most of the blame for their declining terms of trade on the ASEAN-China Free Trade Area (ACFTA). ACFTA is based on the premise that greater economic ties could help the Southeast Asian countries benefit by becoming linked into Chinese production networks. However, as the January 2010 date to implement ACFTA drew near, many Indonesian manufacturers demanded a deferred start date. It has been argued that by 2010, the global economic slowdown had resulted in huge stockpiles of manufactured Chinese goods that were being dumped into countries like Indonesia while China erected barriers to its market.[47] Many Indonesians now view China as a predatory economic actor that seeks to keep others down and fails to abide by the rules of the game. According to a 2012 opinion poll, 49 percent of Indonesians believed that economic competition from China poses a "critical" threat to Indonesia while a further 33 percent believed China poses an "important" threat.[48]

In 2012, Indonesia adopted a series of protectionist trade and investment policies.[49] It would be going too far to attribute these policies solely to the rise of China, but they are all driven by a desire to overcome the status of primary commodity exporter that the expansion of Sino-Indonesian trade has made politically salient. Importantly, Indonesia announced that exports of raw materials in the mining sector would be banned beginning in 2014 in an effort to create downstream processing industries. Disincentives for export of raw materials in the plantation sector would also be raised. Mohamad S. Hidayat, Indonesia's minister of industry, acknowledged that Chinese businesspeople have opposed the bans but argued "this only benefits their side."[50]

China has also "become a major financier to mega projects in Indonesia, the role played by the World Bank, Asian Development Bank, Europe, Japan, and the United States in the past."[51] Chinese loans do not come with political conditions, but are often tied to the use of Chinese companies, which typically bring in Chinese workers. Chinese top the ranks of foreign workers in Indonesia.[52] This has generated concern in Indonesia, with its huge pool of unemployed and underemployed, and also triggered criticism that Indonesia fails to benefit from upgrading skills and technology.

China has attempted to alleviate Indonesian concerns by pledging to relocate manufacturing plans to Indonesia.[53] In 2011, China agreed to provide export credits and $9 billion in soft and commercial loans, primarily for infrastructure projects, but little has been realized to date.[54] In sum, China's economic rise may have benefited Indonesian consumers, but has negatively impacted the manufacturing sector and produced policies to halt or limit the export of raw materials that make up the bulk of Indonesian exports to China. Whether the two sides can devise creative ways to manage their economic relationship or whether it will continue to raise tensions remains to be seen.

Diplomatically, Indonesia uses ASEAN as a tool to pursue its key interest in Southeast Asia: promoting regional stability and ensuring that the region retains its autonomy from great power influence. In the broader Asia-Pacific, Indonesia seeks what Foreign Minister Marty Natalegawa calls a "dynamic equilibrium" or "state of affairs where there is not one preponderant country."[55] In pursuit of this, it has engaged in classic middle power initiatives, including through the Jakarta International Defense Dialogue among defense officials of the region, held annually since 2011. However, Jakarta's main strategy to ensure that regional architecture is built upon ASEAN, which gives its members agenda-setting influence and helps prevent their domination by larger powers. Indonesia's purported ability to lead ASEAN is an important source of its international influence.

China poses a threat to Indonesia's regional leadership. Normally institutions are created and run by powerful states. In the Asia-Pacific, long-standing tensions between Asia's larger countries such as China and Japan created an opening for ASEAN. Retaining ASEAN centrality will require balancing the interests of the larger powers, something possible if they value the status quo but not if they harbor revisionist ambitions.

To date, Indonesia and its ASEAN partners have rebuffed Chinese attempts to usurp ASEAN's formal agenda-setting role. ASEAN members rejected China's proposal to host the second East Asia Summit because they feared China would use the organization as a vehicle for Chinese leadership. All East Asia Summit meetings are hosted by the ASEAN chairman. China has long pushed for regional institution building to take place on a "pan-Asian" basis that would exclude the United States, Australia, and New Zealand while Indonesia advocates institution building along pan-Pacific lines that included them. China objected behind the scenes to the expansion of the East Asia Summit to include the United States and Russia, but under Indonesia's ASEAN chairmanship both became members in 2011.

The ASEAN chairmanship rotates annually, but outsiders, particularly the United States, expect Indonesia to ensure that the organization balances the competing pressures upon it. This is particularly true when small countries like Cambodia with weak institutions, limited diplomatic capacity, and close ties to China chair the organization. At the July 2012 ASEAN meeting, however, China's willingness to use its influence over Cambodia to intervene directly in ASEAN affairs over the South China Sea issue illustrated that it was unwilling to abide by regional norms when Beijing believed key interests were at stake. China's intervention caused ASEAN to fail to issue a chairman's statement for the first time in its forty-five-year history, something Indonesian Foreign Minister Marty Natalegawa called "utterly irresponsible."[56] Virtually all aspects of China's threat to Indonesia—control over its waterways and exclusive economic zones (EEZs), the sanctity of international law, ASEAN cohesion, and the centrality of ASEAN in broader regional institutions—are challenged on the South China Sea issue.

China poses its greatest challenge to Indonesia in the area of maritime security. An archipelagic state sitting astride vital sea lanes of communication (SLOCs) connecting the Pacific and Indian Oceans, protecting the sovereignty of its waters is critical to Indonesian national defense. In contrast, China, the United States, and other actors have a strategic interest in ensuring freedom of navigation through and safety of these SLOCs, particularly the Malacca Strait. Over 60 percent of Chinese oil imports pass through the Malacca or Lombok/Makassar Strait, which cuts through the Indonesian archipelago. China refers to its vulnerability to a closure of the strait as its "Malacca Dilemma."[57] The Malacca Strait, however, is not an international waterway. Sovereignty is shared by the littoral states of Indonesia, Malaysia, and Singapore. Indonesia has rejected proposals from China as well as the United States and Japan for a role in patrolling it, contending that foreign operations in Indonesia's territorial waters are challenges to its sovereignty.[58]

Beyond the vital sea lanes, Indonesia is increasingly concerned about foreign encroachment in its waters, the potential for which its 2008 Defense White Paper calls "very high."[59] First, Indonesia is concerned about its waterways serving as conduits for illicit activities such as drug and people trafficking. Second, Indonesia is concerned about illegal fishing by foreign parties, which costs Indonesia $3 billion annually.[60] In 2009, Indonesia's detention of seventy-five Chinese fishermen off the Natuna Islands triggered such an angry response from China that Indonesia acquiesced to Chinese pressure and sent the majority of the fishermen home.[61] Third, Indonesia is concerned about overlapping territorial claims to islands and EEZs.

China's development of a blue-water navy and its designation of virtually the entire South China Sea as a "core" interest directly threaten Indonesia. China does not claim sovereignty over any Indonesian islands, but does claim waters in Indonesia's Natuna Islands EEZ, an area rich in carbon resources. In July 2010, Indonesia protested China's claim to the UN, contending that it "clearly lacks any international legal basis."[62] As an archipelagic state lacking the naval capacity to protect itself, Indonesia has a strong interest in ensuring that major naval powers abide by UNCLOS.[63]

China's increasingly assertive behavior—including harassment of the USS *Impeccable*, detention of Japanese boats in the disputed Senkaku Islands, the cutting of survey cables of Vietnamese exploration ships, and the 2012 military confrontation with the Philippines over Scarborough Shoal—appears to indicate a policy of deterrence and denial through the South China Sea.[64] Since threats are a function of both capacity and intentions, China's recent actions have undermined its "peaceful rise" rhetoric and convinced many Indonesians that China is in fact a threat. According to a 2012 opinion poll, 56 percent of Indonesians say it is likely that China will become a military threat to Indonesia in the next twenty years.[65]

Indonesia has responded to China's maritime provocations by raising them in regional organizations where Jakarta can harness the influence of other actors behind its goals. US participation in ASEAN-centered organizations is a prerequisite for Indonesian attempts to respond to China's rise by multilateral diplomatic balancing. Indonesia, therefore, has sought to ensure that the United States remains engaged in the region and supports ASEAN-led institutions. The United States shares Indonesia's goal of promoting regional stability but has not always been an enthusiastic supporter of ASEAN-centric institutions. Contending that ASEAN's consensus decision-making privileges process over substance, the US secretary of state skipped a number of ASEAN meetings during the Bush administration. Indonesia interpreted this absence as a sign that ASEAN might have to meet the China challenge without the United States as a counterweight. Indonesia therefore welcomed the Obama administration's attention to Southeast Asia. Hillary Clinton became the first secretary of state to visit the ASEAN secretariat, attended all ASEAN meetings, and called ASEAN "a fulcrum of the region's emerging regional architecture."[66] The United States signed the Treaty of Amity and Cooperation in 2009 and joined the East Asia Summit in November 2011. Indonesia is aware that the United States' newfound appreciation of ASEAN is driven largely by its concern with China. Sino-American rivalry enhances ASEAN's regional status, but risks ASEAN becoming a forum for Sino-American competition, something Indonesia wants to avoid.

Middle Power Diplomacy in the Face of Great Power Competition

Sino-American confrontation is precisely what happened at the 2010 ASEAN Regional Forum (ARF) meeting, when Vietnam used its position as

ASEAN chair to confront China. China lobbied ASEAN not to raise the South China Sea issue, but twelve of the twenty-seven delegations did, including Indonesia and the United States.[67] Secretary Clinton used the occasion to state that the United States had a "national interest in freedom of navigation, open access to Asia's maritime commons, and respect for international law in the South China Sea."[68] Clinton also stated that while the United States did not take sides, it wanted to see the disputes resolved peacefully, through a collaborative process in accordance with UNCLOS, and offered to facilitate negotiations.[69] Clinton's statement supported Indonesia's position, but challenged China's long-standing policy that the South China Sea disputes should be resolved bilaterally. Chinese foreign minister Yang Yiechi, blindsided by the coordination between the United States and ASEAN, responded furiously to the "internationalization" of the issue.

As the 2011 ASEAN chair, a key Indonesian goal was to produce guidelines to transform ASEAN's nonbinding 2002 Declaration on the Conduct of Parties in the South China Sea (DOC) into a legally binding code of conduct, something that China agreed to begin in 2013. Indonesia, unlike fellow ASEAN members Vietnam, Malaysia, Brunei, and the Philippines, has no territorial claims to the South China Sea, which Jakarta has traditionally believed positions it as an independent mediator. While it is true that Indonesia does not claim islands in the South China Sea, Jakarta's decision to lodge a protest against China's 2009 filing of its "9-dotted line" map with the UN and its calls for resolution of the dispute according to UNCLOS clearly conflict with China's positions.

In July 2011, ASEAN and China did agree on a set of guidelines for the DOC, but they studiously avoided the issue of sovereignty.[70] Hopes that the guidelines would include concrete proposals to reduce the potential for clashes, such as advance notification of military exercises and rules of conduct for parties on the high seas, were disappointed. Chinese officials called the guidelines a "milestone."[71] Secretary Clinton called them an "important first step" but also called for follow-up negotiations between ASEAN and China while reiterating that "the rest of the world needs to weigh in" because "all of us" have a stake in ensuring that the conflicts do not escalate.[72]

Indonesia must seek to balance not only the interests of China and the United States but also those of its fellow ASEAN members. Vietnam and the Philippines have borne the brunt of recent Chinese naval assertiveness. They have called for greater ASEAN backing and also sought outside support, particularly from the United States. In November 2011, Secretary Clinton made a strong gesture of US support for the Philippines by referring to the disputed waters as the "West Philippine Sea" during a speech made from the deck of an American warship in Manila Bay.[73] China reacted strongly to the speech, illustrating that the challenges Indonesia faces in maintaining ASEAN cohesion and balancing the interests of China and the United States are intricately intertwined.

Chinese analysts are aware of the dilemma facing Indonesia and have been explicit in laying out the costs to Indonesia of contravening China. In one editorial titled "On the South China Sea, an ASEAN United Front Won't Help Anyone, Especially Indonesia," the consequences of advocating anything other than China's current policy of "setting aside disputes and pursuing joint development" are enumerated.[74] First, China will weaken its support for ASEAN as an organization. Second, it would challenge ASEAN centrality in regional organizations because "China is becoming the focal point of regional integration." Third, China would pursue a subregional approach to economic integration, rather than an ASEAN-centered one. Chinese analysts argue that the Greater Mekong Subregion is geographically and economically more integrated than ASEAN. Given China's strong influence in tiny Laos and Cambodia, such a threat means that ASEAN's long-standing geographic divisions between mainland and island Southeast Asia could be reinforced geostrategically. Any threat to ASEAN cohesion, a perquisite for ASEAN centrality in regional architecture, threatens a key aspect of Indonesia's regional leadership.

Indonesia's task of leading ASEAN from behind when the ASEAN chairman is closely linked to China and China chooses to play hardball was illustrated in 2012. Cambodia failed to include the South China Sea dispute on its list of key agenda items for its chairmanship, in contrast to the 2011 and 2010 chairs. A visit by Chinese president Hu Jintao just ahead of the April 2012 ASEAN Summit triggered speculation that China was pressuring Cambodia to promote its interests. Cambodian prime minister Hun Sen denied such allegations, but Cambodia's proposal that China be included in the drafting of procedures to implement the DOC suggests otherwise. ASEAN's traditional position is that its members should agree on a policy draft first, then share it with outsiders. Any drafting role for China is starkly opposed by many ASEAN members and triggered what Philippines foreign secretary Albert del Rosario called a "big disagreement" at the summit.[75]

China's willingness to intervene in ASEAN affairs through Cambodia was clearly illustrated at the July 2012 ASEAN meetings in Phnom Penh. At issue was whether and how to mention conflicts in the South China Sea, particularly a tense 2012 military standoff between China and the Philippines over Scarborough Shoal.[76] Despite the desire of other ASEAN members to include a reference to the South China Sea, Cambodia—reportedly after conferring with Chinese officials—refused to do so and announced that

ASEAN would not issue a joint statement for the first time in forty-five years. China's actions contravene ASEAN's norm of noninterference in the organization's affairs and illustrate that ASEAN efforts to socialize China had failed.

Recognizing China's threat to ASEAN cohesion and its own regional leadership, Natalegawa embarked on a round of shuttle diplomacy to ASEAN capitals to secure agreement on six points that would be issued in place of the final statement. The points included a desire to observe the Declaration on Conduct of Parties in the South China Sea and guidelines for its implementation; work toward an early adoption of a code of conduct; exercise self-restraint and avoid using force; and uphold the peaceful settlement of disputes in keeping with universally recognized principles of international law, including UNCLOS.

Natalegawa's diplomatic efforts have papered over ASEAN's differences but not resolved them. Moreover, Indonesia's forging of an ASEAN agreement on the six principles does not appear to be having the desired middle power effect of inducing greater Chinese concern for ASEAN's position. Instead, on July 20, 2012, the same day that Natalegawa announced the agreement, China announced that its Central Military Commission has authorized the People's Liberation Army to form a Sansha garrison command over the Paracel and Spratly Islands and that the new command's duties would include "defense mobilization" and carrying out military activities.[77]

Conclusion

In response to the four key questions posed by this book, this chapter concludes that (1) Indonesia is a complete middle power by virtue of its robust middle power capabilities and behavior as well as a self-identity as a critical or above-average middle power; (2) China's rise has significantly challenged Indonesian interests in the areas of economic development, regional leadership, and maritime security; (3) Indonesia's response to China's rise reflects classic middle power attempts to protect national interests and defuse great power conflicts through the use of multilateralism and an emphasis on norm-creation; (4) Indonesia played a positive role by encouraging China's post-1977 charm offensive and preventing Beijing from usurping ASEAN in regional diplomacy, while also encouraging a nonzero sum view of the Sino-US rivalry in Southeast Asia.

Indonesia's policy toward China has shifted in response to the changing impact of China's rise on Indonesia. In the early 1990s, Indonesia engaged China bilaterally to secure economic benefits and multilaterally to socialize

China into ASEAN norms. In the mid-1990s, Indonesia responded to China's maritime provocations by mounting a massive military exercise and balancing diplomatically through ASEAN. Following the financial crisis, Indonesia sought China's support and viewed Beijing as a counterweight to US hegemony. Since then, China's South China Sea claims, its willingness to pursue them forcefully, and to intervene directly in ASEAN threaten Indonesia.

China's rise has been a double-edged sword for Indonesia in Asia. By triggering concerns in Washington, Tokyo, Canberra, and elsewhere, China's rise has helped raise Indonesia's stature. At the same time, it has made mediating the interests of the great powers increasingly difficult. Great power rivalry creates space for middle powers. As Gilley and O'Neil note in chapter 1 about theories linking the structure of the international system to middle power influence, there is a tipping point in US-China rivalry beyond which middle power influence declines as great powers pressure others to choose sides.

Indonesian foreign policy has long epitomized the behavioral dimensions of middle power diplomacy, such as peace initiatives, conflict mediation, support for international institutions, rule building, and leadership in regional institutions. As Indonesia promotes its own rise, it has done so in classic middle power fashion, emphasizing soft power and seeking to promote a dynamic equilibrium between great powers in the Asia Pacific region. This chapter has identified at least two ways that Indonesia has reshaped China's rise: encouraging China's post-1997 "charm offensive" in Southeast Asia, and preventing China from usurping the role of ASEAN in East Asian affairs.

Nevertheless, there is a sense that Indonesia should not be content to be a middle power because doing so means Indonesia "relegates itself to inferiority" and its behavior would "constitute subservience to the politics of great powers."[78] There is a strong tension, therefore, between Indonesia's middle power behavior and the desire for recognition as an important international actor that many Indonesians believe their country's size justifies.

Indonesian leaders clearly believe middle powers *should* have an effect on great powers. In his 2012 speech to the Shangri-La Security Dialogue, President Yudhoyono stated that "the relations of major powers are not entirely up to them." Instead, "middle and small powers can help lock these powers into a durable [regional] architecture through a variety of instruments."[79] However, Rizal Sukma, one of Indonesia's most prominent strategic thinkers, argues that Indonesia needs to stop believing that ASEAN-led multilateral processes, based as they are on soft power, are sufficient to sustain regional order.[80] Sukma argues that ASEAN can function as a source of regional order only when a stable balance of power exists. China's rise has upset the balance of power. If Indonesia hopes to exert a "middle power influence" on China's rise, it will depend on the simultaneous role of the United States in providing the stable balance of power in the region.

Notes

1. Michael Taylor, "World Bank Sees Indonesia Growth at 6.1 Percent in 2012," *Reuters*, October 14, 2012.

2. "The Archipelego Economy: Unleashing Indonesia's Economic Potential," McKinsey Global Institute, September 2012, www.mckinsey.com/insights/mgi/research/asia/the_archipelago_economy.

3. Zachary Abuza, "Indonesian Counter-Terrorism: The Great Leap Forward," *Terrorism Monitor* 8, no. 2 (2010): 6–8.

4. Rizal Sukma, "Indonesia's Security Outlook, Defense Policy and Regional Cooperation," in *Asia Pacific Countries' Security Outlook and Its Implications for the Defense Sector*, ed. Eiichi Katahara (Tokyo: National Institute of Defense Studies, 2011), 3–18, 12.

5. Ibid., 20.

6. Ibid.,13.

7. Arientha Primanita, "Indonesia Pledges to Raise Defense Spending," *Jakarta Globe*, October 6, 2011.

8. The classic work on Indonesia's worldview is Franklin Weinstein, *Indonesian Foreign Policy and the Dilemma of Dependence: From Sukarno to Suharto* (Ithaca, NY: Cornell University Press, 1976).

9. Paige Johnson Tan, "Navigating a Turbulent Ocean: Indonesia's Worldview and Foreign Policy," *Asian Perspective* 31, no. 3 (2007): 147–81.

10. "Preamble to the 1945 Constitution," in *Indonesian Political Thinking, 1945–1965*, 49–50, eds. Herbert Feith and Lance Castles (Jakarta: Equinox, 2007).

11. Michael Leifer,"Indonesia's Encounters with China and the Dilemmas of Engagement," in *Engaging China: The Management of an Emerging Power*, eds. Alastair Iain Johnston and Robert S. Ross (New York: Routledge, 1999), 87–108, 91.

12. Ibid., 93.

13. For a discussion of the triple threat, see Rizal Sukma, *Indonesia and China* (New York: Routledge, 1999), 47–53.

14. Singapore, with a Chinese-majority population, was well aware that Indonesia would view its establishment of diplomatic ties with China as a potential source of subversion. It therefore did not establish relations with China until after Indonesia did so.

15. Weinstein, *Indonesian Foreign Policy and the Dilemma of Dependence.*

16. John Bresnan, *Managing Indonesia* (New York: Columbia University Press, 2003).

17. Rizal Sukma, "Indonesia's Response to the Rise of China: Growing Comfort Amid Uncertainties," in *The Rise of China: Responses from Southeast Asia and Japan*, 139–56, 142, ed. Jun Tsunekawa (Tokyo: National Institute for Defense Studies, 2004).

18. Interview with ASEAN official present at the Hangzhou meeting, who also states that it is difficult to imagine the blunt language used being used now, in part due to China's rising power and in part due to the admission of Laos, Cambodia, and Burma into ASEAN since then.

19. Ian Storey, "Indonesia's China Policy in the New Order and Beyond: Problems and Prospects," *Contemporary Southeast Asia* 22, no. 1 (2000): 145–74, 161.

20. Rizal Sukma, "Indonesia-China Relations: The Politics of Reengagement," *Asian Survey* 49, no. 4 (2009): 591–608.

21. Thomas Christensen, "Fostering Stability or Creating a Monster? The Rise of China and US Policy toward East Asia," *International Security* 31, no. 1 (2006): 81–126.

22. Michael A. Glosny, "Heading toward a Win-Win Future? Recent Developments in China's Policy toward Southeast Asia," *Asian Security* 2, no. 1 (2006): 24–57, 27.

23. Storey, "Indonesia's China Policy," 156.

24. Sukma, "Indonesia's Response to the Rise of China," 144.

25. Storey, "Indonesia's China Policy."

26. Sukma, "Indonesia's Response to the Rise of China," 152.

27. Ibid., 151.

28. Ibid.

29. Aulia R. Sungkar, "Chinese Challenge: More Indonesians Learning Mandarin," *Jakarta Globe*, May 2, 2012.

30. For a discussion of Indonesian perceptions of China, see Daniel Novotny, *Torn between America and China: Elite Perceptions and Indonesian Foreign Policy* (Singapore: ISEAS, 2010).

31. Susilo Bambang Yudhoyono, speech before the Indonesian Council on World Affairs, May 19, 2005, www.presidenri.go.id/index.php/pidato/2005/05/19/332.html.

32. Evan Laksmana, "Indonesia's Rising Regional and Global Profile: Does Size Really Matter?" *Contemporary Southeast Asia* 33, no. 2 (2011): 157–82.

33. Ann Marie Murphy, "US Rapprochement with Indonesia: From Problem State to Partner," *Contemporary Southeast Asia* 32, no. 3 (2010): 362–87.

34. Author's interview with Defense Minister Juwono Sudarsono, Jakarta, Indonesia, January 7, 2006.

35. Gretta Nabbs-Keller, "Growing Convergence, Greater Consequence: The Strategic Implications of Closer Indonesia-China Relations," *Security Challenges* 7, no. 3 (2011): 23–42, 30.

36. Prashnath Parameswaran, "The Limits to Sino-Indonesian Relations," *China Brief* 12, no. 8 (2012): 2–5, 3.

37. "Strengthen Good-Neighbourly Relations and Deepen Mutually Beneficial Cooperation: Speech by Premier Wen Jiabao at Balai Kartini," Xinhua News Agency, April 30, 2011.

38. Parameswaran, "The Limits to Sino-Indonesian Relations," 4.

39. Yeyen Rosiyani, "Another Indonesia-China Cooperation . . . now in Defense," *Republika*, June 8, 2012.

40. Author's interview with senior Ministry of Defense official, Jakarta, January 7, 2008.

41. "Turkey, Indonesia Call for a Ceasefire in Lybia," *Jakarta Globe*, April 5, 2011.

42. Laksmana, "Indonesia's Rising Regional and Global Profile," 171.

43. Anne Booth, "China's Economic Relations with Indonesia: Threats and Opportunities," working paper, revised October 2011, 5.

44. Parameswaran, "The Limits to Sino-Indonesian Relations," 3.

45. Linda Yulisman, "Indonesia Is More Dependent on Chinese Goods," *Jakarta Post*, February 16, 2012.

46. Parameswaran, "The Limits to Sino-Indonesian Relations," 4.

47. Booth, "China's Economic Relations with Indonesia," 7.

48. Fergus Hanson, "Shattering Stereotypes: Public Opinion and Foreign Policy," Lowy Institute Indonesia Poll (2012), 31, www.lowyinstitute.org/files/lowy_indonesia_poll_2012.pdf.

49. Titik Anas, "Indonesia's New Protectionist Trade Policies: A Blast from the Past," *East Asia Forum*, June 18, 2012, www.eastasiaforum.org/2012/06/18/indonesias-new-protectionist-trade-policies-a-blast-from-the-past/.

50. Bagus Saragih, "Indonesia and China Agree to Sort Out Trade Imbalances," *Jakarta Post*, April 9, 2012.

51. "60 Years of Indonesia-China Relations," *Jakarta Post*, April 13, 2010.

52. "China Dominates Foreign Workers in Indonesia," *Tempo Interactive*, March 7, 2012, www.tempointeractive.com/hg/nasional/2012/03/07/brk,20120307-388615,uk.html.

53. Rangga D. Fadillah, "China Affirms Plans to Relocate Factories to Indonesia," *Jakarta Post*, August 13, 2011.

54. Saragih, "Indonesia and China Agree to Sort Out Trade Imbalances."

55. A conversation with Marty Natalegawa, minister of foreign affairs, Republic of Indonesia, Council on Foreign Relations, New York, September 20, 2010, www.cfr.org/indonesia/conversation-marty-natalegawa-minister-foreign-affairs-republic-indonesia/p22984.

56. Sebastian Strangio, "Cambodia as Divide and Rule Pawn," *Asia Times* online, July 18, 2012, www.atimes.com/atimes/Southeast_Asia/NG18Ae03.html.

57. Ian Storey, "China's Malacca Dilemma," *China Brief*, vol. 6, issue 8 (2006): 5–8.

58. Admiral Bernard Kent Sondakh, "National Sovereignty and Security in the Strait of Malacca," presented at a conference at the Maritime Institute of Malaysia, October 11–14, 2004, 3, emphasis in the original, www.mima.gov.my/mima/htmls/conferences/som04/papers/sondakh.pdf.

59. Sukma, "Indonesia's Security Outlook," 7–8.

60. Ibid., 6.

61. Keith Loveard, "The Thinker: China's Tough Talk," *Jakarta Globe*, August 26, 2009.

62. "Indonesia and the South China Sea: Indonesia Wades In," *Economist*, August 2, 2010.

63. The United States has not ratified UNCLOS, but US policy is to conform to it. In contrast, China has ratified UNCLOS, with reservations, but its policies contravene it.

64. See Carlye Thayer, "The United States and Chinese Assertiveness in the South China Sea," *Security Challenges* 6, no. 2 (2010): 69–84.

65. Hanson, "Shattering Stereotypes," 1.

66. Secretary of State Hillary Clinton, "America's Engagement in the Asia–Pacific," address at Kahala Hotel, Honolulu, HI, October 28, 2010, www.state.gov/secretary/rm/2010/10/150141.htm.

67. Donald Emmerson, "China's Frown Diplomacy," *Asia Times*, October 5, 2010, www.atimes.com/atimes/China/LJ05Ad02.html.

68. Ibid.

69. Daniel Tan Kate and Nicole Gaouette, "Clinton Signals US Role in China Territorial Dispute after ASEAN Talks," *Bloomberg News*, July 23, 2010, www.bloomberg.com/news/2010-07-23/u-s-says-settling-south-china-sea-disputes-leading-diplomatic-priority-.html.

70. Walter Lohman, "The US Cannot Rely on ASEAN in the South China Sea," August 5, 2011, www.heritage.org/Research/Reports/2011/08/ASEAN-South-China-Sea-Dispute-and-US-Policy-on-East-Asia#_ftn2.

71. Jian Junbo, "China Averts Collision in South China Sea," *Asia Times*, July 29, 2011, www.atimes.com/atimes/China/MG29Ad01.html.

72. Brian McCarten, "Shallow Agreement on the South China Sea," *Asia Times*, July 30, 2011, www.atimes.com/atimes/Southeast_Asia/MG30Ae03.html.

73. Floyd Haley, "Clinton Reaffirms Military Ties with the Philippines," *New York Times*, November 11, 2011.

74. Xunpeng Shi, "On the South China Sea, an ASEAN United Front Won't Help Anyone, Especially Indonesia," *Jakarta Post*, June 13, 2012.

75. "Cambodia Denies ASEAN Rift over Sea Disputes with China," *Jakarta Globe*, April 4, 2012.

76. Donald Emmerson, "Indonesia Saves ASEAN's Face," *Asia Times*, July 24, 2012.

77. Ibid.

78. See Santo Darmosumrarto, "Indonesia: A New 'Middle Power,'" *Jakarta Post*, October 30, 2009. Over a two-week period in January 2012, the author conducted approximately thirty-five interviews with policymakers and policy analysts, including Santo. Virtually all agreed Indonesian foreign policy behavior was that of a middle power, but also underscored that the Sukarno-era ambition for global leadership remained strong.

79. Bagus T. Saragih, "Yudhoyono Says Region's Stability Not Up to US, China," *Jakarta Post*, June 6, 2012.

80. Sukma's argument was made long ago by his mentor, Michael Leifer, in "The ASEAN Regional Forum: Extending ASEAN's Model of Regional Security," Adelphi Papers No. 302, International Institute for Strategic Studies, 1996.

CHAPTER 8

Australia

A Traditional Middle Power Faces the Asian Century

Thomas S. Wilkins

Introduction

AUSTRALIA, along with Canada, is invariably cited as the archetype of a "traditional middle power," in contradistinction to the "emerging middle powers" examined elsewhere in this book. However, as Bruce Gilley shows in chapter 3, middle power research in China pays close attention to Australia since it seems to be a "traditional" middle power that has learned to act like an "emerging" middle power. Canberra has been firmly wedded to playing such a middle power role ever since the then minister for external affairs, H. V. Evatt, advocated it in the UN at the end of the Second World War. As the 2012 *Australia in the Asian Century* White Paper attests: "Australia's long-standing commitment to active middle power diplomacy, with its focus on practical problem solving, effective implementation and building coalitions with others, will continue to drive our approach."[1] Indeed, in Carl Ungerer's view, "the middle power concept is perhaps the closest that Australia has ever come to articulating a self-conscious theory of foreign policy."[2] Therefore, this chapter will demonstrate how Australia has exemplified, and continues to exemplify, the capabilities and behavior that are generally understood to encapsulate the concept of a middle power.

At the same time, the context within which traditional middle powers arose has changed dramatically since the early Cold War period. At the heart of systemic change, the rise of China creates the prospect of a new and unfamiliar environment, and new dilemmas for these middle powers, since their original middle power modus operandi was predicated upon reinforcing American hegemonic world order, and this order is progressively dissolving. As former Prime Minister Julia Gillard declared: "I summarise our new strategic environment as simply as this. Australia hasn't been here before."[3] This raises the question of whether a traditional middle power like Australia will cope with the challenges triggered by China's rise in a way distinct to the "new" or "emerging" middle powers. As will be clear from the following analysis, Australia has taken a proactive role in what it dubs the "Asian century."[4] At the time of writing, Canberra had just signed a strategic partnership with Beijing. This "provides Australia with organized direct access to the Chinese leadership at a time when the rest of the world is clamoring for their attention."[5] As such, it accentuates Australia's role in the region, and symbolizes Canberra's strategy of *economic* alignment with the People's Republic of China, while maintaining *strategic* alignment with the United States. Also, noteworthy from the *Australia in the Asian Century* White Paper is the recognition that India will also become a major focus of Australian diplomacy, indicating that the country is not preoccupied solely with China. In sum, the Australian government recognizes that "the economic growth and broader international interests of Asia's large powers, especially China and India, are having an impact on the established strategic order."[6]

This chapter thus seeks to examine Australia's exemplary credentials as a "traditional" middle power, and considers how it can navigate the various challenges and opportunities raised by the rise of China in a shifting global and regional security environment, conceived of broadly as the "Asian century." Indeed, it will demonstrate how the notion of claiming such a middle power role is fundamental to Australia's identity, and how Australian governments consciously (or unconsciously) have shaped national policy in accord with its assumptions and principles. Though unsuccessful attempts have been made in the past to rebrand the country as a "pivotal power" or a "considerable nation," these did not successfully dislodge "middle power" as the accepted descriptor.[7]

Based upon the middle power theory elucidated earlier in this book, this chapter characterizes the *capabilities* and *behavior* of Australia in comparison to the "ideal type" of a middle power.[8] Here, the capabilities aspects are termed "middlepowerhood," while the behavioral aspects are dubbed "middlepowermanship."[9] The main body of this chapter analyzes Australia's middle power role and its responses to the rise of China, using both perspectives in turn. The lines between the capabilities and behavioral aspects are not as clear cut in practice as they are in theory. Rather, they represent two sides of the same coin for Australia, and mutually reinforce its claim to be a middle power. The argument therefore proceeds in two parts, which address the ideal type of middle power indicated in the introduction, by looking initially at the middlepowerhood credentials of Australia (capabilities) and how it has exercised them, followed by the practice of middlepowerhood (behavior) as a diplomatic style, and the successes and failures this has entailed. Within this bifurcated framework the discussion considers the ways in which China's rise has affected the domestic, regional, and global environment for Australia, and its responses to these challenges. Also considered is the degree to which Australia has exerted a middle power effect on Beijing's calculations.

As a relevant aside, it has been suggested that Labor governments have been more likely to explicitly embrace middlepowermanship in their rhetoric.[10] This is certainly accurate with regard to the former Labor administration, particularly under former prime minister and foreign minister Kevin Rudd, as we shall see below. On the other hand, while explicitly eschewing the label of "middle power," Liberal governments have been equally attached to maintaining the capabilities aspects of middlepowerhood, and exercising them accordingly, as evidenced by former prime minister John Howard's efforts to support the United States in its war on terror, and act as "deputy sheriff" in the South Pacific. Australia's middle power role therefore enjoys enduring bipartisan support, though the accent may be more on capabilities on the Liberal front, and self-styled "creative middle power" diplomacy on the Labor front. Notwithstanding, the Rudd government's defense policy did not hesitate to flex the muscles of Australia's middlepowerhood, while Howard talked of "bridging" between East and West—a classic element of middlepowermanship.

Middlepowerhood (Capabilities)

Canberra (and Beijing) are acutely aware that in the arena of international politics, capabilities matter. Australia's claim to middlepowerhood is predicated on its possession and projection of material capabilities to achieve its foreign policy goals. These determine its position in the international (and regional) hierarchy of powers. From this angle, it is the *structure* of the system and its resultant power balances that will condition Australia's foreign and security policies, including its responses to the regional power transition. This reflects the realist axiom that "the capacity to enhance security, and effect change on the global or regional stage, will depend on the application of various kinds of power resources."[11] In the Sinic perspective of international and regional order, states can be measured in standing and importance on the basis of their national power. The Chinese have developed a set of complex equations to measure what they dub Comprehensive National Power. The Chinese Academy of Social Sciences and the Academy of Military Science rank Australia twelfth and tenth, respectively, on a global scale.[12] But these rankings need elaboration to be meaningful and to quantify

Australia's undoubted credentials as a middle power, in accord with the metrics stipulated earlier in this book.

Australia is the sixth-largest country in the world with vast strategic depth and the protection of 360-degree maritime borders and exclusive economic zones representing the world's third-largest marine territory.[13] Added to this, Canberra also claims a vast swath of Antarctica as Australian Antarctic Territory (amounting to 5.9 million square kilometers).[14] But the country itself is thinly populated with approximately 21.5 million people (only the fifty-fourth largest in the world).[15] Its GDP is approximately US$1.24 trillion, placing it thirteenth in the world, with an average GDP per capita of $58,000, among the highest in the world.[16] Its key economic strength lies in its natural resource abundance, though it has advanced technology, manufacturing, and service industries—albeit on a medium scale. Australia's role as a resource supplier is crucial to China's continued economic growth and its educational sector is significant in training the Chinese population. It is a highly developed society, ranking second in the UN's Human Development Index (HDI), and its political stability adds further to its high level of "state capacity."[17] Australia's defense budget for 2010 was approximately US$23.2 billion (1.9 percent of GDP), making it the world's fourteenth-largest military spender.[18] It has a modest defense-industrial complex, and the putative ability to develop a nuclear weapons program, but has chosen not to pursue this option.[19]

As argued earlier in this book, such material capabilities place Australia not so much in the "middle" of the international hierarchy of two hundred states, but more accurately position it near the top of the international hierarchy, close to the world's "top 10" great powers. This recognition was behind efforts to rebrand the country as a "pivotal power" under former foreign minister Alexander Downer. According to our definitions, Australia unquestionably qualifies as a middle power.

Moreover, Robert Ayson argues, the 2009 Defense White Paper *Defending Australia in the Asia Pacific Century: Force 2030* is a clear statement of intent that Australia wishes to be taken seriously as a major military actor.[20] It enunciates a strategy of "self-reliance," giving Australia the independent military capabilities needed to resist a direct attack. But the White Paper also illustrates how Australian statecraft, and the capabilities that underwrite it, are integral to its middlepowerhood. First, military power gives Australia a credible profile in the regional security order (described below). It also reaffirms Australia's position in such a regional order by virtue of its power capabilities in relation to others, in a region that is becoming ever-more militarized.[21] Canberra recognizes the currency of a power-political order, noting the need to "back up strategic influence with military power."[22] Second, the White Paper affirms "our responsibility as a capable middle power that is able to contribute to global and regional security, including by way of military means."[23] It also provides the instruments Canberra requires to combat a spectrum of traditional and nontraditional security threats from protection of sea lanes of communication (SLOCs) to nonproliferation, disaster relief, and fighting a major war. Last, such robust capabilities are required to "make tailored contributions to military coalitions."[24] This is manifested through its "followership" of the US alliance, or its independent creation of "minicoalitions" itself when necessary—as it has done, for example, through the International Force East Timor, INTERFET, and the Regional Assistance Mission Solomon Islands, RAMSI.

As the middle power literature predicts, Australia is acutely sensitive to the structural configuration of the international system, and its resultant global and regional security order.[25] James Manicom and Andrew O'Neil note that "as a secondary power in the international system, Australia will remain vulnerable to the changing fortunes of the great powers."[26] It is the shifting balance of power, caused by China's rise, particularly in the Asia-Pacific region, that will significantly impact on Australia's strategic choices.[27] From this perspective, Malcolm Cook et al. assert that "diplomatic 'architecture' matters, but is not of itself a solution: power will shape order and institutions will reflect that order."[28] The rise of China and the resultant power transition have consequentially generated heated debates among Australian strategic analysts.[29] Simply put, Canberra's White Paper assessment states: "The United States will remain the most powerful and influential strategic actor over the period to 2030—politically, economically, and militarily. Its strategic primacy will assist in the maintenance of a stable global strategic environment."[30] However, implicit in this prognostication is that the inexorable rise of China will displace Washington as the preeminent power in the region, and perhaps globally, within a generation. This is already starkly apparent on the economic plane, where China accounts for 18 percent of Australia's trade, as compared with 9 percent for the United States (and 13 percent for Japan).[31] This prominence is reflected in a recent breakthrough deal making the renminbi directly convertible to the Australian dollar, thus further facilitating trading opportunities.[32] However, despite this major step forward, there has been little progress on the desired free-trade agreement negotiations, which began eight years ago.

This "power shift," as analysts have characterized it, if continued, will become manifest on the strategic plane in the future.[33] Indeed, the White Paper notes that "a major power of China's stature can be expected to develop a globally significant military capability. . . . The pace, scope and structure of China's military modernization have the potential to give its neighbors cause for concern if not carefully explained."[34] This will create difficult dilemmas for a middle power like Australia as it seeks to maintain good (strategic) relations with Washington as well as good (economic) relations with Beijing. This is because "China and the United States each seek to promote a different regional order," based upon their own conflicting national values and interests.[35] A future *Pax Sinica* is likely to differ markedly from the present American liberal democratic trading order, as David Kang has recounted.[36] Stuart Harris attests that "the way the regional order has changed since the end of the Cold War, together with the rise of China, does pose challenges as well as offer opportunities for Australia."[37] The difficulties of this complex and contradictory external environment are reflected in Australia's strategic options, considered in detail next. There are three intertwined facets to this policy: continuation of the Australia-New Zealand-United States (ANZUS) alliance, accommodation with China, and a middle power "concert."

Australia continues to strongly adhere to the ANZUS alliance as part of the American "hub-and-spoke" system. Despite Beijing's vehement protestations of its "peaceful rise," Canberra cannot be certain of future Chinese intentions. It has sought to hedge against negative security outcomes by deepening its alliance ties, as the recent agreement to station US Marines in Darwin (on a rotational basis) demonstrates. Melissa Conley-Tyler and Max Feng affirm that this may be conceived as part of Australia's "forward partnering" with the American "rebalancing" to Asia.[38] Australia has also increased its commitment to military interoperability, and its engagement in the hub-and-spoke system, by actively collaborating with Japan in the security sphere, both bilaterally and through the Trilateral Strategic Dialogue. The alliance with the United States will remain fundamental to Australian security strategy, at least while Washington remains the preeminent power, but also for a number of ancillary reasons, including shared culture and values as well as broad domestic public support, none of which apply to China.[39] Canberra is determined to maintain sufficient military force to repel an attack on Australian territory, but sees the United States as a "great and powerful friend" that will ultimately protect the country in a moment of dire peril, if necessary with nuclear weapons.[40] Australia's security ties with Japan are also deepening for similar reasons, though Beijing may not look favorably on Canberra's newfound friendship with Tokyo, given the current tense state of Sino-Japanese relations.[41]

Indeed, the benefits of being part of the US alliance system are integral to Australia's status of middlepowerhood. As Canberra recognizes, "Our defence relationships give Australia an important voice that underpins our credibility as a middle power which is active in promoting security."[42] The alliance also provides Australia with tangible material support to reinforce its claim to be a middle power that can "punch above its weight." Paradoxically, Australian aspirations to "self-reliance" in military defense are actually predicated upon the privileged access to military and intelligence assets (UK-US agreement) made available only through its relationship with Washington.[43] Without the preferential procurement of advanced military hardware (such as the M1 *Abrams* battle tank or F/A-18 *Super Hornet* fighter jet, and the desired F-35 *Joint Strike Fighter*) and valuable intelligence information, the Australian Defense Force would find it difficult—as well as prohibitively costly—to field such an advanced military establishment. Michael Wesley points out that "the alliance gives Australia a military and diplomatic heft it could not otherwise afford."[44] The Australian Defence Force regularly participates in bilateral military exercises with US forces, such as Talisman Sabre, as well as multilateral exercises, such as Kakadu and Malabar.[45] Scholars such as Coral Bell and Alison Broinowski have detailed the "insurance premium" that must be paid for this "followership": acting as "deputy sheriff" in the South Pacific, participation of American "coalitions of the willing" (war on terror: Afghanistan, Iraq), the controversial ballistic missile defense system, and potential "entrapment" in a US conflict involving Taiwan or North Korea, for example.[46] Despite Australia's comfortable distance from these potential war zones, Washington sent a clear signal to Canberra that it would expect unequivocal support in such contingencies, or Canberra would effectively be "abandoned" by its protector, like New Zealand.[47]

But "followership" in the US-led "San Francisco" system of bilateral security alliances and the attendant "Washington consensus" of politico-economic development that has served Australia so admirably during the Cold War is now being undermined. Manicom and O'Neil identify that for secondary states "alignment strategies are manifested primarily, but not wholly in the realm of security policy."[48] But military-strategic theories of pure "threat balancing" are now complicated by economic factors that are more heavily supplementing, or even supplanting, military capabilities as the currency of power over the long term. Wesley points out the conundrum for Australia, as well as many other Asia-Pacific states: "Countries' economic and security interests will pull in different directions, making clear sets of alignments and confrontation impossible."[49] In an environment where China is quietly eroding American strategic primacy and has already displaced American economic leadership, Cook et al. suggest that "medium powers would be well advised to consider hedging."[50] That is, Australia should not place all its eggs in one basket, strategic or economic. Indeed, the White Paper notes that Australia will "hedge and rebalance as required."[51]

There are multiple strands to Canberra's hedging strategy against overdependence on its US ally. First, Australia has sought to "accommodate" the concerns of rising China, thus hedging against American decline, and ensuring continued Australian economic security, thus "bandwagoning" in the economic sphere. Harris points out that "Australia's policy framework tends to see economic and security issues as largely separate," but it is not clear how long this separation will remain tenable.[52] Canberra has been more circumspect than the United States and Japan in pointing to a "China threat," and out of deference to China has been loath to be seen participating in any perceived "encirclement" or "containment" of China. Manicom and O'Neil argue that "there is some evidence that Australia has sought to distance itself from US and Japanese security policy in response to concerns from Beijing."[53] This was evident when Canberra thwarted the expansion of the Trilateral Security Dialogue to include New Delhi, to form a quadrilateral alignment, in deference to Beijing's displeasure at the initiative.[54]

But despite insistent rhetorical efforts to emphasize that its strategic and economic interests are perfectly compatible, doubts remain as to whether as a middle power Australia will not be forced to pick sides. As Hugh White identifies, the question concerns "how Canberra will balance its growing economic, political and even strategic alignment with Beijing with its alliance with Washington."[55] Alan Dupont further notes that "the nightmare scenario is a serious military confrontation between China and the United States over sovereignty or resource issues that forces us to choose between our major trading partner and ally."[56] In fact, Canberra's hedging strategy is designed to avoid an unequivocal choice between the two. But Greg Sheridan plays down the severity of this dilemma, arguing that "some overexcited commentators foretold a fundamental clash between the United States and Australia over China policy. . . . This fear was widely overblown."[57]

Nonetheless, there is plenty of evidence to suggest that Canberra intends to avoid being drawn too deeply into Beijing's sphere of influence. The *Australia in the Asian Century* White Paper affirms that Australia will not compromise its core values, interests, or allies: "We come to the relationship with China as a dependable economic partner, a constructive participant in regional affairs, one of the world's oldest democracies, a good international citizen, and a close ally of the United States. None of these dimensions will change."[58]

There are several indicators that this commitment to retain independence is not simply rhetoric. First, the 2009 White Paper signaled a major increase in Australia's indigenous military potential, with China's military modernization effectively labeled as the driver for this. The degree to which Canberra actually "trusts" Beijing is open to conjecture, with events such as the arrest of Australian nationals in China not raising confidence in the two states' disparate values via-à-vis human rights and rule of law.[59] Second, Australia has sought to deepen and reinforce its military alliance with the United States, particularly through the agreement to host American troops in the port of Darwin. This clearly signals Australia's support of the current US-alliance network as the ultimate guarantor of security and regional stability. And third, by avoiding excessive Chinese economic leverage over its strategic national assets, such as was evidenced in the failure of the proposed bid by the Chinese state-owned metals group Chinalco for a major stake in Australia's mining industry.[60] Indeed, "both the Howard and Rudd governments signaled their discomfort over the prospect of Chinese sovereign wealth funds capturing key areas of Australia's strategic resource market."[61] As Dupont concludes: "Since security always trumps trade, it is highly unlikely that Australia would preference China over the United States if a choice had to be made."[62]

Thus, despite cognizance of a potential Sinic hierarchical order emerging in the future, and the need to prepare for such an eventuality, Gareth Evans considers that Canberra will not be susceptible to "defection" from the US camp into Beijing's orbit—in contrast to the "emerging middle powers," who are not bound into the "Washington consensus"/Western order and are potential "swing states" in China's view. He asserts that "China is hard-headedly realistic about our alliance relationship with the US—in no doubt at all on which side we would be on if the nightmare scenario of a military confrontation were to arise, conscious of the difference between hedging against a possible scenario and talking up a threat, and not inclined to let defense issues inhibit the other dimensions of its relationship with us."[63]

In an alternative form of hedging, Canberra has sought out new "strategic partnerships" in the region, effectively building a coalition with other middle power states.[64] These may be said to constitute a form of "soft balancing" against China in order to preserve a looser regional order not dominated by regional hegemons (or even a US-PRC "G2"). Security declarations with Japan, India, Indonesia, and South Korea are testament to new bilateral strategic partnerships. But these bilateral relationships together are perfectly suited to forming a closer middle power "concert." The 2010 *IISS [International Institute for Strategic Studies] Strategic Survey* notes that "Australia, Indonesia and South Korea appear to be interested in forms of middle-power consultation, to ensure that their interest in a multi-polar Asia is preserved."[65] Carlyle Thayer identifies such a concert as "middle power security cooperation as equals," which might evolve into some form of "a middle power alliance," according to Rod Lyon.[66] Hence, a coalescence of middle powers with similar interests diversifies ("hedges") Canberra's alignment portfolio from absolute dependence on the US alliance and ensures that such powers have a voice in the construction of regional order. This appears a sensible option in line with securing the interests of the region's middle powers multilaterally—including those examined elsewhere in this book—thus avoiding a China-dominated, or "G2," hegemony in which their concerns are overruled.

Middlepowermanship (Behavior)

Middlepowermanship considers the compound of behaviors that define so-called "middle power diplomacy"—multilateralism and coalition-building, order reinforcement, "bridging," and "niche" diplomacy. It is through the practice of such diplomacy that a state *identity* based upon middlepowermanship emerges, or is deliberately crafted. As Robert Cox reminds us: "Possessing middle-range capabilities is a necessary condition of the ability to play the role, but it is not an adequate predictor of the disposition to play it."[67] This section gives a brief sketch of Canberra's general diplomatic stance, before focusing in on its major responses to China's rise, operating at a regional level. Lastly, it considers how "soft power" and behavioral elements constitute integral elements of middlepowermanship for Australia.

Australia has been a major advocate of global and regional multilateral institutions. Along with other middle powers, its effects on the rise of China are far more likely to be felt in the ways it shapes the regional and global context in which China rises than through its direct initiatives in relation to China. Canberra, along with Ottawa, was one of the founders of the UN, where the traditional middle power identity was born. Australia is a significant contributor to the UN's budget (thirteenth) and to peacekeeping operations (twelfth), commensurate with its weight as a middle power.[68] Canberra has gained a rotating seat on the UN Security Council, pointing to its role as a "good international citizen" as a qualification. Australia was also a major advocate for the more recent G20 grouping, formed to overcome the American financial crisis of 2008–9, and displacing the G7/8 as a tool of global governance. It will host the G20 meeting in 2014. Thus, Australia is present in virtually every important global multilateral institution. Ungerer also observes that "coalition-building with other 'like-minded' countries became a key feature that distinguished Australian diplomacy from the growing ranks of secondary powers in the post-Cold War world."[69] This can be seen, for example, in Canberra's role in the formation of the "Cairns group" of agricultural producers (and further in some of its efforts at niche diplomacy discussed below).[70] As William Tow asserts: "The benefits to

Australia in participating in broad and cooperative multilateral security arrangements are clear: middle powers can often apply meaningful leverage in such groupings.[71]

But it is in the Asia Pacific *regional* multilateral context that Australia has most enthusiastically championed its middle power diplomacy, predicated upon the *Australia in the Asian Century* White Paper. This has been part of a process of "relocating" its policy focus (particularly under former foreign minister Gareth Evans)—and to an extent its identity—to its geographic region, according to Andrew Cooper, Richard Higgott, and Kim Nossal.[72] To this end, Canberra has often led the way in the building of multilateral efforts to reinforce security and stability across the Asia-Pacific region by "enmeshing" greater and lesser powers through various regimes and norms. One of the aims of this multilateralism has been to mold China into a "responsible stakeholder" by tying it into international norms and regimes. Philomena Murray states that "Australia has pursued the notion of a new regional architecture—one that would include security cooperation alongside economic and political cooperation and seek to influence and shape power balances in the region."[73]

Thus, Canberra, potentially in tandem with other regional middle powers, seeks to create systemic conditions that avoid hegemony or bipolarity, even if they are not truly "multipolar." It is in this sphere that we see the agency of middle powers in shaping regional order through their institution-building efforts. Thus, Canberra declares: "To sustain regional prosperity and security, we will continue to work actively with China to advance our shared interests, in regional institutions such as the EAS [East Asia Summit] and APEC [Asia Pacific Economic Cooperation], and globally through the G20 and other bodies."[74] Even if they cannot prevent China from assertive actions on issues such as the South China Sea dispute, they can raise the diplomatic cost for Beijing, which could eventually provoke a coalition of middle and small powers to oppose China, perhaps in collaboration with the United States and Japan.

Gareth Evans, an architect of Canberra's activist multilateral policies beginning in the 1980s, attests that "Australia has worked very hard, and rightly so, over the last couple of decades to put in place regional economic and security mechanisms—from APEC and the ASEAN Regional Forum to the new East Asia Summit—that actually work."[75] APEC and the ASEAN Regional Forum were based on the vision of a desire, led by Evans, to create a "Conference on Security and Cooperation in Asia," modeled on the successful Commission on Security and Cooperation in Europe process.[76] Indeed, Australia's "middle power diplomacy" credentials allowed it to persuade Beijing to tolerate Taiwan as a member of APEC, separate from

China's own participation.[77] In addition to the multilateral forums already noted, Australia's regional engagement also occurs through the proposed Trans-Pacific Partnership, and "Track II" initiatives such as the Council on Security Cooperation in the Asia Pacific, Asia Pacific Centre for Responsibility to Protect, and the IISS Shangri-La Dialogue.[78] Australia also works closely in its immediate region of the South Pacific with the Pacific Island Forum. Tow concludes that these "multilateral security arrangements in the Asia-Pacific have proven to be instruments for cooperation by great powers and have provided 'hedging' opportunities for middle and small powers to offset changing threats."[79] Using Australia's platform as a middle power, Rudd launched his vision for regional security and confidence building, dubbed an "Asia-Pacific Community," though this initiative appears to have met with less success.[80] Nevertheless, Daniel Baldino et al. attest that "although the Asia-Pacific community notion may be practically defunct, Rudd's advocacy of it may have contributed to achieving the US engagement with the region that was one of Rudd's stated objectives. That can be seen as successful middle power agency."[81]

There is further potential for coalition-building in the region. Murray argues that "Australia has the opportunity to present proposals subtly, to build coalitions broadly, to engender discussions informally and to nurture common understandings of norms and values."[82] Options could include some sort of "middle power concert" engaging Indonesia, South Korea, and others, for example. Tow argues: "As the US becomes more discriminating about the type of influences and resources it will apply to the region and as both China and India continue 'growing strong,' Australia, along with ASEAN and South Korea, will need to formulate and apply a collective middle power 'grand strategy' to promote community-building in an increasingly uncertain regional security environment."[83]

The key purpose of this multilateralism and coalition-building as features of middle power diplomacy is to forge and reinforce a liberal global and regional order conducive to Australia's security and prosperity. Rudd declared that "we seek to build and strengthen the global and regional rules-based order."[84] Michael Barnett and Emmanuel Adler note that "Australia's attempt to convince its neighbors of the virtues of open regionalism, multilateralism, and market-led integration may also be considered as a case of attempted (though not quite successful) redefinition of the parameters of politics that are designed to make Asia safe for Australia."[85] This is at odds with the power-based order described above in which national capabilities and alliance potential are the primary concerns.[86] But even the liberal internationalist rules-based order that middle powers such as Australia work to create and maintain may be changing due to the rise of China and other emerging powers. Specifically, "the rising powers may not be comfortable with multilateral institutions that have been established and are being run by the West."[87] Thus, the order that Australia and its allies built in 1945 and maintained throughout the Cold War needs to be recalibrated, as Canberra well understands. In response, Rudd claims that "Australia . . . has looked to enhance the rules-based order through the agency of creative middle power diplomacy."[88] But one may question, as the ranks of non-Western powers grow in importance, whether Australia will be able to maintain its strong stance on its core values (democracy, free trade, human rights), or find itself isolated in a future milieu of "Beijing Consensus," in which noninterference and "Asian values" become the dominant currency.[89] Thus, Nick Bisley concludes that "Asia is moving away from a stable international order towards a hybrid system where elements of the old order remain, hints of the new are visible and uncertainty abounds."[90]

An offshoot of multilateral efforts toward crafting a rules-based order is the typical middle power "bridging" or "facilitating" roles that Canberra has undertaken. Australia in its middle power guise seems well suited to such a role. Analysts assert that "the multitude and variety of its external links enable Australia to see the world from several perspectives, including across the north/south divide."[91] As a result, Australian Labor parliamentarian Mike Kelly asserts that "it can enable us to operate in difficult diplomatic spaces where others may appear threatening and to be a bridge to understanding."[92] To some extent, the desire to "bridge" between China and the United States stems from earlier efforts to provide intermediary services between the USSR and United States during the Cold War and parallels the so-called Seoul Process initiated by South Korea (mentioned by TongFi Kim in chapter 5) that seeks the same.[93] Because the consequences of a zero-sum game relationship between the two superpowers would be highly detrimental for a middle power like Australia, successive governments have sought to mediate tensions between the powers. The *Australia in the Asian Century* White Paper declares that "we will promote cooperative arrangements among major powers in the region as the economic and strategic landscape shifts."[94]

Previously, under prime minister John Howard, Australia introduced the notion that it could play the role of "honest broker" between the two countries. Zhu Feng notes also that "[former] Prime Minister Rudd has stated that Canberra could be a broker between China and the West in the move to foster better understanding in general and to secure Beijing's active participation in emissions reduction cooperation in particular."[95] Perhaps Rudd's effort to play the role of *Zhengyou* (or "friend who is not afraid to criticize") to Beijing overplayed this hand.[96] Rudd's self-appointed role was not particularly appreciated by the Chinese leadership. Murray suggests that Canberra would be ideally placed to serve as an intermediary between the Asian and European sides in the Asia-Europe Meeting or in the ASEAN Regional Forum. Moreover, she argues, "There may be opportunities for Australia to use its middle power and intermediate skills to help soothe historical tensions between Japan and China and between Japan and Korea."[97] Finally, Australia may have more success in less ambitious tasks such as bridging between "traditional" and "emerging" middle powers (i.e., between North and South).

As middle power theory predicts, Australia's middlepowermanship is evident in several fields of so-called "niche" diplomacy. In contrast with the realist emphasis on military security threats, Canberra takes a firm leadership role in combating various nontraditional security challenges, thus fulfilling an important role in stabilizing regional security order. First, Canberra was instrumental in the negotiations for the Comprehensive Test Ban Treaty, the Chemical Weapons Convention, the Non-Proliferation Treaty, and the Nuclear Suppliers Group, and participation in the Proliferation Security Initiative. More recently it has cochaired the International Commission on Nuclear Non-Proliferation and Disarmament, which produced a draft report: *Eliminating Nuclear Threats: A Practical Agenda for Global Policymakers*.[98] Second, in the area of climate change Australia has been a key actor, both domestically and internationally through the UN Framework Convention on Climate Change (1992), the Kyoto Protocol (1997) and championing of a carbon tax. Rudd called climate change "the greatest moral, economic and social challenge of our time."[99] Unfortunately, political momentum has recently been lost on these initiatives. In particular, China has not advanced global efforts on climate change, to the frustration of Australian advocates. Finally, and explicitly linked to this, the *Australia in the Asian Century* White Paper points to Australia's commitment to "human security" issues, a niche highly commensurate with the self-ideational notions of being a "good international citizen." Canberra concludes that "the region will be more sustainable and human security will be strengthened with the development of resilient markets for basic needs such as energy, food and water."[100]

One of the key platforms for launching such middle power diplomatic initiatives is the high standing of Australian "soft power" assets.[101] The country was recently ranked fifth in the world for soft power influence.[102] This is built upon Australia's tradition of multiculturalism, its mix of European history and Asia-Pacific geography, its participation in international organizations and NGOs, peacekeeping, activism in the UN, and stand for economic justice and human rights.[103] In the words of Evans, "being, and being seen to be, a good international citizen should itself be seen as a third category of national interest, right up there alongside the traditional duo of security and economic interests."[104] This "reputational benefit" forms the currency of soft power, which in turn is integral to the behavioral element of middlepowermanship. The self-perception of being a middle power drives the sorts of behavior discussed above. In the words of Rudd, "Australia sees itself as a middle power with global and regional interests."[105] This identity is frequently reinforced by "speech acts" to this effect, in ministerial or prime ministerial addresses, in official statements and documents, including the White Paper, and in the policy and academic discourse on Australia's foreign policy.[106] Based upon many of the policies and actions outlined above, Canberra is at pains to create the perception of Australia both as worthy of its claim to middlepowerhood and as a "good international citizen." Validation by others of entitlement to the label of middle power was achieved under Foreign Minster Evans: Through "a series of high profile policy initiatives ranging from the protection of the Antarctic environment, peace building in Cambodia to arms control and disarmament, Australia's self-proclaimed middle power credentials gained widespread international recognition and support."[107] Perhaps significantly, given the question at hand, Dupont concludes that "Australia is seen by China as an influential middle power."[108]

Conclusion

In response to the four key questions posed by this book, this chapter concludes that (1) Australia is a complete middle power by virtue of its demonstrated capabilities, distinctive middle power behavior, and long-standing identity as a middle power, and it is a rare example of a traditional middle power that by virtue of its proximity to China has retained its global significance; (2) China's rise has profoundly affected Australia's economic, security, and diplomatic environment for reasons similar to those of South Korea—geographic proximity to China and its traditional close alliance with the United States; (3) Australia's response to China's rise involves a complex blend of traditional middle power multilateralism and peace-building initiatives with Beijing as well as more atypical realist power balancing; and (4) Australia has directly shaped China's foreign policy by contributing to Beijing's acceptance of the inevitability of the US presence in the region, as well as indirectly through its efforts in leading multilateral initiatives such as the G20, nontraditional security concerns, and the building of Asian regional institutions.

This chapter demonstrates that Australia may be viewed as serving as the definitive model of a "traditional middle power." It conforms exactly to the "ideal type" identified in the introduction in terms of capabilities and behavior. Unsurprisingly, Baldino et al. note that for Canberra "the middle power framework is supported as an important vehicle to identify national interests, determine the overall shape of the international system and influence regional and global responses in ways that will serve those national interests."[109] What makes Australia distinctive from "former" middle powers such as Canada and Norway, for example, is its success in "relocating" away from its traditional emphasis on its British-European-American cultural and economic ties toward ever-deeper engagement in the Asia Pacific region.[110] Thus Australia appears well poised to reap the benefits of the "Asian century." Now, due to Australia's geographic location, Evans notes, "the tyranny of distance for Australia has become the advantage of proximity."[111] Indeed, perhaps the Australia case suggests an example of successful middle power adaptation in the face of power transitions, calling into question exactly what it means to be a "traditional" middle power in light of the increasing prominence of the "emerging" or "new" middle powers, many of which are examined in this book.

Nonetheless, the continued rise of China creates thorny dilemmas for a traditional middle power seeking to adapt to a changed regional landscape. So far, Manicom and O'Neil argue, Canberra has sought to "actively pursue a strategic policy toward China that balances for security by retaining the US alliance and bandwagons for profit with China through a close economic relationship."[112] This, Medcalf argues, creates a deepening dilemma since "the rapid growth of Chinese military power is confronting Australians with an unfamiliar tension between their economic interest, on the one hand, and their security interest and democratic values on the other."[113] Australia has sought to mitigate this dilemma, first through building closer relations with Beijing through the strategic partnership, as a means of building political trust and economic exchange. This supplements multilateral engagement with China, to "enmesh" and "socialize" China into the kind of liberal rules-based order that its middle power diplomacy champions. Last, this has been supplemented by the founding of security partnerships with "like-minded states" such as Japan, Korea, and India, as a further "hedge" against becoming overawed by China, or overdependent on the United States. Together, these responses typify both the realist and liberalist elements of middle power, making it a good test case, or bellweather, for secondary states' response to China's rising power.[114]

Notes

The author would like to acknowledge and thank Bruce Gilley and Andrew O'Neil for their kind invitation to participate in the middle power project; all my colleagues in the project; and Jenna Heim and Hugh Evans, my interns at the Centre for International Security Studies.

1. Commonwealth of Australia, *Australia in the Asian Century* (Canberra: Department of the Prime Minister and Cabinet, 2012), 227.

2. Carl Ungerer, "The 'Middle Power' Concept in Australian Foreign Policy," *Australian Journal of Politics and History* 53, no. 4 (2007): 538–51, 550.

3. Julia Gillard, "Speech to the AsiaLink and Asia Society Lunch," Melbourne, November 28, 2011.

4. Commonwealth of Australia, *Australia in the Asian Century*.

5. Sid Maher, "China Deal the Cornerstone of Julia Gillard's Asian Century," *Australian*, April 10, 2013.

6. Commonwealth of Australia, *Australia in the Asian Century*, 226.

7. Daniel Baldino et al., *Contemporary Challenges to Australian Security* (London: Palgrave Macmillan, 2011), 115.

8. We might also call them "structural" (realist) versus "normative" (liberal/constructivist) interpretations.

9. The former descriptor could be ascribed to a number of original sources, but apparently Canadian premier Mackenzie-King was one of its progenitors. Lynda Hurst, "On World Stage, a Best Supporting Actor," *Star*, September 29, 2007. The latter probably has its origins in the volume J. King Gordon, ed., *Canada's Role as a Middle Power* (Toronto: Canadian Institute of International Affairs, 1966). It may also be referred to as "middlepowerism."

10. Baldino et al., *Contemporary Challenges to Australian Security*, 111.

11. Ibid., 107.

12. Xuetong Yan, "The Rise of China and Its Power Status," *Chinese Journal of International Politics* 1, no. 1 (2006): 5–33; Michael Pillsbury, *China Debates the Future Security Environment* (Washington, DC: National Defense University, 2000).

13. Central Intelligence Agency, "The World Factbook: Australia," www.cia.gov/library/publications/the-world-factbook/geos/as.html.

14. Australian Government, "Antarctic Territorial Claims," www.antarctica.gov.au/antarctic-law-and-treaty/our-treaty-obligations/antarctic-territorial-claims.

15. Central Intelligence Agency, "The World Factbook: Australia," www.cia.gov/library/publications/the-world-factbook/geos/as.html.

16. International Institute for Strategic Studies, *The Military Balance 2011* (London: Routledge, 2011), 223.

17. United Nations Development Program, *2010 Human Development Report 2010—20th Anniversary Edition* (New York: United Nations, 2011).

18. The Stockholm International Peace Research Institute (SIPRI) Military Expenditure Database, 2012, http://milexdata.sipri.org.

19. Stephan Frühling, "Never Say Never: Considerations about the Possibility of Australia Acquiring Nuclear Weapons," *Asian Security* 6, no. 2 (2010): 146–69; Raoul Heinrichs, "Australia's Nuclear Dilemma: Dependence, Deterrence or Denial?," *Security Challenges* 4, no. 1 (2008): 55–67.

20. Robert Ayson, "Australia's Defense Policy: Medium Power, Even Bigger Ambitions?," *Korean Journal of Defense Analysis* 22, no. 2 (2010): 183–96.

21. Michael Wills, ed., *Strategic Asia 2005–06: Military Modernization in an Era of Uncertainty* (Seattle, WA: National Bureau of Asian Research, 2005).

22. Australian Government Department of Defence, *Defending Australia in the Asia Pacific Century: Force 2030* (Canberra: Australian Government Department of Defence, 2009), 26.

23. Ibid., 47.

24. Ibid., 13.

25. Carsten Holbraad, *Middle Powers in International Politics* (London: Macmillan, 1984).

26. James Manicom and Andrew O'Neil, "Accommodation, Realignment, or Business as Usual? Australia's Response to a Rising China," *Pacific Review* 23, no. 1 (2010): 23–44, 39.

27. Michael Sheehan, *The Balance of Power: Theory and Practice* (London: Routledge, 1995).

28. Malcolm Cook et al., *Power and Choice: Asian Security Futures* (Sydney: Lowy Institute for International Policy, 2010), 78.

29. Carlyle Thayer, "China's Rise and the Passing of US Primacy: Australia Debates Its Future," *Asia Policy* 12, no. 2 (2011): 20–26.

30. Australian Government Department of Defence, *Defending Australia in the Asia Pacific Century*.

31. Rod Lyon, *Forks in the River: Australia's Strategic Options in a Transformational Asia* (Barton: Australian Strategic Policy Institute, 2011), 18.

32. Rowan Callick, "PM Set to Sign China Currency Deal in Boost to Exporters," *Australian*, March 30, 2013.

33. Hugh White, "Power Shift: Australia's Future between Washington and Beijing," *Quarterly*, September 2010.

34. Australian Government Department of Defence, *Defending Australia in the Asia Pacific Century*, 34.

35. Carlyle Thayer, *Southeast Asia: Patterns of Security Cooperation* (Barton: Australian Strategic Policy Institute, 2010), 54.

36. David Kang, *China Rising: Peace, Power, and Order in East Asia* (New York: Columbia University Press, 2008); David Kang, "Getting Asia Wrong: The Need for New Analytical Frameworks," *International Security* 27, no. 4 (2003): 57–85.

37. Stuart Harris, "China-US Relations: A Difficult Balancing Act for Australia?," *Global Change, Peace & Security* 17, no. 3 (2005): 227–38, 235.

38. Melissa Conley-Tyler and Max Feng, "Australia's Choices in the Asian Century," Paper presented at 54th International Studies Association Conference, San Francisco, April 2–6, 2013.

39. Thomas Wilkins, "Towards a 'Trilateral Alliance?'—Understanding the Role of Expediency and Values in American-Japanese-Australian Relations," *Asian Security* 3, no. 3 (2007): 251–78.

40. Hugh White, "Australia in Asia: Exploring the Conditions for Security in the Asian Century," in *International Relations of Asia,* eds. David Shambaugh and Michael Yahuda (New York: Rowman & Littlefield, 2008), 215–33, 215.

41. Thomas Wilkins, "Japan-Australia Security Relations: Building a Real Strategic Partnership?," in *Bilateral Perspectives on Regional Security: Australia, Japan and the Asia-Pacific Region*, 111–27, eds. William Tow and Rikki Kersten (London: Palgrave, 2012).

42. Australian Government Department of Defence, *Defending Australia in the Asia Pacific Century*, 93.

43. Coral Bell, *Dependent Ally* (Oxford: Oxford University Press, 1988).

44. Michael Wesley, *There Goes the Neighbourhood: Australia and the Rise of Asia* (Sydney: University of New South Wales Press, 2011), 165.

45. Australian Government Department of Defence, "Talisman Sabre 2011," www.defence.gov.au/opex/exercises/ts11/.

46. Alison Broinowski, *Allied and Addicted* (Brunswick, Australia: Scribe, 2008).

47. For discussion of the abandonment/entrapment dynamic common to all alliances see Glenn Snyder, *Alliance Politics* (Ithaca, NY: Cornell University Press, 1997). In 2004 Australian foreign minister Alexander Downer appeared to back away from any Australian commitment to assist the United States in the case of a Taiwan Strait conflict. After pressure from Washington and his superiors he reversed course. Hamish McDonald and Tom Allard, "ANZUS Loyalties Fall under China's Shadow," *Sydney Morning Herald*, August 18, 2004. In the case of New Zealand, a degree of rapprochement was under way at the time of writing. Joan Soley, "Panetta Visit Reinforces US-New Zealand Defence Ties," *BBC News Asia*, September 21, 2012.

48. Manicom and O'Neil, "Accommodation, Realignment, or Business as Usual?," 26.

49. Wesley, *There Goes the Neighbourhood*, 163.

50. Cook et al., *Power and Choice*, 5.

51. Australian Government Department of Defence, *Defending Australia in the Asia Pacific Century*, 11.

52. Harris, "China-US Relations," 235.

53. Manicom and O"Neil, "Accommodation, Realignment, or Business as Usual?" 33.

54. Rory Medcalf, "Grand Stakes: Australia's Future between China and India," in *Strategic Asia 2011: Asia Responds to Its Rising Powers*, eds. Ashley Tellis, Travis Tanner, and Jessica Keough (Seattle: National Bureau of Asian Research, 2011), 195–226, 204.

55. Hugh White, "The Limits of Optimism: Australia and the Rise of China," *Australian Journal of International Affairs* 59, no. 4 (2005): 469–80, 470.

56. Alan Dupont, "Living with the Dragon: Why Australia Needs a China Strategy," *Lowy Policy Brief* (2011), 7.

57. Greg Sheridan, "Australia's Pragmatic Approach to Asian Regionalism," in *Asia's New Multilateralism*, 155–71, 167, eds. Michael Green and Bates Gill (Ithaca, NY: Cornell University Press, 2009).

58. Commonwealth of Australia, *Australia in the Asian Century*, 229.

59. "10 Years for Stern Hu," ABC News, March 30, 2010, www.abc.net.au/news/2010-03-29/10-years-for-stern-hu/385268; Michael Sainsbury, "Matthew Ng Charged with Embezzlement in China," *Australian*, December 2, 2010.

60. Terry Macalister, "Rio's Deal with Chinalco Collapses," *Guardian*, June 4, 2009.

61. James Manicom and Andrew O'Neil, "China's Rise and Middle Power Democracies: Canada and Australia Compared," *International Relations of the Asia-Pacific* 12, no. 2 (2012): 199–228, 214.

62. Dupont, "Living with the Dragon," 11.

63. Gareth Evans, "No Power? No Influence? Australia's Middle Power Diplomacy in the Asian Century," 2012 Charteris Lecture, Australian Institute of International Affairs, Sydney, June 6, 2012, 3.

64. Wilkins, "Japan-Australia Security Relations."

65. "Asia's 'Middle Powers' Seek to Balance China: Think Tank," *China Post*, September 8, 2010.

66. Thayer, *Southeast Asia*, 29; Lyon, *Forks in the River*, 8.

67. Robert Cox, "Middlepowermanship, Japan and the Future of World Order," *International Journal* 44, no. 4 (1999): 823–62, 827.

68. Mike Kelly, "Regional Security and Middle Power Diplomacy," Second Dr. John Gee Memorial Lecture, Australian National University, Canberra, August 29, 2008.

69. Ungerer, "The 'Middle Power' Concept in Australian Foreign Policy," 538.

70. Richard Higgott and Andrew Fenton Cooper, "Middle Power Leadership and Coalition Building: Australia, the Cairns Group, and the Uruguay Round of Trade Negotiations," *International Organization* 44, no. 4 (1990): 589–632.

71. William Tow, *Tangled Webs: Security Architectures in Asia* (Barton: Australian Strategic Policy Institute, 2008), 4.

72. Andrew Cooper, Richard Higgott, and Kim Richard Nossal, *Relocating Middle Powers: Australia and Canada in a Changing World Order* (Toronto: University of British Columbia Press, 1993).

73. Philomena Murray, *Regionalism and Community: Australia's Options in the Asia-Pacific* (Barton: Australian Strategic Policy Institute, 2010), 5.

74. Commonwealth of Australia, *Australia in the Asian Century*, 232.

75. Evans, "No Power?," 6.

76. Richard Higgott and Kim Richard Nossal, "Australia and the Search for a Security Community in the 1990s," in *Security Communities*, 265–94, 270, eds. Emanuel Adler and Michael Barnett (Cambridge: Cambridge University Press, 1998).

77. Cooper et al., *Relocating Middle Powers*, 92–94.

78. Tow, "Tangled Webs"; Jeffrey Robertson, "Middle Powers and Korean Normalization: An Australian Perspective Revisited," *Nautilus Institute Policy Forum* 8, no. 34 (2008): 1–18.

79. Tow, "Tangled Webs," 4.

80. Frank Frost, "Australia's Proposal for an 'Asia Pacific Community': Issues and Prospects," *Parliament of Australia Research Papers* 13, no. 10 (2009): 1–27.

81. Baldino et al., *Contemporary Challenges to Australian Security*, 85.

82. Murray, *Regionalism and Community*, 30.

83. Tow, "Tangled Webs," 38–39.

84. Kevin Rudd, "The Rise of the Asia Pacific and the Role of Creative Middle Power Diplomacy," Speech, Oslo University, Norway, May 19, 2011.

85. Emanuel Adler and Michael Barnett, "Studying Security Communities in Theory, Comparison and History," in *Security Communities*, 413–41, 425, eds. Emanuel Adler and Michael Barnett (Cambridge: Cambridge University Press, 1998).

86. Muthiah Alagappa, *Asian Security Order: Instrumental and Normative Features* (Stanford: Stanford University Press, 2003).

87. Melissa Conley-Tyler and Geoff Miller, "Australia as a Middle Power," Manning Clark House Colloquium, September 2007, 7.

88. Rudd, "The Rise of the Asia Pacific and the Role of Creative Middle Power Diplomacy."

89. The "Asian values" debate refers to Singaporean and Malaysian affront at criticisms of their human rights records and authoritarian systems, suggesting that they had the right to adhere to "Asian values" based on Confucianism or Islam respectively, and in juxtaposition to "Western values." See Mark Thompson, "Pacific Asia after 'Asian Values,'" *Third World Quarterly* 25, no. 6 (2004): 1079–95.

90. Nick Bisley, *Building Asia's Security* (New York: Routledge, 2009), 128.

91. Conley-Tyler and Miller, "Australia as a Middle Power," 9.

92. Kelly, "Regional Security and Middle Power Diplomacy."

93. Paul Malone, "Hayden's Arms Talk Plan Poll Coup," *Canberra Times*, November 22, 1984, 1.

94. Commonwealth of Australia, *Australia in the Asian Century*, 223.

95. Zhu Feng, "TSD—Euphemism for Multiple Alliance?," in *Assessing the Trilateral Strategic Dialogue*, eds. William Tow et al. (Seattle, WA: National Bureau of Asian Research, 2008), 41–49, 45.

96. Phillip Coorey, "How *Zhengyou* Kevin Is Keeping Everyone Happy," *Sydney Morning Herald*, April 11, 2008.

97. Murray, *Regionalism and Community*, 27.

98. "Nonproliferation Meeting Working on Concrete Cuts," *Japan Times*, October 19, 2009.

99. Peter von Onselen, "Rule of Reckless Vows," *Weekend Australian*, December 27, 2008.

100. Commonwealth of Australia, *Australia in the Asian Century*, 240.

101. Joseph Nye, *Soft Power: The Means to Success in Global Politics* (New York: Public Affairs, 2004).

102. "Soft Power Survey 5: Australia," *Monocle*, December 2011.

103. Evans, "No Power?," 1.

104. Ibid., 3.

105. Rudd, "The Rise of the Asia Pacific and the Role of Creative Middle Power Diplomacy."

106. A list of these "speech acts" is compiled by Gwilym Croucher, "Australia as a Creative Middle Power, Again?," *Australian Policy Online*, May 4, 2009, 2.

107. Ungerer, "The 'Middle Power' Concept in Australian Foreign Policy," 538.

108. Dupont, "Living with the Dragon," 11.

109. Baldino et al., *Contemporary Challenges to Australian Security*, 118.

110. John Langmore and Jan Egeland, "Learning from Norway: Independent Middle-Power Foreign Policy," *Griffith Review* 32, no. 2 (2011): 97–110; Adam Chapnik, "The Canadian Middle Power Myth," *International Journal* 55, no. 2 (2000): 188–206.

111. Gareth Evans, "Australia in East Asia and the Asia-Pacific: Beyond the Looking Glass," *Australian Journal of International Affairs* 49, no. 1 (1995): 99–113, 112.

112. Manicom and O'Neil, "China's Rise and Middle Power Democracies," 213.

113. Medcalf, "Grand Stakes," 199.

114. Conley-Tyler and Feng, "Australia's Choices in the Asian Century."

CHAPTER 9

South Africa's Middle Power Ambitions

Riding the Dragon or Being Its Pet?

Janis van der Westhuizen and Sven Grimm

Introduction

RESEARCH ON South Africa's role as an emerging middle power has accumulated since the late 1990s.[1] Although one would search in vain for explicit references to, or use of, the middle power concept by government officials, the concept fits South Africa like a glove. Yet the rise of China has brought contradictions and tensions to South Africa's middle power identity and interests. South Africa's engagement with China is fraught with controversy, revealing the complex intersection of diverging ideational and material interests, differences within various domestic constituencies, and pitting Pretoria's regional ambitions against its global goals. This chapter highlights these complexities by first contextualizing South Africa's emergence as a middle power and identifying a distinct shift in orientation *within* this role. Second, we contend that South African state elites' attraction to China dovetailed with this reorientation. The third point, however, is that Beijing's ideological attraction to the ruling African National Congress (ANC) stands in sharp contrast to both a degree of suspicion toward China in civil society and looming economic tensions given China's growing African role and as a possible competitor to South African capital in the region.

South Africa's Emergence as a Middle Power

Although the analysis of South African foreign policy through the prism of middlepowership is popular, most tend to assume that such a role appeared after 1994.[2] However, the country's multilateral tradition predates even the apartheid era of 1948 to 1994 with the internationalism of the Jan C. Smuts era (he held various cabinet posts including prime minister between 1919 and 1948) being the most obvious. Smuts not only took control of the Allied war effort in German East Africa but became a member of the British War Cabinet in 1917 and contributed to the establishment of the League of Nations at the Versailles Peace Conference in 1919.[3] Here were the first signs of South Africa's middle power role exemplified by the attempt to mediate worsening relations between the United Kingdom and Germany. Oswald Pirow, the minister of defense, offered his services as a mediator and met with Neville Chamberlain, Adolf Hitler, and Benito Mussolini. But it bore little fruit since "the idea of South African mediation was unwelcome to Germany and embarrassing to the British Government."[4] The internationalist drive of the Smuts era would reappear, although in different form, in the many initiatives of President Thabo Mbeki eighty years later. To understand and evaluate the legacy of Mbeki in post-apartheid South Africa, however, requires a broader historical canvass, and at least one that contextualizes the rise of South Africa as an emerging middle power since the Nelson Mandela presidency.

Global Bridge-Builder, 1990–98

When Nelson Mandela published his important 1993 article in *Foreign Affairs* that outlined a post-apartheid foreign policy, he emphasized a number of normative considerations that would be cornerstones in South Africa's foreign policy, most notably a demonstrated commitment to human rights.[5] What was interesting about this commitment, as Alison Brysk noted, is that "South Africa provides a role model for other emerging regional powers, demonstrating that underdevelopment, non-Western culture, and historic divisions are not necessarily impediments to an active and principled foreign policy role."[6]

On Mandela's watch this found particular expression in the form of an active, "heroic" form of intervention as a mediator in the immediate region, in Africa, and the world beyond. South Africa (militarily) intervened in the constitutional crisis in Lesotho in 1994, sought to ameliorate tensions in Angola, convinced Frederick Chiluba of Zambia not to prevent his rivals from participating in 1996 elections, and attempted to mediate between Mobutu Sese Seko and Laurent Kabila in Zaire in the same year. Pretoria has tried its hand at peace brokering in the Middle East between Israel and Palestine; the Northern Ireland conflict; the refugee crisis in the Great Lakes; the East Timor question; the conflict in Sudan; and between Tripoli and London over the Lockerbie disaster. It even offered to mediate between the United States and Iraq as tensions over weapons inspection escalated in 1997. In global governance issues such as the nonproliferation treaty, it played a major role as one of the first countries in the world to unilaterally and voluntarily dismantle its own nuclear weapons program (and was held up as a model that Iraq should follow by US Secretary of State Colin Powell shortly before the American invasion of 2003). Playing the role of bridge-builder or mediator internationally also saved Pretoria from having to choose sides in international disputes that may upset or feed into the polarization of a bureaucracy in which past incumbents of the apartheid state still worked alongside the newly appointed pro-ANC administrators.

Given that many nations made economic sacrifices in the international struggle against apartheid, South Africa was seen to have a "manifest destiny" to give something to the world in return. As the ANC's electoral manifesto at the time declared:

> Because of our long concern for these issues, an ANC government will immediately take steps to become a fully-fledged member and vital member of that section of the family of nations who hold human rights issues close to the centre of their foreign policy. Some of these steps we will take are symbolic but, in our efforts to canonise human rights in our international relations, we regard them as far more than this.[7]

Yet, what many consider to have been the highpoint of South Africa's commitment to human rights soon proved also to be a watershed event that catapulted Pretoria's diplomacy toward a decidedly less prohuman rights approach. In 1995, when Nigerian ruler Sani Abacha executed nine environmental activists, including Ken Saro Wiwa, in clear defiance of international pressure (and after a personal assurance to Mandela that he would not do so), the latter, enraged, unilaterally called for a boycott of Nigeria's oil and its expulsion from the Commonwealth. Being the only country in the developing world to have recalled its high commissioner from Abuja in protest and thereby moving ahead of other African governments meant that Pretoria infringed the solidarity norm among African states. Even more detrimentally, it strengthened the hand of those who had accused it of blindly following London and Washington. A poisoned chalice was created when a Nigerian foreign minister described South Africa as a "white country with a black president."

Nevertheless, one of the most interesting paradoxes of the Mandela years was the extent to which notions of exceptionalism often underpinned foreign policy initiatives. The myth of exceptionalism common to the South African psyche finds its origins in the country's history of isolation, the celebratory discourse surrounding its democratic transition, Mandela's iconic stature, and of course, the country's degree of infrastructural and industrial capacity relative to the rest of the continent. Yet it also constitutes the fountainhead of the country's soft power and the belief especially in the early 1990s that South Africa could somehow maneuver itself out of the rules of the global diplomatic game. Just as South Africa believed it could retain diplomatic links with both China and Taiwan (it was forced to end official relations with Taipei in 1998 after it recognized Beijing), it believed it could forcefully promote human rights while remaining in solidarity with other African states. In short, the paradox of the Mandela years was that South Africa's relative *lack of socialization* within the accepted rules of international and regional society allowed it to deliver some of the most *innovative* modes of statecraft in its history.

Post-Mandela Era

Arguably, South Africa's innovative interlocutory role in foreign affairs during the Nelson Mandela years was an external reflection of the negotiated nature of the domestic political settlement that ended apartheid. Under Mbeki (president from 1999 to 2008), by contrast, the effects of that domestic moment faded. South African foreign policy became more reformist in seeking to change institutions of global governance, especially the Bretton Woods institutions, and in a host of multilateral initiatives aimed at creating a more equal world order.

Between 1994 and 2000, the country acceded to nearly seventy multilateral treaties and joined or rejoined more than forty intergovernmental organizations.[8] It played an innovative role in brokering deadlocks over landmines (1997), the creation of the International Criminal Court (1998), and the Kimberley process regarding the regulation of "blood diamonds" (2000). Indeed, Mbeki himself had been the prime architect behind the transformation of the Organization of African Unity (OAU) to the African Union (AU) and incorporation (with Nigeria, Senegal, and Algeria) of restrictions on the participation of African leaders who achieved power by nonconstitutional means. Consistent with its middle power role, South Africa was the key driver of the New Partnership for Africa's Development (NEPAD) and with it, the incorporation of "good governance" requirements as a precondition for increased international aid, trade, and investment.[9] Moreover, South Africa began to participate in peacekeeping operations, which led it into Burundi, Ivory Coast, Ethiopia, the Comores, Liberia, and later the Democratic Republic of Congo, Sudan (Darfur), and the Central African Republic.

During Mbeki's second term and especially from 2004 to 2008, the country's erstwhile bridge-building role took a secondary position in favor of an openly Africanist orientation.[10] Three cases in particular—the country's opposition, while a member of the Security Council, to a formal briefing on the situation in Zimbabwe in 2007, to a resolution condemning human rights violations in Myanmar, and to a visit to the country by the Dalai Lama in 2009—highlighted concerns particularly in the West that the politics of pragmatism and international horse-trading now stood paramount over the country's initial commitment to human rights.

The refusal to grant a visa to the Dalai Lama to attend a forum with fellow Nobel laureates Desmond Tutu, Nelson Mandela, and F. W. de Klerk in 2009 on the grounds that it would "distract attention" from the festivities planned in the run-up to the 2010 Soccer World Cup triggered an outcry—largely among civil society. As the decision prompted questions about South African subservience to Chinese sensitivities across radio talk shows, both Tutu and de Klerk withdrew from the event, forcing organizers to cancel it. South African diplomats sought to explain the decisions based on a fear of a potential incident given that the Dalai Lama would be in the country on the anniversary of the date he had left Tibet in 1959. Interestingly, the Dalai Lama had visited the country before, with much less controversy.

Rather than opting for the low-key, bridge-building role that Pretoria had so strategically employed in the past, these developments during its membership of the UN Security Council revealed that South Africa's core identity consisted of three concentric and overlapping circles: "African" at the core, "anti-imperialism" second, and "human rights" the outer ring. The prioritization of these rings does not suggest that these identity conceptions are competing, rather that in those cases where their attendant norms collide—say between anti-imperialism and human rights—the former is likely to enjoy precedence.[11] What has been the effect of this shift in orientation in South Africa's middle power role vis-à-vis China's rise?

More "Africanist" Middle Power

South Africa's diplomatic relationship with the People's Republic of China is relatively recent. The relationship was preceded by a courtship period during the apartheid regime in the 1980s when Pretoria sent signals of wanting to establish relations. In 1994, allegiance was switched from Taiwan to the PRC (formal relations began in 1998), despite an alleged large-scale donation to the ANC from Taiwan before that year's election campaign.[12] In December 2001, a binational commission was established and subsequently several memoranda of understanding were signed for various areas. Since 2010, both countries have been linked by a *Comprehensive Strategic Partnership*. During the Jacob Zuma presidency (from 2009), relations intensified, despite some economic competition between China and South Africa, which we address below.[13]

Chinese observers discuss South Africa's position in Africa as that of a "reluctant hegemon" or "middle power facilitator" with a "global south and emerging power diplomacy."[14] Given both South Africa's and China's security interests on the African continent, it is not surprising that the relationship includes a security component. Even though Egypt (before the fall of President Hosni Mubarak in 2011) received the highest number of senior military delegations from China, South Africa and China also held regular security consultations after 2003.[15] Yet it is the ideational appeal that constitutes the more significant dimension. In this regard we focus on two dimensions, namely the systemic (counterhegemonic or promultipolar) behavioral role of South Africa as a middle power, and second, China's ideational appeal as an economic model.

Pursuit of Counterhegemony

Unlike traditional middle powers, one constitutive characteristic of emerging middle powers is that they seek to redistribute power in the international system by reforming both norms and institutions of global governance. Hence China may at times bandwagon with these middle powers to effect reformist global change. Although China is committed to a relatively liberal international trading order, it does not necessarily underwrite the principles and practices of what Robert Cox describes as an American-led empire.[16] Rather, Beijing is far more likely to assert and call upon the norms, practices, and power capacities of the Westphalian interstate system.[17] Chinese engagement in the current world order is marked by an expressed wish to reform and transcend the current order in the long run, thereby emphasizing its "defense against absorption into the empire" with as little confrontation as possible with the United States, hence Chinese interest in cooperating with multilaterally minded middle powers.[18]

The Chinese understanding of the Westphalian interstate system has developed into a doctrine of noninterference in internal affairs of other states. This doctrine can be understood as a threefold signal: First, it is a signal to other powers that it no longer wants to export its revolution, contrary to the revolutionary internationalism of the Mao era, thus respecting the autonomy of states in the international order as a signal to avoid ideological conflict with democracies.[19] Second, it is a way for China to rebuff criticism of its own human rights situation, and thus constitutes a lesson from the post-Tiananmen situation, thereby following its own interpretation of (legitimate) authority over its own population. And last, for some partner countries, this insistence on noninterference and the orthodox understanding of the Westphalian system is a signal that China will not push for internal reforms as multilateral or Western agencies are doing, thereby portraying China as an "all-weather friend" without specific demands—or, per the formulation in Beijing, "no strings attached."

This third aspect emphasizes the autonomy of states in the international system, catering for an audience in the developing world, not least in Africa. Accordingly, China lends political support to the independence of African states in the international system, an independence that Clapham has discussed as a reflection of international recognition rather than as a reflection of identified state functions within African states, with the international system guaranteeing state survival from the outside.[20] Given Beijing's espousal of more Westphalian norms, and the significance of "anti-imperialism" as a core identity construct among South African state elites, China's appeal to the ANC is that it enables Pretoria to ideationally play the global and regional game simultaneously. Connecting to the global via a closer engagement with China (and thereby the BRICS [Brazil, Russia, India, China, South Africa], which China invited South Africa to join in 2010), while espousing values resonant in many African capitals—nonintervention, sovereignty, anti-imperialism—casts South Africa's international ambitions somewhat more favorably. However, this does not suggest the absence of any inconsistencies in relation to South Africa's broader foreign policy, nor does it preclude occasional criticism as demonstrated during Mbeki's presidency and President Zuma's criticism of a trade relationship that was not sustainable in its current form, as mentioned in Beijing in 2012.[21]

While the upholding of an orthodox understanding of the Westphalian state system might be attractive to a number of African states, it sits uneasily with elements of South Africa's continental policies. For instance, it can be argued, the absolutist, orthodox understanding of noninterference is in contradiction to article 4h of the African Union's Charter that defines instances where "internal affairs" are becoming an international issue and require the AU to intervene in African states (namely, gross human rights violations, genocide, and war crimes). This AU clause reflects discussion on the "Responsibility to Protect" as lessons from the Balkan wars in the 1990s and, importantly, from the genocide in Rwanda in 1994.

In several instances, as a nonpermanent member of the UN Security Council in 2011–12, South Africa did not vote with Chinese priorities as South Africa followed its multilateral commitments and voted according to African Union recommendations. In the case of UNSC Resolution 1973, declaring a no-fly zone over Libya and legitimizing humanitarian support to the Libyan population during the civil war in 2011, South Africa (and the other two African members of the UNSC, Nigeria and Gabon) voted in favor (China abstained along with Brazil, India, Russia, and Germany). Similarly, South Africa voted in favor of a UNSC resolution condemning the violence in Syria in the first half of 2012. Specifically in the latter case, Pretoria faced public pressure from Tunisia (a recently democratized AU member state) to "make up its mind" in support of the Arab spring. In both cases, South Africa's approval of the resolutions did not follow the Chinese vote of abstention.

The potential conflict of Chinese and African understanding of norms has not yet materialized in an open clash of votes; China thus far has never vetoed any UNSC decisions supported by the African Union; it has thereby cautiously avoided open conflict with African states within the UN. Chinese voting in the UN Security Council follows a nonobstructionist stance toward the African position, not necessarily a proactive policy of support. In rare cases of more interventionist joint position by the AU, China has not blocked these positions despite contradictions to its policies. Furthermore, the independence of South Sudan after AU endorsement was accepted somewhat reluctantly, but ultimately pragmatically, even though it was not easy for Beijing to support a policy that is in sharp contrast to its internal control over "separatism" in its Western provinces. In fact, China has pragmatically softened the Westphalian dogmatism by being the biggest supplier of UN peace troops in Africa from outside the continent, insisting on clear UN mandates as a precondition for its engagement, and using the African Union benchmark that nonintervention not be seen as indifference. Discussions on norms and their interpretations, however, prevail over the International Criminal Court (ICC) and whether the ICC is an "imperialist tool," as some Chinese scholars argue, or a needed international institution, as some African scholars argue.[22]

State-Led Development Model

China has been quick to capitalize on the new economic growth trends in Africa that have boosted Africa's self-confidence. Chinese actors emphasize their dynamism in the economy and some allegedly innovative combinations of investments, trade, and aid as a new force for global development—sometimes amounting to the statement that "they" have brought growth back to Africa.[23] Yet overall, cautious voices are predominant, and the Chinese leadership was quick in replacing the slogan of a "peaceful rise" with that of "peaceful development."[24] It is noteworthy that Chinese actors are careful to avoid speaking of a "Chinese model" or the alleged "Beijing consensus."[25] African debates, however, involve discussions about a Chinese model and what to learn from China. The impatience in the "global South" to bring about reforms in the international system appears to be growing, at least in political discussion documents, where the impatience is quite openly expressed.[26] Despite the complex and at times even ambiguous relations between Pretoria and Beijing, the latter is especially serving as a rhetorical point of reference in the realm of an economic policy with appeal to South African state elites.

By 2002, Pretoria's broadly or "soft" neoliberal approach increasingly made way for a shift in policy thinking that increasingly emphasized a more interventionist role. Both domestic and international conditions in tandem set the scene for this shift. Domestically, factional divisions within the ANC ultimately led to the party's 2007 Polokwane Conference becoming the fulcrum whereby a resurgent left seemed to regain ascendancy, a move repeated across most parts of South America. The notion of a "developmental state" emerged vociferously in the run-up to the conference and was supposedly strongly supported by Jacob Zuma, who challenged and finally ushered Mbeki from the presidency.[27] Internationally, the aftermath of the 2008–9 global financial crisis, the massive recapitalization of banks in Europe and the United States, restoring liquidity to the international system (with its attendant inflationary risks) and the worldwide recession, increasingly eroded the ideological confidence of neoliberal economic models. The extent to which many of the world's largest "emerging markets" were relatively better insulated against the *immediate* effects of the financial contagion and their ability to weather the storm relatively better than their northern counterparts, loomed large throughout the crisis. That the world turned to the BRIC countries—with their pronounced role for state-driven capitalism—to help underwrite the continued stability of the global financial system also pointed toward the realignment of global power centers. Throughout all of this, China's role has been central.

Although China has not explicitly sought to articulate a "Beijing consensus," the model of a strong and economically interventionist state has made an impact within ANC policy circles. Since 2009, the ANC has sent numerous delegations, including from its top decision-making structure, the National Executive Committee (NEC), to learn how the Chinese run their party and government, how they train their cadres, and about China's economic situation. "The ANC has relationships with all progressive parties around the world. We share experiences and views and perspectives on issues of international governance," ANC spokesperson Keith Khoza said after one visit in 2011.[28] NEC member and Gauteng ANC leader Paul Mashatile confirmed that NEC members traveled to China for "political lessons," while another party official noted that the ANC "wants to know how the party (CCP) manages itself" given the internal problems of discipline and governance in the ANC.[29] ANC secretary-general Gwede Mantashe also admonished Western investors to realize "South Africa does not need their money" given that it can turn to India and China to fund economic development. "Sometimes when you deal with the IMF or the World Bank or anything, they feel that you must stop thinking because they have money and they will tell you what to do with the money. . . . As long as that is the case, you are going to see the fast growth of the 'Look East' policy."[30] More dangerous is that policy-peddling in terms of an undefined notion of a "developmental state" may set the scene for the justification of a discourse citing democracy as an impediment to rapid development.[31] An opinion poll conducted in 2012 asked respondents to rank countries they thought could be considered as South Africa's ally or "close friends." China scored the highest at 26 percent, followed by the United States at 20 percent. Asked which countries South Africa could learn the most from about alleviating poverty, China again emerged as first at 26 percent, followed by Brazil and Botswana at 20 percent.[32]

It is in this context that the symbolic value of the invitation by Beijing into the club of BRIC states (Brazil, Russia, India, and China) during the summit in Sanya/China in 2011 looms large. A major gain in prestige and in the claim for "autonomy from empire," Pretoria's membership of the renamed BRICS and hosting the grouping's fifth summit in Durban in 2013, signaled its commitment to working toward a more multipolar world order. Rather than hiding in a group, however, gaining this kind of recognition as being part of a group of aspirant powers was seen as a major gain, despite the fact that South Africa is essentially running behind its league. This grouping with existent and emerging great powers can be seen as bandwagoning with global power rather than forming a coalition of (equal) middle powers. President Jacob Zuma seems to distinguish himself from his predecessor by emphasizing the BRICS agenda, somewhat at the expense of the African agenda and at the expense of the previously formed IBSA (India, Brazil, South Africa) grouping. The latter can be understood as a grouping of middle or great powers from the developing world without a UN Security Council permanent seat. Also, the process of coalition-building on the African continent seems to be gaining less attention. Even though interactions are conducted at regional summits, Zuma tellingly had not been on state visits to Nigeria or Ethiopia since his accession to the presidency (through mid-2013), despite both being meaningful regional players on the continent. Mbeki in contrast was often critical of China's role in Africa, setting it akin to the colonial and neocolonial relationships of Europe and the United States.[33] In fact, the Mbeki administration seems to have been uncomfortable being the junior partner in both the BRIC and IBSA groups, "preferring instead to retain its independence, play the powers off against each other, and thereby maximise the development concessions both for South Africa and the continent."[34]

Beijing has also repeatedly lowered expectations toward the BRICS grouping. While it has been agreed to establish a bank as an alternative to the Bretton Woods institutions, disagreements remain regarding where it is to be located and the modalities of partner contributions. South Africa and India objected to shareholdings in proportion to the size of economies, which would give China overwhelming control. More progress had however been achieved in creating a foreign exchange reserve pool to relieve short-term liquidity pressures. However, concerns by Brazil, South Africa, and India about the imbalances created by the undervalued renminbi remained off the agenda.[35] In short, the grouping is rather a pragmatic tool for Beijing. For China, besides helping to minimize dependence on the United States and possibly to constrain American unilateralism, BRIC cooperation serves several other functions. China also benefits from this cooperation by stabilizing its international environment, helping other developing countries, strengthening its identity as a developing country, coordinating its position with others to maximize leverage, and hiding in a group to avoid negative attention.

While South Africa's accession to the BRICS club might be high in symbolic value, it will not per se solve potentially existing, underlying tensions and competition between Chinese economic inroads into the African continent as a reflection of its global power and South Africa's middle power role in the subregion.[36] For example, Sanusi Lamido Sanusi, the governor of the Central Bank of Nigeria, wrote in London's *Financial Times* that "China is no longer a fellow underdeveloped economy—it is the world's second biggest, capable of the same forms of exploitation as the West. It is a significant contributor to Africa's deindustrialisation and underdevelopment."[37]

China's Impact on South Africa's Regional Role

China is attracted to South Africa—as it is to other mineral-rich middle powers like Australia, Brazil, and Canada—but it also bears directly upon the role of the so-called "minerals-energy complex" (MEC) that has been central to the history of South Africa's economy and its role in southern Africa. For example, at the "epicenter" of the MEC, finance has emerged as "a separate but related" set of economic activities closely associated with minerals and related sectors "but in which corporate restructuring and financial speculation have occurred at the expense of providing funds for investment for the expansion and restructuring of production itself."[38]

The $5.5 billion purchase of a 20 percent stake in South Africa's Standard Bank by China's Industrial and Commercial Bank of China (ICBC) in 2008 was an attempt to service other Chinese interests and investment across Africa using a bank with an existing continental reach. Moreover, South Africa's relatively advanced financial sector exposes Chinese firms to a tightly regulated environment—an experience that is worth undergoing in some sort of "test case" when aspiring for more lucrative markets in the Western world. Yet the ICBC investment—probably the most significant foreign direct investment by size—is symptomatic of the proliferation of the large variety of "producer service firms" that emerged in the late 1990s. These "service the centralization requirements of globalized manufacturing and industrial companies (including mining). Most notable among these are accounting, law, advertising, corporate travel, security, public relations, management consulting, information technology, real estate, storage, data processing, and insurance companies."[39] Increasingly, South Africa's role as a middle power is shaped by its position in the global economy to perform what Carmody describes as fulfilling both global and regional interests by promoting economic liberalization for regional market access by its own corporate elites as well as for other major countries and transnational capital.[40] This is more colloquially known as the "gateway to Africa" argument.

However, like other emerging middle powers (notably Brazil and perhaps Turkey), South Africa also faces the complexities that arise from being a part of what Garrett describes as the global "missing middle": the many upper-middle-income economies of Latin America and Central Europe that are neither low-wage economies in which labor executes routine tasks at the lowest possible cost nor knowledge-based economies based on cutting edge technological innovation.[41] In short, because of South Africa's global and regional role, the vast inequalities generated by the country's deep integration with the global economy are mirrored by the enormous skills gaps between on the one hand the small but affluent indigenous capitalist class, the increasingly multiracial middle class, and the organized working class; and on the other hand an enormous subordinate class, reliant on precarious employment and the informal sector. This configuration of class dynamics means that a relatively powerful (but declining) labor movement prohibits a low-wage, mass-manufacturing process based on "flexible" labor, while massive and fundamental skill deficiencies in key sectors also forestall adoption of a relatively productive but high-wage, value-added trajectory.

Desperate to overcome being stuck between this Scylla and Charybdis, Pretoria pursues two strategies. First, it uses sub-Saharan Africa as the base for its manufacturing and service-related exports; and second, it adopts a program of heavily state-financed infrastructural development programs to position South Africa as the pivotal center of African transport, logistics, telecommunications facilities, and related services. Paradoxically, China's role in Africa both complements and complicates these strategies. For example, President Zuma's announcement of a R1 trillion infrastructure-driven model in his 2012 State of the Nation address was cited as drawing on the Chinese model of state capitalism.[42] As Enoch Godonwana, head of the ANC's economic transformation committee, noted at the time, "The Chinese model of building infrastructure and growing jobs will be a key focus of the ANC's economic policy."[43] With the emergence of new growth economies and the impact of these on trade flows, many African states have seen a commodity price boom that resulted in GDP growth figures long unseen in Africa. Yet current growth paths have led to a diversification of economic activity.[44] To the contrary, new partners with a demand for resources have dulled the urge to diversify. This "cashing in" by elites is at the core of the "resource curse."[45] This may also in part explain ANC state and business elites, with close connections to the resource and finance industries, being reluctant to forego lucrative opportunities for their companies to act as intermediaries to Chinese exploration of African wealth.[46]

Beyond the inner circles of the ruling elite, discussions about Chinese interests in Africa and South Africa tend to be much more cautious. Many African states—although not always South Africa—might have some advantages in market access to the United States and to Europe. But they have not been able to exploit these advantages at the same time that China, India, and other competitors were pushing into European and American markets.[47] Few South African enterprises have made it into the Chinese market, with notable exceptions such as SABMiller breweries, Sasol in energy technology, Barloworld Logistics, or the Naspers media corporation—with estimates of investment values ranging between US$1 and 2 billion.[48] While these investments might ensure competitiveness of some South African enterprises on the global market, they do not solve the employment crisis in South Africa, nor do they move meaningful proportions of South Africa's domestic economy up the global production value chain, as export statistics show.

Although trade between South Africa and China has grown tremendously over the past ten years, Pretoria has had a substantial and significant deficit with China. South African exports to China are overwhelmingly based on primary products and resource-based manufactures, while imports from China are nearly entirely manufactured goods, especially consumer goods and capital goods. Beijing's share of South African imports of manufactures increased from 2 percent in 1995 to more than 18 percent by 2010. Yet China accounted for only 5 percent of South African manufactured exports in 2010.[49] While Chinese imports accounted for only 6 percent of total consumption of manufactured products in 2010, these had different impacts across different industries. The industries with the highest levels of Chinese import penetration are also traditional labor-intensive sectors.[50] Unskilled South African workers are thus most likely to bear the brunt of the effects following China's accession to the World Trade Organization. In 2007, the ongoing crisis in the garment industry triggered the imposition of quotas in response to the surge of Chinese imports. Although industrial production in South Africa increased by 14 percent between 2001 and 2010, it is estimated that this figure would have increased by 19 percent had it not been for the effects of Chinese import penetration.[51] Similar "crowding out" effects have been reported in South Africa's previously "uncaptured" markets elsewhere in Africa that account for over a fifth of the country's total industrial exports.[52] While the value of South African exports increased during the past ten years, its share of total exports has declined.

Whereas there was little competition with China in the late 1990s, it is estimated that on average South African exports to ten key African economies "would have been almost 10 percent higher (US$ 900 million more) had it not lost market share to China between 2001 and 2010."[53] These effects feed into the constant tensions between the government and its ally, the Congress of South African Trade Unions (COSATU), particularly regarding domestic social and economic reforms around a more "flexible" labor regime. It is little wonder that in welcoming South Africa's admission to the BRICS, COSATU remained cautious, citing specifically the potential danger of China's impact on domestic industry.[54]

Scepticism over Pretoria's pro-Chinese orientation is not limited to differences between government and organized labor but also exists between government and civil society. These tensions were highlighted by the Chinese cargo vessel *An Yue Jiang*'s attempt to deliver arms and ammunition to Zimbabwe in the aftermath of the domestic tensions there following disputed elections in 2008.[55] Citing South African legislation that prohibits trade and movement of weapons suspected of violating human rights, a court prevented the cargo from being unloaded in South Africa's Durban port. Even before taking legal action, the dock worker's labor union, SATAWU (South African

Transport and Allied Workers Union), refused to unload it.[56] Through coordinated legal action by civil society groups across Southern Africa, the ship was ultimately forced to return to China with its cargo unloaded.[57] The shipment negatively affected China's image among trade unions that were supportive of the initially labor-based opposition to Zimbabwe's president Robert Mugabe.

If the case of the *An Yue Jiang* fueled civil society and public outrage, South Africans' reaction to the Dalai Lama's difficulty in obtaining a visa in 2011 triggered even more public interest in a foreign policy issue. Emeritus archbishop Desmond Tutu invited the Dalai Lama—in his capacity as a fellow Nobel laureate—to Tutu's eightieth birthday celebrations. However, bureaucratic foot-dragging prevented the Dalai Lama from obtaining a visa in time, triggering widespread accusations as well as protest marches against Pretoria's clearly calculated attempts to prevent the Dalai Lama from visiting. Opposition political parties, the Inkatha Freedom Party (IFP) and Congress of the People (Cope), applied for a court order to declare the handling of the matter unlawful.[58] That a foreign policy issue—seemingly so remote from people's material interests—could trigger such a public outcry indicates that concerns were not about Tibetan autonomy or the Dalai Lama per se. The visa request coincided with one of the ANC's NEC study trips to China and with a state visit to China by the deputy president, and it followed shortly after South Africa's accession to BRICS membership sponsored by the Chinese. Moreover, the incident symbolized to many the dangerous extent to which South Africa had become beholden to Chinese interests.

South African appeals at the highest levels to prevent the execution by Chinese authorities of Janice Linden, convicted of smuggling 3 kg of methamphetamine in 2008, fell on deaf ears. As an editorial lamented, the incident illustrated the fundamental asymmetry of the relationship. Pretoria's refusal of a visa to the Dalai Lama was not reciprocated by any gesture by China. Beijing did not act according to expectations of honoring South Africa's objections to the death penalty.[59]

Ridicule of South Africa as being China's "pet" was heard around Africa and was particularly malicious in Nigeria, the continent's other heavyweight. Numerous South African foreign policy scholars cautioned against the perception of Pretoria being seen as too close to China and emphasized the need to strike a more independent foreign policy.[60]

Conclusion

In response to the four key questions posed by this volume, this chapter concludes that (1) South Africa is a more or less complete middle power by virtue of its capabilities, behavior, and emergent self-identity as a middle power; (2) China's rise has been significant in bolstering South Africa's status economically and diplomatically yet has also presented challenges to its democratic identity and to its African regional relationships despite the attractions of the Chinese model to state elites; (3) South Africa's response to China's rise has involved attempts to "ride the dragon without becoming its pet," a strategy of pursuing South African middle power ambitions and narrower economic goals while asserting South Africa's independence as an actor; and (4) South Africa's effect on China's foreign policy is felt mainly through Pretoria's leadership role in the African Union and its policies in support of humanitarian intervention, policies that China has reluctantly not opposed, even in cases such as the independence of South Sudan that directly contravene Beijing's established positions.

By interrelating the impact of different conceptions of world order with South Africa's position in the global production structure and its state-societal complex, it becomes apparent that Beijing casts a powerful ideational presence on South African state elites. China is far more likely to assert and call upon the norms, practices, and power capacities of the Westphalian interstate system as its conception of world order than to push for post-Westphalian issues like humanitarian intervention or good governance norms. Many of these norms—particularly those that relate to nonintervention, sovereignty, and anti-imperialism—resonate well in many African capitals. Additionally, they cast South Africa's international ambitions in a somewhat more favorable, more "progressive" mold if directly compared to Beijing by Western observers. Being chosen by Beijing as the leading African power (as Bruce Gilley notes in chapter 3 is common among the international relations thinkers in China) not only confers upon Pretoria much sought-after "non-Western" recognition, but enables it to play global and regional games simultaneously.

Yet punching above its weight by accommodating China comes at a price. South Africa's engagement with China is often fraught with controversy and even encounters, at times, resistance within civil society, as the instances of the Dalai Lama's intended visit and the *An Yue Jiang* cargo ship incident illustrate. As a result, it will in the future become more difficult for South Africa to dissociate itself from China and contain external actors in pursuit of a "truly African" agenda. Finally, in material terms, despite closer trade and investment ties, South Africa's predominant role as a commodity supplier to China is unlikely to reduce and may even exacerbate existing structural inefficiencies so that South Africa remains part of the global "missing middle." South Africa's middle power capacities and ambitions mean it will never be reduced to a client state of China. However, it is likely to continue to bandwagon with China on many issues as a means of enhancing both its regional and global roles. The challenge for South Africa's middlepowermanship is how to ride the dragon without becoming its pet.

Notes

1. Hussein Solomon, "South African Foreign Policy and Middle Power Leadership," in *Fairy-Godmother, Hegemon or Partner? In Search of a South African Foreign Policy*, 39–48, ed. Hussein Solomon (Pretoria: Institute for Security Studies, 1997); Janis van der Westhuizen, "South Africa's Emergence as a Middle Power," *Third World Quarterly* 19, no. 3 (1998): 435–56; Maxi Schoeman, "South Africa as an Emerging Middle Power," *African Security Review* 9, no. 3 (2000): 47–58; James Hamill and Donna Lee, "A Middle Power Paradox? South African Diplomacy in the Post-Apartheid Era," *International Relations* 15, no. 4 (2001): 33–59; Ian Taylor, *Stuck in Middle GEAR: South Africa's Post-Apartheid Foreign Relations* (Westport, CT: Praeger, 2001); Paul-Henri Bischoff, "External and Domestic Sources of Foreign Policy Ambiguity: South African Foreign Policy and the Projection of Pluralist Middle Power," *Politikon: South African Journal of Political Studies* 30, no. 1 (2003): 183–201.

2. Parts of this section draw on Janis van der Westhuizen, "A Fine and Delicate Balance: South Africa's Middle Power Complexities, 1994–2009," in *Regional Powers and Regional Orders*, 209–29, eds. Nadine Godehardt and Dirk Nabers (New York: Routledge, 2011).

3. It is instructive that Smuts was alone among the other dominion powers to be accorded the honor of attending meetings of the War Cabinet whenever he happened to be in London. Deon Geldenhuys, *The Diplomacy of Isolation: South African Foreign Policy Making* (Johannesburg: Macmillan, 1981), 6.

4. Ibid., 7.

5. Others were the promotion of democracy worldwide, justice, and respect for international law; peace as a goal to which all countries should strive, including effective arms control regimes, the priority of African concerns in policy choices, and the growing importance of economic cooperation in an interdependent world.

6. Alison Brysk, *Global Good Samaritans: Human Rights as Foreign Policy* (Cambridge: Cambridge University Press, 2009), 171.

7. Peter Vale, "Upstairs and Downstairs: Understanding the 'New' South Africa in the 'New' World," Paper presented to the seminar on Reconceptualizing peace in the Indian Ocean, Organized by the Centre for Area Studies, Osmania University, Hyderabad, March 5–6, 1993, 14–15.

8. The most notable at this time included being chair of the Southern African Development Community from 1995 to 1999, president of the UN Conference on Trade and Development (UNCTAD) between 1996 and 1999, chair of the Non-Aligned Movement (NAM) from 1998 to 2001, chair of the UN Commission on Human Rights between 1998 and 1999, and chair of the Commonwealth from 1999 to 2002. In 1999, the country was appointed to the G20 and elected to the boards

of the UN Educational, Scientific, and Cultural Organization (UNESCO), UN Development Program (UNDP), UN Population Fund (UNFPA), UN Children's Fund (UNICEF), and UN High Commissioner for Refugees (UNHCR).

9. Eduard Jordaan, "The Concept of a Middle Power in International Relations: Distinguishing between Emerging and Traditional Emerging Powers," *Politikon: South African Journal of Political Science* 30, no. 2 (2003): 165–81, 169.

10. Heidi Hudson, "When Foreign Policy Meets Foreigners: Xenophobia and the Case of South African Exceptionalism," Paper presented at the ISA-ABRI Joint International Meeting of the Pontifical Catholic University of Rio de Janeiro, July 22–25, 2009, 9.

11. Laurie Nathan, "Consistency and Inconsistencies in South African Foreign Policy," *International Affairs* 81, no. 2 (2005): 361–72.

12. Garth Shelton, "South Africa and China: A Strategic Partnership?," in *China Returns to Africa*, 257–73, 258, eds. Christopher Alden, Daniel Large, and Ricardo Soares de Oliveira (New York: Columbia University Press, 2009).

13. Lucy Corkin, "Competition or Collaboration? Chinese and South African Transnational Companies in Africa," *Review of African Political Economy* 35, no. 115 (2008): 128–33.

14. Haibin Niu, *A Chinese Perspective on South Africa as an Emerging Power: Global, Regional and Bilateral Implications* (Stellenbosch, South Africa: Centre for Chinese Studies, 2011).

15. Zhiqun Zhu, *China's New Diplomacy—Rationale, Strategies and Significance* (Farnham, UK: Ashgate, 2010), 33; David Shinn and Joshua Eisenman, *China and Africa—A Century of Engagement* (Philadelphia: University of Pennsylvania Press, 2012), 348.

16. It refers to the complex confluence of economic, military, and ideational capacities whereby the empire penetrates across borders of sovereign territorial states and includes, among others, the restructuring of a vast market for goods, capital, and services with transnational corporations and international organizations wielding considerable influence over local business elites. Much of the ideational justification for the norms, practices, and rules upon which the empire operates is facilitated by a ubiquitous media network, while military cooperation among allies facilitates integration of military forces under the aegis of the empire. "Hard power" increasingly makes way for "soft power" in those parts of the empire where economic coercion and military dominance are assured. In short, "[E]mpire constitutes a movement towards convergence in political, economic and social practices and in basic cultural attitudes—a movement tending to absorb the whole world into one civilization. Its governing principle is unity and homogeneity." Robert Cox, "A Canadian Dilemma: The United States or the World?," *International Journal* 60, no. 3 (2005): 667–84, 672–73.

17. The central feature of the Westphalian system is the sanctity of the sovereign state, yet marked by the duality of autonomy. The first involves the autonomy of each state as part of a society of nations and the second, the authority of each state in relation to its own territory and population, with both aspects protected by respect for the principle of nonintervention in the internal affairs of other states.

18. Cox, "A Canadian Dilemma."

19. Bruce Larkin, *China and Africa, 1949–1970: The Foreign Policy of the People's Republic of China* (Berkeley: University of California Press, 1971).

20. Christopher Clapham, *Africa and the International System: The Politics of State Survival* (New York: Cambridge University Press, 1996).

21. Shinn and Eisenman, *China and Africa*, 347.

22. The lines of discussion are by no means clear-cut within Africa. Yet the above discussion occurred, for instance, at a meeting of the 1st China-Africa Think Tank Forum in Hangzhou in October 2011. While a Chinese presentation condemned the International Criminal Court, colleagues from Kenya, Nigeria, and South Africa clearly argued for the ICC as a needed "neutral" external institution that can act as a needed element for upholding the "rule of law" in the follow-up of entrenched and violent African political conflicts (Grimm, personal observation, October 2011).

23. Beijing's demand for raw materials to fuel its own growth has arguably somewhat triggered some of the booms in Africa; there is, indeed, a somewhat complementary role in the global economy. Debates revolve around whether this growth is fostering African *development* in the long run (cf. Grimm 2011).

24. Zhu, *China's New Diplomacy*, 12.

25. Chun Zhang and Sven Grimm, "South-South Cooperation and the Millennium Development Goals (MDGs): Preparing for a Post-2015 Setting," Background paper for the European Report on Development 2013, *Post 2015: Global Action for an Inclusive and Sustainable Future* (Brussels: European Commission, 2013).

26. African National Congress, *International Relations: Policy Discussion Document*, March 2012.

27. The extent to which Zuma truly represented a recovery of the ANC's more radical ideals reminiscent of the 1969 Morogoro consultative conference, as many on the left had hoped, remains unclear. Many fundamentals espoused in the new euphoria for a "developmental state" were already echoed in the 2006 Accelerated and Shared Growth Initiative for South Africa (ASGISA) under Mbeki. See Carolyn Bassett and Marlea Clarke, "The Zuma Affair: Labour and the Future of Democracy in South Africa," *Third World Quarterly* 29, no. 4 (2008): 787–803.

28. "South African Party Delegation Meets Chinese Counterparts to Boost Ties," Xinhua News Agency, October 10, 2011; "SAfrica: 'Leaked' Report Gives Details, Insights on ANC's 'Study Trips' to China," *Mail & Guardian* (Johannesburg), November 29, 2010.

29. Marc Rossouw, "ANC's Secret China Trip," *City Press*, October 9, 2011. The Chinese party, for its part, extended relations also to other South African parties and also invited a delegation of the opposition Democratic Alliance, which is the provincial governing party in South Africa's Western Cape province, and the Inkatha Freedom Party. These study visits are part of China's broader foreign policy, preparing contacts and agreements at a later stage. Shinn and Eisenman, *China and Africa*, 82.

30. "ANC Says Turning to China, India," Reuters News Agency, May 23, 2012.

31. W. Gumede, "FPC Briefing: Challenges Facing South Africa-China Relations," Foreign Policy Centre, August 25, 2012, http://fpc.org.uk/fsblob/1465.pdf.

32. Unpublished survey data, "Project Saruman," Ipsos Research Surveys, commissioned by Jannis van der Westhuizen, December 2012.

33. Shinn and Eisenman, *China and Africa*, 347.

34. Adam Habib, "South Africa's Foreign Policy: Hegemonic Aspirations, Neoliberal Orientations and Global Transformation," *South African Journal of International Affairs* 16, no. 2 (2009): 143–59, 152.

35. "The BRICS Didn't Break Out the Bank," *Africa-Asia Confidential* 6, no. 6 (2013): 2.

36. S. Grimm, "Dabei Sein Ist Alles," in *AfrikaSüd, Zeitschrift zum südlichen Afrika* (February 2012); S. Grimm, "Southern Africa: Under the Influence," *ISN [International Relations and Security Network]*, ETH Zurich, May 28, 2012, www.isn.ethz.ch.

37. Less stridently, Elias Masilela, the CEO of South Africa's Public Investment Corporation, called for greater regulation of Chinese investments in Africa. "The BRICS Didn't Break Out the Bank," 1, 8.

38. David Macdonald, "Electric Capitalism: Conceptualising Electricity and Capital Accumulation in (South) Africa," in *Electric Capitalism: Recolonising Africa on the Power Grid*, 1–49, 9, ed. David Macdonald (London: Earthscan, 2009).

39. Ibid.

40. Padraig Carmody, "Another BRIC in the Wall? South Africa's Developmental Impact and Contradictory Rise in Africa and Beyond," *European Journal of Development Research* 19, no. 1 (2012): 1–19.

41. Geoffrey Garrett, "Globalization's Missing Middle," *Foreign Affairs* 83, no. 6 (2004): 84–96.

42. "State of the Nation: Zuma Adopts Chinese Model," *Mail & Guardian*, February 3, 2012. Yet there is nothing particularly Chinese about this "model." South African contexts are very different and, say, Germany or France could also have been cited. What is intriguing, however, is that the budget plan was "packaged" as being consistent with the Chinese growth model.

43. Ibid.

44. Greg Mills, *Why Africa Is Poor—and What Africans Can Do about It* (Johannesburg: Penguin Books, 2010).

45. Paul Collier, *The Bottom Billion: Why the Poorest Countries Are Failing and What Can Be Done about It* (Oxford: Oxford University Press, 2007).

46. Anthony Butler, "Why Is China so Influential over ANC Politicians?," *Business Day*, October 7, 2011.

47. While larger producers such as South Africa did find it difficult to adjust to a changing global competition, in time, for least-developed countries, some of the small print in the trade regimes, such as the EU's everything-but-arms, was also not fully opening markets and thus limited investment incentives in Africa with its difficult economic environments.

48. Shinn and Eisenman, *China and Africa*, 349.

49. "Chinese Competition and the Restructuring of South African Manufacturing," *DEV Research Briefing* 4, August 2012, School of International Development, University of East Anglia, 1.

50. The most notable being footwear, 46 percent; knitted and crocheted fabrics, 42 percent; electronic equipment, 32 percent; electric lamps, 31 percent; and clothing, 28 percent.

51. *DEV Research Briefing* 4, 3. The Chinese Embassy in Pretoria refutes these figures and contends that South African exports increased 115.2 percent from 2010 to 2011 and imports from China rose 76.7 percent. "Letter: Unfair to Blame China," *Business Day*, September 5, 2012.

52. In order of importance, in 2010 these were Zimbabwe, Zambia, Mozambique, Democractic Republic of the Congo, Kenya, Angola, Nigeria, Tanzania, Malawi, and Ghana.

53. In Angola and Tanzania these losses were about 20 percent of South African exports but less severe in Zimbabwe, Zambia, and Malawi. *DEV Research Briefing*, 4.

54. Petronel Smit, "Cosatu Expresses Reservations over Benefits of SA Joining BRICS," April 15, 2011, http://polity.org.za/print-version/cosatu-expresses-concern-over-benefits-of-joining.

55. Nicole Fritz, "People Power: How Civil Society Blocked an Arms Shipment for Zimbabwe," *South Africa Institute for International Affairs*, Occasional Paper, no. 36 (2009).

56. Some reports suggest that the cargo may have been docked beyond Luanda such as Guinea-Bissau, and the Zimbabwean government has claimed that it received the weapons.

57. Fritz, "People Power."

58. "Dalai Lama Visa Issue 'Dead in the Water,'" *Mail & Guardian*, December 6, 2011.

59. "SA Must Ride the Dragon," *Mail & Guardian*, December 15, 2011.

60. Butler, "Why Is China so Influential over ANC Politicians?"; Janis van der Westhuizen, "Has South Africa Lost Its Soft Power?" *Foreign Policy*, April 14, 2009.

CHAPTER 10

Turkey and China in the Post-Cold War World

Great Expectations

Yitzhak Shichor

Introduction

IN 2012, Turkish prime minister Recep Tayyip Erdoğan held a long meeting with US president Barack Obama ahead of the Nuclear Security Summit in Seoul. The discussions between the two men reflected the expansion of Turkey's global impact beyond the Middle East region. Turkey had long depended heavily on the United States. But in the 2000s, Washington increasingly solicited Ankara's services, both political and military. A few days after the meeting, Erdoğan became the first Turkish prime minister to pay an official visit to China in twenty-seven years. This was Erdoğan's *second* visit to China. In 2003—after his party had won a landslide victory in the election but before he officially became prime minister—Erdoğan rushed to China heading a huge delegation of officials and businessmen aiming at improving bilateral relations. This was the beginning of a dramatic transformation in Sino-Turkish relations. Ten years later, Turkey is treated by China (and many others) as a middle power. Indeed, the relationship with China is one reason for Turkey's middle power emergence. Ankara named 2012 as "Year of Chinese Culture in Turkey" and Beijing named 2013 as "Year of Turkish Culture in China."

It is no coincidence that the issue of middle powers has emerged—especially in Beijing's perspective—mainly after the end of the Cold War. Throughout the Cold War the Chinese, in a rather dogmatic way, insisted that all countries had to choose between Washington and Moscow: "Art thou for us, or for our enemies?" (*Joshua* 5:13). Still, since the early 1940s, Mao Zedong had recognized the existence of an "intermediate zone" (*zhongjian didai*), or several intermediate zones, that were neither East nor West. The end of the Cold War, accompanied by China's rise, offered countries in this intermediate zone a new option: *both* East and West. Post-Mao China's rise is one reason that middle powers like Turkey are and can be more proactive. As Lislotte Odgaard puts it: "China's position as a political great power increases the power of secondary and small states. These powers have extraordinary influence because China offers them strategic partnerships either in addition to or instead of the US alliance system."[1] Turkey provides one example.

While China's credentials as a great power are by now a fait accompli, Turkey, as a relative newcomer on the world stage, has yet to prove that it deserves the title middle power.[2] In recent years most of the media, and some leaders, have been hailing Turkey's progress, in particular economic, and greater salience not only in regional politics but also worldwide. The *Economist* wrote that "Turkey was the sick man of Europe, but now it has become one of the fastest growing economies." It is like "a new China in Europe."[3] Some define Turkey as a "global swing power."[4] Ostensibly, the definition of Turkey as a "global swing state" is appropriate. Like swing parties that can tip the outcome of domestic politics, swing states like Brazil, Indonesia, and Turkey can shape the landscape of world affairs. All represent growing economies, strategic locations, democratic governments, and states with reservations about the existing international order. Maintaining their regional and global independence, they avoid identification with the great powers and decline to take sides. Allegedly, Turkey qualifies as a "swing state" on all these accounts.

Where is China in this equation? Does Beijing consider Turkey a middle power that can positively affect the international system? What are the implications of China's emergence for Turkey, strategically, militarily, and economically? How does Turkey respond to China's rise and what are the implications of Turkey's emergence as a middle power on China? These are the main questions dealt with in this chapter. Both China and Turkey are relative newcomers as active global players whose achievements are still limited. Also, China's relations with middle powers reflect necessarily a built-in asymmetry that is underlined in the case of Turkey whose status as a "middle power" is still in doubt.[5] China-Turkey relations are based on mutual "great expectations" and the two sides, primarily Turkey, have still to deliver the goods. From being pawns (*qizi*) on the Cold War chessboard, the two have become full-fledged players (*qishou*).[6]

Beijing's Perspective

Unlike other countries discussed in this book, Turkey's designation as a middle power is a fairly recent phenomenon. While its origins can be traced to the end of the Cold War, it was referred to as a middle power only at the beginning of the twenty-first century or, more precisely, after Erdoğan became prime minister in 2003.[7]

For over two decades after the People's Republic of China was founded in 1949, Beijing regarded Turkey as a crucial link in the US-led Western front against communism and as a lackey of American imperialism. These definitions were rooted in Ankara's participation in the Korean War that engaged North Korean and Chinese troops in bloody confrontations; in Ankara's decision to take part in regional Western-orchestrated defense alliance systems (such as the North Atlantic Treaty Organization and Central Eastern Treaty Organization) and provide Washington with military and intelligence facilities; and in Ankara's offer of a substitute homeland, shelter, and base of operations for a number of Uyghur nationalist leaders who had managed to escape Xinjiang on the eve of its "peaceful liberation" by Chinese communist forces in late 1949.[8] Until the mid-1990s, Turkey was the headquarters of Uyghur nationalism, which Beijing refers to as "separatism" or "splittism" (*fenliezhuyi*).[9]

Infected by Cold War paranoia, Beijing believed—with good reasons—that a Washington-organized Middle East Islamic pact, including Turkey, could lead to the subversion of the PRC by a Muslim fifth column. In retrospect, no such attempt was ever made. Yet Turkey remained tarnished. Unlike other Middle Eastern countries that, in Beijing's view, demonstrated initial signs of "resistance to imperialism," Turkey had been categorized from the early 1950s as hopelessly pro-Western.[10] In the following years Ankara consistently supported Washington-sponsored resolutions to postpone discussion of any proposal to unseat Taiwan from the UN and to admit the PRC instead.

Throughout these years Beijing emphasized that Turkey's dependence on the United States undermined not only world and regional order but also Turkey's domestic affairs, generating political crises and economic difficulties. Beijing argued that American aid had increased Turkey's foreign trade deficit. Ironically foreshadowing China's own impact on the Turkish economy half a century later, the Chinese pointed out:

> The flooding of Turkish markets with US goods has been a serious blow to Turkey's weak national industry. Production has dwindled constantly in the textile, leather, tobacco and other industries, and factories have closed down in large numbers. The dumping of US surplus farm produce has forced Turkey's backward agriculture still further down.[11]

Beijing repeatedly urged Ankara to adopt a "peaceful and independent policy of neutrality" as the only way to overcome its economic difficulties and political crises, yet to no avail. In fact, two years later, a deterioration that had led Turkey and Syria to the brink of a border war prompted Mao Zedong to condemn the "Turkish aggressor."[12] In the early 1960s, the Chinese still regarded Ankara as oppressive internally and as a collaborator of "US imperialism" externally.[13] In the next few years, as the Cultural Revolution evolved, Beijing's negative view of Turkey increased. By the late 1960s, Maoist groups ideologically committed to the Chinese version of Marxism had begun to emerge in Turkey. The first Maoist organization in Turkey, the Communist Party of Turkey (Marxist-Leninist), was launched in 1972.[14]

Nonetheless, the Sino-US rapprochement had led to the establishment of Sino-Turkish diplomatic relations in 1971. Ankara supported the PRC's admission to the UN and as a permanent member of its Security Council. In its first thirty years, however, the diplomatic relationship drew little attention from either side. Beijing continued to concentrate on facing the "Soviet threat" at its doorstep. Turkey was too remote, marginal, and irrelevant to attract Chinese attention. Turkey, meanwhile, viewed China's "reform and opening" drive with skepticism, something that the 1989 Tiananmen massacre reinforced. Beijing, not to say Ankara, did not predict China's dramatic emergence.

It was not until the early 2000s that the relationship changed fundamentally, something that China's "middle power expert," Ding Gong of the Central Party School, has pointed out.[15] Beijing's assertive foreign policy and greater involvement in international affairs is in part related to economic considerations, growth and development, and the pursuit of mineral resources and commodities.[16] But it also reflects concern about world politics and great power constellations, primarily the role of the United States. The Chinese attitude is ultimately determined by strategic considerations rather than by economic ones. Its policy toward Turkey is no exception.

Ankara has begun to attract Beijing's attention only in recent years, following the far-reaching reforms initiated by Erdoğan. Less enthusiastic about his domestic politics, especially Turkey's growing Islamization,[17] the Chinese have been more impressed by his innovative external orientation, economically and strategically. On the eve of his visit to Turkey in 2012, Xi Jinping, then still PRC vice president, underscored economic considerations when he defined both countries as "important newly emerging market countries" and mentioned "Turkey's goal to rank among the world's top 10 economic countries by 2023." But he also pointed out that "Turkey enjoys a superior geographical position" and added:

> Turkey is a member of G20 and is also an important newly emerging country and a large country in the Middle East region. It has for long done a great deal

> in safeguarding regional stability and promoting common development. In recent years, Turkey has participated in resolving the Afghanistan issue, the Iran nuclear issue, the Middle East peace process, and other international and regional hot issues. . . . It will host the 2015 G20 summit. Turkey's proactive, flexible, and all-dimensional foreign policy has enabled the country to play a more and more important role in international and regional affairs. The Chinese side appreciates this.[18]

These are the ingredients of a middle power. Yet as important as Turkey is, the Chinese appear cautious in labeling it as a middle power—unlike other countries that are occasionally mentioned as such: Canada, South Africa, Spain, Mexico, Australia, and Brazil.[19] Still, more recently, Chinese scholars have begun to pay more attention to Turkey, designated as "intermediate country" (*zhongdeng guojia*), "middle power" (*zhongdeng qiangguo*), as well as "emerging power" or "minor power."[20] In their view, Turkey deserves these labels not so much for its tangible "hard power" (*yingshili*) in areas like population, economic size, and military power as much as for its less tangible "soft power" (*ruanshili*) in areas like values, culture, education, will, diplomacy, scientific achievements, and leadership.[21] Beijing expects middle powers to be proactive in restraining great powers, mediating between them and other countries; in facilitating peaceful settlements of regional conflicts; and in contributing to multipolarity. As Xi Jinping mentioned, Turkey fits these definitions nicely, mainly following the end of the Cold War and even more so since the emergence of Erdoğan. As an Islamic country that represents a great civilization that had undergone a "bourgeois democratic revolution," and at the same time is a NATO member, Turkey provides not only a bridge but also a "model" (*moshi*) for Middle Eastern and Central Asian countries.[22]

The Chinese also appreciated Erdoğan as a Putin-style leader, all the more so after his landslide victory in the 2011 election. He was the only prime minister in Turkish history to win three consecutive general elections, each time with more votes. These victories enabled him to govern Turkey single-handedly, sidestepping his crippled opposition. An iron-fisted regime is, after all, something familiar to Beijing and easier for it to do business with. Beijing may also identify with Erdoğan's decapitation of the military establishment and high-ranking officers—traditionally considered pro-American—and, not least, his policy of keeping a distance from the United States. The Chinese implicitly welcome Ankara's contribution to the further weakening of the US regional (and global) posture, primarily because it is done—unlike Tehran's style—in a responsible way. The sudden and total removal of US presence and influence in the Middle East would undermine China's fundamental interests—first of all the pursuit of stability—and would entail growing demands for greater Chinese activism in regional affairs, something

Beijing is not yet ready to undertake. Beijing prefers Washington to bleed a little and friendly countries like Turkey to lead a little.

Public opinion polls in Turkey show a consistent decline in approval of the United States. Confidence in President Obama, for example, fell to 12 percent in 2011. Turkish people were the least confident in Obama among twenty-three countries surveyed. In 2000, 52 percent regarded the United States in positive terms but by 2011, only 10 percent had a favorable attitude toward the United States (the lowest among twenty-two countries) while 77 percent had a negative attitude. Still, only 21 percent said that China will eventually replace the United States as the world's leading power, the lowest rank. China is by no means considered a substitute for the United States, now or in the future.[23]

Constraints on Relations

Needless to say, the Chinese are aware of "constraining elements" (*zhiyue yinsu*) in Turkey's middle power diplomacy. These include its long-blocked accession to the European Union; its Kurdish conflict; its entangled (*jiujie*) politics and military intervention in its domestic affairs; and its perceived vacillation between East and West, which reflects inability or unwillingness to make a choice.[24] Beijing also worries about Turkey's growing Islamization; ongoing squabbles with Cyprus, Greece, and Syria; approval of the Arab Spring; friction with Iran; and the revival (actual or virtual) of Pan-Turkism, a vision resuscitated in recent years not just in China's perceptions (or nightmares) but mainly by Turkish generals and politicians who still wish to revive Turkey's past greatness, mostly in Central Asia.[25] Paradoxically, some of those who promote Pan-Turkism advocate closer collaboration with the East.[26] Erdoğan's rejection of Mustafa Kemal Atatürk's legacy—including a renunciation of Turkish custody over Central Asia's Muslims—may explain Turkey's growing regional and global activism, not always to Beijing's taste.[27]

By far the most pressing constraint is Ankara's sympathy for, and identification with, the Uyghurs of western China.[28] In 2009, Abdullah Gül became the first Turkish president to visit China in fourteen years, and the first ever to visit Urumqi, the capital of the Uyghur-populated far-western territory of Xinjiang. In the past, Beijing had discouraged Turkish statesmen and politicians from visiting this troublesome region, whose Turkic ethnicities make up the majority of the population, rejecting Ankara's requests to set up a consulate there. Within a week after Gül left, violent riots broke out in Urumqi, leaving many (both Uyghurs and Han Chinese) dead. In what appeared to be an uncontrolled outburst of fury, Erdoğan said that the Xinjiang incidents "look like genocide." It is possible that Erdoğan's outburst reflected instinctive feelings against China.[29] There were official calls to boycott imported Chinese goods and resignations from the China-Turkey Inter-Parliamentary Friendship Group.[30] Yet within a month, relations had returned to normal.[31]

This Turkish retreat reflected one of the outstanding outcomes of China's rise: its ability to affect Ankara's attitude toward the Uyghurs. Throughout the Cold War, and for a few years afterwards, the Turkish governments offered shelter and aid to Uyghur transnational organizations and leaders who had escaped Xinjiang and promoted their vision of independence for "Eastern Turkestan" (the Uyghur term for a region that includes most of Xinjiang). China began to pay attention to Uyghur international activism only in the mid-1990s, after Central Asia gained independence following the Soviet collapse and after its borders with Central Asia opened. This change; Beijing's own open-door policy; the US-led campaign to promote human rights and democracy; and the advanced computer-mediated communication technologies turned Uyghur nationalism from an internal Chinese affair into an international issue. Turkey suddenly found itself the headquarters of Uyghur transnational activism.

Following Uyghur demonstrations and acts of violence against Chinese in Turkey in 1999, the Turkish police arrested ten members of the so-called Eastern Turkestan Liberation Organization. According to Chinese sources, the organization was founded in 1996 by Mehmet Emin Hazret, a Uyghur from Khotan Prefecture in Xinjiang, who had escaped to Turkey in 1989.[32] This led to the first Sino-Turkish security cooperation agreement, signed in 2000. Among other things, it facilitated public security coordination and stipulated that measures would be taken against separatist activities jeopardizing the territorial integrity of both Turkey and the PRC. The Turkish interior minister (who signed the accord in Beijing) stated that "his country will never tolerate any form of anti-China activities or terrorism in Turkey."[33] These and other measures intended to limit Uyghur activism in Turkey were a result of Beijing's pressure.

Beijing has long used Turkey as one of the most active stations of the Third Bureau (military attachés) of the People's Liberation Army (PLA) General Staff Second Department (military intelligence).[34] The Chinese not only collect political and military intelligence in Turkey, but they also infiltrate Uyghur organizations through moles, sleepers, and collaborators. Uncertainty and suspicions about their own activists often cause Eastern Turkestan organizations to fall into paralysis and passivity, exactly what Beijing wants. Monitoring Uyghur activism in Turkey (and elsewhere) is also undertaken by the 610 Office (a Ministry of State Security unit operating under the Foreign Ministry's overseas embassies). Launched on June 10, 1999 (hence their name), in response to the rise of the Falun Gong religious sect, 610 Offices are an extralegal police force formed to suppress "illegal organizations" in the PRC and abroad. Reacting to human rights critics, in 2004 the 610 Office was renamed the Department of External Security Affairs (*Shewai anquan shiwu si*, or *guanli si*, literally the Department of Managing Foreign-Related Security). It "aimed at coping with increasing non-traditional security factors" (i.e., terrorism), with the safety of Chinese personnel abroad, and also at "dealing with Eastern Turkistan groups."[35]

However, and despite China's pressure and Ankara's compliance, Turkish public opinion, as well as some parties and the police, sympathize with the Uyghurs—in both China and Turkey. Moreover, given the balance of power in Xinjiang and the nearly universal (including Taiwan's) recognition of Xinjiang as an integral part of China, it is doubtful that Beijing is *really* concerned about the chances of Uyghur separatism or independence. It is more likely that the Chinese exploit the Uyghur issue to intimidate foreign governments and organizations to underwrite positive dispositions for Beijing's policies and demands.

For Turkey there are also constraints on closer ties to China. Ankara rejected China's appeal to boycott the Liu Xiaobo Nobel Peace Prize ceremony; began to distance itself from Iran; and criticized China's (and Russia's) UN Security Council veto on the proposal to condemn the government of Syria as responsible for the atrocities and violence there in 2012 and 2013.[36] In a live television interview, Erdoğan harshly criticized Russia and went on: "China stands by Russia and although Hu Jintao had told me they wouldn't veto the [safe zone] plan for a third time, they did at the UN vote."[37] An article in the Turkish daily *Hürriyet*, titled "The Gang of Four: Syria, Iran, Russia, China," said:

> The still-communist China is the fourth member of the gang. Here, I don't even need to explain that "human rights"—including the most basic one, the right to life—means nothing for Beijing. This is simply a mercantilist dictatorship without any principles. "It doesn't matter whether a cat is black or white," the late Deng Xiaoping once said, "as long as it catches mice." Apparently, it doesn't matter how many innocents die while the cat gets fed.[38]

Turkish public opinion toward China has become more and more negative over time. The percentage of those with a favorable view of China has gradually declined from 40 percent in 2005 to 22 percent in 2012, nearly the lowest among twenty-one countries surveyed. At the same time, while more and more people in Turkey regarded China as the world's leading economy

(7 percent in 2008 gradually growing to 22 percent in 2012), this was almost the lowest among thirty-four countries surveyed (Germany and Britain came first and second with 62 and 58 percent, respectively).[39]

These "constraints" and disagreements by no means imply that Turkey is less a middle power in Beijing's perspective. On the contrary, the principal feature of a middle power is that it is *in the middle*. It does not identify with a sponsor power on all issues nor does it discard a sponsor power on all issues; it goes along with some and rejects some. This is an indication of independence, exactly what the Chinese promote. As seen in other country studies in this book, China's rise is paradoxical because not only has it promoted middle power influence, it has also thereby created more complex and constraining regional and global governance that Beijing must negotiate.

Military and Strategic Implications

China's emergence as a great power has affected Turkey in a number of ways, some positive, some negative. Unlike the Cold War period when Turkey had practically no choice but to take Washington's side against Moscow, the post–Cold War period has transformed the international system and created new options. Ironically, the uncompromising EU rejection of Turkey's membership not only may have spared the Turks grave economic difficulties, but has also expanded their room of maneuver. These new and unprecedented political, military, and economic opportunities and possibilities have enabled Turkey to adopt a more independent foreign policy—not only in a regional context but also in a global one.

For Turkey, China is not just a means of economic growth or cultural exchange; it is primarily a tool for demonstrating Turkey's freedom of choice—by no means a substitute to the United States but a counterbalance, and not necessarily at the expense of its EU option but on top of it as part of Ankara's so-called "eastern orientation."[40] The "eastern orientation" came up dramatically in 2012, when Erdoğan suggested in jest that Turkey would abandon its EU efforts if Russia and China allowed it to join their organization for development and security in Central Asia, the Shanghai Cooperation Organization (SCO). However, he repeated the idea more seriously in 2013: "The SCO is better and more powerful, and we have common values with them . . . in terms of population and markets. This organization [SCO] significantly surpasses the European Union in every way."[41] Turkey became an SCO dialogue partner in 2013, the first NATO country to participate in the organization.

The SCO issue is reflective of deeper geostrategic issues, none of which necessarily draw Turkey closer to China. China likely prefers that Turkey become part of the EU because it would make Turkey a more valuable partner for China. The United States, meanwhile, may have supported Turkish participation in the SCO because it prefers that Russia, rather than China, should be the most influential power in Central Asia. Turkey's participation in the SCO under Russian sponsorship will advance Russian leadership of the organization.

Closely aligned with the United States and NATO, Ankara—affected by a time-honored Cold War mentality and the legacy of the Korean War—had never considered Beijing a military supplier, let alone a substitute to the United States. It was only by the mid-1990s, more than twenty years after the establishment of diplomatic relations, that Turkey became interested in China as a strategic and military partner, if not an ally. This came after the United States refused to provide Ankara with the production license and technology for the M-270 Multiple Launch Rocket System. Washington criticized Ankara for using US-made weapons for human rights abuses; restricted arms sales to Turkey; and cut off grants earlier offered to Turkey for arms acquisitions from the United States. Ankara had no choice but to turn to its military industry and to look elsewhere for arms and military technology. China—whose military hardware was definitely inferior and incompatible—has always divorced arms transfers from political conditions. Its main incentive in transferring arms and defense technology to Turkey has been political and strategic: to drive a wedge between Ankara and Washington.[42]

Based on Chinese technology, in 1997, Turkey began to license-produce different types of missiles and rockets and to upgrade armored infantry combat vehicles.[43] In a dramatic turn of events, Turkey announced in 2013 that it had chosen initially a $3.4 billion missile defense system made by China Precision Machinery Import Export Corporation, a company under US sanctions, over rival Russian, US, and European systems, because it was cheaper and came with offers of technology transfer and coproduction. Whatever the final decision, the announcement signified a new independence in Turkish security policy. Nevertheless, China still is a marginal military supplier to Turkey. According to Stockholm International Peace Research Institute (SIPRI) data, the estimated value of the PRC arms transfers to Turkey between 1998 and 2011 (no Chinese arms sales to Turkey had been reported before 1998) is as low as US$43 million or 0.3 percent of Turkey's total arms acquisitions in that period, and no higher than 2.7 percent if unconfirmed deals are included.[44] Increased Chinese arms sales to Turkey are unlikely because of incompatibility with NATO systems, and probably also because of concern about possible leaks of secrets and intelligence.[45] Still, as mentioned, Beijing's incentive is not only military or economic but primarily political and symbolic—and the same goes for Turkey, whose commitment to NATO has been eroded since the Soviet collapse.[46] A poll of the Turkish public's attitude toward NATO in 2011 revealed that 64 percent held an unfavorable view (the highest among ten countries) and only 18 percent held a favorable view (the lowest among ten countries).[47]

While Sino-Turkish arms transactions are limited, remain mostly confidential, and fail to appear in the UN Register of Conventional Arms, joint exercises gain more publicity and are, therefore, more politically—and symbolically—significant. They originated in a military training and cooperation protocol signed in 1999, when the Turkish army deputy chief of staff visited China.[48] Apparently no more than a formality at that time, it became meaningful in 2009, when General Hasan Aksay, commander of the Turkish military academies (and air force commander from 2009) visited China. The two countries agreed to upgrade their military cooperation to provide for joint military exercises and training and also to promote defense industrial projects. PLA deputy chief of staff Ge Zhenfeng praised the smooth development of military relations between the two militaries, their friendly exchanges, and their "pragmatic cooperation."[49] This, however, by no means implies a favorable Turkish attitude toward China's military power. Asked how China's growing military power affects Turkey, only 9 percent of Turks surveyed responded positively, whereas 66 percent responded negatively. Also, to the question whether it would be good or bad if China became as powerful militarily as the United States, 54 percent of the Turkish public responded negatively and 20 percent positively.[50]

It is within this context that, following Israel's exclusion, Ankara invited the PLA's air force to join the 2010 Anatolian Eagle aerial military exercises.[51] The fact that the United States for the first time *did not* participate in the annual exercise—as a protest against Israel's exclusion—conformed to both China's and Turkey's interests: to keep a distance from Washington as an indication of independence, a message Ankara had already delivered during the 2003 Iraq War when the United States was not allowed to use its Turkish bases for military operations against Iraq.[52] As soon as China's fighters left Turkey, Wen Jiabao arrived in Ankara—the first Chinese prime minister to visit Turkey in eight years. A month later, Chinese and Turkish special forces exercised counterterrorism and assault tactics in the mountainous parts of Turkey, the first time that Chinese troops operated in a NATO member country.[53]

Economic Implications

One of the reasons Turkey belongs to the middle power category is its fast economic growth since the beginning of the twenty-first century that elevated it to the G20 elite group.[54] Yet, impressive as it is, Turkey's economy has been vulnerable to the growth of China. China's exports accounted for 89 percent of Sino-Turkish trade in 2012.[55] Visiting Turkey in 2002, PRC vice premier Zhu Rongji said: "China attaches great importance to Turkey's trade deficit with China and is working hard to take measures to increase imports from Turkey."[56] Turkish trade circles explained that while Turkey exports raw materials to China, the Chinese place customs duties on Turkish-made products. "Accordingly," said Kürşad Tüzmen, Turkish state minister responsible for foreign trade, "we cannot sell much to China. We must find ways to sell more to China. At a time when our exports are increasing rapidly, why can't we sell to China?"[57] One reason is that Chinese firms are more efficient and therefore more competitive than the Turkish ones, leading to "negative expectations from Chinese economic boom in Turkish manufacturing industry."[58] During his visit to Turkey in 2012, Xi Jinping reiterated that "the Chinese side . . . continues to seek a comprehensive way to solve our trade imbalance problems."[59] Ten years after Zhu Rongji's comments quoted above, all attempts to close this gap have, however, failed. In fact, the gap has widened.

Certain sectors of the Turkish economy, in particular textiles and electronics, have been crippled. In 2006, the Turkish *Milli Gazete* blamed China for the recession in the textile sector, "the flagship of the Turkish economy."[60] A 2003 poll conducted by the Ankara Chamber of Commerce uncovered that twenty-five sectors of the Turkish economy are overflowing with Chinese products; some 80 percent of the ready-made garments and toys industry are dominated by Chinese products and *all* of the leather goods manufacturing are under Chinese control.[61] China's penetration has reached such proportions that "each ship full of Chinese products that docks at the Turkish ports is causing the closure of a Turkish factory."

One reflection of the official response is that the share of antidumping cases against China in Turkey's total antidumping cases in the World Trade Organization is the highest in the world.[62] Beijing has called Ankara's actions "one-sided and unacceptable" and added: "Turkey was attempting to make China a scapegoat by using dubious figures and hasty generalizations."[63] On the eve of his visit to Turkey in 2012, Vice President Xi Jinping did not hide his irritation: "We hope that the Turkish side will provide a better environment and more convenient working conditions for Chinese enterprises."[64]

In addition to trade, Beijing has also been diversifying its investments in Turkey, mainly contracted projects and engineering services. PRC official statistics claim that between 2001 and 2011, China invested US$10 billion in Turkish projects, 40 percent of which were already completed.[65] Despite these achievements, however, Turkey still falls far behind other markets as a target for Chinese investments and construction contracts and its share in China's overall foreign economic relations is still relatively small, reaching a peak of 1.59 percent in 2009 but falling to 0.89 percent the next year.[66]

Although Xi Jinping wrote that "China and Turkey are strongly complementary to each other in terms of capital, technology, and market," actually they are not.[67] In fact, they represent competitive economies not only bilaterally but also worldwide, mainly in the fields of textile and leather goods, electrical equipment, and notably, construction (a major Turkish international economic activity).[68] Furthermore, any planned increase in bilateral trade as advertised during the recent visits inevitably means an increase in the Turkish trade deficit. In China's economic relations with Turkey, the latter is definitely the underdog. The Turkish government regards the integration of China (as well as India) into the global economy as an "unfavorable development" that implies a negative impact on the Turkish economy.[69] A Pew public opinion poll conducted in 2011 reinforces this conclusion. To the question how China's growing economic power affects Turkey, only 13 percent responded positively (the lowest among twenty countries) while 64 percent (the highest) responded negatively.[70]

Turkey's Rise: Implications for China

Given the asymmetry between the two, it is understandable that Turkey's impact on China would be considerably smaller than China's impact on Turkey. Turkey—unlike other middle powers like Australia discussed in this book—has nothing to offer the Chinese in terms of commodities and raw materials, let alone military or political benefits. Turkey's main value as a middle power for the Chinese is strategic: a contribution to multipolarity, a weakening of the United States, and a foothold in the crucial junction between Asia, the Middle East, and Europe. This is the main reason why Beijing offered to upgrade their bilateral relations to the level of a "strategic relationship of cooperation" (*zhanlue hezuo guanxi*), which China maintains with few other countries (e.g., Pakistan, India, Australia, Russia). Concluded during Wen Jiabao's 2010 visit to Turkey, this partnership is another foothold in Beijing's attempt to expand its presence and influence in the world.

In the narrow sense, it is directed, according to Beijing, against the "threat of the three evil forces of terrorism, separatism and extremism" that the two face and reflects their common interests "in safeguarding the integrity of territory and sovereignty." Yet behind these slogans lies the real and wider incentive, namely, that China's leaders "attached importance" to Turkey's "influence in regional and international affairs."[71]

Is this partnership really about strategy or is it only a smoke screen for hiding the *real* Chinese interest in economic expansion, as some believe?[72] To be sure, this agreement was immediately followed by eight cooperation pacts in the areas of trade (to be increased from US$10 billion in 2009 "to US$50 billion in 2015 and to US$100 billion in 2020"!), infrastructure, and communications. These led Erdoğan to say that relations between Turkey and China "are now entering a new stage of development." As mentioned, in the Joint Declaration on Establishing Strategic Relationship of Cooperation of 2010, the two sides defined themselves as "emerging developing countries."[73] Yet Beijing could have signed these documents without offering Turkey strategic partnership, however of limited value. The fact that it did indicates that its interests go beyond economics and that it was ready to modify its policies.

One indication of Beijing's growing respect for Turkey is the reversal of its policy that had blocked Turkish leaders' visits to Xinjiang. As mentioned above, in 2009 Abdullah Gül became the first Turkish president to visit Urumqi. In 2010, Ahmet Davutoğlu became the first Turkish foreign minister to visit Kashgar, the heart of the Uyghur community. He was bold enough to admit Turkey's "close historic and cultural bonds" with the "Uyghur Turks," adding that "China is almost a continent for us. We want to increase the number of Turkish consulates. . . . We are determined to take every step that will bring the Turkish and Chinese peoples closer and open consulates all over China," presumably including Xinjiang.[74] As of now, Beijing still rejects Turkey's application but in 2011 allowed Hainan Airlines to start direct Istanbul-Urumqi flights, an act of political goodwill that involves few political risks and many economic benefits.[75]

Finally, another benefit for Beijing is its participation in the Anatolian Eagle aerial military exercise and the counterterrorism exercise held in Turkey in late 2010. It is hardly conceivable that middle powers like Australia and Canada would invite PLA units to participate in military exercises in their territories. It should be noted that the "military" significance of China's participation was limited but its symbolic value was huge. Ankara offered Beijing an entry ticket to the international league, recognizing China as a legitimate global player. The rules have changed.

Conclusion

In response to the four key questions posed by this volume, this chapter concludes that (1) Turkey is an incomplete middle power both because of its still-tentative embrace of classic middle power diplomacy and because of uncertainties about the durability of its capabilities; (2) China's rise, which has entangled it in the Middle East far more than expected, has both bolstered Turkey's regional role and geostrategic options as well as causing typical concerns about economic hollowing-out and human rights softness; (3) Turkey's response has reflected its tangled relationship with the European Union in particular, embracing China as part of an "eastern option" while seeking to maintain its autonomy; and (4) Turkey's most direct effects on China relate to the softening of its policy on pan-Turkic links between Xinjiang and Central Asia and Turkey, while its indirect effects center on Turkey's "honest broker" role in Middle East security issues, which China has often supported or accepted.

Turkey's designation as a middle power reflects primarily its impressive growth in recent years. Some observers, however, are still skeptical and believe that the Turkish economy is on the verge of collapse and that its acceleration is artificial, representing an outburst of expenses fed by low-interest loans and credits.[76] Furthermore, the average annual foreign direct investment has declined considerably since 2008 and may decline even more in view of the global economic slowdown. Still, Turkey is highly dependent on external loans, which means that in case of insolvency crisis, Turkey, which does not belong to the European Union or the Euro Bloc, nor to any other regional organization, cannot expect to be rescued from outside—except perhaps by China, which has not been eager so far to save failing economies.

Turkey's accelerated growth policy is based on "hot money."[77] According to OECD data, Turkey is the highest risk among the middle powers discussed in this book, as far as export credits are concerned, ranking 4 (Australia and South Korea rank 0—no risk at all—Malaysia ranks 2, and Indonesia, Brazil, and South Africa rank 3).[78] As a result, Turkey's middle power capabilities have still to be tested and proved as sustainable.

Meanwhile, Turkey's proactive middle power behavior is based on relatively fragile economic foundations. It is a "contingent middle power," still on parole. Is Turkey going to survive as a middle power? Turkish foreign policy, in the words of one journalist, "suffers from its inability to meet the raised expectations in national and global politics."[79] Still, as with other middle powers considered in this book, the case of Turkey is useful both for providing a prism to understand the rise of China and to direct our attention to issues of world politics "beyond hegemony." China's rise has brought it into new and complicated relationships with countries like Turkey and with the regional and global foreign policies that they pursue. Far beyond the attention of most Western analysts of international affairs, this is one relationship that should be watched closely.

Notes

1. Lislotte Odgaard, "China's National Security Strategy and Its UNSC Policy on Libya," in *The Situation in West Asia and North Africa and Its Impact on the International Strategic Configuration, Conference Report*, 74–78, 74, ed. David Mulrooney (Stockholm: Institute for Security and Development Policy, 2012).

2. Some claim that Turkey had already been a middle power. See Dilek Barlas, "Turkish Diplomacy in the Balkans and the Mediterranean: Opportunites and Limits for Middle Power Activism in the 1930s," *Journal of Contemporary History* 40, no. 3 (2005): 441–64; Serhat Güvenç, *Turkey in the Mediterranean in the Interwar Era: The Paradox of Middle Power Diplomacy and Minor Power Naval Policy* (Indiana: Indiana University Turkish Studies, 2010); Hasan Basri Yalçın, "The Concept of 'Middle Power' and Recent Turkish Foreign Policy Activism," *Afro Eurasian Studies* 1, no. 1 (2012): 195–213.

3. John Peet, "Special Report: Turkey," *Economist*, October 21, 2010.

4. Daniel M. Kliman and Richard Fontaine, "Turkey: A Global Swing State," *German Marshall Fund Analysis Reports*, April 13, 2012.

5. For a different perspective see Rosita Dellios and Nadir Kemal Yilmaz, "Turkey and China: A Study in Symmetry," *Journal of Middle Eastern and Islamic Studies (in Asia)* 2, no. 1 (2008): 13–30.

6. Xian Xiao and Wenzhang Wang, "Zhongguo yu Tuerqi guanxi de yanbian, wenti yu weilai" [The evolution of Sino-Turkish relations: problems and the future], *Waijiao Pinglun* [*Foreign Affairs Review*], no. 95 (2007): 32–38, 35.

7. Zia Meral and Jonathan Paris, "Decoding Turkish Foreign Policy Hyperactivity," *Washington Quarterly* 33, no. 4 (2010): 75–86.

8. Çağdaş Üngör, "Perceptions of China in the Turkish Korean War Narratives," *Turkish Studies* 7, no. 5 (2006): 405–20; Füsun Türkmen, "Turkey and the Korean War," *Turkish Studies* 3, no. 2 (2002): 161–80.

9. Yitzhak Shichor, *Ethno-Diplomacy: The Uyghur Hitch in Sino-Turkish Relations* (Honolulu: East-West Center, 2009); Shih Chien-yu, "Xinjiang zai Zhongguo yu Tuerqi guanxi jiande jiaose" [The role of Xinjiang in China-Turkey relations], *Taibei Luntan* [*Taipei Forum*], July 5, 2012; and "Turkish-Chinese Relations in the Shadow of the Uyghur Problem," *Today's Zaman*, March 29, 2010.

10. See, for example, Qing Wang, "Meidi nuyi xia de Tuerqi" [Turkey under American imperialist enslavement], *Shijie Zhishi* [*World Knowledge*], no. 17 (1951): 19–20.

11. "Comments," *Renmin Ribao* [*People's Daily*], December 2, 1955.

12. *Renmin Ribao*, November 7, 1957; see also *Renmin Shouce 1958* [*People's Handbook 1958*], 432–33; and *Renmin Ribao* [*People's Daily*], October 18, 1957.

13. *Support the Patriotic and Just Struggle of the Turkish People* (Peking: Foreign Languages Press, 1960).

14. Aydin Çubukçu, "Türkiye'de Maoculuğun Doğuşu Üzerine Bazı Gözlemer" [Observations on certain origins of Maoism in Turkey], *Praksis*, no. 6 (2002): 53–62.

15. Gong Ding, "Zhong-Tu guanxi sishinian: huigu yu zhanwang" [Forty years of Sino-Turkish relations: retrospect and prospect], *Alabo shijie yanjiu* [*Arab World Studies*], no. 3 (2011): 20–28.

16. Richard Weitz, "China-Turkey Summit: Economic Enticements Overshadow Differences," *Turkey Analyst* 5, no. 6 (2012): 4–8, www.silkroadstudies.org/new/inside/turkey/2012/120319B.html.

17. Duygu Atlas, "Turkey in the Face of Creeping Islamization in the Public Sphere," *Middle East Crossroads* 2, no. 9 (2012): 3–9. In December 2012, Yilmaz Şahin Hilal, chairman of the Turkish Islamic Party (a jihadi organization), was interviewed by Turkish television and blamed the Chinese government for continuously perpetrating crimes against Muslims in China. See ICT Jihadi Websites Monitoring Group, *Periodical Review* (December 2012): 41–42.

18. Xinhua News Agency, February 24, 2012. See also Selçuk Çolakoğlu, "Chinese Perceptions of Turkey—Analysis," *Eurasia Review News and Analysis*, October 9, 2012.

19. See, for example, Guangqi Wei, "Zhongdeng guojia yu quanqiu duobian zhili" [Middle powers and global multilateral governance], *Taipingyang xuebao* [*Pacific Journal*] 18, no. 12 (2010): 36–44.

20. Zan Tao, "Uncertainty and Ambiguity: Turkey's Perception of the Rise of China," *Journal of Middle Eastern and Islamic Studies* 3, no. 1 (2009): 66–79, 79. See also Zan Tao, "Zhong-Tu guanxi ji Tuerqi dui Zhongguo jueqi de kanfa" [Sino-Turkish relations and Turkey's perception of China], *Alabo shijie yanjiu* [*Arab World Studies*], no. 4 (2010): 59–66.

21. Yong Zhang and Shulin Wang, "Ruanshili yu yingshili: jingzheng li pingjiade—yige xinlilun kuangjia" [Soft power and hard power: a new framework for the evaluation of competition for power], *Heilongjiang shehui kexue* [*Heilongjiang Social Sciences*], no. 4 (2008): 6–14.

22. Zan Tao, "'Tuerqi moshi': lishi yu xianshi" [Turkey's model: past and present], *Xinjiang shifan daxue xuebao, zhexue shehui kexue ban* [*Journal of Xinjiang Normal University, Philosophy and Social Sciences Edition*] 33, no. 2 (2012): 10–22; Ding, "Prospects and Realities," 64–65; Burhanettin Duran, "Whose Model? Which Turkey?" *Foreign Policy*, February 8, 2011; Graham E. Fuller, "Turkey's Strategic Model: Myth and Realities," *Washington Quarterly* 27, no. 3 (2004): 51–64.

23. Pew Research Center, *Global Attitudes Project* (July 13, 2011), 1, 3, 5, 6, 20, 30. See also "The Root Causes of Turkish Anti-Americanism," *Today's Zaman*, June 10, 2012.

24. Bingzhong Li, "Qianxi Tuerqi jingnei de Kuerderen wenti" [Analysis of the Kurdish people problem inside Turkey's borders], *Shijie minzu* [*World Nationalities*],

no. 3 (2008): 12–22; Shengyan Kuang and Zhihong Chen, "Kuerde gongrendang wenti ji qi dui Tuerqi neiwai zhengce de yingxiang" [The question of the Kurdish workers party and its impact on Turkey's domestic and foreign policy), *Xiya Feizhou* [*Western Asia and Africa*], no. 4 (1995): 19–24; Yitzhak Shichor, "China's Kurdish Policy," *China Brief* 6, no. 1 (2006): 3–6; Ding, "Prospects and Realities," 66–68; Lichen Xie, "Rentong shijiao xiade Tuerqi duiwai zhengce" [Turkish foreign policy in identity perspective], *Xiya Feizhou* [*Western Asia and Africa*], no. 9 (2011): 29–40.

25. John C. K. Daly, "The Rebirth of Pan-Turkism?" *Eurasia Daily Monitor* 5, no. 5 (2008); John C. K. Daly, "Pan-Turkism Takes Step Forward in Eurasia." *Eurasia Daily Monitor* 5, no. 39 (2008).

26. İhsan Daği, "Are the Eurasianists Being Purged?," *Today's Zaman*, July 21, 2008; Hoonman Peimani, "Turkey Hints at Shifting Alliance," *Asia Times*, June 19, 2002; Sait Başer, "The Strategic Importance of the Ascending East," *East and West Studies*, August 6, 2007; see also Ying Ding, "Turkey Turns East," *Beijing Review*, April 22, 2012.

27. The two countries are competitors for influence in Central Asia. See Bariş Adıbelli, *Büyük Avrasya Projesi: Abd, Rusya ve Çin'in Varolma Mücadelesi* [The Grand Euroasia project: the struggle of the USA, Russia, and China] (Istanbul: Iq Kültür Sanat Yayıcılık, 2006); Bariş Adıbelli, *Çin'in Avrasya Stratejisi* [China's Eurasia strategy] (Istanbul: Iq Kültür Sanat Yayıcılık, 2007); Weihua An, "Lun Tuerqi tong zhongya xin duli guojia de guanxi yu Tujue yuzu de lianhe" [On the relations between Turkey and Central Asia's newly independent republics and the unity of Turkic nationalities and languages), in *Xin xingshi xia de zhongya yanjiu* [*Studies on Central Asia's new situation*], eds. Bian Zhu, Weihua An, and Zhenguo Zhang (Beijing: Peking University Asia-Africa Research Institute, 1993), 79–94; see also "Is Turkey Turning Its Back on Atatürk?," *EurasiaNet Weekly Digest*, June 20, 2012; F. Stephen Larrabee, "Turkey's Eurasian Agenda," *Washington Quarterly* 34, no. 1 (2011): 103–20.

28. Zhiping Pan, "Lun Tuerqi yu fantujuezhuyi" [On Turkey and Pan-Turkism], *Shixue jikan* [*Collected papers of history studies*), no. 4 (2004): 60–68; Shichor, *Ethno-Diplomacy*.

29. Üngör, "Perceptions of China," 406, 416; see also Deniz Ülke Ariboğan, *Çin'in Gölgesinde Uzakdoğu Asya* [*Far East Asia under China's Shadow*] (Istanbul: Bağlam Yaınları, 2001).

30. "Turkish Pressure Mounting on China to Stop Killings in Xinjiang," *Today's Zaman*, July 9, 2009.

31. Ambassador [to Turkey] Gong Xiaosheng, "Friendship and Cooperation between China and Turkey in Line with Our Common Interests," August 3, 2009, http://big5.fmprc.gov.cn/gate/big5/tr.china-embassy.org/eng/dsxx/t576720.htm.

32. http://news.sina.com.cn/c/2003-12-15/18471347957s.shtml.

33. Anatolia News Agency (Ankara), February 14, 2000, in *Turkistan Newsletter*, February 16, 2000, and "Open Letter to the President and Prime Minister of Turkey on Eastern Turkestan," *Turkistan Newsletter* 4, no. 79 (2000): 2.

34. Nicholas Eftimiades, *Chinese Intelligence Operations* (Ilford, UK: Frank Cass, 1994), 81. See also *Ming Pao Newspaper* (Hong Kong), October 7, 1998.

35. *People's Daily*, July 6, 2004; see also the testimony of Chen Yonglin, former diplomat in China's Consulate in Sydney, in *Falun Gong and China's Continuing War on Human Rights*, Joint Hearing, U.S. Congress, July 21, 2005 (Washington, DC: U.S. Government Printing Office, 2005), 34–36.

36. "Turkey Rebuffs China on Nobel Rite Boycott," *Hürriyet*, December 9, 2010. Turkey by no means wants Iran to have nuclear weapons. See Dongchao Zheng, "Gongshi yu fenqi: Meiguo he Tuerqidui Yilang hewenti renzhi yanjiu" [Agreement and disagreement: US and Turkey understanding of Iran's nuclear problem], *Heping yu fazhan* [*Peace and Development*] 6, no. 124 (2011): 49–52.

37. "Turkey's Erdoğan Slams Russia, China, Iran over Syria," Reuters News Agency, September 27, 2012.

38. Mustafa Akyol, "The Gang of Four: Syria, Iran, Russia, China," *Hürriyet*, February 8, 2012. See also Şaban Kardaş, "Turkey Confronts Syria Imbroglio," *Eurasia Daily Monitor* 9, no. 23 (2012): 2–3; Barcin Yinanc, "Turkey and Cold War Tactics in Syria," *Hürriyet*, February 14, 2012.

39. PEW, *Global Attitudes Project*, 37.

40. "Turkish FM Says Asia, China Not Alternative to EU," *Hürriyet*, November 1, 2010.

41. Yavuz Baydar, "Towards the Shanghai Five," *Today's Zaman*, January 27, 2013; Emrullah Uslu, "Turkish Prime Minister Suggests SCO Membership Instead of European Integration," *Eurasia Daily Monitor* 10, no. 17 (2013): 4–5.

42. On the deterioration of Turkish-American military relations and China's attempts to exploit it, see Atul Kumar, "Sino-Turkish Strategic Partnership: A Prudent Hedging or an Irreversible Shift," *China Report* 49, no. 1 (2013): 119–41.

43. "A New Birth of Chinese Version BMP3," *Kanwa Defense Review* (Hong Kong), May 12, 2005. For more details on Sino-Turkish arms transactions see Shichor, *Ethno-Diplomacy*, 40–42, and Prasun K. Sengupta, "Eastern Showcase," *Force* (New Delhi), May 16, 2008; *Today's Zaman*, July 16, 2008.

44. Adapted from Stockholm International Peace Research Institute (SIPRI), arms transfer database, www.sipri.org/databases/armstransfers.

45. *Hürriyet Daily News*, December 31, 2010.

46. Tarik Oğuzlu, "Turkey's Eroding Commitment to NATO: From Identity to Interests," *Washington Quarterly* 35, no. 3 (2012): 153–64.

47. Pew, *Global Attitudes Project*, 64.

48. *Jane's Defense Weekly*, June 9, 1999.

49. *Jiefangjun Bao* (PLA Daily), March 25, 2009.

50. Pew, *Global Attitudes Project*, 7, 19, 39.

51. "China Mounts Air Exercise with Turkey, US Says," Reuters News Agency, October 8, 2010. Reportedly, Iran (and Pakistan) opened their airspace to China's warplanes. *Tehran Press TV*, October 4, 2010.

52. Carol Migdalovitz, "Iraq: Turkey, the Deployment of US Forces, and Related Issues," *Report to Congress*, RL31794 (Washington, DC: Congressional Research Service, May 2, 2003); Bingzhong Li, "Haiwan zhanzheng yu Tuerqi zhongdong waijiao zhengce pingxi" [A comment and analysis on the Gulf War and Turkey's Middle East foreign policy], *Shixue jikan* [*Collected Papers of History Studies*], No. 3 (2011): 46–53.

53. More details and references in Chris Zambelis, "Sino-Turkish Strategic Partnership: Implications for Anatolian Eagle 2010," *China Brief* 11, no. 1 (2011): 8–12.

54. "Jim O'Neill of Goldman Sachs, who coined the acronym BRIC to denote the big emerging economies of Brazil, Russia, India and China, has included Turkey in MIST, a second tier of biggish rising stars alongside Mexico, Indonesia and South Korea." *Economist*, April 7, 2012.

55. Based on International Monetary Fund, *Direction of Trade Statistics Yearbook 2000*, 164, 459; *2007*, 131, 483; *Turkish Statistical Yearbook*, various years; *China Statistical Yearbook*, various years.

56. Xinhua News Agency, April 16, 2002.

57. "Tüzmen: '15 Percent of Our Trade Deficit Is Caused by China,'" Anatolia News Agency, December 2, 2005.

58. Nizamettin Bayyurt and Gokhan Duzu, "Performance Measurement of Turkish and Chinese Manufacturing Firms: A Comparative Analysis," *Eurasian Journal of Business and Economics* 1, no. 2 (2008): 75–94, 82.

59. Xinhua News Agency, March 6, 2012.

60. *Milli Gazete*, January 20, 2006.

61. This paragraph is based on Emre Özpeynirci, "25 Turkish Sectors Have Been Conquered by Chinese Products," *Hürriyet*, September 8, 2003.

62. Xiaohua Bao, "Fanqingxiao yingyong de xin qushi ji yingxiang yinsu yanjiu: yi Tuerqi weili" [New trends in using anti-dumping and a study of its motivations: Turkey as an example), *Shanghai lixin huiji xueyuan xuebao* [*Shanghai Accounting Institute Journal*], no. 1 (2011): 77–84.

63. Xinhua News Agency, July 16, 2005.

64. Xinhua News Agency, February 24, 2012.

65. Xi Jinping's Speech at the China-Turkey Economic and Trade Cooperation Forum, Istanbul, February 22, 2012, Xinhua, February 29, 2012; Richard Weitz, "China-Turkey Summit: Economic Enticements Overshadow Differences," *Turkey Analyst* 5, no. 6 (2012): 1–2, www.silkroadstudies.org/new/inside/turkey/2012/120319B.html.

66. *China Statistical Yearbook*, various years.

67. "Written Interview to Turkey's *Morning News*," *Xinhua News Agency*, February 24, 2012.

68. See for example Chun Zhang, "Tuerqi dui Feizhou zhanlue yu zhengce pingxi" [Review and analysis of Turkey's strategy and policy toward Africa], *Xiya Feizhou* [*Western Asia and Africa*], no. 9 (2011): 53–67; Chun Zhang, "Tuerqi dui Feizhou diqu de jingmao hezuo" [Turkey's economic and trade cooperation with the African region), *Alabo shijie yanjiu* [*Arab World Studies*], no. 2 (2012): 86–99.

69. Republic of Turkey, Ministry of Industry and Trade, *Turkish Industrial Strategy Document 2011–2014 (towards EU membership)*, 2010, 12, 22.

70. Pew, *Global Attitudes Project*, 7, 16, 39.

71. Xinhua News Agency, October 9, 2010. See also Xian Xiao, "Goujian Zhongguo yu Tuerqi Xinxing zhanlue hezuo guanxi" [Forging a new cooperation strategy between China and Turkey], *Xiya feizhou* [*Western Asian and Africa*], no. 9 (2011):

14–28; Richard Weitz, "Turkey and China Establish Strategic Partnership," *Turkey Analyst* 3, no. 18 (2010), www.silkroadstudies.org/new/inside/turkey/2012/120319B.html.

72. Selçuk Çolakoğlu, "Turkey and China: Seeking a Sustainable Partnership," *Policy Brief*, no. 41 (SETA: Foundation for Political, Economic and Social Research, January 2010), 12–13.

73. Xinhua News Agency, October 9, 2010.

74. *Hürriyet*, November 2, 2010, quoted in Zambelis, "Sino-Turkish Strategic Partnership," 11. There is a Turkish Consulate only in Shanghai.

75. Selçuk Çolakoğlu, "Turkey-Chinese Relations: Seeking a Strategic Partnership—Analysis," *Eurasia Review News and Analysis*, April 17, 2012.

76. This paragraph is based on Eli Amerilio, "Is Turkey's Economy on the Verge of Collapse?," *Iqtisadi: The Middle East Economy* 2, no. 3 (2012), in Hebrew. See also "Turkey's Economic Success Proves to Be Double-Edged," *International Herald Tribune*, November 22, 2012.

77. "Beware of a Turkish Economic Bust in 2012, and Don't Blame it on Foreigners," *Hürriyet*, December 15, 2011.

78. See www.oecd.org/tad/xcred/crc.htm, June 29, 2012.

79. İhsan Dağı, "From Nasser to Erdoğan: Unfulfilled Promises," *Sunday's Zaman*, November 18, 2012.

CHAPTER 11

Brazil's Rise as a Middle Power

The Chinese Contribution

Anthony Peter Spanakos and Joseph Marques

Introduction

IN THE LAST TWO DECADES Brazil has made considerable improvements in addressing long-term political and economic challenges and has become an increasingly relevant "player" in global politics. Brazil's emergence naturally leads to the question of how to understand its previous and current foreign policy behavior as global power tectonics are shifting away from the United States and Europe, toward Asia—and China in particular.

This chapter will explore Brazil's rise as a middle power, arguing for the relevance of the middle power concept and its usefulness in understanding Brazilian foreign policy. It does this by looking at how the rise of China has affected Brazilian capabilities, behavior, and identity, particularly by analyzing Brazilian activities in sub-Saharan Africa, Brazilian participation in new international groups—for example, Brazil, Russia, India, China, South Africa (BRICS) and Brazil, South Africa, India, China (BASIC)—of which China is a member, and Sino-Brazilian relations. The chapter concludes with comments about how this study may advance certain notions of middle powers more generally.

A middle power, as the term suggests, is a relational concept that can neither be conceived nor exist absent two other categories: great powers and/or super powers, and small/weak countries. The chapters by Gilley and O'Neil (chapter 1) and Manicom and Reeves (chapter 2) suggest that middle powers have capabilities that are commensurate neither with the 8 to 10 most powerful countries in the world nor with the least powerful 165 countries. This is a necessary condition for the authors since while some countries may behave like middle powers (Japan), their capabilities render them great powers.

While there is something that can be identified as middle power behavior, it need not be present in all middle powers (or, even, exclusively in middle powers). This behavior involves efforts to influence a system via multilateral institutions, to encourage a rules-based international system that is multipolar (if not multinodal), support conflict mediation, and promote national interests in regional and global contexts. This behavior implies a certain normative commitment to multipolarity, "democratization" of the international system, and support for legal constraints on great powers. These norms and behavior flow from an identity that is shaped through self-perception and external recognition that the state is a middle power.

For much of the post–World War II era, if not earlier, Brazil has been perceived as either on the verge of development or in disaster. In the past decade and a half there has been sufficient political, macroeconomic, and policy stability to encourage significant growth, leading many to argue that the country has turned the corner.[1] Yet it is important to be cautious about Brazil's material capabilities and the overall capacity of its government to manage an ambitious development agenda for the future.

Brazil occupies a huge territory and borders on ten South American countries, none of which it has faced in battle since the middle of the nineteenth century. While uneven economic growth and price instability have been persistent constraints until the past two decades in the region, Brazil's abundant natural endowments distinguish it from its neighbors. Brazil occupies half of the territory of Latin America and it is the fifth-largest country in the world in terms of population (and the third-largest democracy). It was the only South American country to send soldiers to the First World War and to participate in the Paris Peace conference. It was a founding member of the League of Nations, the United Nations, and the General Agreement on Tariffs and Trade (GATT). Although it was an active participant in debates within the UN Conference on Trade and Development (UNCTAD) beginning in the 1970s, it was noticeably absent from the UN Security Council between 1968 and 1988.[2]

In 2011, Brazil surpassed Great Britain to become the world's seventh-largest economy.[3] It is a leading exporter of oil, soy, coffee, sugar, animal protein, among other commodities, and its rain forest provides an invaluable bundle of ecological resources for the planet. While Brazil has no territorial disagreements with neighbors, it maintains some 314,000 soldiers, more than Spain or Canada, and double that of Colombia, the next-largest military in Latin America.[4]

Brazil unquestionably has the potential and, increasingly, the ability to leverage its capabilities for a larger role in global politics. But despite its substantial capabilities, Brazil has been constrained by historical legacies, state weakness in key areas, and distortions within the economy.[5] Until the end of the twentieth century, the Brazilian government struggled to maintain macroeconomic stability, reduce public debt burdens, and maintain a credible currency regime. It continues to face serious domestic problems as a result of high levels of corruption, considerable urban violence, poor protection of human rights, and high levels of inequality.[6] Additionally, investment remains lower than desirable and high taxation is one of many structural bottlenecks that impede higher rates of growth, investment, and productivity. Since the governments of Fernando Henrique Cardoso (1995–98, 1999–2002), there have been important improvements in many of these areas but each continues to hamper the ability of the Brazilian state to effectively implement government programs and to establish legitimacy domestically, undermining, to a certain extent, its ability to project its influence regionally and domestically.[7]

Brazil's capabilities, therefore, appear to be those of a particularly "powerful middle power" with the potential to contribute to regional public goods and ascend into great power territory. This potential may be realizable in time and much of this depends upon events external to Brazil. Indeed, much of Brazil's rise to prominence is not so much due to changes within Brazil but in the world, such as Chinese demand for commodities, and the effects of a power shift toward Asia.

Behavior

Middle power behavior is generally associated with "the tendency to pursue multilateral solutions to international problems, the tendency to embrace compromise positions in international disputes, and the tendency to embrace notions of 'good international citizenship' to guide diplomacy."[8] Brazil may not always act as a "good global citizen" and it does pursue national interests at the expense of others (including both greater and lesser powers). But in general it engages in multilateral action, supports rules building in the international system, and participates in international organizations and missions.[9]

Susanne Gratius, considering Brazil paradigmatic of a middle power, writes that "all middle powers attempt—albeit through different strategies and instruments—to maximize their influence over small countries, minimize the influence of great powers, and prevent the emergence of other middle powers in their respective regions," and Daniel Flemes notes that middle powers soft-balance against great powers through institutions.[10] As Brazil's capabilities have grown it has consciously attempted to reduce the scope and depth of US influence with which it and its neighbors deal. In response to the US proposal of a Free Trade Area of the Americas, Brazil used Mercosur to have greater leverage and was rewarded with a position as cochair of negotiations. Indeed, Inter-American Dialogue commentator Peter Hakim wrote, "Brazil [seeks] . . . to serve as a counterweight to the United States. At times, it has appeared intent on establishing a South American pole of power in the Western Hemisphere."[11] It has since invested heavily in separating South America *qua* region from Latin America by developing South American-only organizations beyond Mercosur, the Common Market of the South, including Unasur, the Union of South American Nations.

Furthermore, Brazil's support of democracy in the region has become more aggressive in diverging from US support of democracy. This can be seen in Brazil's immediate rejection of the post-coup government of Pedro Carmona that briefly replaced Venezuelan president Hugo Chávez in office in 2002 (while the United States indicated possible support for the new government) and in Brazilian support for ousted Honduran president Manuel Zelaya in 2009.

Brazil's efforts to limit the hegemony of the United States extend beyond its region. Most notably, as a result of frustrated commercial efforts in the Doha Round of World Trade Organization talks and the construction of solidarity with other "emerging powers," it formed the India, Brazil, South Africa group (IBSA), the Brazil, South Africa, India, and China group (BASIC), and later joined the Brazil, Russia, India, China, and later, South Africa, group (the BRIC and BRICS). While their chief purpose is not to frustrate US efforts to influence global politics and trade norms, each group aims to advance the commercial, environmental, and political interests of the group as a counterweight against US and European positions that are seen as discriminating against these countries and others in the developing world. Additionally, Brazil has also been one of the most active supporters of the G20 and empowering it to replace the G8 as the primary forum for discussions of international governance.[12]

Brazil has both offered to mediate and has mediated regional conflict. President Cardoso helped negotiate a border war between Ecuador and Peru, and various Brazilian presidents have helped address political instability in Bolivia (1995, 2000, 2006), Venezuela (2003–4), and Paraguay (1996, 1999, 2000, 2012). President da Silva (2003–10) offered to mediate between the Colombian government and the ELN (*Ejército de Liberación Nacional*) though President Uribe demurred, and, since 1994, Brazil has headed the UN peacekeeping mission in Haiti (MINUSTAH), where it maintains twelve hundred soldiers and police officers. Such interest in peacekeeping can be found among smaller powers that engage in niche diplomacy.[13] What is distinctive about Brazil is that it need not rely on only ideological resources and charismatic suasion, but can project capabilities that facilitate conflict mediation outside of its region. Brazil's membership in the Community of Portuguese Language Countries (CPLP) also gives it privileged access to issues across a wide spectrum given the organization's pluri-continental membership. Additionally, although the nuclear agreement brokered by Brazil between Iran and Turkey in 2010 was eventually undermined by the United States, the fact that Brazil was considered a credible partner by the United States and Iran speaks to the capabilities of an important middle power.

Identity

Brazil is (for the time being) a middle power in terms of capabilities and its foreign policy behavior is generally typical of middle powers. It is slightly more difficult to characterize as a middle power in ideational terms, though on balance the term seems appropriate. Following Manicom and Reeves (chapter 2), Brazil does "1) claim a degree of moralism in . . . foreign policy (the claim of good international citizenship), 2) adhere to liberal internationalist values, 3) frame itself as a leader of South–South solidarity, primarily regarding technical cooperation."[14] To these three components Gilley and O'Neil (chapter 1) suggest self-identity is also important.[15] However, many Brazilian foreign policymakers increasingly do not see Brazil as a middle power but rather as an influential emerging great power. Finally, the recognition of middle power status by others must be considered and here Brazil is seen as a rising but still middle power (due to limits to the transferability of its natural resources power to other spheres of power). The ideational component of a middle power can therefore be understood by the norms that guide its foreign policy, its self-identity, and the identity ascribed to it by others.

While Brazil has long viewed international relations in classical middle power terms (reinforcing norms and building a rules-based system, promoting conflict mediation, weakening unipolarity), a noticeable shift occurred during the Cardoso governments and again with the elevation of Lula da Silva to the presidency in 2003.[16] As macroeconomic conditions stabilized, investment increased, and the export profile of the country expanded through both presidencies, Cardoso aimed to make Brazilian foreign policy more active, engaging in more South-South relations, improving relations in South America, while maintaining friendly relations with the United States and Europe. Under Lula, Brazil adopted a more self-confident foreign policy.[17] Indeed, in his inaugural speech in 2003, Lula declared, "this country has everything to be the equal of any other country in the world. And we will not give up on this goal."[18] Despite the declaration, two of the most influential Brazilian foreign ministers in recent years (Celso Lafer 1992, 2001–2, and minister of commerce 1999) and Celso Amorim (1993–95, 2003–11, and minister of defense 2011 to the present) identify Brazilian foreign policy within the international-society favoring norms typical of middle powers.

Although Brazil's foreign policy tradition has elements that favor dependency and world systems theory, the English School of international relations is dominant in the content and study of Brazilian foreign policy.[19] Celso Lafer writes that "a Grotian vision," the approach generally considered closest to the English School, best fits Brazilian interests.[20] He writes, "[g]iven the interplay of variably shaped alliances allowed for in a world of undefined polarities, multilateral fora constitute, for Brazil, the best chessboards for the country to exercise its competence in the defense of national interests."[21] This vision is complemented by Celso Amorim, who declared that Brazil wanted "to increase, if only by a margin, the degree of multipolarity in the world."[22]

While Brazil has long imagined itself to possess *grandeza* (greatness)—suggesting itself (and ultimately being rejected) for leadership roles in the League of Nations and the UN—during the first presidency of Lula there was a sense that Brazil could become a great power. The Brazilian Foreign Ministry (*Itamaraty*) explains that, since 2003, "foreign policy . . . [has been] oriented by the concept that Brazil ought to assume a growing role in the international scene."[23] Being named a BRIC by Goldman Sachs and receiving support from the United States and France for more prominent roles in global governance through the G20 and possibly a permanent seat at the UN Security Council (UNSC) have helped solidify the image of greatness. And as early as 2004, the US National Intelligence Council's *Mapping the Global Future* identified Brazil as a future great power.[24] But Brazil's "greatness" is best understood, in scholarly terms, as a capable and increasingly assertive middle power.

Lula explained the country's greatness in the following terms: "We are not important because of the amount of money we have, the number of atomic bombs that we have, or the quantity of scientific knowledge that we possess. We are important because of our deportment and, above all, our objectives."[25] Similarly, Burges attempts to explain the rise of Brazilian capabilities and influence, particularly in South America, as "consensual hegemony," a system in which "the role of the hegemon is thus to provide the initial impetus to start the hegemonic process and encourage other countries to participate in the formation of the hegemony."[26] That is, vis-à-vis less developed countries, Brazil aims to exercise a leadership that appears grounded in middle power notions of consensus, legitimacy, and "democratic" participation.[27] However, in relations with Europe and the United States, Brazil similarly aims to insert itself, be proactive, and defend its right (and those of other developing countries), to have a greater voice as well as greater participation in global governance. Drawing on Soares de Lima and Hirst (2006), Burges and Daudelin suggest that Brazil is an "intermediate power" that can be a policy entrepreneur, soft-balance against great powers, and maintain good relations with parties according to its interests.[28]

But it is not clear how so-called "intermediate powers" are distinct from middle powers and whether the introduction of a neologism is particularly helpful.[29] After all, middle powers by definition operate in the space between great and lesser powers, they engage both groups, exercising more influence with the latter while trying to balance against the former, always in pursuit of their own interests. The distinction seems to be one of degree not type. Burges, Daudelin, Soares de Lima, and Hirst are all correct to note that Brazil is distinct from many middle powers in that it has particular material and normative capabilities that other middle powers do not have. But middle powers include roughly twenty countries across which there is variation in capabilities and ambitions, and Brazil is probably better understood as being a particularly able middle power rather than being something different altogether.[30]

Malamud's assessment of Brazil as a global middle power whose influence in its own region is highly contested is particularly helpful.[31] The resistance of neighbors to Brazilian influence is hardly surprising. What is particularly telling, however, is Brazil's insistence that its improved capabilities are not going to be enacted in a way typical of great powers. As Burges notes, Brazil resists hegemony, and Lula has explicitly said, "Brazil does not want to lead anything."[32] Thus, although the self-identity of Brazil is not obviously one of a middle power, the mental maps used to understand and communicate how it perceives its improved capabilities are typical of middle power ideation. Additionally, middle power status is not only self-ascribed, but must be recognized by other states.[33] While some analysts and diplomats speak of Brazil as a future great power, and the language used to describe Brazil is that of an "emerging power" or "emerging global player," the expectation is that the general approach of Brazilian diplomats and foreign policy specialists will remain largely unchanged, pursuing traditional goals of development, nonintervention, regional peace, and diversification of export markets and preferences for diplomacy and multilateralism over coercion and uni/bilateralism.[34] That is, it will continue to think like a middle power, albeit one with substantially greater capabilities.

Rise of China

This book aims to make a double contribution to scholarship in that it explores what is meant by the term "middle power" and it aims to understand how this term may be affected by the rise of China. Although the global context is implicit in understandings of the middle power, emphasis is normally given to relations between categories (great-middle, middle-lesser powers) or to agency (do middle powers have agency, can they affect global power structures?). But it is impossible to think about middle powers without considering how shifting structures facilitate re-visioning of capabilities and behavior, as well as norms, identity, and recognition. The gradual emergence of a number of large Brazilian multinational corporations together with an increase in Brazil's outward foreign direct investment (OFDI) and overseas development assistance are important additional indicators of likely power projection in the near future.[35]

Power transition theory tries to makes sense of how the absolute rise or decline of one power or the relative approximation of the first and second powers in a system can generate new structures, particularly the possibility of war, though a power transition need not lead to conflict, particularly when there is agreement among the rising and declining powers.[36] A considerable amount of scholarship has tried to understand China's rise through the prism of power transition theory in order to understand how the rise affects the United States or the polarity of global politics.[37] Less attention has been given to how third parties are affected by and affect Sino-US dynamics. David Zweig argues that China's relations with African states must be considered with a constant eye on its relations with the United States, as well as US relations with the states in question.[38] Horace Campbell argues that China's activities in the global South most directly challenge US hegemony.[39] In both cases the focus is on Chinese foreign policy and its perception in the United States. Similarly, much of the literature on Chinese foreign policy in the Americas is framed in terms of whether China's rising presence in the region should make US policymakers concerned.[40] Consistent with the other essays in this book, this chapter looks neither at the agency of the rising or declining first and second powers, but on a specific middle power.

The effects of a possible power transition on Brazilian foreign policy and the dynamic of Sino-Brazilian relations are considered below. Before doing so, it is worth recalling a few basic issues. First, the rise or decline of a power is the result of perception of capabilities, material and otherwise. That is, it is an act of interpretation.[41] Second, while there is little debate about whether Chinese capabilities are improving, there is debate as to whether the United States is truly declining, what it means for a developing country to be the world's second-largest economy, whether and how power is being reconfigured, or some combination of both.[42] Third, while it would be convenient for scholars, nearly two hundred countries are not in some cryogenic state simply observing as the gap between the capabilities of China and the United States closes. Not only are other countries—great, middle, and small—constantly responding to changes in global structures, but they are contributing to those changes, though obviously certain countries have more agency in this process than others.

This last point is especially important for middle powers like Brazil. While Brazil was never as constrained as other Latin American countries by US influence, particularly those in Central America and the Caribbean, its struggle with inflation, currency stability, and debt during the 1980s and 1990s necessitated considerable US and International Monetary Fund influence over economic policies. Having firmly established price stability, Brazil has more leeway to pursue autonomy from US policies. This period coincided with the "rise of the left" in Latin America and the alleged "end of the Monroe Doctrine"[43] as countries such as Brazil, Chile, Uruguay, Argentina, Venezuela, Ecuador, and Bolivia pursued self-consciously anti-neoliberal policies and were increasingly vocal in building a South American community that reduced US influence and enhanced regional identity. These policies were both the result of improved domestic economic performance and greater state capacity, as well as a decline in US interest, capacity to manage hemispheric affairs, and an increase in US efforts to encourage regionalism with responsible regional leaders (i.e., Brazil not Venezuela). The massive increase of commercial relations with China occurred only once this process was already under way and it encouraged greater foreign and economic policymaking autonomy in the region.[44] That is, Brazil's perception of a shifting global context in which it could be a more active participant was primarily made possible by domestic conditions (improved state capacity) and reduced US influence and interest in the region and, second, by the rise of Chinese interest in the region and in Brazil more specifically. This is not to say that the latter has not been important.

Brazil has responded to this conjuncture and contributed to the fragmentation of poles and nodes of authority in important ways. As already noted, it has refashioned itself as an emerging "great power" while maintaining continuity through middle power behavior and norms, leveraging greater capability to extend that behavior and diffuse its soft power to other regions, and to act more aggressively in global forums. This can be seen in its increasing presence in sub-Saharan Africa, the subject of the first case study below. It is interesting to note that while Brazil and China have extensive relations and share considerable interest in terms of global governance, this does not prevent Brazil from presenting itself as an alternative to Chinese-style investment in sub-Saharan Africa.

The shift in global context, accelerated by the rise of China, has also increased the proximity of the two countries. This partnership extends beyond commerce into the area of norm creation and diffusion, which can be seen in Brazilian activity in multilateral organizations such as the BRICS, IBSA, the G20, and BASIC. The second case study will address this, while the third will look at the more complicated issue of Sino-Brazilian relations. While Brazilian foreign policymakers (including presidents Lula and Rousseff, 2011–present) have publicly welcomed increased interaction with China (indeed, Rousseff's first international visit was to China), Sino-Brazilian relations are not unambiguously entirely beneficial for Brazil and Brazil's response, typical of a middle power, has been to try not to make China "lose face" in public but to pursue its interests through diplomacy and international institutions such as the World Trade Organization.

Case One: Relations with Africa

As noted earlier, together with a preference for a multipolar world and a multilateral system, Brazil has recently adopted a South–South orientation as a major tenet of its foreign policy, giving extra attention to sub-Saharan Africa. Brazil now sees Africa as a natural extension of its economic interests, diplomatic ambitions, and innovative international assistance. Confirming this perception of closer relations, President Lula referred to Africa sharing a "border" (the Atlantic Ocean) with Brazil. It is worth exploring Brazilian initiatives relative to Chinese and Indian efforts in the continent, as Brazil demonstrates more typically middle power behavior.

The move toward South-South cooperation increased with the Cardoso administrations' prioritization of Brazil's immediate neighbors in the Southern Cone (and partners in Mercosur), followed by the Lula administrations' choice of Africa as a major foreign policy priority. Brazil's commitment to Africa is genuine, due partially to demographics (Brazil has the largest population of African descent outside Nigeria—some 50.7 percent of the population of 191 million declared themselves of mixed race or of African descent in the 2010 census) and extensive historical and cultural ties with many African countries, especially in West Africa and Lusophone Africa. Brazil's "reengagement" with Africa is exemplified by the presidential diplomacy of Lula who made twelve trips to twenty-one African countries in eight years (while Foreign Minister Celso Amorim made sixty-seven trips to thirty-four countries).

The Chinese "going out" (*zou chuqu*) strategy identified sub-Saharan Africa as a place of great power neglect that would be ideal for the extension of Chinese commercial activities and the building of soft power in a context that would not threaten US interests. Indian foreign policy in sub-Saharan Africa is motivated by similar interests, though the US-Indian relationship is characterized by far less danger.[45] Though it lacks the heft of China and to a lesser extent India, Brazil is confident that it has much to offer African nations and it has invested much time and energy in developing a reputation as a reliable partner in the field of technical cooperation.

Similarly, while China and India appear to be interested in the entire continent, Brazil has focused initially on a few countries, mainly Lusophone countries and in West Africa. Chinese efforts are led by state diplomacy and state-owned enterprises and India's presence in Africa by private corporations. Brazilian efforts are, however, primarily the result of presidential and diplomatic action. In these ways, Brazil follows a much more traditional middle power path, whereas Chinese and India, bolstered by greater capabilities, fall more within the boundaries of great powers.

Having faced many developmental challenges itself, Brazil has a better understanding of what many African countries need as well as a comprehensive set of effective social policies and tested development solutions to offer. In this regard Brazil charts a distinct course from both traditional Western donors and the new emerging donors from the South, much as South Korea has done from its own middle power diplomacy perspective (see Kim's chapter 5). Importantly, while China and India can credibly claim familiarity and success with poverty reduction and other issues facing Africa, they lack the demographic, linguistic, and cultural ties to the region that give Brazil an apparent advantage.

Brazil's distinctive development experience has centered on the issues of controlling inflation, dealing with IMF structural adjustment plans, poverty reduction, social inclusion, and affirmative action, all issues that have considerable resonance in Africa. Also like African countries, Brazilian foreign policy has given a premium to national development but, unlike most African countries, Brazil now finds itself sufficiently secure to promote social and economic development internationally both as an expression of its fundamental beliefs as well as a way of projecting its growing soft power and visibility in the world. As of 2012, Brazil had 37 embassies and over 412 cooperation projects throughout Africa (China had 48 embassies in Africa). With much less money than China or India, Brazil has developed a reputation as a reliable and desirable partner for many African countries with whom to share its development know-how.[46] Brazil's success in addressing its developmental challenges through public policies (such as the *Bolsa Família* conditional cash transfer program, Zero Hunger program, and development bank lending) and important technical institutions are being skillfully leveraged by Brazilian diplomats through foreign and international assistance policies in Africa.[47] The Brazilian Enterprise for Agricultural Research (EMBRAPA), for example, which produces policy-relevant research on agricultural subjects such as development and sustainability, coordinates projects in thirty-five different African countries (and has recently opened an office in Ghana). Over time, and with its "horizontal" cooperation whereby Brazil views itself as a partner not a donor, Brazil has developed significant support on which it can rely in important negotiations and elections in international organizations.

Brazilian companies operating in Africa differentiate themselves from Chinese companies by their hiring and training practices. Brazil's national apprenticeship service—National Service for Industrial Training (SENAI)—has established several vocational training centers in the country and this has helped supply Brazilian companies with qualified African workers (whereas Chinese companies often generate complaints for not hiring local workers, particularly skilled workers). Brazilian cooperation in Africa has focused primarily in the fields of agriculture, health, and education mainly through the use of technical advisers from Brazil's specialized agencies. Examples of such technical cooperation include Brazil's help in establishing the first antiretroviral HIV medicine factory in Mozambique, cotton production in Mali, and a vocational training center in Angola. Brazilian foreign policy and corporations are deliberately avoiding major infrastructure projects and sporting arenas (the Chinese strategy) and instead have chosen more targeted projects that aim at social concerns and problems of employment. This reflects the "good citizen" approach expected of middle powers, particularly democratic middle powers.

Also, as a resource-rich country Brazil looks at Africa differently than China. Brazil sees Africa as a potentially large consumer market for its manufactured goods and not as a source of energy. Brazil's privileged position as a growing provider of South–South cooperation and its shared cultural heritage with several African countries bolster its image as a major international power in the eyes of many African nations.

Case Two: International Organizations

Brazil's reinsertion in global affairs in the 1990s, following its democratization and management of price stability, took the form of active participation in major international organizations. There, Brazil quickly assumed a leadership position and leveraged its visibility as both a fast-growing emerging economy as well as a country faced with many of the same development challenges as other less developed countries. Brazil today plays an important, if not the leading, role in groups such as Mercosur, Unasur, BRICS, CPLP, IBSA, and both the G20 (major economies) and G20 (developing nations) groups, among others.

Brazil has been successful in altering the negotiation dynamics at the WTO and other international organizations through a combination of its market size and diplomatic efforts to include India, South Africa, China, and others (in the form of IBSA, BASIC, and the G20 developing groups) as strategic partners in negotiations with the United States, Europe, and Japan. While these groups do not have a clear common platform, they have been able to serve as a powerful counterweight to traditional powers and to highlight how the decline of traditional powers and the shift toward the East and the South necessitates rethinking global governance. Importantly, Brazil does not try to affect world governance by itself but works through coalitions of like-minded states and multilateral institutions.

The term BRIC (Brazil, Russia, India, and China), rapidly growing countries with large domestic markets, was created by a research team at the US investment bank Goldman Sachs.[48] By 2008, the four countries contained 42 percent of the global population and were responsible for 14.6 percent of world GDP and 12.8 percent of global trade.[49] Following the global recession of 2008, the four countries held their first summit in 2009. They have since met annually and, in 2011, South Africa joined the other four countries.[50] The countries share a similar foreign policy orientation to give a greater voice to the developing world, act as a counterweight to developed countries, encourage multipolarity, empower the G20 vis-à-vis the G8, and increase the agency for large developing countries in IMF and World Bank governance, as well as encourage the peaceful mediation of interstate conflicts.[51]

Although the BRICS have not yet defined the role that they will claim in discussions of global governance (they have so far emphasized the importance of the G20), their regular meetings create a space and expectation, engendered by the perception of a global power transition, that this block will be increasingly able to negotiate with declining powers, great (Europe) and super (the United States). There are, of course, important challenges in deepening relations between the BRICS, developing concrete common policies despite national interest divergence, and enacting these policies. But importantly, association with China, Russia, and India has given Brazil a certain degree of prestige on the world stage, enhanced visibility for its financial and equity markets, and won greater attention on the part of analysts, academics, and researchers around the world. That is, Brazil has attempted to validate and improve its status as a result, and through the support, of a risen China—a strategy typical of middle powers.

Case Three: Sino-Brazilian Relations

The BRICS platform creates the possibility for considerable Sino-Brazilian interaction on critical global issues. However, as of yet, Sino-Brazilian relations, like Sino-Latin American relations more generally, are predominantly, though not exclusively, guided by commercial concerns. While trade between the two countries grew from $1 billion in 2000 to $77 billion by 2011, it is quite uneven as some 82 percent of Chinese imports from Brazil are raw materials and commodities, with petroleum, ores, and soy as the most important products.[52]

The China-Brazil strategic partnership dates back to 1993 (during Chinese president Jiang Zemin's visit to Brazil), and was China's first such agreement with a developing country. There was no real "content" behind the term at the time and only much later did mutual interest increase the proximity of the two countries. Since then China has developed a broad strategy for Latin America and counts on Brazil to help achieve its objectives in the region.[53] China's interest in Brazil is primarily to incorporate the country into its international source of suppliers of basic commodities, although China also sees Brazil as a gateway to the Americas and as a regional leader to cultivate. Brazil understands that China has national interests but it will go along so it can benefit from many of the proposed plans (including a $10 billion line of credit to the region for infrastructure projects, a proposed free trade pact between China and Mercosur, and an eventual $60 million currency swap agreement with the region's economies). Common membership in different groups (BRICS, G20, BASIC) has also allowed for continuous and intense dialogue at the highest level of government between both countries. Yet the two countries are neither close nor familiar with one another. There is also no specific convergence of their specific agendas and objectives, be it regarding trade (Doha trade negotiations), international financial governance, or climate change (Rio+20 climate negotiations). The mixing of trade interests and geopolitical aspirations has left Brazil, as the junior partner, somewhat frustrated with the lack of reciprocity on the part of China.

While Brazil has benefited enormously from China's consumption of its commodities, both countries have become serious competitors in global markets following China's accession to the WTO (2001). Brazilian agribusiness (soy, meat, etc.), mining (iron ore, etc.), and energy (oil) concerns are the greatest domestic champions of trade with China perhaps best represented by the China-Brazil Business Council (CBBC). To keep up with China's growing demand for commodities, China will become an essential partner in Brazil's plans to modernize its infrastructure and exporting platforms (rail, ports, etc.). Recent investments include a $3 billion line of credit from Hangzhou Cogeneration to the state of Minas Gerais, and a $1 billion loan by China Development Bank to the Brazilian company LLX to finance equipment for the Southeast Superport project.[54] The strongest critics of trade with China are from the traditional industrial manufacturing side of the business spectrum, such as FIESP—the important Federation of Industries of the state of São Paulo.

Trade with China has provided Brazil with a huge opportunity to increase its exports and virtually escape the brunt of the world crisis since 2008. Brazilian exports to China reached a record $44 billion in 2011 while Chinese exports to Brazil amounted to $33 billion. According to the China-Brazil Business Council the stock of Chinese investments in Brazil stands at around $20 billion while Brazilian investments in China amount to around $500 million.[55] While Brazilian companies are building on their earlier success in China there are no Brazilian companies involved in any sector considered "strategic" by the Chinese government.[56] Brazilian companies still face several significant challenges in establishing themselves in China including a different legal system, lack of clear procedures regarding authorization and approval processes, lack of alignment of strategic objectives between Brazilian and Chinese companies, and lack of knowledge on how to deal with the Chinese government.[57] Overall, there is the impression that Chinese companies have more freedom to invest (and certainly much more state financial support) in Brazil than Brazilian companies in China.

Approximately 93 percent of Chinese investment in Brazil is made through state-owned companies under the direct supervision of the central government and operating in strategic sectors. This suggests that Chinese investment in Brazil may be the result of careful planning and a long-term strategy. No such plan or strategy exists for Brazilian investment in China. Brazilian investment in China (approximately fifty-seven companies) is modest, composed mostly of service providers and manufacturing companies. One of the high-profile Brazilian investments in China is Embraer, the country's aircraft manufacturer, which established a joint venture in China. This highly visible investment is now facing some serious setbacks due to growing hesitation on the part of the Chinese government as to how to move ahead with this project. Another area of mutual cooperation is in the field of scientific cooperation including the satellite industry. Brazil is the first Latin

American country with which China cooperated on a satellite program (China-Brazil Earth Resources, CBER).

Much more worrisome for some in Brazil is the entry by Chinese companies into core industrial sectors. This includes Huawei and ZTE, which have been making inroads in telecommunications sectors across Latin America, as well as Chinese automobile manufacturers including Chery (investing $400 million in a factory in Jacair) and Sany Heavy Industry (investing in a factory to build construction machinery in São Paulo).[58] Moreover, the $19.4 billion planned bullet train between São Paulo and Brazil will likely involve China Railway Construction and China Northern Locomotive. Chinese investment has become more aggressive in the petroleum sector where Brazilian state-owned Petrobras received some $10 billion from Sinopec to secure a flow of two hundred thousand barrels per day. The agreement involves Sinopec taking as much as 20 percent stakes in two offshore oil platforms. Additionally, Sinochem has agreed to purchase 40 percent of Norway's Statoil ASA holding in off-shore fields in Brazil for $3 billion.[59] Sinopec has also completed a $1.3 billion pipeline linking "key northern and southern portions of the Brazilian natural gas infrastructure" and it invested $7.1 billion "in Repsol Brazil to capitalize its operations in the Campos, Santos, and Espirto Santo basins."[60] Indicative of other constraints to future substantial Chinese investment in Brazil was a recent remark from the vice chairman of the China Investment Corp. (CIC), who expressed reservations regarding Brazil's tax structure and unpredictability of government plans in Brazil. Regarding Brazil's investment environment and "unlike in some of the emerging market countries, the Brazilian government sometimes shifts its policies in terms of taxation."[61]

Trade between the two countries is clearly unbalanced in the sense that China buys primarily low-value-added commodities from Brazil and Brazil buys higher-value-added products from China. The trade relationship between the two countries is not sustainable as Chinese demand for Brazilian commodities contributes toward skewing Brazilian exports away from industrial and service sectors.[62] The commoditization of exports—generalized across the region although Brazil is better equipped than most to weather it—runs the risk of not only deindustrializing Brazil but it engenders a "middle income trap," since Brazilian companies cannot compete against Chinese companies in terms of labor cost, but are also unable to compete against South Korean and German firms in terms of productivity and technological inputs.[63] This is especially important because Brazilian firms have lost market share to Chinese competitors in crucial third markets, such as the United States and in South America, where Brazilian exporters had been gaining market share. One study shows that Chinese competition is responsible for 30 percent of Brazilian losses in the United States and Chilean markets, and 11 percent and 14 percent losses in Argentine and Mexican markets, respectively. These losses are especially acute in certain industrial sectors, such as the shoe market where Chinese competition is blamed for 90 percent of Brazilian losses in the US shoe market.[64]

China, in this regard, poses a major challenge to Brazil, as the latter must greatly improve its overall competitiveness. Although the Brazilian government has resisted industrialist demands for protection, it has slowly increased protectionist measures. In "June 2011 the Brazilian government took legal steps toward implementing a special 25% 'participation tax' on the mining sector. The states of Minas Gerais, Pará, and Amapá have announced a further levy of up to $4 per ton of iron ore and other metals."[65] Simultaneously, Brazil has pursued a number of antidumping cases against Chinese companies, though it is wary not to provoke retaliation from China.[66]

An additional growing issue is the disparity between the two currencies. The Chinese currency is commonly viewed as underappreciated while the Brazilian *real* is an appreciating currency. Brazil's government has been vocal about the possibility of a "currency war" referring primarily to quantitative easing policies of many developed economies as well as in the case of China. Leaders from noncommodity sectors in Brazil have become vocal about their concerns and suspicions regarding China. Many of the same industrialists had earlier been severe critics of the Brazilian government's decision to qualify China as a market economy. The governments have discussed trading in local currencies (rather than using the US dollar as an intermediary currency) and China has offered swaps to make *yuan* more readily available. Nevertheless, the Chinese policy of maintaining a competitive exchange rate has the unintended effect of contributing to an overvalued *real*, further exacerbating the sectoral asymmetry in Sino-Brazilian trade. Moving beyond trade, both countries are working closely regarding an increase in voting shares in the IMF but have differed regarding negotiations in the Doha trade round whereby Brazil has pushed for a broader agenda (including industrial issues) while China has pushed for a more limited agenda. Different energy matrices also limit the potential for broad agreement regarding climate change negotiations.

In sum, despite its significant potential, the strategic partnership between China and Brazil has had limited global influence to date. These are still two big, rather inward-looking countries—slowly overcoming protectionist and anti-imperialist legacies—trying to find their place on the world stage. More importantly, while China is vested in increasing the visibility, and viability, of Brazil as a regional and global leader, China refuses to support Brazil's quest for a permanent seat on the UN Security Council (UNSC), which is among the most important priorities of Brazilian foreign policy. Chinese hesitance is linked largely to concern that increasing the size of the UNSC would likely include Japan and India, and absent Chinese support, UNSC reform is unlikely. Thus, while China supports Brazil's increased relevance in global affairs, its failure to endorse Brazil's major aspiration can effectively constrain Brazil's ambitions. This highlights a significant difference between the two countries.

Similarly, in commercial matters, while China is Brazil's main export market, Brazil is not among China's main trading partners. Thus, though Brazil still enjoys a large trade surplus with China, China is the dominant member of the relationship. Brazil, relative to China, remains a middle power and a junior partner that is brought in on some but not all deliberations and agendas, illustrating that China as a great power has a greater ability to "act alone" than does Brazil.

Reshaping Because of China?

In response to the four key questions posed by this volume, this chapter concludes that (1) Brazil is best characterized as a middle power, despite its great power capabilities along some dimensions, since it is acting more like a middle power than a great power at present; (2) while it is geographically distant, China's rise has had notable effects on Brazil both economically, competing as a large middle income country in key strategic sectors like aircraft, and diplomatically, by challenging Brazil's traditional role as a leader of the global South; (3) Brazil's response to the challenge of China has in many ways forced it to live up to its potential as a "global" middle power, taking an increased interest in global financial and economic issues, relations with Africa, and peace-building operations, behavior that has reinforced Brazil's middle power status; (4) Brazil's effect on China's foreign policy has so far been limited because of the clear asymmetries in the bilateral relationship. However, over time Brazil is likely to become more of an equal partner with China and, as a result, its approaches to global governance issues will reshape China's positions.

This chapter has followed the typology and framework set out in the first two chapters in this book to explore how Brazil's capabilities, foreign policy behavior, and ideational framing fit within the concept of middle power, highlighting how changes in global power structures, made possible by a power transition, and increased relations between China and Brazil, have contributed to a more confident and assertive Brazilian foreign policy. Brazil is indeed a middle power. It is more capable, more global, and more recognized than in the past, but it remains a middle power. The rise of China both makes it possible for it to have more agency while highlighting that Brazil is a middle, not great, power.

Brazilian analysts, politicians, and citizens do not spend much time wondering whether the country is a "middle" power or not. While they all agree that the country suffers from a long list of structural and political weaknesses, they believe that Brazil's place among the major powers in the world is essentially guaranteed. For them the question is not so much whether Brazil is a middle power but rather how and when the country will achieve its full potential, its innate *grandeza*. At the same time, this same community of scholars and analysts accepts the fact that though Brazil is an agricultural power, this does not translate to other types of power and it has yet to learn how to transform power resources into international influence. It remains to be seen whether Brazil will lead a consolidated regional response to China. When it does, perhaps it will no longer be a middle power.

Sino-Brazilian relations are complex, beneficial, and asymmetrical. China buys Brazilian products but skews the economy toward low-value-added commodities. It elevates Brazilian status in global environments but not on fundamental matters such as UN governance and environmental constraints. While relations between the two countries are warm and are deepening through increased participation in a number of multilateral forums, they relate to one another primarily as trade partners and, for the time being, China behaves as the major partner in the relationship. Brazil is not yet an effective partner in global political matters in its own right. China, by contrast, is Brazil's primary export market and a partner whose prestige can be leveraged for greater global relevance.

For the time being, Brazil will seek to maximize China's role in assisting with the urgent modernization of the country's infrastructure. Over time China's focus will gradually shift from natural resources to other sectors posing additional challenges to Brazil's industrial sector. Brazil's ties to China highlight Brazil's major development challenges: greater industrial competitiveness, diversification of its economy, and the need for more technology and greater innovation in the management of its natural resource endowment. Thus, despite the real improvements in capabilities and perceptions of status that Brazil has enjoyed in the last decade and a half, the comparison with China is illustrative of the conceptual distinction this chapter has advanced. China is a great power. Brazil is not.

That said, Brazil remains an important partner for China with much to offer. Both countries stand to benefit from greater knowledge of one another and closer cultural ties. By leveraging its expertise in energy, health, and poverty, Brazil can provide assistance in the prevention of environmental degradation and the reduction of social injustice, inequality, and poverty. There is cause for optimism regarding sharing development models and further discussion of multilateral aspirations. Brazilian capabilities, behavior, and identity may change over time, and hosting the World Cup in 2014 and the Olympic Games in 2016 may be important in redefining Brazilian foreign policy strategy and identity. It is likely, however, that Brazil will continue the path of an increasingly emboldened middle power and that China will be interested in a Brazil that remains as such, a junior partner whose presence helps legitimize Chinese claims to speak and act multilaterally, on behalf of the developing world. Brazil will also be useful for Beijing's aim to further regionalize the global economy so that China's importance vis-à-vis the United States in Asia grows.

Much of this agenda benefits Brazil, which hopes that an increased status will follow its greater capabilities. Fully aware of the limitations of Chinese support, Brazil is investing in relations with India, South Africa, other countries in South America and sub-Saharan Africa, to carve out a space for itself. In pursuing regional and multipolar approaches to global governance against the backdrop of a rising China, Brazil, like South Korea, exhibits strong traits of being a middle power with global ambitions.

Notes

1. Albert Fishlow, *Starting Over: Brazil since 1985* (Washington, DC: Brookings Institute Press, 2011); Paulo Leme, "The 'B' in BRICs: Unlocking Brazil's Growth Potential," in *BRICs and Beyond* (New York: Goldman Sachs, 2007), 75–84.

2. Maria Regina Soares de Lima and Mônica Hirst, "Brazil as an Intermediate State and Regional Power: Action, Choice and Responsibilities," *International Affairs* 82, no.1 (2006): 21–40, 25, 28.

3. After the United States, China, India, Japan, Germany, and Russia. International Monetary Fund, World Economic Database, 2011.

4. Susanne Gratius, "Brazil in the Americas: A Regional Peace Broker?," Foundation for International Relations and External Dialogue (Madrid) Working Paper 35, April 2007, 8

5. Ibid.

6. Although there has been improvement in some of these areas, most notably inequality.

7. See Andrés Malamud, "A Leader without Followers? The Growing Divergence between the Regional and Global Performance of Brazilian Foreign Policy," *Latin American Politics & Society* 53, no. 3 (2011): 1–24.

8. Andrew F. Cooper, Richard A. Higgott, and Kim R. Nossal, *Relocating Middle Powers: Australia and Canada in a Changing World Order* (Vancouver: University of British Columbia Press, 1993), 19.

9. Sean W. Burges, *Brazilian Foreign Policy after the Cold War* (Gainesville: University of Florida Press, 2009).

10. Gratius, "Brazil in the Americas," 5; Daniel Flemes, "Emerging Middle Powers' Soft Balancing Strategy: State and Perspectives of the IBSA Dialogue Forum," Leibniz: German Institute of Global and Area Studies, Research Programme: Violence, Power and Security, no. 57 (2007).

11. Ibid., 369.

12. This was formalized in the Pittsburgh declaration of the G20 in September 2008.

13. Andrew Fenton Cooper, *Niche Diplomacy: Middle Powers after the Cold War* (New York: St. Martin's Press, 1997).

14. See Manicom and Reeves, chapter 2, in this book.

15. See Gilley and O'Neil, chapter 1, in this book.

16. Soares de Lima and Hirst, "Brazil as an Intermediate State and Regional Power," 24–25; Paulo Roberto Almeida, "Lula's Foreign Policy: Regional and Global Strategies," in *Brazil under Lula: Economy, Politics, and Society under the Worker-President*, 167–83, eds. Joseph L. Love and Werner Baer (New York: Palgrave-Macmillan, 2009).

17. Burges, *Brazilian Foreign Policy*; Almeida, "Lula's Foreign Policy"; Henrique Altemani de Oliveira, "Brazil and China: From South-South Cooperation to Competition?," in *Latin America Facing China: South-South Relations beyond the Washington Consensus*, 33–53, eds. Alex E. Fernández Jilberto and Barbara Hogenboom (New York: Berghahn Books, 2010).

18. Andrew Hurrell, "Brazil and the New Global Order," *Current History* 109, no. 724 (2010): 60–66.

19. Almeida, "Lula's Foreign Policy"; Tullo Vigevani and Gabriel Cepaluni, *Brazilian Foreign Policy in Changing Times: The Quest for Autonomy from Sarney to Lula* (Lanham, MD: Lexington Books, 2009).

20. Although they considered their approach to include elements of all three approaches, the English School over time has been most in line with a "Grotian" analysis. See Celso Lafer, "Brazilian International Identity and Foreign Policy: Past, Present, and Future," *Daedalus* 129, no. 2 (2000): 207–38, 222.

21. Ibid., 229.

22. Andrew Hurrell, "Hegemony, Liberalism and Global Order: What Space for Would-Be Great Powers?," *International Affairs* 82, no. 1 (2006): 1–19, 15.

23. Itamaraty, "Resumo Executivo," *Balanço de Política Externa 2003/2010*, www.itamaraty.gov.br/temas/balanco-de-politica-externa-2003-2010/resumo-executivo/view.

24. National Intelligence Council, *Mapping the Global Future* (Washington, DC: National Intelligence Council, 2004).

25. Leslie Elliott Armijo and Sean W. Burges, "Brazil, the Entrepreneurial and Democratic BRIC," *Polity* 42, no. 1 (2010): 14–37, 15.

26. Burges, *Brazilian Foreign Policy*, 10.

27. Martha Finnemore, "Legitimacy, Hypocrisy, and the Social Structure of Unipolarity: Why Being a Unipole Isn't All It's Cracked Up to Be," *World Politics* 61, no. 1 (2009): 58–85.

28. Sean Burges, "Mistaking Brazil for a Middle Power," *Journal of Iberian and Latin American Research* (in press).

29. David Collier and Steven Levitksy, "Democracy with Adjectives: Conceptual Innovation in Comparative Research," *World Politics* 49, no. 3 (1997): 430–51; Giovanni Sartori, "Concept Misformation in Comparative Politics," *American Political Science Review* 64, no. 4 (1970): 1033–53.

30. See Gilley and O'Neil, chapter 1, in this book.

31. Malamud, "A Leader without Followers?"

32. Lula quoted in Gratius, "Brazil in the Americas," 23.

33. Malamud, "A Leader without Followers?," 3.

34. See Vigevani and Cepaluni, *Brazilian Foreign Policy in Changing Times*.

35. José Flávio Sombra Saraiva, "A Nova África e o Brasil na Era Lula: o Renascimento da Política Atlântica Brasileira" [The new Africa and Brazil's Lula era: the renaissance of Brazilian political Atlanticism), *Revista Brasileira de Política Internacional* [*Brazilian Journal of International Politics*] 53, no. 2 (2010): 169–82.

36. See A. F. K. Organski and Jacek Kugler, *The War Ledger* (Chicago: University of Chicago Press, 1981); Michael Mastanduno, "Preserving the Unipolar Moment: Realist Theories and US Grand Strategy after the Cold War," in *Unipolar Politics: Realism and State Strategies after the Cold War*, 138–81, 148, eds. Ethan B. Kapstein and Michael Mastanduno (New York: Columbia University Press, 1999).

37. John J. Mearsheimer, "The Gathering Storm: China's Challenge to US Power in Asia," *Chinese Journal of International Politics* 3, no. 4 (2010): 381–96, 382; Kenneth N. Waltz, "The Emerging Structure of International Politics," *International Security* 18, no. 2 (1993): 44–79; Benjamin Miller, *States, Nations, and the Great Powers: The Sources of Regional War and Peace* (New York: Cambridge University Press, 2007), 59; Barry Buzan and Gerald Segal, "Rethinking East Asian Security," *Survival* 36, no. 2 (1994): 3–21, 6; Dingding Chen and Jianwei Wang, "Lying Low No More? China's New Thinking on the *Tao Guang Yang Hui* Strategy," *China: An International Journal* 9, no. 2 (2011): 195–216, 215; Robert J. Art, "The United States and the Rise of China: Implications for the Long Haul," *Political Science Quarterly* 125, no. 3 (2010): 359–91; Rex Li, "The China Challenge: Theoretical Perspectives and Policy Implications," *Journal of Contemporary China* 8, no. 22 (1999): 443–76.

38. David Zweig, "'Resource Diplomacy' under Hegemony: The Sources of Sino-American Competition in the 21st_Century?," Center on China's Transnational Relations Working Paper No. 18, www.cctr.ust.hk/articles/pdf/WorkingPaper18_DavidZweig.pdf.

39. Horace Campbell, "China in Africa: Challenging US Global Hegemony," *Third World Quarterly* 29, no. 1 (2008): 89–105; Deborah Brautigam, *The Dragon's Gift: The Real Story of China in Africa* (Oxford: Oxford University Press, 2009), offers a challenge to this.

40. Richard Feinberg, "China, Latin America, and the United States: Congruent Interests or Tectonic Turbulence?," *Latin American Research Review* 46, no. 2 (2011): 215–24, 215–17; Francisco Santibañes, "An End to US Hegemony? The Strategic Implications of China's Growing Presence in Latin America," *Comparative Strategy* 28, no.1 (2009): 17–36, 18.

41. William A. Callahan, "How to Understand China: The Dangers and Opportunities of Being a Rising Power," *Review of International Studies* 31, no. 4 (2005): 701–14, 703.

42. Robert Jervis, "Unipolarity: A Structural Perspective," *World Politics* 61, no. 1 (2009): 188–213; see also Brantly Womack, "First among Unequals: China in a Multinodal World Order," Paper prepared for the annual meeting of the American Political Science Association, New Orleans, August 27–September 1, 2012.

43. Parag Khanna, *The Second World: Empires and Influence in the New Global Order* (New York: Random House, 2008), 122.

44. He Li, "China's Growing Influence in Latin America: Challenges and Opportunities," *East Asian Institute (Singapore) Background Briefs*, no. 411 (2008); R. Evan Ellis, *China in Latin America: The Whats and Wherefores* (Boulder: Lynne Rienner, 2009); Shixue Jiang, "The Panda Hugs the Tucano: China's Relations with Brazil," *China Brief* 9, no. 91 (2009): 7–10; Anthony Peter Spanakos and Yu Xiao, "Has the Rise of China Made Latin America More Unsafe?," in *China and International Relations: The Chinese View and the Contribution of Wang Gungwu*, 221–41, ed. Yongnian Zheng (London: Routledge, 2010).

45. J. Peter Pham, "India's Expanding Relations with Africa and Their Implications for US Interests," *American Foreign Policy Interests* 29, no. 5 (2007): 341–52.

46. China has announced a $5 billion fund to invest in infrastructure in Africa. See China-Brazil Business Council, *Chinese Investments in Brazil* (Rio de Janeiro: CBBC, 2011), 17.

47. Major government agencies used by the Foreign Ministry include ABC–Brazilian Cooperation Agency; EMBRAPA (agricultural research), FIOCRUZ (tropical medicine), and SENAI (vocational training), among others.

48. See Leslie Elliott Armijo, "The BRICs Countries (Brazil, Russia, India, and China) as Analytical Category: Mirage or Insight?," *Asian Perspective* 31, no. 4 (2007): 7–44; Jim O'Neil et al., "How Solid Are the BRICs?" *Goldman Sachs Global Economics Papers*, no. 134 (2005); Dominic Wilson, Alex L. Kelston, and Swarnali Ahmed, "Is This the BRIC Decade?," *BRICs Monthly* 10, no. 3 (2010).

49. Anthony P. Spanakos, "China and Brazil: Potential Allies or Just BRICs in the Wall?," *East Asian Policy* 2, no. 2 (2010): 81–89. By 2010, the BRIC share of global GDP was 25 percent and is expected to rise to 40 percent in 2050. See Dominic Wilson et al., "The BRICs 10 Years On: Halfway through the Great Transformation," *Goldman Sachs Global Economics Papers*, no. 208 (2011), 5.

50. The addition of South Africa, which has been ignored by Goldman Sachs and other financial analysts who continue to write about the BRICs, is significant not because it increases the amount of global GDP or trade of the group, but because it adds political legitimacy to the group as it now includes an African country and can more legitimately claim to speak as a voice of the developing world.

51. Anthony P. Spanakos, "China and the Rise of the BRICS," in *China: Development and Governance*, eds. Gungwu Wang and Yongnian Zheng (Singapore: World Scientific, 2012), 491–97.

52. Michel Temer, *Brasil e China: Uma Reunião de Concertacão e Cooperecão (Valor Econômica)*, February 13, 2012, Itamaray.gov.br, www.itamaraty.gov.br/sala

-de-imprensa/discursos-artigos-entrevistas-e-outras-comunicacoes/vice-presidente-da-republica-federtativa-do-brazil/brasil-e-china-uma-reuniao-de-concertaco-e-cooperacao-valor-economic-13-02-2012/?Searchterm;china%202012; Stephanie Lloyd, "Brazil and China Commercial Ties Blossom despite Limitations, While Brazil-U.S. Diplomatic Ties Remain on Course, with Some Exceptions," *Council on Hemispheric Activities*, June 8, 2010; Spanakos, "China and Brazil"; Kevin P. Gallagher and Roberto Porzecanski, *The Dragon in the Room: China & the Future of Latin American Industrialization* (Stanford: Stanford University Press, 2010).

53. See "China's Policy Paper on Latin America and the Caribbean," 2008, http://news.xinhuanet.com/english/2008-11/05/content_10308117.htm.

54. See "Chinese Investments in Brazil: A New Phase in the China-Brazil Relationship," China-Brazil Business Council (CBBC), São Paulo, May 2011, 25.

55. China-Brazil Business Council, *Brazilian Companies in China: Presence and Experience* (Rio de Janeiro: CBBC, 2012), 3.

56. Ibid., 12.

57. Ibid., 14.

58. Ellis, *China in Latin America*, 3.

59. Lloyd, "Brazil and China Commercial Ties."

60. Ellis, *China in Latin America*, 3.

61. Quoted in Maureen Farrell, "Tricky Allegiances among Emerging Superpowers," CNNMoney, May 1, 2012, http://money.cnn.com/2012/05/01/markets/china-brazil/index.htm.

62. See Enrique Dussel Peters, "Latin America, Mexico, and China: Economic Conditions and Challenges," in *Setting the Agenda: Asia and Latin America in the 21st Century*, 59–61, ed. Ariel C. Armony (Miami: Center for Latin American Studies, University of Miami, 2012).

63. Eva Paus, "The Rise of China: Implications for Latin American Development," *Development Policy Review* 27, no. 4 (2009): 419–56.

64. Quoted in Rodrigo Maciel, "The Economic Relationship between China and Brazil," in *Enter the Dragon: China's Presence in Latin America*, 27–41, eds. Cynthia Arnson et al. (Washington, DC: Woodrow Wilson International Center for Scholars, 2007).

65. Adrian Hearn, "What Can South America and Australia Learn from Each Other in Relation to China?," in *Setting the Agenda: Asia and Latin America in the 21st Century*, 33–38, 34, ed. Ariel C. Armony (Miami: Center for Latin American Studies, University of Miami, 2012),.

66. Raymond Colitt, "Brazil Anti-Dumping Tariffs Rise Sharply," Reuters News Agency, August 20, 2008.

CHAPTER 12

Conclusion

Seeing beyond Hegemony

Bruce Gilley and Andrew O'Neil

Introduction

THIS BOOK began with a simple premise: that understanding international politics in the twenty-first century requires seeing beyond the hegemony of great powers. That is not a normative hope but an empirical reality. A world in which great power hegemony is challenged by new global forces may or may not be a better one. Nonetheless, it is imperative for analysts and policymakers to grasp the complex webs of power and influence that will guide global governance for the foreseeable future.

One of the dimensions of this new global governance system is the role of states with capabilities that rank them as the immediate neighbors of great powers. We have used the term "middle powers" throughout this book to refer to these states. But as is clear from the preceding chapters, the role and influence of these states puts them in the top bracket of all states. They are seen as key partners of the great powers and typically exert leadership roles in their regions.

All too frequently, the role of nongreat powers has been dismissed by students of international relations. Great powers determine the shape of the international system, it is argued, and other states have little choice but to fall into the "order" that is created by these larger states. Even those who acknowledge the influence of some secondary states in the day-to-day ferment of the international system tend to privilege great powers in their analysis of long-term systemic change. Ultimately, from this perspective, it is great powers that determine the nature of international order and that are the primary agents of change in world politics.

By contrast, there is a body of evidence that shows that a recurrent feature of international relations is the role of middle powers in shaping international order. As noted by James Manicom and Jeffrey Reeves in chapter 2, this book advances that body of evidence by moving beyond the traditional focus on "first-generation" middle powers (Australia being the lone example here) to focus on "second-generation" middle powers such as South Korea, Indonesia, Brazil, Turkey, South Africa, Malaysia, and Thailand. These states are seen—and see themselves—as increasingly important actors at both the regional and global levels. Assuming a leadership role in regional multilateral initiatives and playing an active part in new global institutions such as the G20, which themselves mirror the changing distribution of international economic power and political influence, these second-generation middle powers are not content to define their roles in relation to the increasingly explicit US-China rivalry. Nor are they satisfied with playing only "bridge-building" roles to bring the great powers together, although this remains a key agenda item. As Amy Freedman notes in chapter 6, they often seek to redefine great power foreign policies and great power relations with one another. These countries see themselves as *leaders* in international affairs and their national role conceptions are defined in accordance with this view.

An inquiry into the role of middle powers in global governance could consider many issues at the regional and international levels. We chose in this collection to focus on the rise of China as the lens through which to understand the contemporary characteristics of "middle powermanship." Not only is the rise of China arguably the preeminent issue of contemporary international relations, but the broad global impact of China's rise also allows us to peer into the many regional and international issues where middle powers may shape China's rise.

Against this background, this book has been concerned with the following four questions: What are the capabilities and behavior of middle powers in practice when compared with the ideal typology? How has China's rise affected the domestic, regional, and global environment for middle powers? How have middle powers responded to the rise of China? Is there evidence of a "middle power effect" in China's rise? The chapters in this book have addressed these questions from a wide variety of perspectives, each one providing a succinct response to these four questions in the opening paragraph of the concluding section. The findings are summarized in table 12.1. What have we learned?

Capabilities and Middle Powerhood

We began by defining middle powers positionally, meaning the group of states that have the material capabilities to make a difference in global governance when acting in concert with like-minded states. The cases here

Table 12.1 Summary of Findings

1. **What are the capabilities and behavior of middle powers in practice when compared with the ideal threefold typology (positional, behavioral, ideational)?**
   - Whether middle powers emphasize material capabilities or behavioral dimensions of their national role, conception is contingent on the type of domestic government they have at any given time.
   - Compared with Australia, Indonesia, South Africa, and South Korea, Turkey, Thailand, and Malaysia are incomplete middle powers given their patchy track record in the ideational realm.
   - Middle powers today have unprecedented influence to shape international institutions and to provide international leadership on key policy issues.

2. **How has China's rise affected the domestic, regional, and global environment for middle powers?**
   - Perceptions among middle powers regarding China's rise are diverse but strong themes of concern are the potential for China exerting adverse pressure economically and apprehension about possible security and diplomatic threats from Beijing.
   - Interdependence is a double-edged sword from the perspective of middle powers. Asymmetry in relationships with China encourages anxiety regarding potential pressure from Beijing.
   - Middle powers are torn between the rewards and risks of engagement. Preserving future autonomy is a key theme.
   - The impact of China's rise on individual middle powers tends to be strongest in proportion to geographical proximity.

3. **How have middle powers responded to the rise of China?**
   - There is a strong emphasis on mitigating threats and maximizing opportunities. Opportunities have been seen primarily in economic terms and threats in political and security terms.
   - China's rise has sharpened middle powers' preference for multilateralism to avoid great power domination.
   - Middle powers have focused on reforming international institutions as a means of constraining and socializing China's influence at the regional level. Including China in global governance mechanisms is a major theme.
   - Most middle powers are hedging against China's rise rather than balancing against it or bandwagoning with China. Uncertainty over China's long-term intentions promotes the tendency to hedge.
   - Middle powers are wary of a possible "G2" between Beijing and Washington. They want a stable US-China relationship, but want to avoid a condominium.

4. **Is there evidence of a "middle power effect" in China's rise?**
   - China remains sensitized to the views of middle powers because it regards these countries as key players in helping Beijing achieve its aims in important regions.
   - But there is no evidence that China has changed any of its policies as a direct response to the behavior or influence of middle powers.
   - China strongly resists proposals for middle powers to play a mediating role with respect to territorial issues in Asia.
   - The middle power impact on China has been expressed less in bilateral terms and more in terms of shaping the broader international environment in which China operates, particularly concerning new rules and institutions.
   - Over time, middle powers will become more important in shaping the context in which Chinese foreign policy operates.

include a wide cross section of middle powers, so defined. Brazil, sometimes touted as a future great power, is a "particularly powerful middle power," as Spanakos and Marques note in their chapter. In terms of capabilities, Malaysia and Thailand are, as Amy Freedman points out, "near the bottom of the middle power cohort." South Korea, Australia, and Turkey are firmly located at the mid-level, while South Africa and Indonesia are also mid-level but are regional leaders in their own right, in large part by dint of their respective capabilities.

James Manicom and Jeffery Reeves provide a threefold typology of middle powers: "positional middle powers" that are expected to exercise influence due to their size and contribute to building international order in a way that promotes their interests; "behavioral middle powers," which, in addition to exerting influence and promoting interests, build coalitions with the like-minded, engage in niche diplomacy, and build bridges between the great powers in pursuit of substantive ends, which Gilley and O'Neil identify as multipolarity, rules and institutions, and peace building; and "ideational middle powers" that also claim to be good international citizens and leaders, as well as adhering to liberal-internationalist ideals. As several chapters show, middle powers often move among these definitions depending on who is in power domestically at any given time. At times, often when conservative or realist voices are strongest, middle powers tend to emphasize their material capabilities. At others, often when left or liberal voices are strongest, they emphasize good international behavior. A fully formed middle power combines capabilities, behavior, and idealism.

Among our cases, some fit the threefold typology more fully than others. Australia, for instance, has an established track record across all three descriptors of middle powers, which can be traced to its early active postwar involvement in UN institutions.[1] As Thomas Wilkins observes in chapter 8, Australia in many respects exemplifies the characteristics outlined in ideal typologies of middle powers. Part of the reason for this is that the theory and practice surrounding middle powers in international relations tend to be mutually reinforcing. Many of the contemporary middle power attributes are drawn from the traditional empirical cases including Australia, while policymakers in these same countries cite elements of the ideal typology to strengthen their own claims about middle power status. It is no coincidence that some of the most influential texts on the role of middle powers in international relations have been written by individuals with experience in the policy world.

With the exception of South Korea—whose middle power attributes were emerging during the 1970s under the leadership of Park Chung-hee—and Brazil—which, notwithstanding its great power ambitions, has for some time possessed both the capabilities and ideational outlook indicative of middle power status—the other cases covered in this book have been relative latecomers to the middle power game. Indeed, in the case of Turkey, Yitzhak Shichor notes that its status as a middle power is a twenty-first-century phenomenon that can be directly linked to the rise of Recep Tayyip Erdoğan as prime minister in 2003. However, Turkey, like Thailand and Malaysia, can be classified as an incomplete middle power given its patchy track record in the ideational realm. All three states have democratic traditions, but in the contemporary context they are struggling to fulfill a role as behavioral middle powers in light of their governments' domestic performance on human rights. According to the threefold typology employed in this book, Turkey, Thailand, and Malaysia are incomplete middle powers.

Indonesia and South Africa, by contrast, can be regarded as fully fledged middle powers. These two cases are interesting because their respective rise as middle powers with influence can be seen as a corollary of the demise of authoritarian regimes and the process of democratic transition in both countries. The end of the Suharto regime in 1998 and the formal termination of apartheid four years earlier conferred an important degree of moral authority on Indonesia and South Africa, respectively, which underpinned their foreign policy ambitions in their regions and beyond. For Indonesia, as Ann Marie Murphy reminds us in her chapter, its weight in international relations "is enhanced by factors not captured in traditional middle power rankings." For Indonesia's political elites, a strong commitment to democracy domestically has formed an explicit element of foreign policy, which reflects an important ideational dimension of Indonesia's middle power status.[2] While South Africa's foreign policy priorities have shifted away from global concerns toward addressing a more explicit African leadership agenda, Nelson Mandela's early vision of his country as a moral and ethical leader still remains a key strain in South African foreign policy. As Janis van der Westhuizen and Sven Grimm point out in chapter 9, South Africa's "core identity construct" is framed by a concentric-circles approach, with Africa at the center, "anti-imperialism" next, and "human rights" making up the outer core.

Nonetheless, all of the cases considered here find themselves natural allies in international relations. "We see ourselves as an activist middle power, a member of the Group of 20, and try to play a constructive role in relation to that . . . . [T]hat's something we share with South Africa," Australia's parliamentary secretary for foreign affairs Richard Marles said on a 2013 visit to South Africa.[3] South Korea's former ambassador to Australia, Kim Woo-sang, meanwhile said in 2012: "The time has come for Korea to take a leading role in resolving global issues by reinforcing multilateral diplomatic ties with developing countries . . . particularly with those middle power countries."[4] Australia, South Korea, and Indonesia—the three Asian member of the five-country Mexico-Indonesia-South Korea-Turkey-Australia Initiative announced in 2013—increasingly style themselves as "middle power partners" in Asian security, a recognition of their similar approaches to international issues despite widely different contexts.[5] Studying middle power dyads—such as recent works looking at Canada-South Africa[6] or Iran-Turkey[7] relations—is thus a potentially fruitful area of research in international relations for explaining when and how these "natural allies" cooperate on specific issues.

Seen in the context of a rising China, we have learned several further things about this definition of middle powers. The contributions of South Korea, Indonesia, and Australia in shaping the context of China's rise are a reminder that geography still matters. As Wilkins notes, "the tyranny of distance" from the traditional Atlantic center of power has become "the advantage of proximity" for these nations as power shifts to the Pacific. China is predominantly an Asian power with global aspirations, which is reflected by the fact that its military and political power-projection capabilities are felt most acutely in its own region. China's ability to project power further afield, in Africa, Europe, the Americas, and the Middle East, remains circumscribed by its own material and soft power limitations, as well as by US endeavors to actively counter Chinese influence regionally.

At the same time, since power is relational as well as positional, China's rise has led some middle powers that have closer ties to Beijing to emerge as stronger than middle power rivals (Turkey vs. Saudi Arabia, for instance, or South Africa vs. Nigeria). This makes it especially imperative to study great power debates on middle powers. David Cooper and Toshi Yoshihara argue in chapter 4 that the currency of the middle power concept in US foreign policy thinking remains low. This is in contrast to China where, rhetorically at least, the role of middle powers has been acknowledged and continues to be canvassed in various policy and academic outlets. As Bruce Gilley asserts, Chinese conceptions of what constitutes a middle power in international relations have traditionally been quite different from the typologies presented in the Western academic literature. Middle powers tend to be nonaligned in China's view and are "swing states" that transfer these allegiances at regular intervals to maximize national interest considerations. In this sense, US allies such as Canada and Australia are perceived among some Chinese analysts as an anachronism in the context of the rise of "second-generation" middle powers such as South Africa and Indonesia.

While China exhibits all of the hallmarks of contemporary great power status—permanent membership of the UN Security Council, a "dialogue of equals" with the United States, economic scale and influence—it remains sensitized to the views of middle powers, partly because of its foreign policy traditions, but also because it sees these states as important players in helping Beijing achieve its aims in key regions. China may be an intrinsically realist foreign policy actor, but it nevertheless appreciates the key role that non-great powers play in shaping regional environments and the need to coopt these states in order to achieve economic, political, and strategic objectives. If, as Gilley as well as Cooper and Yoshihara argue, middle powers are taken more seriously *as* middle powers by Beijing than by Washington, then relations with China will support conventional middle power behavior while relations with Washington will not.

Thus great power alliances have a variable influence on middle power capabilities as well as behavior. As Spanakos and Marques show, China's rise both strengthens Brazil's capacity for initiative in international affairs while reinforcing its status as a middle (not a great) power. As Grimm and van der Westhuizen point out, South Africa's attempt to ally more closely with China under Jacob Zuma has in many ways constrained its middle power role in Africa.

It should come as no surprise that great power alliances are neither a consistent impediment nor a consistent boon to middle powers. After all, the premise of middle power theory is that middle power capabilities and behavior cannot be read off as derivative functions of great power alignments. In many cases, great power alliances are a net asset. Turkey's honest-broker role in the Middle East depends closely on its links to the European Union and North Atlantic Treaty Organization (NATO), while South Korea's US alliance and Pakistan's close ties to China make both of those states more capable than they would otherwise be. On the other hand, Canada is often seen as a middle power whose deep integration with the United States makes a middle power activism more difficult.[8]

Effect on Middle Powers

Gauging how a rising China is affecting middle powers is a tricky assignment. Establishing cause and effect is difficult and often contingent on the particular issue. Merely because of its rapid rise, China has altered the behavior of other states in the international system. The impact of China's rise has been increasingly global in scope and its capacity to project economic power to far-flung regions in Africa and the Americas has been a hallmark of its rise. The "going out" strategy of economic engagement—driven significantly by energy security imperatives—has seen Chinese state-owned enterprises

(SOEs) acquire enormous influence in parts of Africa and in the Americas, regions traditionally dominated by the United States and Brazil.[9] This influence has not always been positive, with the close relationship between SOEs and regimes with egregious human rights records causing concern throughout sub-Saharan Africa in particular.[10]

The chapters in this book underscore the plurality of perceptions among middle powers about China's rise. Conventional realist power transition theories make an assumption that threats from rising great powers are perceived by secondary states to be exclusively security related in nature. There is certainly evidence in this book to support the proposition that middle powers are nervous about China's rise from a security perspective (of which more below).

However, one of the salient findings of this book is that even from a purely economic perspective, a number of middle powers regard deepening interdependence with Beijing in the trade and investment spheres as threatening. In particular, the massive scale of cheap Chinese imports into domestic markets has generated resentment among key sectoral interests. As Yitzhak Shichor illustrates in chapter 10, the textile sector in Turkey has been particularly impacted by cheap Chinese imports and the Turkish government's attempts to reintroduce quotas on these imports have provoked tensions with Beijing. Similarly, in Brazil, as Spanakos and Marques note in chapter 11, a substantial trade deficit with China and perceptions that investing in China is excessively problematic have raised questions about the net benefits of economic integration. In chapter 7, Anne Marie Murphy points out that, while major Chinese investment in large-scale projects in Indonesia may benefit consumers in that country, Beijing's insistence on tying this investment with the use of Chinese companies and workers has triggered heated criticism from Indonesia's manufacturing sector. This has promoted a broader perspective that China is, in effect, contributing to the "hollowing out" of the Indonesian economy. While aware of the central role of trade with China in inoculating Australia against the worst effects of the global financial crisis, Australian public opinion is showing signs of discomfort with rising Chinese investment in the country, especially in the agricultural and telecommunications sectors. This stems from unease over the intentions of China's state-owned enterprises, but it is also a corollary of long-standing Australian suspicions about foreign investment generally.

These developments have the potential to harm China's broader relations with these middle powers. The more dependent these countries become on China's economic growth and close trade and investment ties, the more resentful general publics may become. Such resentments may spill over into the political dimension of relationships. In chapter 9, Janis van der Westhuizen and Sven Grimm point out that South Africa has lost significant market share in Africa to China, and that imports of low-cost Chinese manufactured goods have had a deleterious impact on the most labor-intensive sectors of the South African economy, including manufacturing. Public resentment over China's increasingly long economic shadow has had the effect of feeding accusations that the government in Pretoria is exhibiting "pro-China" characteristics by not being sufficiently critical of China's approach to human rights.

As major economic powers in their own right, middle powers are deeply integrated with the consequences of China's global rise. But unlike the United States, the European Union, and even Japan, these states are the junior partners in their economic relationships with China. Despite Beijing's well-established disavowal of linking economics with politics, it is clearly easier to have smoother economic relations with China if political relations are solid. The asymmetry inherent in the relationships middle powers have with Beijing means that they will remain vulnerable to Chinese pressure not just economically, but also in the political realm.

This may explain why the debates on China in middle power countries so often pit claims of "sell-out," often raised by civil society voices, against claims of "strategy," often raised by diplomatic and business voices. We see this in the chapters here on South Africa, Turkey, Australia, and Brazil. Other middle power countries not covered in this book, like Canada and Pakistan, have similar debates. Powerful enough to influence China through engagement but not so powerful to avoid undue influence in return, middle powers find their relations with China constantly torn between the risks and rewards of engagement.

Behavior and Middle Powermanship

In a neatly ordered world, these "independent variables"—the capabilities of middle powers and the systemic effects of a rising China—could be used to predict the "dependent variable" of middle power behavior. The hypotheses we set out were that middle powers would be probabilistically more likely than great or small powers to initiate with coalitions of like-minded states foreign policies that sought increased multipolarity, new rules and institutions for global governance, and the advancement of human security and peace building.

Of course, each middle power is different in many respects and their relations with China reflect that. The evolution of Indonesia's relationship with

China cannot be understood without reference to the history of bilateral tensions between the two countries that came to a head in the 1960s over accusations of Chinese interference in domestic Indonesian affairs. Similarly, China's intervention in the Korean War has continued to color perceptions of Beijing in South Korea. For Australia, history is perhaps less important than the deep degree of economic interdependence with China, particularly in the all-important resources sector, which in turn has raised questions about whether Australia can effectively "balance" this interdependent economic relationship with the formal security alliance it has with the United States. A similar resource factor figures into South Africa's relations with China.[11] Brazil, for its part, sees China largely through the prism of the BRICS (Brazil, Russia, India, China, South Africa) framework and global institutions, particularly the G20, as well as Brasilia's regional leadership role in the Americas.

Yet, notwithstanding the important differences among the country cases, some common findings emerge.

Middle powers have responded to China's rise in a variety of ways, but ultimately these can be boiled down to the dual strategy of mitigating threat and maximizing opportunity. Typically, the threat dimension has been associated with suspicions that China has expansionist objectives while the opportunities are seen as being overwhelmingly economic. As Amy Freedman notes, in the cases of Thailand and Malaysia, neither country sees close relations with Beijing as precluding a close relationship with Washington.

The fact that a wide variety of middle powers are actively engaging and seeking to manage China is evidence of the systemic implications of China's rise. Middle powers, as this book shows, share hopes and fears about China's rise. The hope is that it will advance their traditional concerns with multipolarity and middle power influence. The fear is that China will prove to be an overwhelming force, forcing them to fall back into the embrace of Washington and losing the autonomy they have carefully nurtured. But if middle power behavior is a measure of systemic change in the international system, then China's rise surely qualifies.

Middle power responses to China's rise involve contextual permutations of the generic middle power emphasis in using the forms of multilateralism, bridging, consensus-building, niche diplomacy, and acting within like-minded coalitions to pursue the substantive ends of multipolarity, rules and institutions, and peace building or human security.

The pursuit of multipolarity in the context of China's rise has been one of accepting the end of American preeminence yet avoiding the emergence of a new G2. Multipolarity is perhaps the wrong term. As Spanakos and Marques point out, middle powers want to increase multipolarity, but only at the margins—a G20 to be sure, but not a G80. As in 1945, they want their unique contributions to global governance recognized with unique, not broad, inclusion. The rise of China has presented middle powers with an opportunity to advance and institutionalize their special status in global governance. Embracing China has also meant enmeshing it in new institutions and norms, of which the Association of Southeast Asian Nations (ASEAN) approach to regional affairs is the best example.

As norm entrepreneurs, middle powers have responded creatively to the implicit model of the so-called "Beijing Consensus" by formulating their own regionally sensitive alternatives that combine their democratic credentials with their "new middle power" emphasis on reforming international institutions to serve the developing world. Turkey in the Middle East, South Africa in Africa, the ASEAN middle powers and South Korea in Asia, and Brazil in Latin America have all pushed back against the Beijing Consensus even as they engage Beijing in regional affairs.[12]

Brazil and South Korea, for instance, have separately initiated attempts to bridge great power divides over development assistance by introducing new approaches that marry the accountability, civil society, and poverty-alleviation of Western approaches with the state-led and pro-growth approaches of China. Moreover, South Korea is explicit in seeking to bridge the Organization for Economic Cooperation and Development (OECD) donors and emerging donors like China. Again, power transition theory might suggest a warm welcome for the Beijing Consensus approach to development in regions hoping to gain from China's rise. But instead we see middle powers defining their own developmental agendas and norms. To paraphrase Margaret Thatcher, having rolled back the frontiers of authoritarianism at home, middle powers are not willing to see it reimposed by China.

Finally, the peace-building portfolio of middle powers is being fundamentally transformed in part because of the sorts of threats to peace that China's rise has highlighted. Security and balance-of-power concerns are preeminent. But new nontraditional security concerns in areas like climate change, global health, cybersecurity, humanitarian intervention, and resource management are all areas where middle powers have made new contributions.

Managing and Reframing Power Transitions

The rapid rise of a new great power inevitably provokes changes in the global environment. States not only react to the behavior of the rising power, they also seek to anticipate and preempt changes to their external environment. This is an imperative for secondary states whose challenge is to shape, or be shaped by, their external environment. For middle powers, the rise of great powers poses significant challenges, which are evident at two main levels. The first level relates to the process of systemic transition precipitated by the new great power. Much of the period since the end of the Cold War has been characterized by unipolarity and the rise of China raises the real prospect of a return to a bipolar international system. The key question is how, indeed whether, Washington and Beijing can effectively manage this transition as rivals. Some, most notably Hugh White, have argued that the United States must cede power in Asia to accommodate China's ambitions in order to avoid conflict, while others claim that America needs to reassert its primacy and that the US decline/China rise narrative is excessively simplistic.[13] The scale and pace of China's rise has injected a sense of urgency into these debates in the policy world as well as throughout academia.

Whatever the merits of the arguments, middle powers have a major stake in ensuring that a stable transition to a bipolar order takes place. During the Cold War, middle powers often took the lead to moderate the Soviet-US rivalry. That peace-building function has now been redefined in terms of moderating the Sino-US rivalry.

What can middle powers do to help effect such a transition? As a range of literature confirms—including the chapters in this book—most middle powers are hedging against China's rise as distinct from actively balancing against it or bandwagoning with China. This should not come as a particular surprise; the natural reflex for most states is to hedge during periods of uncertainty and transition. The inscrutable nature of China's intentions—does it seek hegemony or will it be content with primacy?—merely promotes the tendency to hedge.

Given that China's power-projection capabilities are focused on Asia, this is of particular salience for middle powers located in that region. We should expect that the response of US allies such as Australia and South Korea will be to strengthen their bilateral alliances with Washington, which is what has occurred in recent years (although Seoul's motives have also been driven by anxieties over North Korea's behavior). Yet what is interesting is that nonaligned Indonesia, Malaysia, and Thailand have been quietly gratified by the Obama administration's "rebalance" of its global commitments to Asia. These three states have also sought to use ASEAN more instrumentally as a means of engaging China in a multilateral forum with a view to constraining Beijing's tendency to act unilaterally on maritime territorial issues in the South China Sea.

A second response has been to include China in existing and emerging multilateral institutions. The latter are central to middle power strategy, both for systemic reasons (by definition, multilateralism provides greater opportunities for nongreat powers to shape the international system) and for stability reasons (multilateralism serves to bind a wide range of states to commitments, not just the dominant players). Middle powers, moreover, tend to have an ideational commitment to multilateralism as part of their established identities among domestic constituents and in international relations more broadly. An attempt to bind China to multilateral institutions is not necessarily aimed at socializing Beijing into extant norms and practices on specific issues in particular contexts—although such an outcome is seen as preferred—it is aimed more at persuading China that middle powers are themselves key actors in the contemporary global order.[14]

The four chapters on Asian middle powers make clear that despite various degrees of alignment with the United States, none of Asia's middle powers is willing to accede to Washington's hopes for continued US primacy in the region. China is to be included as an equal, not a "responsible stakeholder" of a US-led system. Indonesia, South Korea, and Australia have taken the view that they will not work on an Asian security architecture that does not treat China and the United States as equals. Middle powers are seeking actively to break the "zero sum" approaches of US-China power transitions theory to create opportunities for positive sum approaches on military, economic, and new governance issues like climate change and maritime safety. They want not the United States *or* China but the United States *and* China in Asia. As Marles said on his visit to South Africa in 2013: "Australia thinks it's important that we don't construct a world which has an inevitability about competitiveness and contest between the US and China. I just don't think that's how the world is nor does it have to be."[15]

The advent of the G20 is important in this context. Previous iterations of the various global economic groupings (G7 and G8) have been dominated by the Europeans and North Americans—with Japan as the only Asian power—while the G20 exemplifies above all else the shift of economic power from the west to east of the international system. China's G20 membership and the inclusion of most of the middle powers examined as cases in this book represent a significant step toward multilaterizing China's cooperation with other states in the realm of global economic governance.

The challenge for middle powers is to avoid a situation where their role and influence are constrained. The high-profile, but ill-fated, proposal for a "G2" arrangement between the United States and China was highly antithetical to the interests of middle powers, suggesting as it did a great power condominium in international relations. While middle powers want Beijing to have a stable relationship with Washington, they are not keen on the relationship being too close. As Hedley Bull wrote more than forty years ago, great power condominiums have the effect of marginalizing middle powers in key deliberations and decision making in respect to global and regional orders.[16] This strengthens even further the case for multilateralism in the eyes of middle powers, particularly those that do not have alliance with the United States, which would (at least in theory) provide these states with slightly more scope to exert some influence in a G2-type arrangement. The enthusiasm on the part of Indonesia, Thailand, and Malaysia for China's active involvement in ASEAN's expanding institutional mechanisms can be partly explained by the motive of maintaining their own relevance as regional players in Beijing's eyes. Persuading China of the relevance of engaging middle powers as key actors in their own right is informed by the broader strategy of avoiding marginalization in the decision-making process regionally and globally.

In a real sense, China's rise has sharpened the traditional aspects of middle power behavior that were evident during the Cold War—an insistence on multilateralism to avoid great power domination and ideas of bridge building between the great powers—as well as heightening anxiety domestically with respect to the "unknown" factor in China's ascent to great power status. As Thomas Wilkins outlines in chapter 8, Australia has pursued an array of different strategies in relation to China—ranging from selective accommodation in its decision to terminate quadrilateral security cooperation with the United States, India, and Japan, to evidence of so-called "hard balancing" in agreeing to base US marines in-country—which tend to reflect the contradictory impulses in Australian domestic opinion about China.[17]

Interestingly, conservative and social democratic governments in Australia have canvassed the potential for Australia to play a bridging role between Washington and Beijing, in spite of its formal security alliance with the United States and persistent ambivalence about China's strategic intentions in Asia. Indonesia, too, albeit in different circumstances, has sought to play a bridging role in relation to China. The ASEAN Summit meeting in 2012, which showcased a major split between ASEAN members over the various competing claims involving China in the South China Sea, led to intensive shuttle diplomacy on the part of the Indonesian foreign minister aimed at repairing damaged relations between key ASEAN members and Beijing.[18] It is fair to say that, of all the ASEAN members, only Indonesia has the stature to play such a role.

The real litmus test of this may come in the disputes over the South China Sea in which the United States has declared it has a national interest. Our authors and others are divided on the question of whether middle powers have moderated Chinese behavior on this issue. On the one hand, China has abandoned its insistence on dealing with the issues on a bilateral basis and agreed to work toward a legally binding code of conduct to replace the nonbinding code it signed in 2002. On the other hand, Beijing continues to press its claims in a variety of aggressive ways (legal, military, diplomatic, economic, and administrative).

A Middle Power Effect?

Andrew Carr has recently pointed out that although it is relatively easy to identify middle power policy outputs, it is far more difficult to measure their impact.[19] If one examines the direct, bilateral impact of middle powers on China, one would have to conclude that their impact is little to nil. There is no evidence that Beijing has changed its policies in explicit and direct reference to middle power behavior. One example can be found in the classic mediation role that is frequently earmarked for middle powers. Arguably the most acute territorial issues for China in the contemporary context are located in maritime Southeast Asia and the East China Sea. Rival claimants in the South China Sea, Vietnam and the Philippines, and Japan over the Diaoyu/Senkaku Islands, are equally as adamant as Beijing regarding the legitimacy of their competing claims. Many analysts agree these represent major flashpoints for conflict and that any conflict would have disastrous implications for the passage of trade through strategic waterways. Yet China has steadfastly resisted any suggestion that middle powers such as Australia or Indonesia could potentially play a mediating role in defusing these disputes, and has made a regular point of signaling to external parties that they have no mediation role to play.[20] China's approach to middle power participation in regional security architectures in Asia has stemmed more from the goal of minimizing US influence in the context of bilateral rivalry between Washington and Beijing than it has from an objective of configuring architecture that is representative of middle powers across Asia. Notably, Beijing was insistent that Australia not be included in the newly instituted East Asia Summit (EAS) process in 2005, despite general support among ASEAN states (the United States was not a founding member of EAS). China's opposition was circumvented only by strong support for Australia's inclusion from Japan.[21]

As we discussed in chapter 1, any middle power effect on China's rise will be of modest magnitude, difficult to observe, and mostly indirect. As the collection of essays in this book confirms, middle powers today have more scope than ever to influence the contours of international institutions and provide meaningful regional leadership in response to key policy challenges. China seeks to engage more fully in regions across the international system where the influence of middle powers is increasing in scope. For instance,

South Africa's role as a regional leader is something China must navigate in its attempts to deepen engagement with African states economically and politically, both through and independent from the African Union. Similarly, China's relationship with Indonesia is central to Beijing's efforts to engage states in Southeast Asia on a range of issues, including China's role in the region. And China can achieve only limited economic and political outcomes in the Americas without a positive relationship with Brazil. In short, middle powers loom increasingly large in China's foreign policy and Beijing has no choice but to engage with these states and cultivate deeper relations with them.

Thus, the middle power impact on China arises not directly but indirectly from the ways that middle powers shape China's international environment. As we have seen, middle powers are important actors in their own right, and can no longer be defined merely in terms of how they interact with the great powers (if indeed they ever could be). One good example is the prominent role of middle powers in the evolution of norms regarding humanitarian intervention. Along with the African Union, Australia and Canada played a key role in promoting the emergence of the Responsibility to Protect (R2P) doctrine in 2005.[22] More recently, Brazil has championed the related "Responsibility While Protecting" initiative that builds on the earlier R2P doctrine.[23] The increasingly powerful norm that state sovereignty entails a moral obligation to safeguard the human rights of all citizens has obvious implications for authoritarian states like China, which house significant minority populations within their borders. It also makes life more difficult for Beijing in terms of justifying continuing support for those regimes (e.g., Syria, North Korea) that commit egregious human rights abuses against their own citizens on a daily basis.

New rules and institutions are probably the most important ways that middle powers will reshape the rise of China. The G20, ASEAN, and the Global Green Growth Initiative are all examples of middle power rules and institution-building with profound implications for the context in which China is rising. Evelyn Goh's term is "enmeshment," and a broader statement would be that middle powers are responding to China's rise by enmeshing it in regional and global institutions.[24] While limited in their ability to reshape China through direct bilateral relations, middle powers in concert with others have a leading role in shaping the global governance systems with which China will have to contend. This is perhaps most clear in the case of South Korea, whose "Global Korea" ambitions so far include redefining the development aid agenda, creating norms in the area of cybersecurity, initiating an inclusive "Seoul Process" to manage the power transition in

Northeast Asia, and bridging pro-growth and pro-environment lobbies with its "green growth" initiative.

As China's view of its own international status evolves, and as it becomes more ambitious as its material power capabilities expand, it is likely that middle powers will become more important in Chinese foreign policy. However, Beijing will become even more discriminating in favoring second-generation middle powers such as Brazil, Indonesia, and South Africa and increasingly critical of first-generation middle powers that are US allies, including Australia and South Korea. As bilateral rivalry with Washington deepens over time, Beijing will tend to see the international system increasingly through this prism. This will probably lead to greater emphasis on how middle powers can be enlisted, or in some cases marginalized, to weaken US influence. It is true that China's leaders are largely preoccupied with domestic challenges, the scale of which dwarfs the challenges most other countries have to face, but it is equally accurate that China has a clear set of aims about what it wants to achieve in its foreign policy. Defending its territorial claims, limiting US influence, and securing long-term energy supplies are all near the top of the list, but so too is achieving widespread respect for what Beijing sees as its rightful place in the world. Due deference is something Chinese leaders continue to crave, and the influence of this in shaping Chinese foreign policy should not be underestimated. Over time, middle powers will be regarded less in terms of actors that should be engaged in their own right in terms of their material and behavioral attributes, and seen more in terms of their position in respect to US-China rivalry in international relations.

Beyond Hegemony

Traditional realist approaches to international relations direct attention to great power initiative and secondary power passivity. Moreover, they often set up a tragic vision of great power conflict. The middle power prism reminds us not only of the dispersion of power in the international system but also of the alternative visions that are equally plausible interpretations of reality.

This book has, by design, spent little time examining US or Chinese foreign policy because of our view that seeing beyond hegemony requires looking at the world through a different lens that does not revolve around great power orderings. We have examined the world as a hive of cells rather than as competing webs of great power alliances. Both China's rise and America's preeminence are treated here as the background, not the center, of international politics. There is no center, only a hive of adjacent cells that interact through complex networks.

By definition, the prism of middle power theory, like all theories of international politics, is a way to simplify reality so as to provide meaningful interpretations of diverse phenomena. No one doubts the signal importance of great powers in international politics. All things considered, as a category, great powers probably still matter more than any other single category of actors—whether middle powers, small powers, international institutions, or nonstate actors. But middle power theory reminds us that great powers cannot do as they please and are themselves caught in the hive, or webs not of their making. Middle powers have reframed and initiated policies that realist theories centered on great powers cannot predict: the operation of ASEAN, the role of regional leadership, and the human security agenda are all evidence that great power approaches are insufficient for explaining contemporary international politics. We need to see and move "beyond hegemony," at least as an adjunct to traditional approaches if not as an alternative.

The contemporary international system is risky, multipolar, and competitive. In this new context, many new actors can make use of creative and persuasive behavior to forge new governance regimes—what Yves Tiberghien calls "Minervian actors" for the Greek goddess of creativity, law, justice, and inventiveness, or what Avant, Finnemore, and Sell call the "new global governors."[25] Middle powers are not the only Minervian actors or new governors in contemporary international politics but they are among the most important. They pursue what Richard Higgot and Mark Beeson have termed "games of skill rather than games of will"; for them, "middle power theory is thus premised on being not a giant but a good dancer skilled in persuasion, coalition-building, and the 'art of the indirect' playing the role of (i) catalyst, (ii) facilitator, and (iii) manager."[26]

In many ways, this new international system is one in which middle powers will thrive because while the system is "decompressed" from great power hegemony, it is not disorderly enough to require a great power concert. A 2012 report issued by the US-based Atlantic Council argues that "there is a burgeoning strata of pivotal states, dynamic rising middle powers (most prominently, Turkey, Brazil, South Korea, Indonesia, Saudi Arabia, and South Africa) likely to play an increasingly important role in regional security and global ruleshaping."[27] Although not a US (or China)-centered view of international politics, this does not mean that the United States and China cannot thrive in this context. The same Atlantic Council report argues that the United States could still retain primacy and influence although now only in concert with these others. By rethinking their great power status in middle power terms, the United States and China could make a decisive contribution to overcoming the global governance deficit.

To be sure, as a friendly critic of this book has put it, the middle power concept should not be "overcooked." It cannot bear the analytic weight as a paradigmatic theory of international politics. Rather, it provides a useful adjunct to other approaches. If the middle power theory did not exist, we would have to invent it because of the repeated intrusion of this class of states into the spotlight of international politics. As an aspirational category of policy learning and diffusion, it is also indispensable to these states in making foreign policy and, not incidentally, for great powers seeking to align themselves with the complex new world of global governance of which the rise of China is a key part.

Notes

1. For contemporary reflections on this theme, see the collection of essays in James Cotton and John Ravenhill, eds., *Middle Power Dreaming: Australia in World Affairs, 2006–2010* (Melbourne: Oxford University Press, 2011).

2. On this point, see Greta Nabbs-Keller, "Reforming Indonesia's Foreign Ministry: Ideas, Organization and Leadership," *Contemporary Southeast Asia* 35, no. 1 (2013): 56–82.

3. "Australia Is Much Like South Africa, Says Minister Drawing Parallels," *Pretoria News*, February 19, 2013.

4. Cho Chung-un, "Korea Foundation to Bolster 'Soft Power' on Global Stage," *Korea Herald*, May 11, 2012.

5. "Indonesia, S. Korea Build Middle Power Partnership," *Tempo (Jakarta)*, May 23, 2013; "Australia-Republic of Korea Foreign and Defence Ministers (2 + 2) Meeting," *ForeignAffairs.co.nz*, July 5, 2013.

6. David J. Hornsby and Oscar van Heerden, "South Africa-Canada Relations: A Case of Middle Power (Non)Cooperation?," *Commonwealth & Comparative Politics* 51, no. 2 (2013): 153–72.

7. Suleyman Elik, *Iran-Turkey Relations, 1979–2011: Conceptualising the Dynamics of Politics, Religion, and Security in Middle-Power States* (New York: Routledge, 2010).

8. Bruce Gilley, "Middle Powers during Great Power Transitions: The Rise of China and Canada-U.S. Relations," *International Journal* 66, no. 2 (2011): 245–64.

9. See Evan Ellis, "The Expanding Chinese Footprint in Latin America: New Challenges for China, and Dilemmas for the US," *IFRI [French Institute of International Relations] Center for Asian Studies Paper*, February 2012, www.ifri.org/?page=contribution-detail&id=7014.

10. For discussion see Uche Ofodile, "Trade, Aid and Human Rights: China's Africa Policy in Perspective," *Journal of International Commercial Law and Technology* 4, no. 2 (2009): 86–99.

11. Mark Beeson, Soko Mills, and Yong Wang, "The New Resource Politics: Can Australia and South Africa Accommodate China?," *International Affairs* 87, no. 6 (2011): 1365–84.

12. André Bank and Roy Karadag, "The 'Ankara Moment': The Politics of Turkey's Regional Power in the Middle East, 2007–11," *Third World Quarterly* 34, no. 2 (2013): 287–304.

13. Hugh White, *The China Choice: Why America Should Share Power* (Melbourne: Black, 2012); see, for instance, Michael Beckley, "China's Century? Why America's Edge Will Endure," *International Security* 36, no. 3 (2011): 41–78.

14. For a useful treatment of socialization in the ASEAN context, see Alistair Iain Johnston, "Socialization in International Institutions: The ASEAN Way and International Relations Theory," in *International Relations Theory and the Asia-Pacific*, 107–62, eds. G. John Ikenberry and Michael Mastanduno (New York: Columbia University Press, 2003).

15. "Australia Is Much Like South Africa, Says Minister Drawing Parallels," *Pretoria News*, February 19, 2013.

16. Hedley Bull, "The New Balance of Power in Asia and the Pacific," *Foreign Affairs* 49, no. 4 (1971): 669–81.

17. Polling regularly shows that while Australians perceive great opportunity in engaging actively with China, they are simultaneously dubious about China's authoritarianism and its capacity to pose a future security threat as its power increases. For the most authoritative public opinion surveys on the China question, see successive reports by the Lowy Institute for International Policy, www.lowyinstitute.org/programs-and-projects/programs/polling.

18. Vikram Nehru, "Shuttle Diplomacy in the South China Sea," *Jakarta Post*, August 30, 2012.

19. Andrew Carr, "Is Australia a Middle Power? A Systemic Impact Approach," *Australian Journal of International Affairs* (in press).

20. For instance, see "China Rejects Philippine UN Mediation Effort," *Sydney Morning Herald*, February 20, 2013.

21. See Mohan Malik, "The East Asia Summit," *Australian Journal of International Affairs* 60, no. 2 (2006): 207–11.

22. For a detailed account of the emergence of the R2P doctrine, see Alex Bellamy, *Responsibility to Protect: The Global Effort to End Mass Atrocities* (Cambridge, UK: Polity Press, 2009).

23. See Thorsten Benner, "Brazil as a Norm Entrepreneur: The 'Responsibility While Protecting' Initiative," *GPPI [Global Public Policy Institute] Working Paper*, March 2013, www.gppi.net/fileadmin/media/pub/2013/Benner_2013_Working-Paper_Brazil-R WP.pdf.

24. Evelyn Goh, "Institutions and the Great Power Bargain in East Asia: Asean's Limited 'Brokerage' Role," *International Relations of the Asia-Pacific* 11, no. 3 (2011): 373–401.

25. Yves Tiberghien, ed. *Leadership in Global Institution Building: Minerva's Rule* (New York: Palgrave, 2013); Deborah D. Avant, Martha Finnemore, and Susan K. Sell, *Who Governs the Globe?* (New York: Cambridge University Press, 2010).

26. Mark Beeson and Richard Higgott, "The Changing Architecture of Politics in the Asia-Pacific: Another (Lost) Middle Power Moment?," Paper given at conference The Role of Middle Powers in 21st Century International Relations, Seoul, April 19–20, 2013.

27. Atlantic Council, *Envisioning 2030: US Strategy for a Post-Western World* (New York: Atlantic Council, 2012), 25, 30.

Contributors

David A. Cooper is professor and chair of national security affairs at the US Naval War College. His areas of scholarly and professional expertise include nonproliferation, disarmament, weapons of mass destruction, multilateral negotiations and organizations, international relations, and foreign policy analysis. He served for nearly two decades on the professional staff within the US Office of the Secretary of Defense. He is the author of *Competing Western Strategies against the Proliferation of Weapons of Mass Destruction: Comparing the United States to a Close Ally* (2001), in addition to articles including most recently in the journals *Foreign Policy Analysis* and *The Nonproliferation Review*.

Amy L. Freedman is professor and department chair of political science and international studies at Long Island University—Post. She is also an adjunct associate research scholar at Columbia University's Weatherhead East Asian Institute, and an editor of the journal *Asian Security*. Her current research looks at questions of nontraditional security threats in Southeast Asia. She has also published widely on questions of democracy in Indonesia and Malaysia, and on matters of international political economy in the region. She has published articles in a diverse array of journals and is the editor and a contributor of a forthcoming book on the internationalization of internal conflicts.

Bruce Gilley is associate professor of political science and director of the doctoral program in public affairs and policy in the Mark O. Hatfield School of Government at Portland State University. His research centers on the comparative and international politics of China and Asia as well as more general questions of legitimacy, democratization, and international relations. His books include *The Right to Rule: How States Win and Lose Legitimacy* (2009) and *The Nature of Asian Politics* (2014).

Sven Grimm is director of the Centre for Chinese Studies at Stellenbosch University and editor-in-chief of *African East-Asian Affairs*. His research interests are the political and developmental relations between China and African countries. Recent publications include *Coordinating China and DAC Development Partners—Challenges to the Aid Architecture in Rwanda* (2011) and the chapter "Emerging Partners and Their Impact on African Development" in the edited book *Africa towards 2030: Challenges for Development Cooperation* (2013).

TongFi Kim is a research fellow at the Griffith Asia Institute and the Centre for Governance and Public Policy, Griffith University. He received his PhD in political science from Ohio State University in 2010, and worked as a visiting assistant professor at Purdue University before coming to Griffith. His research centers on security studies and the international relations of East Asia. He is currently revising his book manuscript on intra-alliance bargaining and US alliances in East Asia.

James Manicom is a research fellow at the Centre for International Governance Innovation in Waterloo, Canada. He is the author of *Bridging Troubled Waters: China, Japan and Maritime Order in the East China Sea* (2014). He is interested in the politics of maritime space in East Asia and the Arctic. His research interests include East Asian international relations and strategic studies, maritime security, energy security, nationalism, and territorial disputes.

Joseph Marques is a research fellow at the Brazil Institute at King's College, London. He has been a frequent visitor to Brazil over the last two decades as an international banker including a four-year stint living in São Paulo and traveling extensively throughout the country. His research interests include Brazilian foreign policy, Brazilian international trade relations, the internationalization of Brazilian companies, Brazil's growing role in global governance and relations with Africa. He has also been a visiting scholar at the Latin American Centre at the University of Oxford and received his PhD from the Graduate Institute of International and Development Studies, University of Geneva (Switzerland).

Ann Marie Murphy is an associate professor at the School of Diplomacy and International Relations, Seton Hall University; a senior research scholar at the Weatherhead East Asian Institute, Columbia University; and an associate fellow of the Asia Society. She monitored Indonesia's first direct presidential election as a member of the Carter Center delegation and was the US representative on the 2008 Presidential Friends of Indonesia delegation. She has been a visiting scholar at the Centre for Strategic and International Studies, Jakarta.

Andrew O'Neil is director of the Griffith Asia Institute and professor in the School of Government and International Relations at Griffith University. He has served on the Australian Foreign Minister's National Consultative Committee for International Security Issues and is former editor-in-chief of the *Australian Journal of International Affairs*. His most recent book is *Asia, the US and Extended Nuclear Deterrence: Atomic Umbrellas in the Twenty-First Century* (Routledge 2013).

Jeffrey Reeves is an associate professor at the Asia-Pacific Center for Security Studies in Honolulu, Hawaii. He received his PhD from the London School of Economics in 2010. His main areas of research, teaching, and outreach are Northeast Asian security issues, Chinese politics, political economics, transnational crime and terrorism in Asia, Mongolia, and nontraditional security in China and Asia.

Yitzhak Shichor is the Michael William Lipson Professor Emeritus of Chinese Studies at Hebrew University of Jerusalem and professor of political science and Asian studies at the University of Haifa. He studies China's Middle East policy; international energy relations; defense conversion; labor export; democratization; Xinjiang; and the Uyghur diaspora. His publications include *Ethno-Diplomacy: The Uyghur Hitch in Sino-Turkish Relations* (2009). He is chief editor of *All under Heaven: A History of the Chinese Empire* (3 vols., 2011–13) and editor of the Hebrew edition of *China and Israel 1948–2012*, in press.

Anthony Peter Spanakos is an associate professor of political science and law at Montclair State University. He has been a Fulbright Visiting Faculty member (Brazil 2002, Venezuela 2008) and a visiting researcher at the East Asia Institute (Singapore). He is coeditor of the book series Conceptualizing Comparative Politics and the coeditor of *Reforming Brazil* (2004). His scholarly articles on comparative politics, foreign policy, and political theory have been published in *Comparative Political Studies*, *New Political Science*, *Latin American Politics and Society*, and *Latin American Perspectives*.

Janis van der Westhuizen is associate professor of political science and coordinator of the B.A. International Studies program at the University of Stellenbosch. His current research project focuses on the political economy of South Africa and Brazil's foreign policy. He has authored and coedited *Adapting to Globalization: Malaysia, South Africa and the Challenges of Ethnic Redistribution with Growth* (2002), *South Africa's Multilateralism and Global Change: The Limits of Reformism* (2001), and *Democratizing Foreign Policy: Lessons from South Africa* (2004).

Thomas S. Wilkins is a senior lecturer in international security at the University of Sydney. He received his PhD from the University of Birmingham, UK (during which he was an exchange visitor at Johns Hopkins University, School of Advanced International Studies). Recent career highlights include postdoctoral fellowships at the University of San Francisco and East West Center, visiting positions at Nanyang Technical University and University of British Columbia, and research fellowships at Taiwan Nation University and the University of Tokyo. He has published in journals such as *Review of International Studies*, *Australian Journal of International Affairs*, and *International Relations of the Asia Pacific*.

Toshi Yoshihara is the John A. van Beuren Chair of Asia-Pacific Studies and an affiliate member of the China Maritime Studies Institute at the US Naval War College. He has also served as an analyst at the Institute for Foreign Policy Analysis, RAND, and the American Enterprise Institute. He is the coauthor of *Red Star over the Pacific: China's Rise and the Challenge to US Maritime Strategy* (2010), *Indian Naval Strategy in the Twenty-first Century* (2009), *Chinese Naval Strategy in the Twenty-first Century: The Turn to Mahan* (2008), and coeditor, with James Holmes, of *Strategy in the Second Nuclear Age: Power, Ambition, and the Ultimate Weapon* (2012).

Index

www.ingramcontent.com/pod-product-compliance
Lightning Source LLC
Chambersburg PA
CBHW031413270326
41929CB00010BA/1436
9781626160842